D0475503

Where the
Orange Blooms

THOMAS TAYLOR

Where the Orange Blooms

One Man's War and Escape in Vietnam

McGraw-Hill Publishing Company

New York   St. Louis   San Francisco   Bogotá   Hamburg   Madrid
Milan   Mexico   Paris   São Paulo   Tokyo   Montreal   Toronto

1 2 3 4 5 6 7 8 9 DOC DOC 8 9 2 1 0 9

ISBN 0-07-063193-X

Library of Congress Cataloging-in-Publication Data

Taylor, Thomas
    Where the orange blooms: one man's war and escape in Vietnam /
Thomas H. Taylor.
        p.   cm.
    ISBN 0-07-063193-X
    1. Cai Lam.   2. Vietnam—Politics and government—1975–
3. Refugees, Political—Vietnam—Biography.   4. Refugees, Political—
United States—Biography.   I. Title.
DS559.914.C35T39   1989
959.704′4′092—dc20
    [B]   89-2595
                                                                                  CIP

Book design by Eve L. Kirch

Ben Cai Lam dedicates this book to the resistance—
to those still fighting communism in Vietnam.

CONTENTS

ACKNOWLEDGMENTS

The permission of the following authors and publishers is gratefully acknowledged for passages I have edited:

The Aurora Foundation, for their publication of the investigations of Amnesty International in *Violations of Human Rights in the Socialist Republic of Vietnam.*

John Del Vecchio, *The 13th Valley*, Bantam Books.

Albert Garland, *Infantry in Vietnam*, Battery Press.

Nguyen Long, *After Saigon Fell—Daily Life under the Vietnamese Communists*, published by the Institute of East Asian Studies, University of California, Berkeley.

Nguyen Van Canh, *Vietnam under Communism, 1975–1982*, published by Hoover Press of Stanford University.

Truong Nhu Tang, *Vietcong Memoir*, Harcourt Brace Jovanovich.

William Westmoreland, *A Soldier Reports*, Doubleday.

Sources used from the public domain include Cao Van Vien's *The Final Collapse*, William Le Gro's *Vietnam from Cease-Fire to Capitulation*, both published by the U.S. Government Printing Office; *Rendezvous with Destiny*, a magazine series published by the 101st Airborne Division in Vietnam and provided to the author by Wade Stewart of Smithfield, North Carolina. I obtained press accounts from a Vietnam era army publication called *Scrapbook for Fighting Men Too Busy to Keep Their Own.*

Combat photos were made available from *Vietnam Odyssey*, copyrighted by the 101st Airborne Division Association. Pictures from the SRV were kindly provided by Ms. Brenda Reed Sutton, who reserves all rights, as does Ben for his personal collection. Other photo credits are as shown. The cover photo is from a 1971 edition of *Rendezvous with Destiny*, taken in the Ashau valley.

In oriental societies, surnames precede given names and that convention is followed in this book. To protect identities still at risk in the SRV, some fictitious names have been used.

The author owes special thanks to Bill Laurie of Mesa, Arizona, for his research guidance, and to John Del Vecchio, for his comments. I also received first-hand recollections from a number of veterans of the Oh-deuce, notably Hank Emerson, Frank Dietrich, Steve Baka, as well as Dave Hackworth about the circumstances surrounding Operation Gibraltar and Dak To I. The reader is advised that my own Vietnam experience is related in chapters 5 through 8.

Ben is particularly indebted, most of all to Hank Emerson, but also to the generous townspeople of Dillon, Montana, and the faculty of Western Montana State College, who have done so much to fulfill his American dream.

S O U T H E A S T   A S I A

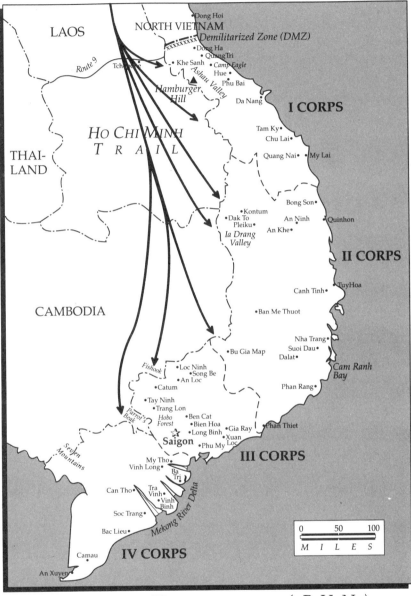

LAOS

NORTH VIETNAM

• Dong Hoi

Demilitarized Zone (DMZ)

xxxxxxx

Route 9

Tchepone •

• Dong Ha

• Quang Tri

• Khe Sanh   • *Camp Eagle*

Hue •

A Shau Valley

Hamburger Hill

Phu Bai •

Da Nang •

I CORPS

HO CHI MINH

T R A I L

Tam Ky •

Chu Lai •

Quang Nai •   • My Lai

THAI-LAND

Bong Son •

• Kontum

• Dak To

Pleiku •

Ia Drang Valley

An Ninh •   • Quinhon

An Khe •

II CORPS

CAMBODIA

Canh Tinh •   • TuyHoa

• Ban Me Thuot

Nha Trang •

Suoi Dau •

Dalat •

Cam Ranh Bay

• Bu Gia Map

Fishook •

• Loc Ninh

• Song Be

• An Loc

Phan Rang •

• Catum

• Tay Ninh

• Trang Lon

Parrot's Beak

Hobo Forest

• Ben Cat

• Bien Hoa

Long Binh •   • Gia Ray

• Xuan

✪ **Saigon**   Phu My •   Loc

III CORPS

Seven Mountains

My Tho •

Vinh Long •

Ba Tri •

Can Tho •   Tra Vinh •

• Vinh Binh

Soc Trang •

Bac Lieu •

Mekong River Delta

Camau •

IV CORPS

An Xuyen •

```
0        50       100
|_____|_____|
    M I L E S
```

S O U T H   V I E T N A M   (R V N)

Wherever snow falls man is free, but where the orange blooms, man is the foe of man.

—Ralph Waldo Emerson

PART I

"Any place better than Vietnam now"

Chapter
One

By 1983 nails were scarce, and had been extracted from the planks that tipped like seesaws. The moldering pier, no larger than a kitchen table, teetered beside the river, which had sluggishly reversed its flow during the hours Cai watched and waited. Mosquitos, rising to feed at twilight, drew his blood but could not distract his thoughts from the country he was trying to escape.

Something like bayou country, his brother now safe in Louisiana would call it. In Vietnam it was called "the delta": reedy tidelands carved into islands by meandering waterways, a flat profile from every shore receding to a flat horizon between still water and pearly sky. Below his sandals the tide turned back the river as it had for millennia, fresh water and brine alternating their dominance gently and forever.

The incoming tide was his signal to embark, and reminder of a lesson from failure. Two attempts ago the fishing boat had slipped its moorings at ebb tide, the organizers believing the river's current would speed the passage to sea. They knew nothing about enlisting nature to aid an escape. Nor did they care. They were gone with the money before the boat ever started.

Everyone knew the odds were twenty to one against reaching freedom. If they were not caught by the coastal police, they faced a belt of storms, and beyond, an armada of pirates. Yet each boat was overloaded, every joint venture toward freedom oversubscribed, and all the maritime provinces of conquered Vietnam were gold markets for organizers like the one who had misused the tide.

"The boat goes faster," Cai had heard him say.

Faster, but not as fast as the tide that night that left the boat stranded on a mud bank a quarter mile offshore. At dawn they were still suspended, the boat tipped on its side, the rudder flapping as uselessly as the fin of a beached shark. The debate on board was whether to struggle back to shore through the muck or wait for a new tide to refloat them. The lives of eighty-eight escapees awaited the decision of the men speaking for their wives and children who huddled under the deck of the thirty-foot fishing smack.

Cai had urged everyone to stay below deck. Stranded as it was, neither the communist coast guard nor the shore patrols could reach the boat, and none had appeared with daybreak. The best to be made of the situation, Cai counseled, was the impression of a careless fisherman who had let his boat go aground. To add to the deception, he would impersonate the fisherman and wallow back to shore. His footprints would make it seem the boat was temporarily abandoned. Once ashore, he would watch for shore patrols, and if one looked like it might investigate the boat, he would signal the passengers to flee as best they could. That was the only plan anyone could think of, so Cai went over the side and the escapees sprawled face to foot under the deck as the sun poached them in bilge water. For an hour, using both arms to pull his legs out of the sucking, hip-deep mud, Cai floundered toward shore.

In the boat, the cramped fugitives were succumbing to thirst. But one family must have been as concerned for food as for water. A child was sent over the side to gather little crabs that scurried on the mud flat. A second child, then three more, joined the hunt. The appearance of a stranded fisherman evaporated.

As if to confirm his fear, Cai saw a single figure down the shore, binoculars at his eyes. Though his own twelve-year-old son was aboard, Cai had to flee. Before he did, he rose and waved the signal that the police had discovered them. Cai was nearly in their net too: the police knew every trail between the coast and the highway. When he started to run someone opened fire on him from 100 meters away.

Racing along levee trails, shielded by five-foot reeds, Cai thought he had enough of a lead to reach the highway several miles away. Though unarmed, he darted through the swamp with confidence developed from fighting the Vietcong in similar wetlands.

"*Dung lai!*" a young voice ordered.

A guerrilla, as the local communists were still called, stepped out of the reeds. Five years ago, when they were known as the Vietcong (VC), Cai had pursued them. This one seemed to recognize him as a former enemy. The war was over, but in the new communist society everyone was a capitalist. Cai pulled out a bundle of piasters.

The guerrilla took the money and gestured for Cai to go, folding into the reeds like a Venus flytrap waiting for more fugitives. The bribe from Cai, less than $3, was as much as a quarter of the guerrilla's monthly pay. For the equivalent of another dollar, he told Cai the best route to the highway.

He received a third bonus by steering Cai toward the uniformed police. Now near the highway where other activity made him less conspicuous, Cai tried to walk away from a checkpoint. But he forgot that his legs were caked with mud. Casually, a police sergeant approached him and gestured to stop. Cai blanched. Bribing a sergeant would surely be expensive.

Instead of taking him to the checkpoint where other police were loitering, the sergeant nodded for Cai to follow him back into the reeds. He had searched escapees before and knew all the hiding places. Cai had hidden two gold rings (the standard black market currency) in a pouch sewn into his shorts. The sergeant found and removed them as if he had hidden the gold himself. He flicked out a penknife and cut the seam of the fly to reveal a long, thin gold necklace. A fast shakedown convinced him that Cai had nothing more.

"Where are you from?" the sergeant asked conversationally.

"Saigon . . . I mean Ho Chi Minh City."

That was a true but unrevealing answer, for the city teemed with three million Vietnamese, tens of thousands of them homeless. If the sergeant had asked for an address, Cai could have told him any of a dozen inventions he had memorized.

"Now you've got no money," the sergeant rightly observed, then tossed him bus fare to Saigon.

The gesture's purpose was twofold: Cai with his fly and shorts slit was evidence of a shakedown. If another policeman searched him, this could lead to examination of the journal at the checkpoint. If no escapees were reported captured that day, suspicion might focus on the sergeant. Cai amounted to evidence that must be removed. He could shoot him now with no more thought than he would give to lighting a cigarette; but Cai also represented future revenue.

"Next time you try," said the sergeant with a pat on the rump, "see me first."

Cai nodded with due respect, and feigned gratitude as if the sergeant had recommended a local restaurant.

Back in Saigon, Cai had melted into the dangerous life of the transient population. A year before he had escaped from a "re-education" camp. As a former Army of Vietnam (ARVN) officer, he was worth a high bounty for anyone who betrayed him. The communist government rewarded snitches on their output; informing for the government, even part-time, was the steadiest source of income throughout the country. Even using many aliases, Cai could never stay in a neighborhood long enough to arouse anyone's interest in him. Beggars, lepers, amputees, food vendors, prostitutes, orphans, pedicabbers, black marketeers, escape organizers, draft dodgers, money changers, anyone and everyone was a potential informer.

To keep on the move, Cai had to move among other fugitives. In the collapsed economy, thousands of the jobless had turned to crime. Women particularly had been shoved out of work so that prostitution was even more rampant than at the height of the war, when a quarter of a million GIs had turned Saigon into a sprawling honky-tonk.

But it was robbers and cutthroats with whom Cai had to rub shoulders and exchange appraising glances. He slept by day on the waterfront, in alleys, on roofs during the dry season, under gutter eaves in the monsoon. By night he prowled, edging closer to the thoroughfares where street lights still eked out some illumination. The police made their arrests by night, so street lights aided them, but in the dark squalor where the slums spread larger each week like ink blots, violent crime overrode even the danger of police surveillance.

Police surveillance but not police protection. They watched for political criminals, ignoring the rest. For the citizen who caught a thief in the act, the police would make the arrest but charge the citizen for food the thief was fed in jail. In an informer society, everyone was responsible for everything, while the government was responsible for nothing except keeping itself in power, and the Socialist Republic of Vietnam (SRV) did so more comprehensively and diligently than any other in the world.

This was the Saigon (officially Ho Chi Minh City) to which Cai returned after his sixth attempt to sail to freedom. It was the city of his boyhood, the city where his own boy was to be imprisoned, for everyone on the boat was captured. Only a complex pattern of graft could get his son out in less than a month. And Cai was penniless; he had staked all his gold and money on this attempt because he had heard that corruption continued even when refugees reached foreign shores.

Once more he had to make contact with his parents; once more advise them of failure, and this time catastrophe—the capture of their grandson. The anguish turned him weak, the guilt ended every nap as he searched the slums for fleeting rest. When he dreamed, the events of April 29, 1975 were repeated. That was the last day he could have escaped with his whole family. The day Saigon fell.

Now on the tiny pier another critical day was ending while the tide slipped upriver below his feet. Cai's parents' bribes had bought his son a lenient three-week sentence. As he waited for his release, Cai had decided to work into an escape organization rather than submit to its haphazard process.

The escape process, in constant evolution all along the Vietnamese coast, always involved three components: capital formation, bribery, and seaworthiness. That was the process of legitimate, though perilously illegal escape attempts. Cai had already been victimized by bogus escape networks, ones that had no purpose but to raise capital for organizers who then vanished.

Cai was fortunate he had parents who could cobble together more gold to slowly replace that lost to cheating organizers. Cai's two brothers had escaped six years before. One was in California, one in Louisiana, and both were successful enough in their new lives to send their parents regular money orders. The communists were happy enough to tax repatriated money and transmit receipts back to the U.S. so more would be sent. Indeed, if the government had prevented all escapes, Vietnam's source of hard currency would dry up quickly.

Organizers charged on a scale based upon the potential for success. For example, $1500 in gold better ensured that the requisite bribes reached police authorities on the coast: vital officials like the sergeant who had searched Cai. The whole police apparatus could not be bought, for there were genuine and fervent communists throughout its chain of command. But a well-heeled organizer could nearly guarantee an escape window if he developed a well-planned timetable. Thus, escapees were willing to pay a premium for strategic bribery even though organizers never refunded money for failed escapes.

It was in the third vital component that Cai gained entry into an organization. Seaworthiness was the combination of boat and crew. Most of the escapees' money went toward purchasing or—since fishing smacks had become scarce—building a boat. This had to be done secretly as boat building was now a government monopoly, an illegal activity for anyone else. Even more scarce were reliable marine engines, for these were only manufactured abroad.

The crew for a promising escape, as important as hull and engine, was a good mechanic and savvy navigator. Competent marine mechanics were as rare as Americans, for most had already escaped. Even harder to find was an experienced high seas navigator. Navigation was an officer's skill in the former navy, and nearly all of them had fled before their government and lives tumbled down in 1975.

Except one. Cai had been in prison with him. They had slept on racks so close that they warmed each other with their body heat. Huong was his name, a lieutenant commander in charge of shipboard radar, but also competent in basic seamanship. Huong and Cai had often whispered together at night, planning their freedom.

The nub, of course, was navigation. Only years at sea developed the skill of dead reckoning, but the navigation required was elementally simple. Indeed, Huong convinced him that sun and stars were probably sufficient to make landfall somewhere in Thailand or Malaysia. Furthermore, Cai already was a relative expert with the pocket (lensatic) compass after navigating with it on wartime patrols. The principles of deflection, azimuth, and back azimuth were the same in featureless jungles or on featureless seas.

After investigating several organizations, Cai offered one his navigational skill. They queried him about his background but he refused to discuss it except to claim some nautical experience and imply that it was in the navy. The organizer had to respect his silence in this world of informers, but he had a simple test for Cai.

At a cost of a hundred dollars, Cai had bought a U.S. Army lensatic compass on the black market. It was in his pocket when the organizer took him to a sampan on the Saigon River.

"I will row," said the organizer. "Tell me the way to go southeast."

Referring to his compass, he pointed in the right direction. The organizer was pleased. Previous candidates had stood facing the correct direction but could not comprehend that the boat's prow must face that way as well. By demonstrating this boy-scout level of proficiency, Cai was named navigator and skipper for a first-class escape.

The organizer presented him to several representatives of families who would pay more to be escaping with an experienced navigator. Cai impressed them: a handsome Hainan Chinese, with a beard hiding a distinctive chin dimple, he was taller and heavier than the wispy Vietnamese and thus an appropriate figure of authority on ship. Moreover, he spoke English, the international language of the high seas, and from the war he had much experience in sleepless vigilance, the kind required for the five-day passage across the Gulf of Siam. To reinforce the escapees' confidence, Cai would be bringing his family, so no one could doubt that he would press on to the limit of endurance.

Cai strained to hear the boat approach but hoped he would not. The less noise it made, the less chance of alerting police checkpoints downriver. The necessary bribes had been paid but sometimes shifts were changed and the wrong men were on duty.

Piloted by the mechanic, the squat nine-meter boat drifted into sight.

The single piston chugged lazily and almost inaudibly. The prow went by. Cai jumped aboard, thinking how his feet were leaving Vietnam for the last time.

The mechanic knew the river and would navigate to its mouth. He stood in what looked like a low outhouse with a window on the door. Inside there was nothing but a wheel. At sea the mechanic would stay at the stern with the diesel drums. There would be little need for conversation between the two, for their tasks were simple and separate: Cai would steer while the mechanic kept the engine running.

They slipped downriver, the engine turning only enough to withstand the opposing current and one mile per hour more. They crept along so that even slower sampans could bring the passengers by threes from hiding places along the shore. Cai had separated his wife and two children so that all were not lost if one sampan was discovered by a river patrol.

It was a moonless night, all the more difficult for the eight sampans to spot the blacked out boat on the broad river. Against the dark sky the boat still made a silhouette to guide the sampans, but Cai could see nothing of them. One by one he heard the dip of their oars and felt the gentle bump of the prows.

Wordlessly the dark-clothed figures climbed on deck and slithered into the hold. Cai helped them up and confirmed that his family was aboard.

The sampans were loaded with rocks. A short blow at the water line and they gurgled, disappearing like sodden leaves to the river bottom.

The fishing boat's gunwales also sank. Cai's suspicion was confirmed by a muffled argument below deck. One of the two families had brought several additional relatives, paying off the organizer, who had not told the others. His higher profit lowered the waterline and the margin of safety in high seas.

Cai knew some passengers should be put ashore, but he also knew they would kill to stay in the boat. And there could be no sounds of mutiny as the boat drifted by police checkpoints. Their only hope, their collective salvation, was in kind weather and that alone. At least the sea and skies would receive more prayers, Cai thought, as he remembered that there were Catholics, Buddhists, and Confucians aboard.

He had searched for maritime forecasts on the organizer's short-wave radio but had heard nothing useful. Clouds were low and stationary as the boat slipped out from the mouth of the river. Cai traded places with the mechanic, who accelerated the engine. The boat plowed ahead into the shallow sea, passing over the mud bank that had grounded Cai's last attempt. This time they were on their way, a slight curl in the bow wake as he aligned the luminous figures on his pocket compass to a heading south-southwest.

Eight men, six women, and nine children, ranging from three months to twelve years old, remained packed in the hull space twenty feet by seven with a chair-sized hatch for ventilation and nothing for sanitation. At first, Cai would not permit anyone above deck for fear of tipping the overloaded vessel.

He scanned the horizon for the low silhouette of Con Son, an island prison made famous by its "tiger cages" for South Vietnam's political prisoners. Now the prisoners were the South Vietnamese themselves, and the island was a base for the communist coast guard. Cai gave Con Son a twenty-mile berth. When it passed behind him, he took up an azimuth of 220 degrees, the course for the rest of the 800-mile voyage.

The night passed quickly as the boat chugged along. The sea rolled lazily out of the dawn. Cai allowed the passengers on deck one at a time. Pale with worry and fright, they looked into the breeze to cool their faces.

But it was a headwind that freshened as the day warmed. The diesel fumes streamed straight behind like a plume.

He had never been to sea, nor had any of the passengers, but he felt the unfettered sweep of the sky as much as he felt the wind. And as he did Cai thought about his long association with the Americans and a bit of their earliest history, how America's first seekers of freedom had braved the ocean to reach a new life. He knew they were called pilgrims, but the word had a different connotation in Vietnam's largely Buddhist population. Cai himself was Confucian, the religion of his Chinese ancestors on Hainan. Ancestors were worshipped there. He invoked their memory but only to protest that this opportunity to join them was premature.

The unfriendly wind continued through a dehydrating day. The mechanic guarded the five-gallon jerry can of water. This would be rationed to a half cup per person over four days. Cai and the mechanic could drink when they pleased but Cai did not take more than his share, for thirst would help keep him awake during the next night. His only other stimulant was ginseng, though it parched his throat even more. Every hour he drew his knees to his chest, and also bent backward, exercises he had learned in prison when he was kept doubled over in shackles twenty-three hours each day.

The babies did not cry. It was as if everyone on board had taken a deep breath and would not make a sound until they reached land. By the end of the second day, standing at the wheel the entire time, Cai made his first announcement to the passengers: if his estimate was right, they were halfway to freedom. There was no reaction from them. Their odds had improved but they did not know by how much. One successful attempt out of twenty was still a daunting statistic. No one mentioned it; everyone thought of it.

On the third day the human cargo was limp from dehydration. One arm wedged in a corner, one on the wheel, Cai tried to focus on the compass. The needle seemed to waver; his eyes blinked off and on as he drifted between hallucination and upright sleep. He tried to sing but his mouth was too dry. It was the buffeting wind that jarred him to full consciousness.

While his mind drifted, black clouds were materializing on the forward horizon. Low on the water, they seemed to incline the sea into a ramp the boat must climb. Semidelirious, Cai thought that on the backside of the ramp the boat would slide down, gathering speed to approach land.

But the ramp rose into a wall of black clouds, which hurled flicks and then gusts of rain before them. The boat lost headway, rocking on its beam in deeper and deeper furrows.

Waves began to sound against the hull, smacking at first, then hitting like a fist. From his vantage point, Cai saw them come on as if from tiers of water, each higher than the one in front. The crests of the farthest tiers danced with foam.

White water surged over the gunwales. As the waves crashed harder, foam shot into the air, the wind sweeping it in Cai's face. The wall was upon them now, blackening the sky. Cai looked back to see if the mechanic was lashed to the stern. He was doubled over, holding his stomach.

Cai popped three motion sickness pills. Below, the passengers rolled in vomit. Some began to shriek, a counterpoint to the howling wind.

The wind seemed to carry as much water as the invading sea. Faces crammed the passenger hatch, mouths open to catch water. Cai too was lapping the rain, which was heavier than any that had drenched him on land. In battle he had seen death close by, heard it in the crack of bullets, and knew the smell of the rain as it poured through the jungle. A smile of gallows humor came over him: a soldier for eighteen years, he was facing a sailor's death. The thought lingered that the sea kills more sailors than do other navies.

The sea's roar reminded him of the endless American artillery barrages. The wave troughs narrowed, pushing the boat aloft, then smashing it down on what felt like concrete. The beam shuddered, the boards quivered, the gunwales wallowed awash, and the deck funneled water down the hold until Cai screamed to slam the hatch. He could feel the boat slowly yaw, the engine a trifling power against the storm.

As the boat came under the control of the elements, Cai could feel it sinking in a corkscrew motion. Slowly the stern was coming about. When it pointed into the storm, the engine would flood. He held full rudder while the mechanic leaned over into the swell to jam it in place. Cai looked up to see the hatch forced open against the water surging over the deck. It was the father of one of the families.

"Go back!" he cried over the wind.

Another head popped out beside his. "Go on!" the other father screamed.

Below deck the two families were arguing: life or freedom.

The choice would be nature's. Cai stopped and started the engine as the waves dictated; the only hope was to keep the boat pointed into the storm. Somehow the boat absorbed the shivering impacts.

But it was sinking; Cai could tell from its leaden feel and the lower freeboard when it rose from the troughs. He leaped when the vertical drop of a wave shattered the bow. Water boiled on deck, then sucked into the hole like a sink. Cai felt the boat tip forward as if it were a plane in a banking dive. He felt the center of gravity shift.

If it shifted forward another meter, the boat would tip down beyond recovery and shoot like an arrow for the bottom. Cai wondered for a moment if the bottom was hard or soft, imagined for an instant the sudden growing cold, the dropping darkness, and how he would only feel, not see, the surging mud as it enveloped the wheelhouse, while bodies and giant bubbles burped up from the crushed deck.

While he imagined his death, the boat's deck struggled to the surface. The trough was a wide one; the boat wallowed awash long enough for the mechanic to dump a fuel drum, roll it miraculously to the jagged hole and dip the drum below. A dozen hands shoved it up sloshing with brine to be dumped over the side. As the boat climbed a more gradual swell, the drum was dipped and dumped as fast as it could be lifted. The slope to the next trough was also gradual.

Succeeding waves smacked the keel down hard; the wind howled on but at a lower pitch. Shipping water, losing water, the boat struggled to a standoff with the storm.

One family shouted at the change of course and waved in the direction of Malaysia. The other family was silent, sensing that the wind would drive them where it would. No one had cried except in terror; now tears flowed as children clung to parents and each other.

"Better to drown!" someone shouted to Cai, and there was murmured agreement. The mechanic was on his knees blowing out the pump in the flooded engine compartment. He looked up at Cai, then west toward freedom. That was where he would go, or to the bottom with his engine.

Cai wanted to steer back to the west as soon as he could, preferring a two-minute death in the deep to another four years of re-education, but for now to stay afloat the boat must run before the waning storm. As it did, Cai had to appraise three crucial questions. In ascending importance they were: water, fuel, and seaworthiness.

The five-day voyage would now be at least six (there was no telling how far off course the storm had driven them). Some fuel had been dumped to use the drum for bailing. There had been only enough fuel at the beginning for five days.

Children might die of thirst, the boat might drift powerless, but still survival was possible if it did not sink. With the bow deck stoved in, the boat could weather only mild seas, nothing half as high as the storm that was driving them back to the east. And there was probably other damage concealed by the knee-deep water in the hold.

Cai called for the two fathers. Both wanted to go on, to turn west, but both realized nothing could be done until the storm passed. Cai explained the three factors for survival—survival, not necessarily escape.

Both fathers said their families would go on until they died, so there would be no turning back for lack of water. Death by thirst is excruciating, but they would both see every child die in their arms rather than return to Vietnam.

Fuel was no reason either. This wind that was blowing them back could reverse and drive them to Malaysia.

"With what sails?" Cai asked.

With their shirts, was the reply, and each man stripped to the waist.

So seaworthiness was the only determinant. The boat would be watched, the boat would decide. It would obey the wind, but when Cai could reverse course he would. He was the captain but those were the instructions from his passengers.

As the boat wallowed on, Cai shivered through the night, watching the needle swing back and forth across an easterly azimuth. He estimated the storm had cost a hundred retrograde miles, and it was sweeping him away not only from Malaysia but from Vietnam and any chance of return.

The winds leaped beyond them in the night but the sea rolled on against the boat. He reckoned to be close to "no place to go," somewhere in the South China Sea, with not enough fuel to reach either his destination or his departure point. There was a chance that if another storm pushed them they could reach the Philippine Islands, but they could also easily miss them and disappear into the Pacific.

Groggy, cold, and exhausted, Cai summoned the fathers just before dawn. All night he had heard the scrape of bailing in the hold, yet the boat had not risen an inch. Briefly the fathers spoke of jettisoning the passengers who could not survive another day. No, said one father, the ones to go overboard should be those who were not to come in the first place.

"We all go together," Cai decided. "Now where do we go?"

One father tried to speak, but words would not come. He shook his head, stared at the sky, then went below as if to announce it was time for all to leap into the sea.

"Where do we go?" Cai repeated to the other father in a hoarse whisper.

"Where can we go?"

"The only place—back to land."

"Vietnam?" He spoke the word like a curse.

Cai could not even nod. The father turned away from him, weeping.

Chapter
Two

"What will you do now?" the mechanic asked after the fathers went below. The deck inclined slowly as if waiting for the answer. Cai knew there was but one thing he could do—follow the back azimuth of the escape course. As the wind whistled out of the west, he was able to point the boat at 40 degrees.

Huddled over the wheel, he thought of the irony the storm had created. He was now sailing for Vietnam. On an unremembered voyage in his infancy, he had sailed for the same destination. That was in 1949, when China fell to Mao's red armies.

Vietnam, under the French, was the landfall for his parents. Now, thirty-four years later, sight of the Vietnamese coast was like returning to a prison's gate. Admission would be easy because inbound boats were assumed to be fishermen and were never inspected.

"The gates of hell are always open," he remembered an American chaplain once saying.

By the next night the beacon on Con Son flashed distantly in cruel welcome. By daylight it was behind them and the Vietnamese coast was only a few hours away.

His parents' flight had been part of a clan's diaspora. Lam was the clan's name, and they fled almost as a fleet; two uncles to Thailand, one to Hong Kong, and Vu Xuol, his father, across the Gulf of Tonkin to Vietnam. There the corrupt and ousted regime of Chiang Kai-shek (called the Kuomintang) was still recognized as China's legitimate government. Though the Lams were not sorry about its downfall, they had to seek sanction from the Kuomintang Embassy in order to remain in Vietnam. The Lams bribed the ambassador and were given passports with resident visas.

The visas were extended until 1954, when the French declared South Vietnam to be independent and installed its first president, Diem, who declared that all foreign nationals doing business in his country must become Vietnamese citizens. In a group naturalization, Cai's parents, his three sisters, and three brothers became Vietnamese. As further proof of assimilation, each adopted a Vietnamese name, and Cai, who had been born Lam Minh Ben became Lam Minh Cai.

The muggy Mekong littoral emerged from the haze. The sea floor tapered upward, its color merging with that of the vast estuary. Cai was uncertain of the tide, and turned north hoping to spot other fishing boats. Luckily one crossed his course a few miles ahead. With a good catch it was low in the water like the refugee boat; moreover, it seemed to know where to go. Cai followed the boat until he saw a familiar river mouth, the very same from which he had put to sea beginning a span of four days and eternity.

The mechanic, slumped by the engine compartment, looked up wonderingly. It seemed Cai had performed a navigational miracle by hitting the point of departure as if guided by radar. But Cai knew it was luck. Luck that was as good as his previous luck had been bad.

He remembered some escapes that had relied so much on luck that he had spurned them, attempts with neither mechanic nor navigator, putting to sea in homemade boats so crowded the hundred passengers had to stand. Escapes with no destination except the sea lanes where the only hope of rescue was by passing freighters.

Who had made it? Who had not? These were questions rarely answered unless a letter was received from abroad. The few that arrived were the only source of hope. Hope was what Cai needed now, what he needed to revive after being turned back halfway to freedom.

He could not ponder the ways of fate for long. As the boat

approached the river mouth he had to think of a way to "unescape," a contingency he had never considered. For the moment he would head for the very pier from which he had departed. He relinquished the wheel to the mechanic and thought of what to do next.

First off, the twenty-two refugees must disperse, for large groups of any kind attracted police attention. There were no sampans; so the boat had to moor until dark, when the refugees could slip ashore and become fugitives once more. Sensing loss of hope, babies cried all day in the soggy oven of the hold.

Cai watched his son for signs of heat exhaustion as they sweated through the day crouched in a foot of bilge and diesel. The airless vault compressed them until temples throbbed and coughs became gasps. Cai often lapsed into fitful unconsciousness, reviving to the memory of failure. The long simmer of this day would end his seventeenth attempt to escape. On the first attempt he could have gotten away so easily.

Two of his brothers had begged him to leave with them. Phat and Tho had seen the final North Vietnamese invasion coming and grew more certain it would succeed. Cai was commanding an infantry company in the delta, where there had been no recent fighting; consequently, he did not share their alarm.

In retrospect, he saw how he was wrong:

Beginning in April 1975, I talked to my brothers every night. They said things in II Corps are getting worse all the time. I tell them Americans come back if things get too bad. They say no, no more American troops or planes, ever.

I don't believe that because I was with the Americans so long.

But it was the Americans who were telling his brothers what his brothers were telling Cai. It had been four years since "Vietnamization," and the war had been turned over to ARVN; the paratroopers Cai had served with were home in the U.S. to stay. Only intelligence specialists remained in Saigon with the job of monitoring the war and reporting the outcome to Washington, where the astonishing Watergate revelations had crowded news of Southeast Asia from the headlines.

Cai's brothers worked for American intelligence specialists. They knew the end was near but could not convince him. The Americans in Saigon knew that President Ford was in no position to honor the U.S. commitments to South Vietnam, the commitments embodied in the Paris peace accords.

North Vietnam had tested U.S. sincerity to those commitments in 1972. The result of the test had heartened Cai. Hanoi's troops and tanks had streamed across the demilitarized zone on the border between the countries but were turned back by U.S. bombers and ARVN plentifully supplied by American logisticians.

Cai had read that some U.S. politicians sided with the north, even saying that the 1972 invasion was merely a "probe," and that the North Vietnamese Army (NVA) were really not in the south at all. Senator McGovern had said such things, but Nixon had trounced him in the presidential election. In Vietnam there was local opposition to the war but it was inconsequential, and so too seemed the antiwar movement in America. Only one state voted for McGovern. Even when he resigned, Nixon was more popular in the U.S. than was President Thieu in South Vietnam. Cai could not understand what the Americans in Saigon were telling his brothers.

Nevertheless, he knew the invasion that followed in 1975 was the most serious threat to South Vietnam since the famous Tet offensive of 1968. Though ARVN and the Americans had thrown back the NVA and Vietcong in one of the most one-sided military victories in modern history, the American antiwar movement had thrived on TV coverage of a suicide raid against the U.S. Embassy and the long siege of Hue, which the NVA held for nearly a month. What Cai saw and heard during Tet was the wrath of the GIs against the antiwar movement. If the GIs felt that way, what did it matter if the longhairs in San Francisco protested? Saigon had its protestors too—Buddhist monks who occasionally cremated themselves—but they meant little to the war.

But in 1975, the GIs were gone. His brothers said NVA divisions were rolling down from the highlands and there was little to stop them. That news steeled Cai for a fight, not for flight. He had beaten the NVA before, easily with the Americans, but his own ARVN company had not done badly without them.

And who was there to stop the NVA if not men like Cai? American bombs and artillery were important but not so much as riflemen who were as willing to fight as the NVA. Cai was responsible for about 150 such riflemen. They looked to him for an example. His brothers did not have such responsibilities. One was in the air force, one in the navy, both with desk jobs. Cai did not blame them for looking first to their families and future; he just recognized that he had an additional obligation.

The rotted pilings groaned as one by one the passengers crossed the tiny pier into the reeds. Everyone would disperse now, go their own ways back to wherever they had come from. They had not known each others' names while they were together, and there were no farewells as the families melted into the night. But both of the fathers, though hostile toward each other, gripped Cai's hand, saying they wished to be with him again.

I want to cry, but then I think it so funny what they say. They say I am a great seaman. They believe that no one else can come back, right to this place the way I did. One guy wants me to go to his town and wait till we get another boat, and I will be navigator. The other father gives me his address and says he has money if I will take his family when I try again. They don't believe it when I tell them how lucky I was.

It would take more luck just to redisperse his own family. His daughters had remained with his parents, a wrenching decision to ensure that one of his children, consequently his line of the family, would survive if Cai and his son perished at sea. Dat now had to be infiltrated back to Cai's parents' home in the Chinese quarter of Saigon.

For a boy of twelve, he would need considerable luck himself. His own playmates might mention his five-day absence to the neighborhood informers. Both children and neighbors would be rewarded if Dat's interrogation uncovered an escape network or led to the arrest of Cai, a fugitive with a price on his head, and assassin of one of the regime's secret policemen.

Cai had nowhere to go. He could not approach his parents. They were under police surveillance for no other reason than being his parents.

Yet he had to contact them. He was broke and they still had some gold, the currency of the black market. Sometimes he felt his continued dependence on them was the most bitter aspect of being a fugitive: his escape attempts had cost them more than they spent to live. And not just his parents made sacrifices for Cai. Phat and Tho in America were sending money back to Vietnam even as they scratched out a living for their families in a new and bewildering country.

He seemed to be straddled between the extremes of luck. The mud bank, and then the storm, had stopped him at the verge of success, but the miraculous landfall and his family's ability to finance his escapes made him uniquely fortunate in Vietnam's captive population. For would-be refugees who could raise only enough for one attempt, a fraudulent organization meant a fate so cruel that no amount of the vaunted Oriental fatalism could withstand loss of the singular leap for freedom. Defrauded families consequently disintegrated, the females to prostitution, the males to penury.

Escape scams were so profitable the government devised the biggest one:

In one delta province the cadre say, "Okay, if anybody does not want to build socialism, they can leave. We don't want them here. Pay twelve leaves of gold. We give you a good boat, then you can take off. But first you donate all property to the party." This province is rich. Lots of landowners want to get out. For the first boat, they even pay twice what the party asked for. They sign over everything—house, rice acres, cars—all they own in Vietnam. There is a big show when they leave. A coast guard boat takes them out to international water, and shows them the way to go.

In a few weeks, relatives in the province get letters from these people. They made it and are happy. The communists are happy too because the cadre has collected lots of money. They say, "Who wants to go on next boat?" Hundreds of rich people sign up. They turn over everything, like the first group, and get ready to go. Then the cadre said, "Too bad, but there is delay. No boats ready yet. While you wait, better go to new economic zone. We let you know when the next boat is ready." These people know NEZ is just a concentration camp in the jungle, so they run away. There is never another boat.

Cai's stomach churned with hunger as he waited by the roadside. Dat looked at him uncomplainingly, for kids rarely complain in Vietnam. At a curve in the road, there was an intercity bus stop fifty meters away. A few women emerged in the dawn balancing baskets of live chickens on poles across their shoulders. Other nondescript peasants gathered in the first hour. The bus had only a vague schedule, dependent on hit-or-miss maintenance, subject to the availability of watered fuel, and the deterioration of the road that was now more rubble than asphalt. Cai kept his distance from the bus stop; he wanted no one to notice him.

He was waiting on Route 1, the spinal cord of both Vietnams. From French times it had connected Saigon with Hanoi and all the coastal cities in between. Route 1 was studded with names briefly famous from war, beginning with the stretch in Quang Tri that the French had called the "street without joy." Cai knew much of Route 1 from his six years with the American army: Cam Ranh Bay, where they first came ashore, Phan Thiet, Tuy Hoa, and Bong Son, where they had clashed in early encounters with the NVA.

American trucks and armor had rolled and ruled on Route 1 since Cai was a teenager. American engineers had improved and maintained it until it handled more traffic more efficiently than any two-lane highway in the U.S.A. Now there was nothing left over from the Americans except the people who had worked for them.

People like Cai. And he knew one other. He would have to see Nguyen Ba Nam soon. They had been interpreters for the Americans; Cai with one battalion of the First Brigade, 101st Airborne, and Nguyen in a sister battalion. For six years they had helped the paratroopers defeat the army that now occupied the country. Seeking revenge, the NVA had looked for veterans like Cai and Nguyen. Seeking refuge, they had looked for each other.

Cai would be back to visit Nguyen after he returned Dat to Saigon.

Without any travel papers, he and Dat would have to hitch a ride. The morning bus would be sagging with passengers, top heavy with produce and fowl for the Saigon markets. The driver might not see who scrambled onto the racks or clung to the windows.

Rumbling, spewing black smoke, the tarnished tinsel-colored bus swayed around the curve from Vung Tau, once a resort named Cape St. Jacques by the French. Hand in hand, Cai and Dat walked toward the bus, avoiding the driver's sight in the rearview mirror. As the bus heaved back into motion, they tucked themselves on the rear baggage rack.

They had no fare, and if expelled they would wait for the next bus. But Cai's luck held as they rode back to where he would need it greatly—to Saigon, the most transmogrified city in the world.

It was also the city of his childhood and his happiest memories.

In Vietnam, as in many countries, the Chinese were among the hardest workers and the most deft entrepreneurs. Cai's father, Lam Vu Xuol, was both. With little money, or fluency in the Vietnamese language, he set up a photography store in Tra Vinh. It was primitive photography—a huge box on a tripod, a black hood, and long exposures for frozen poses—but it was a modern miracle for rural Vietnamese who had never seen a photograph that was not of a government official. Vu Xuol became prosperous making wedding albums. He was helped by his parents, who had immigrated earlier. They were restaurateurs, and soon Vu Xuol entered the business himself, opening a Chinese kitchen in the old market region of Saigon a block from the original U.S. Embassy.

With most of the Vietnamese economy run by Chinese, Vu Xuol was able to branch out farther, first into textiles and later to Japanese motorcycles. By any standards, especially those of laid-back South Vietnam, he was a stellar success. But such success aroused jealousy and triggered discrimination; nevertheless, he strove for assimilation, realizing that China under Mao could never again be his homeland. With this realization, he moved Cai from a Chinese private school to a Vietnamese public school.

Memories of Saigon always revived whenever Cai approached his parents' old house. He was there when Vu Xuol lost it in 1975.

That was the first time I saw my father weep. It was not because South Vietnam fell into communist hands. He was sad inside about that. It was because the communists took away his house. That was the old house my father bought when I was young.

It was three floors and built of concrete with windows as big as I was, and a heavy teak door. The floor and roof were made with large red brick tile. In America this was not a modern house, but it was built by the French.

In the front yard were many huge old trees. When the wind blew, the clashes of the bamboo made strange noises like a whistle. When my father wanted to buy this house, my mother disagreed because it looked like a little castle in a fairy tale.

This was why I always remember the house. The evening dinners, the young people who came on weekends, my wedding party, were all the strongest memories of my life. For my father, this house was where he raised his children and from where they all went away when the communists came.

My father had run from the communists when he was young in China. When they came again in Vietnam, he was too old, and stayed. After they took the house they let my parents live in a garage across the street.

Cai kept Dat close as they wound through the back streets of Saigon. Along the river, what the French once called the "Paris of the Orient" had crumbled into a seedy casbah, further decaying into slums that the few foreign visitors were now comparing to Calcutta. Here the scattered street lights were as dim as the economy; identification was difficult and neighborhood watchers were less vigilant because even the police hesitated to enter this quarter at night.

Cai wished he was armed in this part of Saigon. For a while he had carried a pistol here, but the peril at night had been outweighed by the danger of being stopped by the police during the day. He had no fixed place where he lived; no place where he could leave anything. For months he had not spent two consecutive nights in a single location.

When they reached a neighborhood where Dat knew the rest of the way, Cai turned back to the slums. Usually he slept by day, in abandoned tool sheds, under docks, between shacks, but after his vigil at sea he had to sleep that night.

He knew a wharf with a warehouse inhabited only by rats. It would be hard for prowlers to see him; under a gutter eave he would look like a sack in the darkness. Stumbling with fatigue, he found his place for the night.

Cai awoke as he always did in Ho Chi Minh City—hungry. He had a "leaf" of gold (approximately $200) that was to have gotten him started in Malaysia. Stiffly he trudged back from the river toward the market, where mobile money changers were always ready to trade. The communist piaster was increasingly worthless, even in local transactions; today his gold would be worth another handful of paper.

Every morning when I have gold, I try to help my morale. I say, "Cai, you are richer than last night."

The market was a curious mixture of bustle and torpor. It seemed the Vietnamese congregated for subsistence rather than profit. Because most transactions were barter, profit was hard to quantify and saving was impossible, for money saved was money lost to inflation. Banks had died with the republic, and all private phones were disconnected so that commodity prices in the countryside could only be guessed.

Cai flashed the thin gold leaf in his palm. His signal quickly drew two men, soon joined by a third—more attention than he wanted. He ignored them as he seemed to browse through the produce stalls, repeating an astronomical figure in a low voice. He was testing the market; the money changers protested loudly. Cai's eyes flashed anger. One man reassured him that he had paid off the police and so there was no cause for worry. The second man promised to meet Cai's price but would need to get more piasters from nearby. He would have to have the gold, however, before a major money changer provided the cash. Would Cai please accompany him?

The oldest scam in the black market. Cai shoved him away. He himself was shoved toward a corner by a mother and daughter. Either or both of them would love him indefinitely and in any way he enjoyed. They jabbered about their cleanliness and class, saying they had worked for South Vietnam's last president in the Independence Palace.

The transaction with its unwelcome attention was going on too long. Cai demanded a cup of noodles and privacy or else he would go to another market. One of the money changers called his woman out of her sleeping stall and sent her scurrying to a Chinese food stand. Like a policeman, he practically dragged Cai into the stall. Figures bounced between them like a Ping-Pong ball, Cai scoffing, the money changer pleading and protesting.

"Forty thousand!" Cai called through the reed-thin wall to the second money changer he knew was waiting outside. The man would not go higher, so Cai settled with his host for 40,000. But not without some fringe benefits. The woman approached bowing, to hand Cai a steaming bowl topped with chopsticks.

"I want to sleep here," he announced as he watched the money changer count off stacks of rumpled, grimy bills.

"Yes, she is a fine woman. Almost virgin."

"Send her out. I want to sleep now."

Chapter
Three

He needed to talk with Nguyen; he needed to talk with anyone, and Nguyen was the only person who could both understand and keep the secrets. Cai had to release what he felt; to describe how close he had come, how far he had returned, to be right back where he started.

He could not bear Saigon with its memories. The despair of the city felt like a crowded cell that he thought he had escaped. For the moment, Cai could not face it, and would even sacrifice some security to go out in the countryside where there were fewer people, and where strangers were watched more closely. When Cai dropped in on Nguyen every few weeks, the two drank heavily and visibly. Thus, when Cai spent the night, he had the excuse of having passed out.

It was at night that the communists always looked in on their subjects. At 6 p.m., the neighborhood watchman went around to all the dwellings for a head count and ID card check. Any visitors, and their reason for being there, were reported to the district police.

Every night, in every dwelling in the country.

A one-night drunk would go unnoted. A second night might bring a district inspector around. What Nguyen had going for him was rapport with the district inspector—they were partners in the black market. Nguyen dealt in contraband gasoline and vehicle parts, some of which he gave to the inspector.

Nguyen lived on the highway, part of an extended village that was one shack wide and ten miles long. Cai got off the bus far away so he could scout in both directions for any unusual police presence. It was hot at midday, time for the traditional nap called *pac*. In the distance the communist flag hung limply above the police station.

Nguyen sat cross-legged under the awning of his shack. Ostensibly he was a bicycle mechanic, so he idly fiddled with a battered rim and bent spokes. The war veterans greeted each other casually as if Cai's visits were routine.

They crawled into the shadows of the shack, sprawled side by side on an oil-grimy tarpaulin, and spoke in English, so softly no one outside the hooch could hear.

"Airborne!" said Nguyen cheerily, but Cai's eyes were red and downcast.

"Airborne." He dispiritedly returned the greeting of American paratroopers.

"How 'bout some wine?" It was thick, puce Vietnamese moonshine.

"Thanks."

"What happened?"

"I tried again. Almost made it."

"*Xing loi*." It was the Vietnamese expression, once in vogue with Americans, meaning both "too bad" and "it doesn't matter."

Cai related the adventure. Nguyen nodded complacently, as if listening to a story of success. Cai never told him beforehand when he was starting an escape. Nguyen would not want that knowledge. But each meeting, they realized, could be the last.

Cai had tried to interest him in joining an escape. It was hard for Nguyen to decline, but eventually he did, even though he could have raised the money: his business was good, so good that even the chance for freedom could not call him away.

He dealt with the NVA at the giant supply base at Long Binh. It was a shriveling giant however, as captured American stores were drawn down. Nguyen knew a little about how U.S. trucks were run and maintained—a little bit, but a lot more than the NVA knew.

They understood that broken parts should be replaced with new ones, but had no idea how to keep parts from breaking or how to service them.

They brought components like clutches to Nguyen, who sometimes could rig them to work. The low-ranking NVA whose job he was doing brought him more, especially machinery requiring simple periodic maintenance. He also showed them how to do oil changes.

His reward was a steady supply of gas and the opportunity to take new parts from NVA trucks and replace them with worn parts salvaged from the civilian economy. This exchange enlarged both his maintenance business and stock of material, especially tires, for the black market.

"So why you look like you step on your dick?" Nguyen inquired when Cai had told his story.

"My parents run out of money."

"So now you get money from organizer, man."

"He's not the 1/327." When Nguyen had mustered out of First Battalion, 327th Airborne, the paratroopers had crammed his baggy pockets with piasters.

"You got skill, Cai—better than gold. You tell him you'll pilot his next boat—if he pay you enough."

"Hey, you maybe smart, Nguyen."

"Fucking aye, GI. You tell him navy guys good if they find Thailand. You go twice that far and find a place small as this hooch."

"Just luck, I tell you."

"Don't tell him that."

"Okay."

"Tell him you number-one navigator. Say you'll work for him if he give you a number-one boat and pay you like navy officer."

"Good idea," Cai mused.

"Don't forget—send me a postcard."

"You better come too."

"Eight kids, Cai. I gotta sell a lotta carburetors."

Cai had made his original contact with the organizer in Soc Trang, a fair-sized city 200 road miles south of Saigon on the Mekong River. As Nguyen suggested, Cai would offer to navigate for pay. The organizer had no fixed address, but Cai felt he could find him through the black market grapevine. By bus he traveled to Soc Trang, a journey of memories, for the route went through Tra Vinh, his first home in Vietnam.

His childhood coincided with that of his adopted country. When South Vietnam was "born" in the Geneva Treaty of 1954, Cai was living with his grandparents in Tra Vinh. Across from their house in the center of the city was one of the largest buildings in the province, a hunkering gray compound surrounded by a concrete wall, like it had secrets.

It did, because it was the province headquarters for the French Bureaux #2. Cai was too young to know what that meant, but his older brother told him that "if I am against the white people, I shall be held in that building."

Those who were brought there suffered. The French, recently suppressed and oppressed themselves by the Nazis, were again the occupying power, replacing the Japanese (and briefly the British and Kuomintang Chinese) from World War II. Fighting them all in sequence were the Viet Minh, the nationalist guerrillas of Ho Chi Minh, who had appealed to the United States for assistance to gain independence. Because of his slaughter of non-communist nationalists, the American reply had been silence, so Ho—a Marxist from the start—had turned permanently to the U.S.S.R. for help.

Soviet material aid was scant, but they had dispensed Marxist ideology freely, and it had been useful for Ho to adapt the arguments of class struggle and anticolonialism for the Vietnamese situation. Ho was later to exempt South Vietnam from the slogan of self-determination, but when Cai was in elementary school that was the war cry of the Viet Minh, a paraphrase of Patrick Henry's "Give me liberty or give me death!"

Cai heard many die in the Bureaux #2 building. For a nine-year-old child, their voices could bring on nightmares.

After a big roundup, people cry in there all night. We heard one voice for about an hour, then a new one for next hour, then more. Before morning the first voice starts again. One night I even heard the beating: the French were real mad—they lost some guys in an ambush. I think they wanted the people outside to hear what they do to prisoners. When it was so bad, we were afraid to look at the building.

But on the way to school each day, Cai passed the main gate where the French guard sometimes gave him candy or chocolates. French was taught in school so Cai was able to thank the guards properly.

French patrols went into the countryside around midnight, returning at sunup with suspected Viet Minh sympathizers tied together in a long line, all badly beaten, some hobbling on broken legs. The townspeople avoided such scenes, fearing that the French might detect some sign of sympathy for the prisoners. It became second nature for the Vietnamese to conceal their reactions to what they saw. Later, with the American army, Cai many times had to explain this ingrained characteristic of his people.

In 1983 it took Cai a half day to reach Tra Vinh, a distance of about ninety miles, due to bus breakdowns and detours for washed-out roads. In 1953 the trip had taken just as long because of French checkpoints, typically at bridges where the passengers were required to walk across so they could be checked for papers and identification. The checkpoints also provided shacks for the French to rape women.

The Vietnamese found out that French and Americans do some same things, but also much is different. If American rapes a girl—big court martial. I was interpreter for a court martial in 1970. I told the girl's story in English. In French times, a soldier rapes girls even if an officer is looking. No big deal because they think girls like it. Vietnamese learn to tell an American officer if a GI rapes. When the French rape, the girl tells nobody, not even her husband. Then there is a big surprise when she has a white-skin baby.

Other big difference was about schools. Americans like to build schools. They think education is important to win people over against communism. The French never build schools; they build pagodas for people instead. If a district asked for cement to build a school, the French said no cement. But if they ask for a pagoda, army engineers come right out and build it.

Pagodas are good for superstition and keeping people calm. But Viet Minh were smarter than the French sometimes. Every pagoda has a Buddha. Religion says Buddha must have the best view around, so people asked the French to build on a hill or where canals cross. Great view, so Viet Minh use for outposts and lookouts.

Though Confucians, Cai's grandparents regularly visited a pagoda in the countryside because of its lovely view and tranquility for prayer to the Lam ancestors. It was also inhabited by two propitious snakes, arm-sized when they took up residence, but coiled after fattening they looked like tractor tires. The monks wisely called them god-snakes, holy protectors of the Buddha. Boys like Cai were not always respecters of Buddhist traditions, especially when the onset of puberty drew them to girls and the seclusion of the pagoda.

I think the monks brought the snakes. When people go into a pagoda, they must be on bare feet and knees in front of Buddha for praying. These two god-snakes liked the shade from Buddha, so they always hung around him. They made the people pay more respect.

When I grew up, I found out these two snakes got so big and fat and lazy because they were overfed. That's why they didn't want to move. People fed them twice a month with ducks. I could not understand why these hungry people saved their best fresh meat for snakes. They should kill them and eat like a sausage.

Once I saw the snakes very pissed. Once a year people threw expensive cologne on the Buddha. This was a big ceremony when peasants gathered around him for good luck. The cologne woke up the snakes and they hissed. Stuff got in their eyes, I think, and made them mad. I saw them make hoods, then I knew these snakes are cobras.

Monks said Buddha was tired of cologne every year—that's why the snakes hissed and made hoods. People should give money now instead of cologne.

When the Viet Minh lost a battle near the city, they ran into the pagoda. The French called in an air strike. It blew away a squad of communists—and also those Buddhist god-

snakes. So for a while then I thought Viet Minh were good for the people.

From events like the bombed pagoda, Cai became politically sensitive, even by the age of ten. Vaguely he sensed the social order: colonialism overlayed on feudalism. It seemed a natural order; the French governmental and commercial apparatus was like the ropes of a tent spreading from the top, supporting and enclosing the shape of society. Within their enclosure was the ancient social hierarchy. Though immigrants, Cai's family was near the top.

The person with me the most while I was in Tra Vinh elementary school was Doe. Doe means servant. I was small boy and did not know this was not her real name. She looked after me, ran errands, and did odd jobs for my family. Chi Sen ("old maid") was the old woman who took care of all our cooking and laundry. Doe was just a few years older than me.

I asked my grandparents why Doe always came home after she took me to school. They told me, "a good boy does not ask too many questions." Then I thought she does not go to school because her clothes are not nice. But I think she is lucky because when we play together after school, she can get her clothes dirty and not be criticized.

She only cried twice. Once when I was trying to spell a word, I got upset and saw her watching me. She lived behind the kitchen with Chi Sen. Her eyes were wet, so I thought I said something that hurt her feelings when I was upset about learning to spell.

I said I was sorry, but Doe looked away so I think it must be some other reason. But I can't understand what because my grandparents treated her very fair.

Doe was my best friend in childhood. One day I brought home a piece of chocolate that the French guard gave to me. I saved it for Doe. When I gave it to her she shook her head and walked away. I was so surprised because when I gave her things before it made her happy. This time, she cried.

In high school I learned there are three classes. The French, the landlords, and the peasants. Rich Vietnamese are allowed to send their children to French schools or sometimes to France. These Vietnamese helped run the government for the French. Some became officers in the French army.

Peasants were in debt for their land, but also for their fathers and grandfathers. So they must work for the landlords and remain very poor. Most peasants could not feed all their children. They raised them up to age of eleven or twelve, then sold them to rich families for servants. This happened to Doe I find out later. My family paid her father five years of her wages in advance.

Doe wept when she saw me study because she was sorry for herself, her family, and the class system. When I asked my parents what happened to her after I went to Saigon for school, they told me she took off a few months later and nobody knew where she went. I find out later that she went to join the Viet Minh. I can understand that. Doe was like a lot of people who were at the bottom of society.

Cai's bus to Soc Trang stopped in Tra Vinh across the street from the old Bureaux #2 building. The walls of the compound were newly covered with communist slogans, but the building had retained its function continuously from the colonial era. Its cells were never empty: first filled by prisoners of the French, then those of the South Vietnamese government (GVN), followed by the Vietcong (as the Viet Minh were renamed after the Geneva Treaty), and finally the NVA. Ironically, a considerable number of the NVA's prisoners were Vietcong who resisted domination by the northerners. "Liberation," Cai could see everywhere, had a different meaning for the former allies.

Tra Vinh was still garrisoned by the NVA, for this part of the delta was traditionally independent—sort of a Scotland within Vietnam's Great Britain. The delta had always been Southeast Asia's rice bowl, and the reason Indochina had once been a major rice exporter. Now it was not producing, and the price of rice had soared throughout the country.

Cai was not sure why. His last assignment with ARVN was in

the delta, and he remembered that even when the Vietcong were at their peak of strength, farmers produced sufficient rice and got it to market in spite of ambushes, intimidation, land mines, and destroyed bridges.

Now, after eight years of Hanoi's peace, rice was hoarded and bartered on the black market. He learned the reason in re-education camp:

There was a prisoner who worked for GVN, and later for communist crops plan. He saw what happens. Big surprise for him that communists want people to have little rice. Rice is wealth in Vietnam. Communists don't want anyone else to have it. People who know a lot about growing and shipping rice are eliminated because communists say that knowledge is power. That's what happen to this guy: northerners used him till they find out what he knows, then they put him in prison. He told me Hanoi made a rice shortage in the south so people look for food all the time and do not think about politics.

Even from the bus, Cai could see the black market in action. Stray soldiers around the station ignored the illegal transactions or else participated in them with scarcely a glance over the shoulder. It seemed as if the communists wished for everyone to become criminals—so long as the crimes were not political. Political penology was the reason the old Bureaux #2 building had continued its uninterrupted function.

Certain advantages derived from a sanctioned criminal society. For one thing, everyone was guilty so anyone could be arrested with evidence of a crime. Whether it was a legalistic trait inherited from the French, or rationalizations of communist doctrine, the North Vietnamese always went through the formality of charging that a crime was in progress when they made their arrests.

A second advantage for condoning a black market economy was that it privately subsidized the military and police forces. The NVA who were in Nguyen's black market ring received pay from the government of about $12 per month. The black market supplement tripled their income. Better for Hanoi that the South Vietnamese populace pay the troops than the government itself.

Finally, the North Vietnamese—so resolutely efficient and ultimately successful in waging war—had no idea how to manage a potentially rich economy. They could have put former ARVN engineers to work in repairing the roads but would not because it was more important to re-educate them politically. Cai had been in a re-education prison camp for five years. Even prisoners who were doctors had not been allowed to use their medical training until their brains were washed and dried. Like his countrymen everywhere, Cai could not understand the purposes behind the policies of the new rulers.

He slumped down as if asleep all the while the bus was in his old hometown. In Ho Chi Minh City he could have concealed his face by burying it in the official newspaper (there was nothing else to read), but here in the countryside, literacy set a person apart. Anonymity was always the surest safeguard against curiosity.

Especially in the town where his grandparents were once prominent. In prison Cai had a cellmate who had been betrayed by a woman who had not seen him in twenty-six years. And Cai had that dimple, that telltale dimple in his chin that the girls of Tra Vinh had found so cute. It was buried in his beard now, but Cai cupped his hand over his chin. He stayed that way until the bus rumbled off for Soc Trang, stirring chickens turned yellow by dust.

Soc Trang was a treacherous town. It was once an American base that seemed to be built on an anthill. Cai felt uneasy as he pushed his way off the bus. His survival senses were extra alert, as when he had patrolled in ambush country.

He arrived a little after *pac*, a time when market activity usually resumed quickly as early risers got a jump on competition, and buyer resistance might be a little lower from recent sleep. But the crowd seemed thinner than Cai expected. He could scan a marketplace wherever he was, spot the nexus in foot traffic where deals were underway, the strategic coves and vantage points where business was expedited.

There did not seem to be a perceptible drift to this crowd in Soc

Trang. People were ignoring likely trading points. There was no locus of activity and Cai could not understand why.

He glanced around and had a strong urge to get back on the bus. But he was here to find the organizer. It had been a long trip and he could not stay in an unfamiliar town for long.

He drifted toward the hardware stalls. Black market action usually centered around the men who dealt in motor and bicycle parts.

Two policemen in shabby khaki uniforms appeared on a corner. Unhurriedly, one began to roll tape across the narrow dirt street. Peasants scurried to pass him before he reached the other side and raised the tape waist high. He exchanged faint smiles with some peasants who slipped by. This was a random seal and search, a rare police practice in Ho Chi Minh City, and apparently the important people in Soc Trang had been tipped off.

Cai turned, but not so quickly that his movement would be noticed. He strode back to the bus but then turned again. A policeman was already talking to the driver, listening to his complaint with an indifferent shrug.

Cai had counted the streets leading into the market before he got off the bus. Two made a V as they entered the market. Instinctively he headed for the V, a double chance to get away.

Around him people sighed and sat down in patient clusters or drifted toward the shade of the stalls. Groups began to thicken by the fruit vendors, a sign this would be a long and thirsty wait as everyone enclosed in the taped-off square was inspected and questioned.

Cai glanced down three streets as he traversed the market. The tapes were up, causing the crowd to ooze back into the square. A whistle blew as a cyclist darted around an almost completed barricade. He got away. The local police were not armed and seemed unconcerned by the escape.

But a small group of province police were in charge. Cai could see their military-style hats moving about. He was close to the V. People were already grumbling as they turned back from one of the streets he had hoped to reach. He quickened his stride, pushing people aside as if he were a plainclothes official involved in the operation.

The street was the most shady, the least visible from the square.

The tape was still at a small angle, for a young cop was holding it slightly open next to a wooden house. But he was turning peasants away. Still, Cai approached.

Three people in front of him. He could see over them; the face of the pimply faced cop kept glancing nervously at the square. He turned a man away. He let the next man pass without looking at him, but Cai knew there had been a transaction. He dug into his pockets as a complaining woman, holding two naked infants, recoiled before the cop. Cai shoved her aside. His eyes met the cop's for an instant as their hands met and the bundle of piasters was appraised by touch.

It was big enough. Cai always kept a 1000 piaster note visible over a roll of much smaller bills. Before the cop's head turned, Cai was gone.

Chapter Four

Such narrow escapes reminded him of prison—re-education—the result of giving himself up to the communists after the fall of Saigon. Another Vietcong had been his interrogator, but Ai had been his indoctrinator, his pedagogue in re-education. In Cai's study group, Ai always focused on him, the "student" who had worked for the Americans.

"Who fought the Japanese?" Ai had demanded.

"The Viet Minh!" Cai found it wise to be the first to respond, with as much enthusiasm as he could feign. Answers repeated often enough became reflexive.

"The French?"

"No!"

"Did the Americans know this?"

"Yes!"

"Stand up and tell the group."

Before re-education, Cai had been vaguely aware of the brief Viet Minh–American detente; in prison Ai embedded the history until it seemed to Cai that it had always been in his memory.

"The Americans asked Ho Chi Minh to be their ally. They sent representatives and requested help against the Japanese. The Viet Minh were the only soldiers against the Japanese and forced them to surrender."

"What was the American promise for the Japanese surrender?"

"To make Vietnam a free country after World War II. To make Vietnam independent from the French."

"Did this happen?"

"No! There was treachery. The Americans were corrupted by the French."

"Are all Americans corrupt and imperialistic, Cai?"

"No! Not the first ones. George Washington was like Ho Chi Minh. The American declaration of independence is like ours."

"What did the American Major Petty say after he saluted our flag in 1945?"

"The white man was finished in Indochina!"

"Was he right?"

"Yes!"

"Was he believed?"

"No!"

"Why?"

"The Americans forgot the spirit of freedom in Vietnamese people . . ."

"That we will not be controlled by foreigners! Not by Japanese, Chinese, or British. Not by French and not by Americans. Why did you forget this?"

Such questions began the litany of self-criticism, at first heavily directed by the indoctrinator, but after months of drill and punishment, correct responses to the communist catechism were truly unfeigned, and the group criticized itself, collectively and individually, with a self-generated momentum that Ai needed only to modulate with the emphases of the day. Cai found the experience closest to that of learning another language:

You think one word but must say another. When Ai said something, I translated in my mind. Like when he said "imperialist" I have to think if he means French or Americans. Most words are easy. Like "imperialist puppets" or "running dogs of imperialists." They always mean the South Vietnamese government.

I learned new words, too, like "lackey." Ai told me that I was

*a lackey of Americans. When I was an officer in ARVN, I was a
lackey of the ruling class and a "false soldier."*

The jargon was useful for Cai to evade the communists as he did
in Soc Trang. Every man his age, and most women, too, had been
involved in the anti-imperialist wars either on the right or the wrong
side. In brushes with the authorities, Cai knew the role to play. He
could play the part of a Vietcong veteran but he did not: a believable
family background of a guerrilla was too intricate to fabricate and
back up with forged documents. Instead he played the penitent
ARVN. He even admitted to having been a captain, for his speech
was too educated for that of an enlisted soldier.

And by Vietnamese standards he had indeed been born to the
purple. One of his relatives had become chief of a village in Tra
Vinh Province. It was his influence that enabled Cai's father to
become a naturalized Vietnamese. A wide web of good fortune and
prosperity had been spun by the Lams and the extended clans in
which they intermarried. Cai was one of the few members of the
family still searching for the *ma*, the pot of gold under the rainbow
that seemed always to arch over the Lams no matter what conflict
or pestilence raged in the country around them.

*My sister Lanh never finished junior high, but she loved to buy
and sell things. She was not pretty, but she smiled all day long
and had good relations with everybody.*

*On a trip back to Tra Vinh with my mother she met Chung
Hong Duc, the Chinese man she married. First she opened a
small utilities store, then a pawn shop, then a jewelry store. She
also had four sons and four daughters.*

*Duc got a position on the village council so he was never
drafted into the military. When I tell young American infantry
that, sometimes they were pissed. But Duc also worked for the
Province Reconnaissance Unit and raised chickens for fighting
so people in his village could bet money on them.*

*When the GVN fell, communists arrest Duc because he was
in PRU (Province Reconnaissance Unit). It took more than one*

year for Lanh to bribe him out of re-education camp. Even though communists took her jewelry store, she buried gold in many places. In 1978 they let everyone who paid fifteen gold leaves leave Vietnam. She and Duc and three sons got to Malaysia. Phat, my older brother, was already in California so he sponsored them. Because they came out legal, they brought some wealth. Now they make window frames in California and pretty good money.

Lanh was very lucky because only one time, in 1978, the communists let people buy out. Next time, people paid, but then the communists said no, they can't go, but they don't get their money back. Many people killed themselves after that.

Another sister, Hong, did not get a good deal like Lanh. She was cashier in MACV PX for many years. Her husband was captain like me in ARVN, with a division in central highlands where NVA started the last invasion. When his division pulled out, he was missing in action. Because she had no money, Hong accepted communist Vietnam. Her sister Lanh was willing to help her get out, but Hong decided to stay.

My youngest brother, Phuoc, finished junior high, then worked for the U.S. boat club next to Club Nautique on the Saigon River. He later was interpreter for U.S. forces, like me. When the U.S. pulled out, Phuoc joined the Vietnamese Navy and became intelligence officer to work for Mr. McGill in the Defense Attaché Office, U.S. Embassy. McGill was married to a Vietnamese lady and lived in Vietnam many years. Once I captured a .44 Smith & Wesson Magnum pistol from VC. It was too big for my hand so I trade it to McGill for his .38 snub nose.

Phuoc and McGill told me in March 1975 that things look pretty bad. They already got my brothers Phat and Tho out of the country. Then they called me on the phone. I was with Twenty-first Division in delta. They said go to a secret point on top of a building near Saigon's airport. Last words they told me: "Any place better than Vietnam now."

Twenty years earlier, when Cai was a high school student in Saigon, he thought no place could be better than Vietnam. The

French with their racial condescension were gone, beaten in the showdown battle of Dien Bien Phu. They left behind Bao Dai, the "Boy Emperor" of all Vietnam, installed by the French in 1932. The Japanese had used him as a figurehead as well. When he abdicated, the monarchy was dissolved, but the French reinstalled Bao as Chief of State. But he had to abdicate again when the Viet Minh moved into the power vacuum caused by the surrender of Japan.

Bao then began a pleasant exile as the "Playboy Emperor" in Hong Kong. With the return of the French after World War II, along came Bao Dai for the third time, to earn a third sobriquet, "Absentee Emperor," because he spent most of his reign in Paris, leaving South Vietnam to be governed by his prime minister, Jean-Baptise Ngo Dinh Diem. Diem was the first Vietnamese most Americans had ever heard of. He nursed the precarious state of South Vietnam from nearly stillbirth into a fairly healthy infancy.

But there was nearly crib death. Cai remembered how with the French departure, most European shops in Saigon closed. The transportation system was in shambles. Foodstuffs could not reach the cities, and a relative's factory in Cholon (the Chinatown of Saigon) could not get enough rice from the countryside to polish and process. Nevertheless, Viet-Chinese like the Lams generally supported Diem in his struggle to preserve South Vietnam from the Vietcong. His myriad problems included a million refugees who fled down from the north to escape communism. Concealed among them were cadres to provide control of the Vietcong from Hanoi. By 1960 they were assassinating 1000 village leaders per month.

While Cai was in high school, the Americans began arriving to bolster Diem's regime. Church agencies for refugee relief, transportation and agricultural technicians, military and infrastructural advisers trickled and then poured in as Diem showed signs of creating a nation.

Many Buddhists didn't like Diem because he was Catholic. Americans didn't know what to do, but finally they dumped him. Diem was assassinated just a couple of weeks before the same thing happened to Kennedy.

Then came a lot of coups because nobody as strong as Diem was. In school, we hear tanks and APCs and sometimes ran out to see who grabs the government. No shooting. Just different units that back different groups.

I was a boy when I watch that, but even so young I wondered why the Americans try to fix up this country that fights so much among itself. Peasants had a lot of trouble when government change all the time, but in the city, Americans brought in a lot of money and jobs, and fix up the streets. Life in Saigon was pretty good.

In this "good" period for Saigon, governments turned over like seats on a ferris wheel:

Gen. Duong Van ("Big") Minh, Diem's chief of staff, led the coup that toppled him in November 1963. The wheel of fortune turned up many ironies in Vietnam: in 1975—after twelve years and a dozen U.S.-backed regimes in Saigon—Big Minh agreed to come back as a figurehead to surrender the country to the NVA. For this service, the communists let him immigrate to France.

Lt. Gen. Nguyen Khanh deposed Minh in January 1964, proclaiming himself president. He was twice overthrown by Buddhist opposition, twice restored, and finally abdicated to become Vietnam's ambassador at large.

Brig. Gen. Lam (no relation) Van Phat ousted Khanh in September 1964 but lasted only a month, to be succeeded by

Tran Van Huong, former mayor of Saigon, who survived until January 1965, followed by

Lt. Gen. Tran Thien Khiem, former Ambassador to Washington, and predecessor to

Air Vice-Marshall Nguyen Cao Ky, a name and face that became familiar to Americans during the war. A swashbuckling, pistol-packing fighter pilot, married to a comely Air Vietnam stewardess, Ky led the first air strike against North Vietnam. But his administration lasted but a few weeks as he gave way to

Col. Pham Ngoc Thao, a one-time press officer at the GVN Embassy in Washington, also a former Viet Minh with a brother serving at a high rank in the Hanoi government. Thao deserves mention as one of history's most remarkable double agents. Eventually exposed, he was executed by GVN security forces, but his remains were later reclaimed by the victorious communists for interment in the "Patriot's Cemetery," Hanoi's equivalent of Arlington.

Next came Phan Huy Quat, an ex-foreign minister. He, Thao, and Ky were all rotated out of office in the month of February 1965.

Then came the "long" tenure of Phan Khac Suu—from February to June. He was toppled by the tandem of Ky and Maj. Gen. Nguyen Van Thieu, who resigned and fled his country in fateful ides of March 1975.

Who lead the government did not make much difference to the people. Factions fought all the time. The Vietcong did not make much trouble while coups were going on. They think it is better to let South Vietnamese fight among themselves. The time with Diem was more better. Lots of people opposed him but he did what he thought best for all Vietnam. Diem was honest too, but too bad his brother and sister-in-law were so corrupt. That gives him bad press in U.S. I think. I grew up while Diem was in power: 1954 to 1963. That was the best time for me.

I have a cousin, Thi, son of my father's brother. Thi ran the restaurant at the famous Club Nautique. All the members were high class; they signed chits for expenses at the club. Thi collected their money at the end of the month.

Because my parents stayed in Tra Vinh, I lived with Thi while I went to school in Saigon, and I worked for him too. I kept an eye on the place for him and helped with the chits. My younger brother Phuoc worked next door at the annex. We both learned a lot. Many politicians came, and high-rank officials. Always they talked about Diem and each other. I began to wonder why nobody worried about fighting Vietcong. On Sundays I watched them sail and go water ski or rowing.

My uncle with the best connections is Phu Lam Anh, who owned the floating restaurant on Saigon River. "Phu" means "rich," and I learned why he got that name:

When the Japanese took over Vietnam they captured all French soldiers and made them laborers. Vietnamese people liked to see the French sweep streets, clean up sewer tunnels, and work like that. But Lam Anh was a generous and humble person so he did not enjoy French shame.

One day a French POW ran into his house and asked for refuge. Lam Anh's wife was afraid and told him not to let the Frenchman stay. She knew that when the Japanese catch a pick-pocket, they chop off his hand right away. Hiding a French POW means heads will be chopped off if the Japanese find out. So, she said, run the French guy out. But Lam listened to him and let him hide in his bedroom. Later he got away.

Four years later the Japanese surrender. Lam Anh had a very bad time with them. He was glad to see the French come back. He was also very surprised when French police came and picked him and his wife up. He asked why but they said that's just their orders.

His wife cried because it looks like he will go to Bureaux #2 for interrogation. But the police drove him downtown and to Independence Palace where the governor lives. A French colonel with his lady opened the door, and Lam Anh got the biggest surprise of his life. The guy he hid from the Japanese is now Governor of Saigon! He wore full-dress uniform with a lot of medals. My uncle stayed for a fine French dinner and everything goes good for him after that, so people call him Phu.

Through Phu's connections, Cai could have gone to a university for the sons of Vietnamese civil servants or into a number of his relatives' businesses. But the fast money was with the arriving Americans. During the summer of 1964 there had been a murky engagement in international waters between a U.S. destroyer and a number of North Vietnamese torpedo boats, which became known as the Gulf of Tonkin incident. Fire was exchanged between the warships, and one of the communists' vessels may have been sunk. Curiously, the date of this encounter is now celebrated as "Navy Day" in North Vietnam. The incident, whatever it was, resulted in the U.S. Congress passing the Tonkin Resolution, which gave President Lyndon Johnson virtual war powers in aiding the GVN against North Vietnam.

With the Tonkin Resolution, U.S. men and material flooded

Saigon as they had London before the Normandy invasion, and not just with troops, guns, and planes, but "nation building" resources in the midst of an escalating war and the rash of coups.

All my relatives wondered why Americans were getting in such a big mess, but my older brother Phat said, "Let's make the best of it," and he did that.

Although he had only a high school education, Phat spoke some English and was thus able to pick and choose among offers from the Americans for interpreters. He chose Television Associates of Indiana (TAI), a firm with a huge contract to build and operate a tower antenna system throughout the country for the Vietnamese post office. Phat went on to become a supply contractor, but before he did, he got Cai his first job—mail clerk for TAI. Cai had picked up a smattering of English in high school, which rapidly improved from contact with the Americans.

Secure in his first job at the age of nineteen, Cai could contemplate marriage. He was enraptured with his high school sweetheart, Nguyen Lena, a Chinese girl eight years his junior.

When I first saw her I felt so in love I followed to her classroom and walked in like I was having a dream. All the kids laughed at me because they thought I walked into the wrong class by mistake.

We went out together for five years, even though many other boys liked her because she was so pretty.

In the dry season we walked side by side under big shade trees where the city is not crowded. In monsoon season we shared the same raincoat and laughed at each other. We always told each other the story of what happened that day. She was very good for me because I was a kind of wild kid then. Every weekend she took me with her to a pagoda in the country. I kneel beside her for praying, while she bowed to Buddha and asked that our love be forever.

But events were swirling around the young lovers like a centrifuge. TAI completed their project for the post office; then Cai landed a job as mail clerk at the U.S. Navy's Headquarters Support Activities in Saigon. It was there he learned that American units were coming to join the fight as ARVN was losing a battalion per week to redoubled Vietcong offensives. In 1964 it was Hanoi's strategy to rush for victory before the Americans arrived in strength.

In such a military crisis, Cai was likely to be caught up in a general mobilization. Word circulated around the Navy headquarters that the U.S. units would need interpreters. In that capacity, Cai could enlist in ARVN as a sergeant rather than be drafted as a private. Not only was the pay better, the danger was less, for if there was a safe place to fight the war it was with U.S. combat forces and their awesome fire power and air support—not to mention superb medical facilities for the wounded. So in the midst of his wartime romance, Cai volunteered to serve with the Americans.

After I finished basic training with ARVN and military language school, I left for Cam Ranh Bay with nine other interpreters. We got there on July 28, 1965, the day before the 101st Airborne Brigade came in on their ship.

The night before was the first time Lena and I sleep together. This made her pregnant. She told her parents with happiness but they were ashamed that she is not married and still a schoolgirl. Her mother's crying made her very upset, so on the way to school Lena ran into a car and miscarried the baby. Her family moved to another place to get away from bad rumors about how she was pregnant.

That was how I lost contact with Lena from the time I joined the 101st Airborne till I escaped from re-education camp in 1980. Fifteen years. Very much happened in between while I never stopped looking for her, my love.

I tried to send her letters. All came back. The 101st was always in the field. They were called "fire brigade" because of moving around so much, fighting in II Corps, III Corps, all over. Four months till I could send Lena a letter in Vietnamese mail, but there was no answer.

In December 1965, we did Operation Checkerboard from Ben Cat into War Zone D. That is the closest we ever were to Lena's home. Lieutenant Johnson let me take one day of leave to look for her. His driver took me to the airport so I can get an Air Force plane that lands close to her town.

I dropped off my gear with my parents and they were very glad to see me, but I wanted Lena so much I hurried to her neighborhood. Someone who lived next door told me she miscarried and her family moved a long time ago, but nobody knew where. I came back to the unit next morning still worried about what happened to her.

The 101st kept moving around, fighting guerrillas, Main Force VC, then NVA—never stopped. We are not around towns much, but everywhere we go I looked with hope for Lena. Then I thought she might be with the Buddhists and I start looking in temples and pagodas. No one saw her, but I feel she is alive somewhere waiting for me to find her.

The 101st finally made base camp at Phan Rang. In 1967, I meet Nho—she was high school student there. I was very lonely then because I was looking for Lena so long. Nho looks very much like Lena so I decided to marry her. Things like that happen in the war. I never know if I have children before I get killed.

I was allowed seven days off for the wedding. I have to fly there in C123 from Quang Ngai, where there was an operation. About twenty interpreters go with me, and I think 101st Division Headquarters was sort of pissed because not many interpreters around to translate or question prisoners for a while.

I also borrowed eight army jeeps to pick up Nho and her family for the wedding. The interpreters laughed at each other because we are all in uniform with U.S. equipment so it looked like maybe an American wedding. Right away I had to go back into the war.

PART II

"Names we read in granite"

Chapter
Five

July 29, 1965, was a memorable day in the sands and scrub brush around Cam Ranh Bay. There to meet the 101st under a beating sun was General Westmoreland, once their commander, now CO-MUS MACV, an acronym used, almost like the name of some legendary Scottish warlord, for the chief of the U.S. war effort in Vietnam. He was known as "Westy" to the outgoing U.S. ambassador, Maxwell Taylor, who also had sentimental reasons for greeting the "Screaming Eagles" of the 101st, for he too had been commanding general of the division, its wartime leader through historic campaigns in Normandy, Holland, and Bastogne.

Unknown to each other, Cai and I were also on the shore of Cam Ranh, both awaiting assignment to the brigade about to land. As the author of this book, I'm stepping into its pages for a few chapters as a year of Cai's life coincided with mine. Within two months, we were both to be assigned to the same battalion, 2d of the 502d Parachute Infantry (2/502), known heraldically as the "Strike Force" and colloquially as the "Oh-deuce." Cai became the battalion interpreter; I, the commander of B Company.

On the day of the landing, the press found human interest in another coincidence: my father, the ambassador, was leaving after a year in Vietnam just as I started my year. He, Cai, and I awaited the brigade. All 2000 of them were crammed in what looked like a tramp steamer, the *Leroy Eltinge*, a World War II transport that unloaded the troops, then limped home to be scrapped. On the voyage to Vietnam it had broken down in mid-Pacific during a month-long crossing, so the troops' most visible emotion while debarking was relief.

The colors came ashore to the music of an ARVN band. Immediately the ambiguity of Vietnam took hold. Duffel bags in one hand, weapons in the other, the troops looked confused as to whether they should prepare to defend the beachhead or parade for the VIPs.

It was kind of funny, all these cherries. Right away they asked me if the Vietnamese civilians around are VC. I told 'em, I don't know. Have to wait till nighttime!

Nighttime during the first week sounded like the 101st was once again under siege at Bastogne. Except that there was no enemy surrounding the paratroopers, only the unfamiliar sounds of the tropical night. Nervous outposts fired at shadows and stray dogs. Fire from one sector triggered a chain reaction from others and sometimes provoked firefights between units. To Cai we seemed as erratic and jumpy as the greenest ARVN. He was right—and we were supposed to be the elite of the U.S. Army.

I was the brigade assistant intelligence officer, much perplexed by the "rules of engagement" by which the war was to be fought. There was a nighttime curfew, and the local Vietnamese were supposed to know about it. One of my jobs was to send out patrols at night to observe where there might be VC activity. At its northern end, a tongue of the beautiful Cam Ranh Bay reached up into the brigade sector. Patrols began reporting lights on the water at night and requested permission to destroy the small boats with artillery.

Fortunately there were Vietnamese like Cai assigned to us who found out that a seasonal run of fish was moving to the head of the bay and the Vietnamese always attracted them with lights. "Jacking," such fishing is called in America, and after our patrols recognized the way the Vietnamese jacked, my radio watch at night grew more quiet.

In fact the entire brigade sector fell stultifyingly quiet in the first month ashore. After the war, it was learned that Hanoi had been surprised by the 101st's landing and had no means to counter it. Their strategy of quick victory before U.S. intervention had failed, though they kept ARVN reeling elsewhere in the country.

But battles were only something we read about in *Stars & Stripes*. The Marines at Danang were largely idle, the 173d Airborne Brigade was doing little more than guarding an air base, and we were just watching engineers begin construction of a colossal port facility at Cam Ranh. In my first letter I complained to my father that his old paratroopers were spoiling for a fight. He replied that we would not have long to wait.

But wait we did for nearly two months, fighting only the heat, insects, and the outbreak of venereal disease. Cai was approached to be intermediary for the first international relations, but he would not become involved, for no translations seemed necessary as the term "boom-boom" became part of both languages.

Soon one of the first "strips" for which Vietnam became notorious appeared outside the barbed wire of the brigade perimeter. These were tin shacks made from sheets that were never shaped into beer cans. Where they came from I've never learned, but the shacks sprouted in arrays that looked like giant six packs. Beer cans were also a favorite material for Vietnamese suitcases. Budweiser and Carlings Black Label were favorite colors, and sometimes a shack adopted the name of the brand it featured. Most proprietors chose escapist themes like "Hot Heaven," "Texas Bar," or "Las Vegas."

Colonel Timothy, the Brigade Commander, told Cai to speak with the local authorities to see what could be done about the unwelcome shacks, but that turned out to be little because the local district chief was getting a cut from prostitution profits. This was our introduction to the reality that while the war might be a "cause" for us, it was an opportunity for profiteers among our allies. Patriotism, even nationalism, for most high-ranking Vietnamese was a cynical facade.

Though we hardly clashed with the Vietcong during our months at Cam Ranh, we did hurt them in an unintended way. In reviewing our intelligence input, I received reports of increasing VC intimidation in the villages around the bay. Apparently the communists were beginning to confiscate the farmers' rice. Where before our arrival they had kept good relations with the local farmers by paying for rice, we had driven up the price of everything with our plentiful dollars. Now the VC could not compete in the market that we had inflated beyond their means. With farmers disgruntled by the new VC confiscations, they gave us more information about guerrilla activities.

If, by our spending habits, we helped the war effort, by our living conditions we set it back. The troops came ashore with nothing but their duffel bags. Except for a few headquarters tents, they had no shelter; nothing to sleep on but air mattresses, nothing to sleep under but poncho liners; no showers, no chairs, no laundry facilities or lights for reading and writing.

*E*verybody had jungle boots except the guys in the jungle.

This truth described the state of the troops' uniforms. They wore the cotton fatigues issued to them in Kentucky and all-leather paratrooper boots that took a good shine for stateside parades but were only good as fungus incubators in the jungle. All the advisory personnel in Vietnam had the excellent jungle boots and quick-drying fatigues.

The troops could do little about obtaining functional jungle gear (though there was some on the black market), but they could help themselves—literally—to improve how they lived. All around them the Army Engineers, the Air Force, and American contractors like RMK were building the Cam Ranh base with a cornucopia of construction materials.

Plywood began to disappear from the construction sites as our informal patrols visited them at night. Vehicles as big as 2½-ton trucks appeared in our motor pools with fresh paint and new markings on the bumpers. Cement was "found" in abundance and pierced steel planking (PSP) for the Air Force's runways became our tent floors. A construction manager for RMK told me that the 101st set back his construction timetable more than all the enemy activity in the war.

When we finally went to war, probably no one was sorry to see us leave except the prostitutes.

As his last gamble to win the war in 1965, Ho Chi Minh for the first time moved the NVA in strength against ARVN to cut South Vietnam in half along Route 19. Military Assistance Command, Vietnam (MACV) was aware of the plan and had the First Air Cavalry Division at sea en route to a base at An Khe athwart Route 19. But by late August, it appeared An Khe might fall before the First Cav arrived. Consequently, our brigade was sent to secure the base. As we choppered to our destination, we flew over rusted hulks of French vehicles that the Viet Minh had ambushed in their slaughter of Mobile Group 100 twelve years before.

The highlands here were a bit cooler than Cam Ranh Bay and everyone was ready for a change of clime. Cai had never seen this region of his adopted land, populated more by Montagnards (the French name for the hill tribes) than by Vietnamese. He was with me when the reconnaissance troop recorded their first kill.

A jeep roared into our encampment with a body strapped to the hood like a deer. It drew a crowd, including Colonel Timothy. There it was, this body, still oozing blood onto the radiator grate. A sergeant waved an old American carbine, the dead man's weapon. The corpse also wore a pack and pistol belt so there was no doubt that he had been a full-time guerrilla. He looked young, ignorant, and his jaw flapped loosely as he was untied from the jeep's hood. My strongest impression was how dead he was—heavily dead, so that when his limbs were loosed they fell in a way I'd never seen anyone contorted.

We ordered Cai to translate the blood-soaked papers in the VC's pack. This was to be a job he would repeat a thousand times.

After some back slapping and bravado, we glanced at each other with concealed embarrassment: we had been in Vietnam nearly two months and this was about all the proud Screaming Eagles had to show for it. At this rate, the war would go on to be fought by our grandchildren.

At An Khe the score read: 101st, 1, VC, 0. At least we were ahead.

* * *

Between An Khe and the port of Quinhon (where the First Cav would debark) was a valley some twelve miles long, tapering north from Route 19. The brigade would have to clear this valley so that the First Cav's convoys were not harassed by the VC. We focused our patrols there. Exchanging fire with snipers, disarming booby traps, discovering mines, our patrols began to learn the ways of war in Vietnam.

Some respected military commentators have called our foe the best infantry in the world at that time. As an intelligence officer, that was not my impression. The VC were wily, durable, extremely determined, and frustratingly difficult to bring to battle, but these merits were not so much intrinsic as they were the result of living where they operated. Knowledge of the local terrain permitted them to disappear when we seemed to have them cornered. In this valley, which I named in irony, "Happy Valley," we were playing on the VC's home field, where guerrillas such as the unimpressive one we first killed were dangerous will-o'-the-wisps.

Our first aim was to clear the field of all but the contestants. We did this by sending Cai and others over Happy Valley in light planes to broadcast on loudspeakers for the civilians to move south of the highway. Cai also dropped leaflets with the same instruction and a deadline. The response was scant, but at least we felt we had given fair warning. Luckily, there were few civilians with the VC, so the stage was set to see who would rule the valley.

We staked our claim with waves of small patrols. If the VC operated in small groups, we would too. They were famed as night fighters, and ARVN was known for surrendering the hours of darkness to them. So it was by night that we took the fight to the heretofore unchallenged guerrillas.

The principal VC weakness, temperamentally, was their confusion and lack of initiative in the face of the unexpected. Their administrative network—that is, their tax collecting, medical system, resupply, and most communications—assumed free passage by night. Through night ambushes, we upset their sense of security and the freedom of movement necessary for them to impose their will. Soon we captured documents that described the effect we were having. Cai translated some of the VC's frustrations: ". . . In the day there is artillery that seems to watch us. At night the chicken soldiers with their black rifles hide by our paths." To the VC we were known as the "chicken soldiers" because of the white eagle screaming on our shoulder patch. The "black rifles" refers to the M16, which the VC had never seen. We were learning about each other and the Americans were learning faster. Then the VC made a major mistake and we almost made a greater one.

Around twilight one night my radio crackled with an unfamiliar voice. He was a fighter pilot overflying our area of operations (AO), and he had just received fire from a .51 caliber machine gun from the head of Happy Valley. I had learned from the VC "order of battle" that such a heavy weapon was usually found with a battalion-size force. I went to the map and drew the red symbol for the suspected unit. Maj. David Hackworth was the brigade operations officer at the time and immediately became interested because we had yet to come across a VC company, much less a battalion.

On such a scanty lead, Hackworth did not go after the suspected target with a big force, but he told me to get some patrols out into the head of the valley. The job was given to the Oh-deuce, where Cai had recently been assigned.

The patrols were the job of infantry squads, but in the Oh-deuce there was a Hawaiian cook who wanted nothing more in life than a VC weapon to take home. Consequently, whenever he finished his duties in the kitchen, he volunteered for patrols.

We had never patrolled so deeply into the jungled mountains at the head of Happy Valley. Slithering through the foliage, like stalking Indians, the cook's squad came upon an abandoned Montagnard settlement. He brought up the rear of the squad—as a cook he was not trusted to do the most dangerous scouting. He watched his comrades move through the dilapidated huts with silent caution, covering each other's moves, until it seemed the search was complete. Like all such settlements, the ground was honeycombed with covered pits once used for bomb shelters. But all were now caved in or cobwebbed from long disuse. His squad had disappeared into the jungle when the cook peered into the last of the pits.

A rifle barrel poked out like a periscope. He froze as it leveled on him. He heard the click of the firing pin. The rifle had malfunctioned.

The cook's shout brought his squad back; they surrounded the pit and the VC came out with his hands up. The cook got his souvenir—the rifle that nearly killed him—and we got a lot more.

The VC was an AWOL who had been harassed by the guerrilla battalion's political officer, so our prisoner talked freely. He had deserted the battalion a few days before so he wasn't sure where they were, and furthermore he could not read a map. But his information corroborated the pilot's report. I confidently placed the symbol for the Ninety-fifth VC Main Force Battalion at the head of Happy Valley.

Hackworth quickly cranked up Operation Gibraltar to trap and destroy the Ninety-fifth Battalion. One of our battalions, the 2/327, would move overland to close in on the Ninety-fifth from the southwest while the Oh-deuce choppered in on flat ground to the east, then move up into the mountains on the Ninety-fifth's other flank. My most important job was to recommend the landing zone (LZ) for the Oh-deuce.

The map suggested large clearings around the village of An Ninh ("Calm of Peace" in Vietnamese) suitable for simultaneous landing of a dozen troop-carrying Hueys. I got the Air Force to do a rush job for aerial photos of this LZ. They were in my hands two nights before the assault was to land.

The district chief told us An Ninh had long been abandoned, and indeed the photos showed no signs of life. However, the outskirts of the village were crisscrossed with trenches obviously dug by the VC in case they ever needed to defend it. The Oh-deuce was to land within the network of trenches. If the VC manned them, the Hueys would be ambushed and the Oh-deuce slaughtered.

I searched for more evidence from the photos. There was a rickety flag pole in front of what had once been the village chief's headquarters. I noted this, because it might be an obstacle for the landing choppers, and sent the photo on to the Oh-deuce commander. But I kept a copy for our records and it was with me at brigade headquarters as H hour for Gibraltar drew closer.

I saw that photo too while we got ready. I didn't worry about it till the S3 tells me to go in with the first lift. Then I wondered why he thought we would meet Vietnamese so soon!

These were Cai's thoughts as he prepared for only the second helicopter ride in his life. We expected him to have a safe landing at An Ninh: the Ninety-fifth Battalion was supposed to be in the hills beyond. We were wrong—almost dead wrong: the headquarters of the Oh-deuce (including Cai), and half of the companies landed squarely on the headquarters of the Ninety-fifth Battalion.

Both sides were violently surprised. The VC were not alert for helicopters because ARVN always "prepped" their LZ's by saturating them with artillery fire before a landing. Indeed, Hackworth had planned to prep the Gibraltar landings but had not reckoned with the concealed road craters that hampered movement of our howitzers.

Some months later, the Ninety-fifth Battalion clashed with the First Cav near Bong Son, and the cavalrymen captured the VC report on the battle of An Ninh. It was an astonishing document that chilled our relations with ARVN forever after. As required by allied agreements, Hackworth had submitted the operations plan for Gibraltar—including the LZs we would use—to the province headquarters. There VC spies had copied the plan and sent it posthaste by courier to the Ninety-fifth Battalion commander, who had several days to prepare for our arrival and anticipate the glory of exterminating an elite American unit in an ambush version of Dien Bien Phu. At this introductory stage for U.S. forces in the war, such a disaster would have had incalculable effects on the morale of both sides.

By the mercy of God, and for reasons he cannot remember, Hackworth kicked off Gibraltar a day early. In the bustle of accelerated staff work, he also neglected to inform province headquarters of the change. He thinks he may have told me to do it (I had transmitted the original plan to province), and if so this failure in my duty was of far more benefit to the 101st than any contribution I made thereafter.

For at dawn, when the Oh-deuce swept down from the sky on An Ninh, the VC battalion commander was completing his preparations for our attack he believed would come the next day. His troops were all in place to rehearse the ambush. He had assembled his company commanders to go over final details when the Oh-deuce roared out of the sky.

An air strike cut his field phone lines to the entrenched troops, and due to the rigidity of their discipline, the first flight of choppers was allowed to land as the VC waited for their company commanders' order to open fire. It never came, as fate, which had miraculously spared the unsuspecting Americans, reversed its quirk in the next few moments.

The paratroopers sprinted from the choppers and sprawled into an oval skirmish line. In a stream bed, a machine gunner swiveled his M60 to cover some nearby huts. Six black-clad men burst out of a hut, obviously alarmed. The American could have cut them down point blank but he saw that they were unarmed. In their surprise, they had left their pistols in the hut. There had been no fire on the ground, and according to MACV's rules of engagement —drummed into the troops' minds from the time they boarded the *Eltinge* months before—unarmed Vietnamese could not be fired upon unless they resisted capture.

The six men were the Ninety-fifth Battalion commander and his company commanders. Their early death would have meant quick victory for the Oh-deuce at An Ninh, but the VC leaders scurried away under the sights of the machine gunner. The battle was joined when Cai landed a few minutes later—armed with a .22 caliber derringer.

Down *we come. Bullets zinging all around! I say to myself, "Cai you won't be in this war very long." I jumped into a trench next to Lieutenant Colonel Smith and we don't look out for a long time.*

They would have seen the first group to land lose thirteen men, and a brave captain killed as he tried to wave off the second flight of choppers. Cut off from reinforcements and resupply, the men of the Oh-deuce closed a tight perimeter to fight in all directions as their predecessors had at Bastogne.

For me, the day of their encirclement began at dawn when the fleet of Hueys sailed overhead in a formation of vees. I had never seen such an armada, and a certain eerie feeling seemed to float by with it. It was a foreboding that would return in other circumstances, and I taught myself to recognize it. Some of my point men in B Company possessed this sixth sense and they were never ambushed. This day when the Oh-deuce flew on toward An Ninh, I felt a compulsion to look again at the aerial photo of their LZ. There was a magnifying glass handy. I stared at the enlarged flag pole. There, hanging from it limp as a rag, was a flag.

It could not have been a GVN flag—so it had to be VC.

News of the Oh-deuce's predicament was flashed to Saigon. This was the first time a sizable U.S. unit had been in serious trouble since the war began. The situation was fraught with political as well as military implications, for we were expected to get in and win the war, not reenact Dien Bien Phu.

In silent distress, Timothy, Hackworth, and some of the staff paced around the jeep where I manned the radio receiving the Oh-deuce's reports. Clearly there was not much they could do to influence the faraway siege. The result would be determined by men pulling triggers and hurling grenades.

But Timothy tried in every way he could. Fighter-bombers flew in from all over the country to provide constant support. Round-the-clock bombing was nearly as effective as the absent artillery. Nevertheless, the Oh-deuce's situation grew critical as their ammunition ran low. Soon they relied on the M79 grenade launchers that the VC had never encountered. It looks like a sawed-off shotgun, and with a little practice a man could lob a grenade into a barrel at fifty meters. Cai learned to use one at An Ninh.

Still, without more ammunition, the airhead would go under. There seemed a possibility to get in some supplies by using the First Cav's choppers, which had arrived that day at Qui Nhon after sailing around the world from Georgia. Huge Chinooks, never before seen in Vietnam, soared over the valley en route to An Khe and oblivious to the Oh-deuce's fight for survival.

The First Cav was commanded by Maj. Gen. Harry Kinnard, who soon came out to see Timothy. Their meeting was an indelibly poignant one, especially for me and the 101st heritage.

For Kinnard, as a lieutenant colonel, had been the operations officer for the 101st in World War II. Indeed, he had suggested the immortal reply to the Germans' surrender demand at Bastogne—

"Nuts!" No one in the illustrious history of the division could claim a deeper attachment to the 101st than Kinnard.

The screaming eagle on his right shoulder and the First Cav patch on his left symbolized Kinnard's personal dilemma as Timothy beseeched him to divert a Chinook into the Oh-deuce's airhead. Gravely, Kinnard said "No." The Chinook was a cargo, not an assault chopper, and if small, armed Hueys could not dart into the LZ, what chance was there for the lumbering, defenseless Chinook?

He was right but he was overruled. Westmoreland had sent his deputy, Lt. Gen. John Throckmorton, up from Saigon to appraise the situation and do what he could to salvage it. He told Kinnard to lend Timothy a Chinook. It went in and was shot down in a fiery crash.

I saw B57 drop bombs around our position, then F100's. I felt the ground go up with each bomb. Sergeant Major Strawser then told us to back up to the dry creek bed where there is better cover. We did this while bombs hit.

Time was slow after the Chinook crashed. I saw troopers drag dead bodies toward us. They are left by a dike for later. A guy asked me if I was getting hungry. I said, "Not really." But he thinks it is time for chow, and asks me, "Why don't you crawl over to the bodies, bring a rucksack here, and we might have something to eat." I tell him that is a good idea but I am Confucian and cannot take anything from dead people.

But I must crawl over anyway because Strawser told me I must be on guard that night, and I have only the derringer. I took a K50 Chinese submachine gun from the dead VC, but it has brains and blood on it. I threw up and asked for an M16.

As the bushwhacking battle went on, the afternoon waned. The airhead reported that some of the wounded were dying.

Captain Rawls was hit right when we landed. A very brave medic dragged him into the trench close to us. He did not bleed much—maybe a jigger from his back. But when it got dark, he died. I just joined the unit but I felt real bad. I always remember the sound of a bullet when it hits a man. It sounds like a hard slap. There was a body between the trench and the jungle. Bullets keep hitting it in crossfire—slap, slap, slap.

At the brigade CP we dreaded the onset of night almost as if we were in the airhead. Bombing was difficult to control in the dark, depriving the Oh-deuce of their principal defense against a mass attack.

Finally our artillery was able to get into position. In a thundering greeting, barrage after barrage bracketed the airhead.

Our FO was super good! Even in the dark the shells walk right up to the trenches. I heard VC getting wounded and I think maybe we can get through the nighttime.

Cai's instinct was right. A C130 poured out flares like a fiery waterfall throughout the night. The white glow looked like the dome of light from a distant city. We were braced for catastrophe but the reports from the airhead began to sound almost encouraging. We started to hope, then seriously speculate, that rather than closing in for the kill, the VC were using the night to break contact and get away.

Even though VC tried to take advantage of the night to overrun our position, all their attempts failed. There was no panic. I heard Sergeant Wilhite crawl back and forth and talk to the troops for their morale. Made me think only Lieutenant Colonel Smith and me are scared. With cold wind, firing, and flares falling all the time, I counted every minute till the next morning.

Our other battalion, plus ARVN rangers, battled the jungle all night to break through to the Oh-deuce. By mid-morning, one relief force linked up with the airhead.

Everybody shouted like hell when we saw the 327th come out of the jungle! We were plenty glad to get out of that trench. Sort of laughed because the VC dug it. Saved our ass for sure.

Cai had little time to rest or relax. He was put right to work translating documents found with the VC bodies. My job was to count the bodies from reports that were radioed to me by the patrols that roamed out from An Ninh.

"Body count" was a controversial measure of success in Vietnam. Unjustifiably so. This grizzly statistic has historically been the most valid determinant of victory or defeat. Stalingrad was not a disaster for Hitler because he could not capture the city but because he lost a quarter of a million men trying. El Alamein was not Britain's greatest victory because they seized a desert ridge but because they destroyed Rommel's Afrika Corps in the process. Destruction of the opposing army has always been the principal objective, not the capture of real estate.

This was even more true in Vietnam, where real estate had ephemeral strategic value. What was different about Vietnam was that bodies meant far less to the communists than to us. General Giap, the NVA's counterpart to General Westmoreland, said it himself: "Every minute hundreds of thousands of people die on this earth. The life and death of a hundred, a thousand, tens of thousands of human beings, even our compatriots, means little."

The number of his compatriots whom we killed around An Ninh meant much to us, for there was no other indicator to prove we had won a battle that had begun so badly for us. I felt pressure from higher headquarters to produce a "good" body count.

Much has been made about how body counts were inflated. I can only speak from personal experience, beginning with An Ninh. The figure 226 which I compiled was, I think, pretty accurate and certainly not invalidated by the Ninety-fifth Battalion's own report, captured later by the First Cav. Bodies are not entities, especially those resulting from bombs and artillery. That is how most of the VC at An Ninh were killed. Was a severed arm dangling in a tree a body? Blobs of boney pulp—quickly scavenged of blood and flesh by insects—represented how many bodies? And how many VC should be counted in the comingled remains found strewn in a swamp? The answers are estimates.

In aggregate, our body count for the whole war was low. For this fact we have Giap's own admission in 1989 that he lost a million troops while our body count claimed no more than half a million. His figure does not surprise me. For every enemy we counted as killed, we surely wounded another, no doubt more. The enemy's evacuation and medical system was as primitive as in our Civil War. Consequently, huge numbers of VC and NVA died of their wounds, to be recorded only by their comrades.

Why then, if we inflicted such staggering casualties, were not the communist forces annihilated? Eventually they were—those that were in South Vietnam. But beyond were Cambodia, Laos, and North Vietnam. Sanctuaries, they were called, places of refuge where the NVA could refit, reequip, and receive replacements for the bodies we counted. Without these sanctuaries tolerated by President Johnson, Giap could have never won his war. Even with them he did not succeed until the war was once again "Vietnamized."

But for the next six years the war was largely America's, especially on our home front. Once, while translating VC documents, Cai came across a postage stamp from Hanoi commemorating a contemporary American, Norman Morrison. It took Cai a long time to find someone in the brigade who had heard of Morrison, a Quaker who burned himself to death with kerosene, his infant daughter in his arms, on the stairs of the Pentagon.

Americans are very different from each other. I never think some burn themselves like Buddhist monks in Saigon. But I also never think they leave Vietnam for the communists.

Chapter Six

The brigade moved off to Quinhon to secure the arrival of another incoming division, this time the Korean marines, called ROKs (Republic of Korea). In the case of these marines, the acronym was also a pun because they were all muscular six-footers, hard as rocks.

The ROKs set the tone of their relations with the Vietnamese quite differently than we had by banning beer can shacks around their perimeter. The first Vietnamese thief they caught was summarily executed and hung on the barbed wire, moldering until the district chief prevailed to have the body buried.

Koreans understood the Vietnamese pretty good. They had respect for old people and liked the local food. But they can be very hard on people too. Sometimes they dropped off a few soldiers in a village to spy on VC in the countryside. ROKs told villagers, "If anything happens to our men, we will come back and burn this village." They did that too.

Shortly the ROKs began their great success with "pacification," the term for subverting the populace from VC control. Our investment in the Korean War seemed to pay large dividends when the ROKs came to the aid of South Vietnam.

The Oh-deuce now had new company commanders because two had been killed at An Ninh. Hendrik Lunde, grim and relentless, took over A Company; I had B Company, and Bob Murphy, an intense, commando-type commander, had C. Soon Lieutenant Colonel Smith left, replaced by Hank Emerson, who would be our battalion commander for the next year.

With a rangy build and warmingly volcanic demeanor, Emerson engraved the battalion with a personality that fit his radio call sign —"Gunfighter."

"Every day that Hank did not fight the VC or NVA he wanted to," was Cai's initial and accurate opinion. For this goal, Emerson had three willing company commanders. We knew the enemy had not seen the likes of the Oh-deuce and we were eager to make an introduction.

Cai was the battalion interpreter, but Emerson usually sent him down to the companies where translations were most timely. On paper, he was a sergeant in the ARVN, but he had been accepted as a Screaming Eagle, sharing our rations, hardships—and learning about us.

*S*ometimes the MPs ask me stay on the strip after curfew in order to talk with business there. One night a bar owner came to me with an M14 rifle and said the weapon was left when she closed, and she asked me to bring to whoever lose it. I tell her it does not belong to 101st because all of them carry M16. She said she will get in trouble if she keeps it, so I took it.

I took this rifle to Oh-deuce supply sergeant. He was surprised to see an M14, and said he will give me a Bowie knife and army watch. I told him I just want to return M14, but he say, "You do good, so take the knife and watch for trade."

ARVN issued me an old carbine called a grease gun. Troopers never saw that gun before and always want to play with it and ask for trade. After a while Private First Class Leddelytner came to me with .22 caliber derringer with a few hundred rounds of ammo in an army sock. He asked that I trade for the grease gun.

I told him, what can I shoot with this little pistol? But he said he will give me another revolver later, so I agreed. He did that, but not till a month later, after we were in big battle at An Ninh. There I just had this little lady's pistol and Bowie knife—not much good against main force VC! That was a lesson for me. From that time I get M16 and keep it with me always.

Cai proved himself valuable to us in many ways:

When *we were at Suoi Dau at night we could see the light glow from Nha Trang. The company commander sent me for beer because the days were very hot. I spent all the money he gave me for Bier Larue. Troopers called this beer "tiger piss." It is very strong and well liked. After I bought it, I looked in my pocket but there was no more money because I lost some to the sergeant who teaches blackjack.*

I went to the police checkpoint and asked for help to get a ride. Because I was broke they did not help me so I must beg bus drivers to take me. I asked them how can I walk ten miles with so much beer? They all shook their heads, so I must go back to owner of beer store. I told him if he will take me in his truck, the Americans will give him all the gas he wants. He thought that was a good deal because gas is very expensive for civilians, so he drove me back to the company area. I am very sorry for him because at night the American gas pump is closed, and I am ashamed because I already knew that.

Next day it was also too bad for bus drivers who did not help me. They all got to go through our checkpoint. I told the CO what happened about the beer and he ordered each bus to unload everything for inspection. Drivers asked me for help, but I said, you guys should give rides to help American troops.

While securing the ROKs arrival, the brigade also—it seemed an afterthought—began carving out a base for itself. The first site was called Suoi Dau, a plot of hilly jungle between Nha Trang and

Cam Ranh. When hundreds of local laborers were hired to clear the underbrush with sickles, Cai was one busy interpreter.

I got worried about laborers around the CP and weapons. I told the first sergeant and he said keep an eye on the laborers. But there are so many. Then first sergeant started looking too. One day, sure enough, we find this guy with a grenade in his pocket. He says he stole it, but it is different type grenade than ours. It also has a string around it for making a booby trap. I said this guy is VC for sure, and I think he was shot.

Suoi Dau was abandoned before our base could be built. Someone in Saigon decided that we should instead move down to Phan Rang to collocate with a U.S. fighter squadron that was building an airstrip there. So after four months without a roof over our heads, we packed up for Phan Rang, hoping to build some shelter before the rains came.

It was not until a year after our arrival that concrete slabs were poured at Phan Rang and permanent tents erected. According to General Westmoreland, we spent more time in the field than any U.S. unit in Vietnam. He could have included the NVA.

Ostensibly and officially we were a parachute unit. That meant, according to regulations, that each man was to make one parachute jump per month in order to qualify for "hazardous duty" pay. It seemed there was plenty of hazardous duty in the jungles around us, but for a while the jumping requirement continued in force to the amusement of the VC, who occasionally took pot shots at us dangling in the air. Sometimes Cai, who as an ARVN was exempt from jumping, took our pictures.

Another regulatory relic was the requirement for an honor guard for men killed in action. When MACV consisted of advisers only, and casualties were few, a squad of Americans accompanied each body to Saigon to render honors before the deceased was flown home. Such an honor guard was appropriate for the advisory era, but at An Khe a company that lost four men also lost a platoon for a week! We accomplished little that month at Phan Rang except for removing such anachronisms from our procedures.

* * *

Emerson was a student of irregular warfare and an evangelist for the new tactics he devised. He came up with a concept called "checkerboard" and promoted it widely. Checkerboard was developed to counter the VC practice of moving at night or in dense jungle so as to remain undetected. Despite the poor odds of finding VC in these conditions, the most common method of searching for them was by saturating suspected areas with patrols. Emerson reasoned that such sweeps were an uneconomical use of patrols because an entire area need not be searched in order to make contact with the VC. The probability of contact was multiplied if small patrols were deployed in a checkerboard pattern with gaps between them.

So the principle of checkerboard was that of a minefield: VC might slip through the first row of spaced mines but they would likely "hit a mine" in the second or third row. The laws of probability ruled that no guerrilla force of any size could wriggle through an entire checkerboard without contact. Moreover, a far-flung checkerboard allowed a considerably larger area to be investigated than was possible by saturation patrols. The disadvantage was that the smaller and widely separated patrols might run into bigger VC units than they could handle. Emerson was confident that with our artillery, air support, and helicopter mobility, we could back up a patrol and turn the battle.

Without freedom of movement, the VC disconnected from its infrastructure, and the capillaries of their military-political control would shrivel.

Ideal checkerboard country was flat terrain where the geometry of the concept could be exploited, and in December 1965 Emerson was given such a locale for a test: War Zone D, as the French had called it, beginning some thirty miles north of Saigon. There in the forested plain of a Michelin rubber plantation, a dreaded regiment of VC had overrun an ARVN battalion the previous month.

We suffered most of our casualties—a full squad of men—en route to the base where we would spread the checkerboard. The VC's weapon was a command-detonated mine that exploded under one of our trucks as we convoyed up Route 13 to Ben Cat.

It was a very big mistake not to clear the hooches along that road. A dozer should dig up shoulders and cut wires for mines. Some little guy just waited with a radio battery till our trucks came along. Very sad what happened. Guys all messed up.

Overlapping jurisdictions and official reluctance to dislocate villagers prevented us from following Cai's suggestion. The approaches to Ben Cat were the most populated areas in which the Oh-deuce operated. I was grateful that thereafter we had to contend with only the enemy and the wilderness. Separating guerrillas from the populace was as easy as dehomogenizing milk.

The battalion fanned out into its checkerboard patrols. Movement was swift and easy through even rows of rubber trees, but the alternating sense of concealment and exposure was unnerving. From behind a tree there seemed to be solid wood in one direction but long vistas in others. "Halls and walls," one trooper described it.

My three platoons had not split into their squads when we made our first contact. The opening burst was American fire, a good sign that we had surprised the VC rather than vice versa. But soon small arms cracked back at us, and I moved up to investigate. It was one of Emerson's many appreciated traits that he did not call on the radio when he heard fire but came down to sense the situation himself. I knew my platoon leaders preferred similar noninterference from me, so I tried to get to the action without interrupting their concentration with a call on the radio. A unit's proficiency could be well judged by its silence on the air, because the VC were superb eavesdroppers on our radio conversations, and that was an important reason for their success in eluding us.

So I hurried forward with my artilleryman so he could bring down the heavy fire of howitzers. We quickly came upon a squad of my men who had ducked down on the trail as VC fire shredded the foliage over their heads.

"Get moving," I told the squad leader, who promptly did so as if the firing had stopped. It had not, but he took off, his men close behind him, as if they had only been waiting for my order.

For a moment their obedience amazed me. They did what they were told though they knew their lives were at risk! That was the basic and simplest premise of the army, but it was stunning to experience it personally for the first time.

That first contact started a ripple of others, so I threw artillery all over the abandoned plantation. The VC were protecting rice they had stored but were not prepared to withstand the artillery barrages. Later I heard that Michelin sued the U.S. government for the damage we did to the rubber trees. I will never buy a Michelin tire.

By nightfall we had uncovered a half dozen VC caches, the rice in hundreds of cloth bags decorated with a large insignia featuring the stars and stripes over two clasped hands. By black market or capture, the VC were living off rice the U.S. had given the GVN.

We called in cargo helicopters and hauled out as much rice as we could, giving it to the GVN for the second time. But one cache was so large (several tons) and in such dense forest that the rice could not be evacuated. So I had most of the company go back to the cache, each man pick up a bag, slit it, and walk away in all directions so the rice would sprinkle unrecoverably through the jungle.

Emerson approved my decision, but Cai thought the VC might come back to get their rice even if it was in spoonfuls. This I doubted but decided to ambush the cache anyway.

I chose my senior platoon sergeant for the ambush and told him it might be hairy. He did not think so, kidding Cai about being stabbed with a spoon. With "airborne" insouciance, Sergeant Crowe asked for only three men and a radio to stake out the cache.

My father took quirkish pride in having had a good night's sleep all throughout the hot action of World War II, his point being that a sleep-starved officer is dangerous to everyone under his command. He even claimed to have slept for six hours on the night of June 6, 1944—D Day at Normandy. When it came to catching sleep, I strove to emulate my father, and can only remember a few nights that I was constantly awake. The longest one for me was the night on the radio with Sergeant Crowe.

Darkness, and Crowe's tiny patrol, had hardly settled in when he began to see what appeared to be fireflies drifting in from the forest. He tried to remember any briefings that dealt with the entomology of Vietnam but became increasingly certain that fireflies were not a native insect.

He was right: the ghostly lights were tiny candles held behind leaves by a large number of approaching VC. They were converging on the cache like filings to a magnet, following every gossamer trail of rice my men had strewn. Within an hour the lights had drawn so close Crowe and his men could hear faint scraping. Cai was right: the thrifty VC had returned with spoons.

They were so close Crowe did not dare even whisper into the radio. One of his men claimed to smell the garlic the VC exuded. It was inevitable that in their scraping, they would come upon the holes in which the Americans were hiding.

Before this happened, Crowe touched off his one command-detonated mine, a claymore that blasted the forest like a volley of buckshot. Before the VC recovered from their shock, Crowe told me to fire the artillery until he said stop. He never did, and shells rained over the cache all night, but never quite drove the VC away. I sent a platoon and a change of underwear out to Crowe at daybreak.

The next morning he trudged into the CP looking years older than when he left. By radio I had talked to him throughout the night, asking for his sensings of the artillery's accuracy. Because of his intimate distance from VC prowlers, he could only reply by code, squeezing the microphone once for "yes" and twice for "no." Now he spoke his peace:

"You said it might be hairy, sir. It was."

The VC reacted to the checkerboard the way they reacted to any innovation we threw at them: they backed away to devise stratagems to counter ours. They withdrew deeper into War Zone D, leaving many stores and supplies for us to discover like an Easter egg hunt. In contrast to a conventional army that lives off a "tail" of supplies brought up from the rear, guerrillas live off a logistic "nose" of caches pre-positioned ahead of their advance. The main force VC we engaged in War Zone D were supplied from a logistical corridor that wound down from the Cambodian border. We intruded into the corridor and disrupted their timetable for strangling the approaches to Saigon, but we were the first to realize that when we left the VC would resume progress toward their objective like a stream of transporting ants.

When asked what their objective was, prisoners invariably replied, "Saigon." That amused us at the time.

We were feeling good about ourselves. Generals were calling the brigade a veteran force now, and some said we were the most effective in the country. The press picked up on our exploits, and one day near the end of Operation Checkerboard, a few came out for an appraisal. For us, they turned up at the wrong place at the wrong time.

My "Mexican platoon," as they proudly called themselves because of high Hispanic membership, had skirmished with the VC rear guard. As journalist Malcolm Browne described the contact,

> There was a flicker of movement, and suddenly it was there on the trail—an ugly black grenade with a wisp of smoke shooting from its wooden handle. It was there for only a split second. Chinese-type potato-masher grenades have short fuses. When it went off, four Americans were hurt, one of them screaming in agony.
>
> The crash of the explosion left GIs stunned momentarily, but then some began firing and others charged into the thick of the jungle, intent on getting the Vietcong who had thrown the grenade. He got only a few hundred feet away before a GI found him . . .

The VC was staggering and bleeding from a bullet wound. Rather than shoot him again and possibly draw return fire from other VC, the trooper dispatched him with a hatchet. The kill was in dense jungle. To drag the body back seemed more trouble than it was worth. The trooper realized, however, that identification of this guerrilla might be important, as the GVN had pictures of many VC and would be grateful to know they could remove this one from their "wanted" gallery. So with a few more hacks with his hatchet, the trooper severed the head to return it for identification. Carrying it by its hair like the head of John the Baptist, he came out of the jungle into a clearing where the journalists were gathered.

There was a brief flurry of investigations, and allegations of atrocity, but fortunately the only permanent repercussions were an order to turn in our hatchets, and an article by Browne, "We're Turning into Animals!" We also dropped the nickname "Hatchet Battalion."

We came out of War Zone D and reflected. Even services for the dead were more uplifting than depressing. For me the first knowledge that one of my men had been killed is the only crushing experience, and that for his family more than for the man. To see the body is to think, he is dead—but his family does not know it yet. It was their grief that I felt most.

These are my musings decades after men died under my command. At the time I could not think about them, not for long anyway. The first thing we all did was relax intensely, every man choosing his own way, but all seeking communal relaxation as well. In this, Emerson led us just as he did in combat. There would be a battalion barbecue with plenty of beer in cargo nets drooping from helicopters. Cai was given the mission of locating some VC steers. The district chief showed him an area on the map under the guerrillas' control where any cattle were a food source for the enemy.

The Strike Force would strike once more with a helicopter assault. "Take 'em prisoner" were Emerson's orders to Cai, "but if you can't, bring back the bodies." The communist cattle resisted and were KIA. They were duly embalmed by the Mexican platoon in a sauce that tasted like sauteed fire ants.

The beef was confirmed VC because it was tough and stringy.

We went back to Phan Rang and the chill of the rainy season— "home for Christmas," we called it. Our base looked more like a refugee camp than a military cantonment, a sight that made us envy the stockade for VC prisoners we had seen near Bien Hoa. There, eleven years later, Cai would himself be a prisoner of the communists.

A USO troupe flew in to raise our morale. It was a gallant effort, with rainy gusts flapping the tarpaulin over a flatbed truck. The troops huddled in ponchos while Jackie Deshannon strummed and sang as if in the Hollywood Bowl.

Bob Hope, patron saint of the serviceman, appeared at Cam Ranh, which was now a bustling naval port. Naturally, Emerson wanted everyone to make the thirty-mile trip and catch the show, but of course someone had to stay "home" to guard the base.

The three company commanders drew straws and I lost. In a drizzle, B Company secured the road for the rest of the battalion's excursion. Just to let them know what I thought of our luck, I fired my pistol in the jungle and threw a couple of grenades, simulating a contact with the VC. My jokes were not appreciated nearly as much as Hope's.

About the only other laugh we had during that yuletide was from an international competition. A battalion of Australian artillery was attached temporarily to the brigade. In combat they operated differently from our "redlegs," though there was no difference between their excellent effectiveness and ours. The executive officer for an American artillery battalion stays with the howitzers while his lieutenants are forward observers with the infantry. With the Australians, the arrangement is reversed in the belief that spotting the rounds should be the job of the most experienced officer. I would match my forward observer (FO), Joe Mastreoni, against anyone, but the Aussies were interested in another sort of contest.

They suggested that the reason we Americans did not drink more beer was the quality of our brew. I agreed that it was inferior to that of the rest of the world but that did not mean our capacity was less. In fact—to judge by B Company—our per capita consumption could stand up to anyone's.

Interesting speculation, said the Aussies, and even allowed that with decent brew Americans might be able to match pints with New Zealanders. I said that with Swan Lager, Australia's premium beer, there were guys in B Company who could drink anyone into oblivion. Anyone at all.

Did I mean to include Australians in that generality? I assured them that I did. The snickers I heard led to the terms of a challenge: four American paratroopers versus four Australian artillerymen, all seated at a table with an infinite supply of Swan Lager. There would be an empty oil drum to obviate the need for competitors to leave the table. After four hours, the winning team would be determined by the number of empty beer cans on the respective sides of the table.

If the Americans won, their prize was the Swan Lager they had already consumed. If the Australians won, I would give them all the American beer they could carry away on their feet.

Paratroopers are all volunteers, so I was not surprised at how many stepped forward to champion the honor of the Strike Force. I let the first sergeant pick, for when it came to beer drinking he was probably the most familiar with individual reputations.

I did not want word of the contest to go beyond the company, but Cai got wind of it. Later he reflected on B Company's only defeat:

B Company started too fast, I think because the beer is so good. Our guys fart a lot but Australians only belch because they drink slower. Cheers make our guys drink faster, but Australians know what they're doing. When Barnes got sick, only three of our guys were left. They had to drink faster and got sick too. That's why we lost—the Australians had better strategy.

The Australian victory was convincing. All four of my brave troopers slumped from their chairs before three hours while the opposing team sat intact, sipping steadily. After I saw off the victors with their prize (at least they were too drunk to carry more than a case apiece) my first sergeant said he suspected they had lined their stomachs with cream, and requested a rematch. Fortunately the Aussies left the brigade before that was possible.

Chapter
Seven

*We started moving fast after Christmas. I saw more of Vietnam
than ever before in my life.*

A hundred miles north of Phan Rang is the Tuy Hoa rice bowl,
one of the largest outside the Mekong Delta, and long the chief
source of food for the VC in II Corps. Harvest time was approaching
in January 1966, as was Tet, the lunar new year. The VC expected
to again shake down the farmers for most of the rice crop, and even
more this year because the first NVA regiment to enter South Vietnam had joined the guerrillas hovering in the hills while 40,000 tons
of grain ripened.

The Oh-deuce was flown up to Tuy Hoa to protect the harvest
in an operation called Van Buren. Originally, operations had been
named by the senior commander involved, and most favored warlike
descriptors like "Masher," "Barracuda." But as such names reached
TV viewers at home, some nomenclator in Saigon told us to use
obscure American presidents. While we were in Tuy Hoa, we participated in operations Van Buren, Harrison, and Fillmore. Later it
became vogue for the commander of an operation to name it for an
American town or region.

Brig. Gen. Willard Pearson now took over the brigade, and he dubbed his new command "Diplomats and Warriors." Our diplomatic skills were soon tested by our allies in Van Buren, the ARVN, and Korean marines who had been trying to secure the rice bowl before we arrived.

The allied commanders demarcated boundaries between each others AOs. One of the Oh-deuce's first missions was to kick the VC out of a vast tideland tract that previously had been the responsibility of ARVN. By night, B Company infiltrated into the estuary befogged by the thickest, most vicious clouds of mosquitos I've ever suffered through. Miles away at the Oh-deuce CP, the radio operators could even hear the mosquitos over my whispers on the air.

It seemed our torture that night would be quickly compensated by the reward revealed by the late rising harvest moon. The VC were cruising about in sampans and strolling over the islands as if the war were over.

Stealing out on some sandy bluffs, my patrols reported in chorus that squad-size VC forces were loitering a few hundred yards away. It was incredible—something like the misimpression we had of the night time fishermen at Cam Ranh—so I took my binoculars and went closer for a personal look.

I saw exactly what my patrols had reported; the VC were armed and in uniform. Mastreoni, along with Steve Baka, my heavy mortar observer, began arranging for all the artillery available in the brigade to bring a hellstorm on the unsuspecting guerrillas. I insisted on no adjusting rounds but rather a cloudburst of steel before the VC could scatter. I heard Mastreoni request, "Fire for effect, battalion six volleys," and licked my lips, anticipating 200 rounds to explode in the air, and a VC company to die in a matter of seconds.

But minutes passed as the request was processed at the Oh-deuce CP.

This was a big fire mission for the artillery but I expected them to handle it faster. I called Emerson about the delay. He was fuming—his steam almost transmitted over the radio waves.

Apparently some ARVN general had intervened, demanding confirmation of the target and some irrelevant information. Responsibility for the estuary was not to shift to the Oh-deuce until midnight or some idiocy like that.

I looked at my watch; it showed 11:45. I kept watching the VC; they began to stir as if they had received a movement order. Sure enough, by midnight they disappeared, their weapons at sling arms, leaving Mastreoni only a few sampans to blast out of the water.

Cai was not too surprised by the debacle, especially since the VC seemed to move off into the new ARVN AO.

*V*C *and ARVN sometimes agreed. They knew this was a long war. Sometimes generals paid VC to leave them alone. Sometimes VC left rice for ARVN not to bother them.*

C'est la guerre, Vietnam. We would again meet those VC who sauntered away from us that night, and have to kill them the hard way.

We next moved over to what had been the Koreans' AO. There was plenty of evidence of fighting here—shattered weapons, a helmet or two, even parts of bodies still lying around. I learned the VC had assaulted the ROKs' position, been hurled back and never returned. I congratulated the marine company commander I relieved, and received from him a map overlay of his perimeter that was better than any I had seen since infantry school at Fort Benning. Perfect in every detail, right by the book.

I then expected him to show me the history of his patrols. When he did not offer, I asked him. Embarrassed, he related that his company had not conducted any deep patrols since the big VC attack. I started to ask why, but then I remembered to be a diplomat as well as a warrior, and clearly by his demeanor the Korean did not wish to discuss his company's recent, baffling inactivity.

Emerson, Lunde, Murphy, and I began to suspect that the Americans were the only force willing to fight the war at Tuy Hoa. The NVA regiment was apparently sitting it out in the hills while the VC negotiated with ARVN about how the rice crop would be divided this year. The ROKs had caught on to the game and seemed content with a *modus vivendi*. The Oh-deuce would have to go looking for a fight, and that's what we did.

The mountains fringing the rice bowl were not checkerboard

country, but it was good terrain for our patrols. The eight-man patrol that typified the spirit with which the troopers restarted the war was led by Sgt. Gene Hawthorne of A Company. A newspaper man described it like this:

> Leaving at dusk, the patrol moved 5000 meters, swam a river towing their equipment on a raft, crossed through jungle and over rice paddies, carefully skirting several tiny villages. The patrol was in the hills by daybreak, safely in undergrowth so thick they could not see a thing, but they could hear Vietcong moving around.
>
> "One little rat," said patrol member Robert E. Drake, "walked right into the middle of where we were concealed. Before we could do anything, he was off like a bullet. [Before long] they came at us screaming and shooting. We wasted a bunch and got through their first assault without a scratch.
>
> "The second go 'round, we weren't so lucky. One man was hit, though he kept right on fighting right up to the end. We were hit a third time and came through clean. When we moved again, one of the men triggered a booby trap, killing himself and wounding Hawthorne in both arms.
>
> "We cut down a few more before they withdrew. They didn't hit us again till about nine the next morning. Hawthorne lost a lot of blood during the night, but he still put out a deadly volume of fire. He would collapse, regain consciousness, and fire again. He pinpointed our position on the map for the artillery and adjusted the fire by listening to the bursts."
>
> Soon afterwards, the besieged patrol was reached by a platoon of its comrades, marking the end of the 30-hour ordeal for the eight men, two of whom were now dead and their leader gravely wounded.
>
> As Hawthorne was carried aboard the helicopter, he said, "Give me a couple of quarts of blood! I just need a refill and I'll be back."

A full-blooded Navaho from Shadow Rock, Arizona, Hawthorne was known as "The Indian," as much for his tracking ability as his ancestry. During his "refill," the doctor noticed that his foot was festering with jungle rot. The VC couldn't stop him but the doctor could: he was hospitalized for five days, then limped to a helicopter that was going back to the AO.

We followed the route of Hawthorne's patrol, and the site of their last stand (Hill 51) became B Company's CP. The place stunk.

One of our canine mascots found out why: the patrol had killed thirty-five VC, and some remained unburied.

"We were sitting around, digging in," Steve Baka recalled, "when our puppy comes up growling with a NVA's foot in his mouth. Some cherries had just come into the company, and I said, 'Bad dog, Ajax—we told you—no people bones.'"

We investigated until we found a sprinkle of spider holes—vertical, shoulder-wide pits—containing fully armed guerrillas killed apparently by Hawthorne's artillery. The dead men's uniforms looked so new that we began to wonder if the NVA was entering the fight for the rice crop.

Soon we thought the Chinese were entering the war as advisers. One of our patrols killed a soldier in an unfamiliar uniform, which looked Chinese. This report excited Emerson, who sent his two-seat chopper to pick up the body. It was not the pilot's favorite mission as we could see from his expression when he landed, the dead man strapped in beside him like a passenger asleep. The nationality of the corpse was never confirmed, but he was probably an overseas Chinese, like Cai.

Cai's favorite memory of Tuy Hoa was evacuating a remote Catholic orphanage before it was surrounded by the VC. B Company got the job of securing the landing zone and escorted 137 orphans and nuns to the waiting choppers.

There is supposed to be a cease-fire then for Tet, but VC were setting up mortars to shell the LZ. The gunships are not able to stop them because of cease-fire. What we did is move the LZ out of range of VC mortars.

Only one man was killed, a communist priest. The Oh-deuce sponsored new orphanage in Tuy Hoa. This make VC look very bad because they blew up a bridge at that time and kill a lot of civilians.

During the Tet holiday, my R and R came up—the "rest and recreation" leave granted everyone midway in their year in Vietnam. I put on my unused khakis, flew to Saigon, and boarded a Pan Am charter for Hong Kong. As I enjoyed a hot breakfast in a window seat, we flew right over the AO for Operation Van Buren. I looked down to see our artillery massaging the hills where B Company was patrolling. *C'est la guerre*, Vietnam.

In Hong Kong I rendezvoused with a stewardess I had met en route to Vietnam six months earlier. As I write this, we are about to mark our twentieth wedding anniversary. The war seemed a world away for us until we were in a taxi on Nathan Road. The Chinese were celebrating their new year, and a string of firecrackers sent me diving under the seat!

The week of R and R seemed to be over in minutes. Back on "Hawthorne's Hill," it seemed I had never left, but while I was gone the Ninety-fifth NVA Regiment got hungry. The VC were not seizing enough rice for them, so the NVA slipped down from the hills to get it themselves. We learned of their arrival a few nights after my return.

One of my night patrols called for artillery on four men slipping through the paddies. A document was found on a body, which Cai translated. It requested medical supplies. It read as though the VC was asking the NVA for help, though we could not be certain. The couriers seemed to have come from the vicinity of a twenty-hut village shown on the map as Canh Tinh (4). The parenthetical number meant there were three other clusters of huts with the same name. Canh Tinh, on a deep stream flowing from the jungled mountains into the paddies, looked like a good connecting point between the communist allies, and worth checking out with a patrol.

I sent one out the next night. It ran into a minefield that ARVN had not bothered to tell us about. The patrol leader, Sergeant Pasquale, had his foot blown off. The chopper sent to get him drew fire from Canh Tinh. At dawn I sent a platoon across the paddies to investigate. They were pinned down by fire and one man was killed.

Baka recalled at a Oh-deuce reunion in 1988:

That's when I found out how crazy combat is. We're out in the paddies about a hundred meters from this line of concealed bunkers on the edge of the village. We're firing back, running low on ammo, so Lieutenant Craig radios for resupply. A couple of sling loads drop so much stuff we can't even use it all. Charley [the NVA] must be interested in it, 'cause one pops up and shoots our guy who's trying to get the ammo. Shoots him right through the skin under his chin. He bleeds a lot but he's okay and can't believe what happened.

Rodriguez gets shot through the ass and he's laughing about it. This big pile of ammo is out in the paddy. We crawl around and pick stuff we can use. M79 rounds mostly. Some guy—can't remember his name—a real good E5 [junior sergeant] finds these cartons that say "Light Anti-tank Weapon" (LAW). He yells around if anyone's ever fired a LAW, but nobody has. We weren't fighting tanks in 'Nam! But this E5 thinks the LAW might be good on the bunkers. He props the LAW on a paddy dike, reads the directions on the carton, and all of a sudden there's this big boom like a recoilless rifle.

Damned if that first round didn't poop out there a hundred meters, hit just in front of a bunker, skip into the firing slit and blow shit in the sky!

Everybody just looked at each other, then we started whooping. No one had ever seen anything like that, even in the movies. Charley must have been shook. He must have been sayin', "Who are these guys out there?" I don't think the Ninety-fifth ever recovered. We kept chasing them for the rest of the war, didn't we?

Talk about race relations: Sergeant Rodriguez shot through the ass, right? He's got a couple of Hispanics in his squad. Never gives 'em any slack. Makes sure everyone knows there's no favoritism. Never speaks Spanish with 'em. Now he's on the ground about to be medevaced. He tells one of 'em, "*Deme un cigarro*—gimme a cigarette," and they all start talking Spanish like they've been holding it in for months.

During this action I took a platoon to swing around south of the village, crossing the deep, swift stream with difficulty. As we approached Canh Tinh fanned out like a search party, the villagers began to leave, prodding water buffalo ahead of them. That tipped us off that whoever was still in the village was going to fight us for it.

The VC did not operate that way. They always forced villagers to stay, thereby forcing the attackers to kill civilians with bombs and artillery, thereby creating photo opportunities that the western press so relished.

To me the flight of the villagers meant that NVA, rather than VC, had dug in at Canh Tinh. Before coming any closer, I recommended to Emerson that my third platoon be choppered across the stream to surround the village. He agreed, and gathered some fighter-bombers to support me.

Thus, B Company crept up on Canh Tinh, silent and sinister in the poaching heat. The village looked to be our biggest fight since An Ninh, and this time we were attacking rather than defending.

With my head well down, I could not tell exactly how my other two platoons were deployed; I knew only their general location on the map. Emerson had a better picture from his chopper, and could see that our encirclement of Canh Tinh had a gap, so he landed C Company to complete the seal. Now the Oh-deuce was ready to compress the NVA from all sides. We had to do our work in the next few hours, however, because there were probably escape tunnels somewhere that we would not have much chance of finding in the dark.

We sneaked to within fifty meters of the outlying huts without receiving any fire. I would have thoroughly prepped the village with artillery but without knowing the exact positions of my other platoons, I did not want to risk their safety. The fighter-bombers wove lazy figure eights overhead and could strike any target we marked, so I was not worried about fire power when we needed it.

I began to hear muffled detonations from our grenades thrown into huts, a precaution as the troopers approached them. No response. Some men took that as a signal to relax—a sign the enemy had probably pulled out, and the village could be swept in short order. These were the men killed by short bursts from the well-disciplined NVA.

My first sergeant was among the first to fall. He had been an adviser to ARVN in an earlier era of the war when the VC had orders not to kill Americans so we would not intervene. He stood and surveyed the village as if he were some umpire on a maneuver. I did not even know he was in the field; he did not have to be, for first sergeants usually stay at the CP.

Also brave to a fault were some squad leaders who knew that in battle, the leader should be first to advance. When I looked up after the initial exchange of fire, one lay dead at the edge of a clearing he had sprinted across to get closer to the action.

Dug into undetectable bunkers with firing slits for their automatic weapons, the NVA remained invisible. I had heard one fire no more than twenty meters away, even heard his spent cartridges clink against each other as they were spit out on the ground. There were several low mounds, looking like compost heaps, which could be his position, but there was no sign of him.

Bayonet charges were for movies. The way to get this guy and his comrades was by turning them into landfill. I had one of my men loft a smoke grenade into the center of where I thought this NVA was burrowed and called for a fighter-bomber.

The pilot offered me napalm or a five-hundred-pound bomb. I felt he could be more accurate with the bomb. Fine, he said, then asked me how close I was to the smoke grenade. About twenty meters, I replied. He chuckled, apparently realizing that I did not know what a bomb that size would do.

"Don't slip in the crater," he advised as he soared off for his pass.

He came from directly behind me, and loosed a huge black object resembling a football. Hypnotized, I watched it enlarge to the size of a sports car. For an instant it seemed to hang above the treetops; then the earth erupted equally high, to settle heavily in giant clods, with a deep-toned explosion like one from down a mine shaft.

The ground had lurched from under my feet.

There was a crater with earth sliding down its sides where I had suspected the NVA bunker to be. Indeed, I could not visualize what had been there before. I ordered some riflemen into the new landscape. In a few hours Canh Tinh could have been reduced in this way, but the fighter-bombers carried only one five-hundred-pounder apiece and soon had to return to their base for more.

We could not wait for their return, so the infantry took up the battle. It was slow but steady going, preceded by napalm that seemed to intimidate if not kill the NVA, whose discipline began to work against them.

Each of their soldiers had been assigned a sector to cover with fire. As long as these sectors overlapped, we could not move through them. But as bombs and napalm began to knock out the bunkers that covered the sectors, we found holes in the NVA's well-planned defense. When we filtered through the holes, the NVA did not shift their sectors of fire to counteract us. Orders were orders to them, not to be changed by individual soldiers. Thus we were able to work around some bunkers and take them from the flank or the rear.

One of our troopers burst into a bunker. The NVA glanced at him but never moved his weapon from its firing slit until a nudge from the trooper's M16 convinced him to surrender. Such incidents reminded me of the Japanese in World War II who fought inflexibly until they were destroyed.

We had trapped an NVA company in Canh Tinh, and drew the noose tight during the night so we could mop up in the morning. Exhausted from the fighting, and drained by our losses, I rigged my hammock in a hut a few hours before dawn. A squad led by Sergeant Anglin was beside me in another hut.

I was hardly asleep when I bounced to the sound of a burst from an M16 next to my ear. There had been no fire since dark. I assumed one of the troopers, careless from fatigue, had accidentally triggered his weapon, and proceeded to bawl out Anglin through the thin reed wall that separated us.

"Sir, would you come over here?" he replied with calm respect.

"Can't you handle it yourself?"

"Yes, sir. I handled it all right. Just thought you'd like to see something."

"In the morning. Get some sleep. And, dammit, put your weapons on safe."

"Okay, sir. Just thought you'd like to see this visitor. I think he was looking for you."

Grumbling but curious, I went around to Anglin's hut. Hearth ashes were strewn in the still warm blood of an NVA whose body half emerged from a trap door under the ashes. Anglin had been nearly asleep when the hearth opened before his eyes and the muzzle of an AK-47 protruded. I apologized, went back, searched my hut floor, and discovered a similarly invisible trap door. The next morning we uncovered no NVA except dead ones. The rest had gotten away through a web of tunnels.

The request for medical supplies we had found on the VC couriers hinted there was a medical station nearby, probably in the first range of hills above Canh Tinh. However, the crest of these hills marked the boundary of the ROK AO. As ever, Emerson was eager to pursue the NVA, but it looked as though the boundary would stymie us. I suggested we use the principle of hot pursuit while the NVA blood trails were still warm. Emerson said he would try that with the Koreans and sent us off to be warriors while he was the diplomat.

Crisscrossing the jungle in search of NVA trails, we found them strewn with blood and bandages. At the base of the hill, before it steepened to where we used our hands to scale it, we found a dozen graves, each marked with a name. To confirm the body count, we had to dig up the putrid remains—the only time I ever saw men of B Company balk.

We climbed as silently as we could, for if there were enemy on the hillcrest they could dislodge and destroy us just by rolling grenades down the slope. The trees were arm-thick, the underbrush skimpy. Our packs swayed heavily, throwing us off balance, colliding helmets against branches with *thunks* that seemed audible in Saigon. The temperature was rising with us during the hottest day I experienced in torrid Vietnam.

One man gasped with heat stroke, the first such casualty I ever had. Panting and struggling, we could not stop until we reached the top. Cai was with us that day, and had never climbed such a hill.

I don't worry that NVA are on that ridge. When we climbed up to the top, I think that we are alone.

Blood no longer speckled the trails. The next valley looked dense with foliage, the sort of secure surroundings guerrillas liked. As we descended, we could hear the tantalizing roar of a stream rushing under boulders. Our canteens were empty, so we followed the sound until the stream emerged at the base of the hill. Around this source of scarce water, I circled the company for the night, expecting perhaps that VC would come to fill their canteens.

When camped at night, I put on black pajamas like the VCs in order to get out of sweat-soaked fatigues. Tying off my hammock, I somehow grasped a huge caterpillar covered with filamentary spines too small to extract and too sharp to ignore.

"In Vietnam, the enemy is everywhere," Cai joked, using a hackneyed phrase from his training.

I wanted to search for the medic to see if he had some salve, but dressed like a VC I thought better of looking for him in the dark. I spent much of the night soaking my hand in the stream.

In a mean mood, I started the company off at first light. Emerson called to say the Koreans were upset and might not be able to provide artillery support if we moved much farther into their AO, so I swung along the base of the hill we had descended the day before.

It was a fortunate choice of route because the VC were using the natural caves and huge boulders of the hill for their base. They did not even have any outposts in the direction where we approached. We jumped them like Comanches on a campsite.

Our fire ricocheted around the boulders as in a western movie. It was all over in less than a minute. Twelve dead, including a couple of guerrilla women, slumped among the rocks like discarded scarecrows. We collected their weapons and moved on, doubly alert, for any VC in the valley would have heard the fire.

But our barrels were still hot when three VC came trotting through the trees. Regrettably, we did not see they were carrying only medical kits, and one of my men dropped them in a single burst. I decided to booby trap them by pulling the pins from a grenade and placing it under a body so when other VC came to bury them the grenades would enlarge the funeral.

As we worked our way out toward the Koreans, we surprised two more unwary parties of VC who did not seem to understand that we were behind them rather than coming from the paddies.

B *Company was very good that day. Every contact they win and keep getting around the VC—left, right—always one squad moved while other squad shoot. But I worried that we cannot get back to American AO after it gets dark. That one sniper tried to hold us up.*

The sniper was far off on our flank, so that we had to cross in front of him to get back into the Oh-deuce AO. I had a man wounded in the jaw and was in a hurry. The fighter-bombers came to the rescue again, though this time I was embarrassed to tell them the target was a single sniper. We fired tracers that the Skyraiders followed in with bombs, and the pesky VC was eliminated.

Like insurgent organizations everywhere, the VC had three components: the fully armed, full-time guerrillas; their part-time auxiliaries, who hid weapons where they lived; and an unarmed underground known as the infrastructure, the nervous system of the VC. Our principal task was to eliminate the guerrillas so that the ARVN militia and police could root out the auxiliaries and infrastructure. Around Tuy Hoa by that time, we had ground down the guerrillas to the point where we could help in campaigns against the covert communist elements. Such campaigns often began with the capture or defection of some members of the infrastructure. Cai called them cadres:

On an early morning we went out with some cadres we captured. We covered their faces with sand bags so that the local people could not recognize them. We surrounded the village, then the cadre guy showed us a house and told me that is where the honcho for infrastructure hides.

Our troopers hurried into the house but the man we looked for was not there. The captured cadre guy said, "Look better in bedroom."

I went in myself and checked out that room, but nothing was there except a bamboo bed. Then I was mad and told him not to lie anymore, but he whisper to me, "Get into the room from the roof of the house—but be careful."

There was no way to get in the roof except to tear it open. When we do that we find a very thin room between the walls. Smaller than a closet. No way to find it inside the house. Two VC cadre men wait there very quiet and we captured them with no fight.

Another time we killed a VC tax collector. I was very surprised he is by himself, but that means VC have good control so their tax collector can go around without fear of being robbed.

He rode right down the trail, but B Company was all around.

Plenty of guys shot him before he got away. Brigade was very happy when we turned in so much money, and they let me keep his motorcycle. It was made in Germany and not shot up too bad.

With Cai for a period was an ARVN scout dog handler, a 50-year-old corporal named Hon. As a legionnaire, he had been captured with the French at Dien Bien Phu. In spite of this experience, Hon was convinced that only a mercenary army could prevail over the communists.

Hon said same soldiers must stay for years in Vietnam so they become professional all their life. I did not agree with him. To me the longer the soldiers have been in combat the more scared they get, even if they gain more experience. He sipped C ration coffee and asked me slowly, "What will you do if Americans leave and the VC win?"

Speaking sincerely, I told him I never thought of that.

Chapter
Eight

The NVA decided that Tuy Hoa was not the place to get their rice. We left Hawthorne's Hill to prevent their escape, hopping far and wide in helicopters to search the beautiful range of hills in the back country. Once we ambushed a VC tax collector whose revenue included a pound of heroin as well as thousands of piasters. Once we were almost ambushed by a tiger. On another occasion, Screaming Eagles captured a VC carrier pigeon. The message attached to his leg said the bird was being sent back to a more secure area because the Americans were closing in.

Once we followed up a strike of the weapon the communists feared most, the carpet bombing of B52's.

Soaring invisible and unheard above the clouds, Arc Light missions, as B52 strikes were called, obliterated square kilometers in a rain of 750-pound bombs, leaving a crater field of telephone pole depth with only cordite fumes and a memory of what had been there.

Obviously, the mass destruction of Arc Lights could be inflicted only in the wilderness. As the NVA pulled back from Tuy Hoa, the wilderness was where we searched for them. A battalion was located by its radio transmissions. Rather than take the chance of scaring them off, we were told not to patrol into the NVA's lair, a narrow, winding valley perfect for their ambushes. Instead, B Company would sneak up to within three kilometers of the mouth of the valley.

Then when the Arc Light hit, we would rush in while the NVA's ears were still ringing.

Even the code name Arc Light was secret during that early phase of the war, and no one told us what to expect; however, I was sternly ordered to observe a three-kilometer buffer zone from the bombs' impact area in case the giant Stratofortresses missed their mark.

From studying the map, I became concerned what the buffer zone meant for B Company's follow-up attack. It left us with a belt of jungle and a mile of grassland to cross just as dawn was breaking. Rather than meet an NVA battalion on those terms—even assuming the bombs shook them up—I decided to shrink the buffer zone without telling anyone, including Emerson.

I think he would have winked at what I did, had I told him. For some reason, he never believed Arc Lights were very effective, possibly because there was no evidence left of the target. It was as if the bomb rain drowned the battlefield.

Around 3:00 a.m., I started infiltrating the company into the buffer zone. In utter darkness, we slipped through the jungle up to the edge of the grassland I wanted to cross just as the last bombs fell. The strike was scheduled for 4:30 a.m., and I became fascinated by the luminous sweep of the second hand on my watch as the time approached.

The men joked about the preparations for this attack that seemed a throwback to World War II and their training in conventional warfare. No breaking up into lonely six-man patrols this time; no dropping from helicopters into some jungle clearing they had never seen. This was 150 men, shoulder to shoulder, checking weapons in the predawn as in some black and white movie. Then suddenly the landscape turned technicolor.

Multiple flashes rippled under the indigo sky seconds before a giant gust of compressed air boomed by us. Crouching men rocked back on their haunches; men on their feet staggered as the shock wave surged through the ground like an earthquake. The night bulged with darkly glowing eruptions—wave after wave of them synchronized to the pounding of a mad timpanist.

The hills lit up as if by strobes, and thunder rolled up and down the valleys, flinging the concussions back and forth in a prolonged shudder that left us groping for trees.

The trees swayed while I prayed that the bombers would be as accurate as the ones at Canh Tinh. A quarter million pounds of bombs were re-forming the valley, as when the planet was young. More explosive power than was dropped on Hiroshima obliterated a rectangle one by three kilometers during the twenty-minute mael-strom. When I ordered two platoons to advance abreast across the grassland, the NVA battalion was a minor fear compared to what we had gone through watching and hearing the bombs. An inkling of what it was like to be the target of an Arc Light is found in *Vietcong Memoir* by Truong Nhu Tang:

> The concussive whump-whump-whump came closer and closer, moving in a direct line toward our position. As the cataclysm walked in on us everyone hugged the earth—some screaming quietly, others struggling to suppress attacks of violent, involuntary trembling. Around us the ground began to heave spasmodically, and we were engulfed in a mon-strous roar. Then, abruptly, it stopped, leaving us shaking our heads to clear the pressure from our ears. The last of the bomb craters had opened up less than a kilometer away.
>
> It was as if an enormous scythe had swept through the jungle, felling teak trees like grass in its way, shredding them into billions of scattered splinters. When the B52's found their mark, the complex would be utterly destroyed: food, clothes, supplies, documents, everything. It was not just that things were destroyed; in some awesome way they had ceased to exist. You would come back to where your lean-to and bunker had been, your home, and there would simply be nothing there, just an unrecognizable landscape gouged by immense craters.

My platoons reached the mouth of the valley but could not pen-etrate it for the uprooted trees that had been vomited into the jungle, creating a matted barricade. Down the valley there had been a considerable stream, now a terrace of ponds with waterfalls in be-tween. The air of dawn was full of the smell of fresh earth that collared the rash of craters.

Gradually we worked our way into the moonscape through con-torted piles of wood, silent as mourners after the death of the jungle. There was silence except for the occasional rattle of falling wood and sporadic thuds of giant earth clods dropping from branches.

Emerson wanted a report, but there was none to give him except a description of the tortured terrain. It took a couple of hours for us to move through the impacted area. At the far end we found that the bombs had stopped a little short, for there was a long cluster of huts on stilts, rows of them twenty meters apart, aligned like a permanent military camp. Indeed, that was what it had been, and it had been vacated with understandable haste.

Trash was everywhere: spilled rice bowls, broken chopsticks, tipped wash basins, unlaced boots; warm tea soaked the ground; bullets and grenades were strewn like confetti. There were rifles, carbines, and even a wheeled machine gun abandoned in the litter—a full range of weapons that could start a small war museum.

But nary a body. As best we could determine, the deluge had extinguished two of the battalion's three companies, and the third —the lucky one—had taken to their heels barefooted.

I was at Battalion CP when your report came in. Everybody looked at each other funny. You said you got about twenty weapons, some big stuff too, but no body count. Just one POW. Only time CP ever heard something like that I think. Good thing you showed them the weapons because I think they did not believe you at first.

We torched the huts, then struggled out of the Arc Light's killing field with our booty, and headed for pickup by helicopters. One of my men heard someone crashing through the jungle, making so much noise he must have been a lost paratrooper. So we held fire as the figure struggled toward us. He was the POW I reported, a dazed corporal of the Ninety-fifth Regiment, his ears bleeding from perforated eardrums.

With the NVA dispersed from Tuy Hoa, and the harvest taken in for the civilians, we turned over our AO to ARVN. The Oh-deuce was needed elsewhere, this time along the boundary of II and III Corps, where the VC had long held a redoubt exploiting ARVN's lack of coordination between their two corps.

It was the dry season on the coast when we took up Operation

Austin II. Albert Garland's book *Infantry in Vietnam* describes what
we were up to:

> After careful analysis of the area, the battalion commander sent B
> Company to seize what he considered to be key terrain—a trickling
> creek!
>
> At first glance B Company could have passed for South Vietnamese
> Regional Forces with their conglomeration of jungle uniforms and cel-
> lophane bags of rice slung around their shoulders. In place of the regular
> combat packs, the men trudged along with frameless, battered ruck-
> sacks; rather than air mattresses, they carried lightweight nylon ham-
> mocks captured from the Vietcong. Two Montagnard guides added
> native color to the command group.
>
> Hours later B Company arrived at the objective. To the men it was
> an oasis, for most of them had already drained their meager water
> supply. The area around the creek abounded with signs of recent use
> —the tell-tale signs of the deep tread of "Ho Chi Minh sandals" (slip-
> on tire treads) were everywhere.
>
> Down in the creek bed, the point man disappeared into a shaded
> V-shaped glade. Standing alone in the small sanctuary, he wet his throat
> with the remaining water in his canteen, and, kneeling, refilled the
> canteen and absentmindedly replaced its cover. As he did, he glanced
> up and saw at the other end of the glade another uniformed figure step
> into view. He was looking at an enemy soldier!

My trooper beat the VC to the draw.

> The enemy soldier fell and the point man ducked into the tall grass at
> the water hole; he was soon joined by his squad leader. No words were
> needed as the two men squatted and peered cautiously over the top
> of the grass—they knew that the enemy seldom traveled alone. Where
> were the others?
>
> They did not have long to wait for an answer—a bullet whacked
> into the squad leader's thigh. One by one the paratrooper platoon came
> abreast spraying fire on the treeline ahead. Automatic fire was returned
> from this flank, indicating the enemy had maneuvered quickly through
> the trees and were apparently ready for a fight.
>
> By this time 3d Platoon was coming up, moving to the high ground

on the left under Captain Taylor's directions. He wanted them to wheel onto the rear of the enemy, but when the platoon's machine gun opened fire to support the maneuver, the enemy, sensing defeat, broke contact. A short pursuit found four of their dead—all with empty canteens.

I had only half of B Company with me on this patrol, which cost me a bullet nick on the shin. Cai reproached me for letting one of the Montagnards get away, and I shouldn't have, but he was such a withered, miserable creature I could not bear turning him over to ARVN, though he quite likely betrayed the patrol and helped the VC get away.

Austin II happened in late April 1966. I had commanded B Company for eight months, several longer than the norm, and brigade began to hint it was time for Lunde, Murphy, and me to make way for new captains to get "command time." Emerson would have none of this, for he was content with our performance and, more important, the men benefited from our experience. Nevertheless, Murphy soon moved on with a distinguished record, Lunde— equally able and about to be promoted—got ready to go, and I received an offer from MACV that everyone said I'd be a fool to refuse.

It was to run the MACV R and R program in Hong Kong for sixty days. I'd work in civilian clothes and live in a hotel with a generous per diem. If anyone who ever served in Vietnam could turn down that job, I hope to meet them. Nevertheless, ambivalence remains about my decision to take it. Hong Kong was a unique experience, but so too were some famous battles the Oh-deuce would fight without me. I had no way of knowing.

Like so many decisions in Vietnam, I had to make mine quickly. MACV wanted me in Saigon yesterday for a briefing. There was no time for a formal farewell or even a sendoff evening. As I packed my bags, B Company choppered overhead to a new AO. In my shorts, I rushed up a hill and waved like a shipwrecked sailor. Armed for battle, crouched in the doors of the Hueys, many recognized me by shouting, waving, and saluting.

My feeling for B Company compensates many times over for whatever frustrations and tribulations I experienced in the army. These men put medals on my chest, shrugged off my mistakes, justified my tactics, and while asking for nothing, gave their all. To them, race and even rank were insignificant. A man was judged by what he could do.

They fought ferociously but used arms only against the armed enemy. If, by misassignment, Lieutenant Calley had been a platoon leader in B Company, he would have been killed by the same M16 he turned on civilians. And I would have made sure no one was punished for his death.

We called the Vietnamese dinks, gooks, and slopes, and never cared if Cai was around when we did. No doubt the Vietnamese had similar epithets for us: different races simply think of each other in such stereotypical terms. No one I knew despised the Vietnamese, or loved them. All we wanted was for our ally to get out of the way so we could get on with the war and get out of their country. We did not relate to them, and did not expect them to relate to us. *C'est la guerre*, Vietnam.

When I left, I expected the war would be over in about eighteen months. There seemed no way the VC could survive, much less prevail, as we tore away their hold on the population. Indeed, two years later, the VC essentially perished, leaving only the NVA in the field. Mauled in Giap's misbegotten Tet offensive of 1968, they found sanctuary beyond South Vietnam's international borders. Sanctuary. That, in my optimism, was the trump card I had not counted. Let others more eminent than I explain why sanctuaries were allowed. I will dwell on my memories of B Company.

Two things I told replacements who joined us. First, I waved my pistol to show I was the only infantry company commander in Vietnam not to carry an M16. Such was my confidence in B Company that I never expected to defend myself. If I ever needed an M16, someone was not doing his job. Second, B Company had never engaged the enemy where we did not commence fire first. In other words, we were never surprised, but rather, surprised the other guys. In a war of ambush and counterambush, it was the alert who stayed alive, and we were.

From just staying alive in Vietnam, I took up the good life in Hong Kong. There too I watched the Oh-deuce gain a distinction: in sixty days we had more AWOLs than the rest of MACV combined; i.e., more troopers who overstayed their authorized period in Hong Kong. The statistic chagrined Emerson, who marked it down to our time spent on operations, which was unsurpassed by any other unit. He added that we had done a year's fighting in six months, so the troopers felt entitled to an R and R twice as long!

About 250 servicemen from Vietnam arrived in Hong Kong every day. Most of them were broke after forty-eight hours, so a principal job for me was getting them money orders. But my biggest challenge was to give them a chance to orient themselves before they fell into the clutches of hotel touts. The R and R visitors were the largest constant group of tourists in the city, so in effect I was a travel agent nonpareil. The competition between the hotels for the R and R business got so out of hand that some employed bevies of lovely sirens to lure the servicemen right out of customs before I could brief them.

With help from airport officials, I had the sirens held back. But few GIs paid attention to my briefing while they were being beckoned by the nearby temptresses. Finally I had to ban a hotel from the R and R trade, then the others got the message.

One day the chief of the British vice squad and a ranking public health official approached me with long faces. Was there anything I could do, they asked, to control my compatriots' sexual practices in the city? They were discouraged when I told them that, in Vietnam, VD accounted for as many of our casualties as VC.

It appeared to the epidemiologists that we were importing a particularly virulent and refractory strain of gonorrhea that the British had never seen before. In spite of all precautions, Hong Kong's whores were becoming infected.

Would the men accept complimentary condoms? I was asked. The GIs would be grateful, I answered, because condoms were much valued in the jungle for protecting cigarettes from monsoon rains.

I don't know what became of the potential epidemic, but I did agree to brief the men that their temporary partner should produce a blue card showing she had been inoculated. I even had a sign in front of me, "Make sure she's blue or you could be too."

* * *

Vietnam was barely a stopover before I caught my "freedom bird" for the States, but I wanted to see the Oh-deuce once more before I left. As usual, they were on an operation, this time mopping up after the battles at Dak To concluded with an Arc Light.

Emerson showed me around the Toumorong mountainside, which was hugely pocked like some asteroid after a meteor shower. The jungle skin had been flayed from the earth, its tatters strewn as debris in mammoth craters. Here and there, earth-filled foxholes marked the graves of NVA, who had fought here so tenaciously. Emerson said the few survivors of the Arc Light wandered about insane.

From a hill, he pointed out over rolling acres of craters, reenacting the battle as if on a sand table. With its jungle blasted away, Toumorong was a barren heath, its distances distorted by its nakedness. That it had taken two hours for A Company to move a hundred meters up that hill was impossible to imagine without replacing the jungle. It was a horrendous battle, and its aftermath showed in the faces of everyone.

There were more new than old faces in B Company. In the two months I had been gone they had lost scores of men; relatively few to war wounds, the rest to prolonged exhaustion and exposure, tropical fevers, infections, and the enervating tension of patrolling. Even the fiery spirit of the paratrooper shrinks to its pilot light and must be refueled before it extinguishes. The Oh-deuce looked close to that burnout stage when I left them for the last time.

But the war went on while the warriors—except for Cai—were replaced like horses in the pony express. New leaders arose as old ones departed; last month's cherry was this month's veteran. People change, the unit remains. Drill bits are replaced, but the machine grinds on. *C'est la guerre*, Vietnam and probably all such long wars.

I had much to consider as I started my new assignment as an instructor in the Infantry School at Fort Benning, Georgia. From there the army forecast that I would return to Vietnam, probably as an adviser to ARVN. Then, when I was promoted to major, a first assignment to the Pentagon looked likely.

The two years at Benning gave me time to take stock. There would never be another B Company for me to command, that much was certain. The army tried to rotate all its competent captains into command slots in order that everyone would have a chance to prove oneself and be appraised for promotion.

There is an old army saw that company commander is the best job an officer can ever have. From my experience, this was very true: there is the matchless invigoration from close contact with the men doing the fighting, yet sufficient distance (usually) to use the intellect toward a broader experience than "Kill or be killed."

The company commander's skill is honed quickly, and regularly tested with prompt feedback. If he's good, that is soon recognized from both above and below him in the army hierarchy. There is a straightforward honesty in daily dealings. Responsibility includes authority. There is common purpose and distaste for politics. There is opportunity for originality and unstinting support for ideas that work, be they in combat or in helping civilians. All these qualities of life combined are nearly unique to the wartime company commander.

Moving back into the peacetime (Stateside) army, it was easy to realize that my peak experience—as later acquaintances in Berkeley would call it—was over. If I stayed in the army, everything else would be anticlimax. Better to quit with my best memories than settle for the security of retirement in eleven years, most of them as a bureaucrat in uniform.

Moreover, except in Vietnam, the army did not much value what I prized most about myself—my imagination.

"You can get in more trouble," an officer once told me, "using your imagination than using anything else except cocaine."

Bureaucracies do not nurture imagination because it is difficult to quantify, uncomfortable to accommodate, tends to make light of procedure, and upsets routine. In 1964, I wrote my first novel, *A-18*. I'm grateful that it is now out of print, but at that time it would have been the very first Vietnam novel. As I was in the army then, I had to submit the manuscript to the office at the Pentagon called (with an irony they missed) Freedom of Information. They denied me permission to publish on grounds of "propriety" (e.g., I had related how a sergeant seduced a woman in Hawaii).

Clearly, my fiction did not fit the army's official image of itself. I wanted to write about the war with no editorial assistance from the Pentagon. Though written at Fort Benning, my second novel, *A Piece of This Country*, was published after I resigned.

Getting out of the army meant getting into something else. Having been brought up in the military subculture, I felt tenuously connected to American society at large. I wanted to learn quickly, and also interact with minds grown from different perspectives; to me, that meant an academic setting.

Taken together, my requirements called for graduate school. Then the questions were where, and in what discipline. Well, it seemed sociologists should know the most about society, and the best sociology department, I was advised, was at the University of California in Berkeley.

That I, a "Junker war criminal" as some classmates called me, was accepted into the most radically leftist department of the most radically leftist campus in the country—possibly in the world—is the sort of thing Pope must have had in mind when he started the line, "Fools rush in . . ."

Actually, my two years of grad school comprised my second Vietnam tour, this time in the trenches of the home front, where Hanoi was winning the propaganda war while losing the shooting war, as Cai was to see.

Even after twenty years it remains impossible for me to recall without a degree of loathing the antics that went on in Berkeley under the guise of "student protest" against the war. I had come to oppose the war too, principally because the GVN was so riddled with corruption and so lacking true patriotism that it never proved worthy of America's sacrifices made in its behalf. For that I could respect the VC's determination to topple the Saigon regime.

Respectable too were the VC as fighting men; as brave as they were ruthless, their cruelty matched by self-sacrifice. From my experience against them, I am confident the VC would have found the coddled cry babies of Berkeley as contemptible as I did.

They sacrificed nothing (except others' education) while demanding everything—and now. They wanted their political agenda endorsed without debate, their worldview enforced as if it were divine, their manifestos imposed bypassing democracy, and all this bestowed at taxpayers' expense as part of free education. They wanted "power to the people," so long as the voters of California were not considered to be people.

I did not understand why they wanted to stop the bombing of North Vietnam but not the NVA's slaughter of South Vietnamese.

They wanted "their" professors, and to determine academic qualifications. They wanted "their" campus unpoliced, as if they held title to it. They wanted free speech except for those who dared disagree with them. They wanted ROTC removed, and made their point by burning down the building. They wanted the campus shut down if the students did not turn out for strikes and demonstrations.

All this they wanted summarily, and of course at no personal jeopardy. So most of all they wanted their disruptions condoned by the university administration, blanket amnesty for themselves, and immunity from any sanctions. Theirs was to be a revolution without risk. Power was to be earned by tantrum.

Twenty years later, I showed Cai the campus newspapers from the Berkeley mob era. He noticed that America was spelled with a "k." "Invasion" was raiding Cambodia; "liberation" was the NVA invasion of the south. "Genocide" was our side bombing theirs; "armed struggle" was their side terrorizing ours. "Imperialism" could have only one modifier—"U.S."—and fittingly the mob defined "trash" as a verb.

This sounds like what they taught in re-education camp.

For the most part the Berkeley faculty was cowed. I saw for the first time the distinction between academics and men and women of action. The professors postured a bit about how disruptions encroached on academic freedom, but generally excused the riots because they were so well intended. They wanted their academic freedom, but ROTC off campus too. A feckless chancellor pampered the faculty and appeased the penny-ante bolsheviks.

S*ometimes Radio Hanoi sent greetings to Berkeley. That's when I found out it was in California.*

Berkeley was indeed the toast of Hanoi, as well as capital of the street people, the citadel of self-indulgence, and a disgrace to California. Before long, the taxpayers expressed themselves about what was going on in their Athens of the West. Across the bay in San Francisco, a university president who threw the dilettante VC off his campus was elected U.S. senator, and Ronald Reagan swept in as governor in the draft of the backlash against Berkeley. *C'est la guerre*, Vietnam: Johnson's loss was Reagan's gain.

David Horowitz and Peter Collier, co-editors of *Ramparts*, the national voice of the New Left, remarked on this era:

> The left was hooked on Vietnam. It was an addictive drug whose rush was a potent mix of melodrama, self-importance, and moral rectitude. Vietnam was a universal solvent—the explanation for every evil we saw and justification for every excess we committed.

While I watched the psychological war being lost in America, Cai felt the repercussions in Vietnam. Certain milestones of the war we shared: Nixon's raid into the NVA's Cambodian sanctuary produced as pitched a battle on campus as in the jungle. The televised return of our POWs did indeed "bring the war home," as the rioters had long called for, but with an opposite effect than they had imagined. There, hobbling across the screen, was the evidence of communist torture the Berkeley bolsheviks had so long denied.

The sociology department was a monument to irrelevance in my experiential education. What I learned from them was that what sociologists do is teach other people how to be sociologists.

*   *   *

Berkeley's novelty and distractions pulled my mind away from the war as much as the constant news from Vietnam allowed. I had declined a commission in the army reserves when I resigned, but when the California National Guard began tear-gassing the campus, I offered them my services and worked undercover to help predict riots before they started. It was a pretty easy job picking up the pamphlets calling for antiwar rallies—there seemed to be one every week. I got to know the radical groups' reputations pretty well, and could forecast that the Anarcho-Mystical Bund would produce less violence in their rallies than the Students for a Democratic Society (SDS).

I also did my bit as a counterguerrilla. The local VC took up the practice of painting a yellow star at the border between the red and blue paint on mail boxes, thereby converting them into the Vietcong flag. At night I would paint the star white, returning the mail boxes to an American emblem.

As a teaching assistant in both the sociology and English departments, it was enjoyable to prevent unanimous resolutions by their councils condemning things like the Cambodian incursion and bombing of North Vietnam. It appalled them that there was someone in their midst who dared dispute their antiwar catechism. With attitudes so steeped in hypocrisy, they could not condone dissent from their own dissent.

Even with the propaganda war fought on campus, Vietnam receded in its immediacy for me. The stories of racial tension and drug addiction among our troops were as unbelievable for me as the rumors of atrocities. Thus, for me, the greatest shock came when the horrors of My Lai were uncovered. This was the most ghastly turn of the war, more stunning even than the fall of Saigon.

The National Guard sent me back to Fort Benning, for a reason I've forgotten, during the closing arguments of Lieutenant Calley's trial there. With all the appearance of a well-turned-out officer, Calley was an even more repulsive figure, especially with the motto on his shoulder patch, "Follow Me." He followed orders—that was Calley's disgusting and discredited defense. It was gratifying that he was convicted by fellow soldiers; it was as mortifying when he was pardoned by Nixon as when Nixon was pardoned by Ford.

Though regularly revived by news of its progress, the war became for me a shrinking memory. Now and then I would see a Screaming Eagle on TV. Once Emerson spoke on camera about the raid into North Vietnam to free our POWs. I second-guessed the 101st's tactics at Hamburger Hill, wondering why they did not transform it into Mole Hill with an Arc Light. But in 1968, I was getting on with a new life while Cai continued his in a war that had begun between his adopted people, but was now being fought principally by his adopted army. His new extended family was the 101st, his relatives by blood.

Cai would remain with the 101st for six years, longer than any other man. Just as he had experienced the birth, infancy, and adolescence of South Vietnam, he witnessed the history of America there. His own history and mine would not intersect again for nearly ten years, and we would not meet for twenty.

Chapter
Nine

During May and June of 1966, while I was in Hong Kong, the Oh-deuce clashed with the NVA in some of the most significant battles of the war. The border war, as this perennial campaign has been called, was the implementation of Westmoreland's strategy to block NVA reinforcement of the VC's mauled main forces. Giap's strategy was to keep potent units like the 101st engaged on South Vietnam's borders so that the VC would have only ARVN to contend with. Both generals' strategies succeeded.

For six days in May, the Oh-deuce and a sister battalion, the 1/327, investigated along the Cambodian border where the NVA had been entering South Vietnam through a wide tract of particularly difficult jungle. At first there were only rain and leeches to battle. Cai recalled these conditions:

Everybody had jungle sores. My skin got as white as Americans. No sun at all. We talk about how good Phan Thiet was because after patrol we get nude on the beach. But this country around Bu Gia Map was awful. We still had old cotton fatigues. They rot in a couple of days out there. Leeches too, big as fingers.

These water-borne leeches prompted fast crossing of streams. In the trees was another variety that dropped like tiny caterpillars, attracted to the heat of steaming soldiers thrashing through the jungle.

Bu Gia Map was an abandoned settlement with an airstrip overgrown with grass, and barely suitable for Hueys. This LZ was cold, and soon too were the troopers as the monsoon moved in with daily showers. The Oh-deuce patrols radiated in all directions but made only one light contact, that in the direction of Cambodia a scant fifteen miles away.

Emerson deployed into a checkerboard, and within two days his patrols were reporting small, glancing firefights. He had to be cautious, for the extraordinary thick jungle had few clearings where reinforcements could land in choppers. Moreover, the NVA seemed to be falling back toward Cambodia as they skirmished.

Emerson was one of the first U.S. commanders to experience the frustration of approaching an NVA sanctuary where the communists could skip over the border whenever they chose. The Oh-deuce seemed heading into a no-win operation, or into a major ambush that Giap had longed to spring on an American unit. He had told every NVA regiment to look for such an opportunity, and north of Bu Gia Map exactly such a situation was developing. It was Cai who first learned that a trap for the Oh-deuce was baited and Emerson was nibbling at it.

In close quarters an A Company patrol brushed against a similar reconnaissance force from the NVA. A firefight in dense jungle broke out. One North Vietnamese, a young sergeant, was hit. His squad fled.

He was the first POW we took in the operation. Emerson sent me up right away. This guy got hit in the thigh. Our medic fixed him up real good and gave him a canteen, cigarette, and cookies from a C ration. But this NVA was still real shaky—he held his hands on his head like he thinks we are going to hit him or something. I asked him what's wrong, and he said please take his letter because Americans kill all prisoners. I told him that's not right: we will take good care of him—maybe better than NVA

because he look so hungry. Then he relaxed a lot. I asked him
what he was doing when he got shot. He talked plenty: said his
whole battalion was waiting for us, maybe about an hour away.

This prize prisoner could even read a map, and drew on it a
horseshoe-shaped ambush where his battalion was waiting for patrols
like his to suck in the Oh-deuce. Behind that ambush was another
NVA battalion poised to finish us off.

Terrain and foliage prevented a helicopter force from getting
behind the NVA, so Emerson set about to flank them. Lunde's A
Company advanced cautiously toward the ambush while Capt. Ron
Brown's force broke trail through the jungle to get around and in
back of the horseshoe. Strangling, slippery vines entangled Brown's
troopers. The men grabbed each other's packs, for this kind of "wait
a minute" foliage closed as soon as it was released. Keeping the
flanking force on course was Emerson's main concern.

The NVA had selected their site well. On the sides of the horseshoe were walls of bamboo that the flanking force could not penetrate. They had to swing wider, and this additional jungle bashing
took the rest of the day. Meanwhile, at dusk, Lunde had come upon
the open end of the horseshoe.

"They're all over the place!" he reported to Emerson, just where
the prisoner had said they were.

It took until 10:00 the next morning before the flanking force
was in position in back of the curve of the horseshoe. Then a trap
quite different from what Giap had hoped for began to close as A
Company engaged the shanks of the horseshoe. Both sides thought
they had the other caught. NVA machine guns were as heavy as the
Americans', thundering back and forth against each other at ranges
so close the spurting muzzle flashes seemed connected.

But the fighting raged for only a few hours. With A Company
as the anvil, Brown's flanking force hammered through the back of
the horseshoe, submerging it in 2000 rounds of artillery and deep-
digging bombs that threw up the NVA's bunkers in shards. There
were no escape tunnels this time, and the bamboo thickets became
the walls of a death trap.

The second NVA battalion was idle during the extermination of the first. When the Oh-deuce turned the tables on the ambush, apparently the NVA regimental commander did not know what to do, for on the third morning the regiment backed away toward Cambodia to be caught in an Arc Light just short of the border. As they reeled into the sanctuary, Emerson tried to get in one more punch.

"The border was a river," Emerson recalled. "Lunde got a patrol up there and ambushed a bunch just as they crossed. Caught about twenty in one burst. I got up in a chopper to take a look. I see what looks like a platoon wading across, and the door gunner's about to waste 'em when I see that they're A Company! Going into Cambodia, for Christ's sake! I get Lunde on the horn and tell him there's something called rules of engagement and he's got to stop on an island at midstream. He says he sees trucks on the other bank, and a big administrative assembly area. The NVA over there are giving him the finger.

"I asked the pilot if he'll go over and take a look. He did, and what Lunde described is 101 percent right. There are trucks parked right out in the open, troops loading up like the end of some maneuver. And we couldn't touch 'em. Hell, General Larsen was reprimanded for even saying they were there."

Frustrated at the threshold of the communists' sanctuary, the Oh-deuce trudged back through the rain to the Bu Gia Map airstrip and flew away to Pleiku, the hub of the central highlands, where they became the reserve for II Corps, which was resisting multiple NVA thrusts from the tri-border area. Though no longer under fire, the Oh-deuce suffered two deaths from a frighteningly virulent form of malaria. Non-battle casualties, as such losses were called officially, had sapped the battalion's strength for nearly a year. When I left B Company, thirteen men had been killed by enemy action, and two accidentally. More than ninety, including myself, had been hospitalized for varying lengths of time. Strain, heat, exposure, exhaustion, and lack of rest dropped men in their tracks so that a company at full strength of about 150 rarely could field more than 90.

The NVA were not immune to endemic pestilence either. Nearly half of the prisoners taken at Bu Gia Map had malaria. At Pleiku, Cai came down with his own malady:

I was weak all the time. I ate plenty but didn't get strong. The brigade doctor checked me out and found a tapeworm in my intestines. Twelve feet long! Even when I saw it I didn't believe that thing was inside me.

The doctor saved it in a bottle, but he had bad news for me. He said another one was still in there. It must grow many feet before he can get it. In a couple of months, a doctor in Phan Rang took out that second one. I didn't know, but I think maybe I got the tapeworm from VC cows we eat at the barbecue.

Kontum, a tri-border province (also the name of its capital) and the major portal from the Ho Chi Minh Trail, was to be Giap's main front in his border war. Intelligence reports at brigade indicated the NVA's initial objective to be a militia (CIDG) camp at the village of Dak To, and that was the name given to what became a renowned campaign. On a commanding height in the mountains ringing Dak To was an outpost called Toumorong, where the NVA had encircled and nearly annihilated a CIDG company still under siege.

The invading force was the Twenty-fourth NVA Regiment, and unlike all earlier battles, they were not hard to find. The regiment adhered to the "bear hug" tactic, which meant closing rapidly with the Americans—intermixing with them whenever possible—in order to neutralize the staggering fire power of U.S. bombers and artillery. As the brigade set up to relieve Toumorong, they quickly felt the violent embrace of the NVA's bear hug.

Cai was again with A Company, now commanded by Capt. Ron Brown, and after the counterambush at Bu Gia Map, their job sounded easy. Lieutenant Beach's platoon was detached for security of a fire base for a battery (six howitzers) of artillery supporting a relief force from the 1/327 climbing up to Toumorong.

It got dark and we fired artillery, but I think the rounds are short because the shells came down on the perimeter. Then someone shouts, "Incoming!" This is NVA artillery shooting at us! First time that happened. That's when I knew we tied into a big force, and this would be like a big war.

Under their own rocket barrage, an NVA battalion attacked the fire base, beginning three weeks of some of the most vicious fighting of the entire war. Backed by the howitzers firing at point blank range, Beach's platoon turned back the first assault, but around 2:30 that morning, the NVA slammed into the perimeter again, this time penetrating it, and seized "gun number six," which was to become a famous artillery piece.

In the navy, the motto "Don't give up the ship!" is famous. In the artillery, the equivalent motto is "Defend the guns!" and to lose a gun is like surrendering a ship—something that must be recaptured for the sake of honor. Beach's platoon was responsible for defending the guns at Dak To. No one needed to tell him about venerable military tradition, but for Cai the American counterattack had something new.

There was shooting all over the place. Then I saw troopers put bayonets on the ends of their rifles. I never saw that before. Maybe it's so dark they think NVA run into them, but there are lots of flares and tracers, and I can see pretty good. Jets came in and bombed the NVA who are still outside the perimeter. Then everyone started yelling and going for that howitzer. Helluva fight then, but we got it back and battery commander is very happy.

But the NVA came back a second time. Some were never dislodged from the perimeter, and through the gaps they held, another wave stormed in to dispute ownership of the gun.

Second time the NVA blew on bugles when they attacked. Never heard a thing like that before except in movies. Our guys yelled real loud too—made music like cavalry charge: Ta-ta-ta-ta-ta! People getting shot but laughing too. And that howitzer is no good anymore. Bullets were hitting it all the time—they made it sound like a gong.

Fighting swirled around the howitzer, which changed hands once more, but with the approach of dawn the NVA, no doubt realizing that daylight would expose them to vengeful air strikes, began to back away. They found it hard to break their bear hug. Grenades hurled back and forth at such close quarters that some wounded their throwers. In the morning, smoke rose from the battered fire base as if hell had once more gone underground.

Thirteen NVA bodies in the perimeter. Some of them had long ropes around their feet for their buddies to pull them back into the jungle. But Lieutenant Beach's platoon came out quick— found about a hundred more bodies, and captured some mortars too. Everyone looked at each other and said what a hard fight that was, like regular war. I'm very glad when it's over and we still had the howitzer. The battery commander, Don Whalen, deserved the DSC medal he got.

The battle was over but the campaign had just begun. The 1/327 gained the heights of Toumorong, saved the CIDG outpost, then pressed on against the NVA, who were surprising everyone by their willingness to stand and fight. It became clear that they considered the frontier around Dak To be their property.

It was property they had already developed. From POWs, brigade learned that the Twenty-fourth NVA Regiment had moved into the environs around November 1965, and had spent seven months digging in and fortifying their claim.

A U.S. brigade and an NVA regiment are roughly equal in numbers—about 2000 men. The fire power available to the brigade far exceeds that of the regiment, but at Dak To this advantage was neutralized considerably: first by the bamboo-carpeted mountains with no LZs of any size, and second, by the NVA's long tenancy and familiarity with this terrain, and third, by their skill in subterranean engineering. The U.S. Army's symbolic mascot is a mule; the fitting equivalent for the NVA would be a mole.

One third of the brigade was absent, hundreds of miles away at Tuy Hoa. General Pearson suspected that the Oh-deuce and 1/327 may have bitten off more than they could chew, so he requested reinforcements from MACV. All he got was one company from Tuy Hoa and a semipromise that the First Cav, our old friends from An Khe, could probably send some help if the brigade became over-matched.

A tactical rule of thumb, applicable to any war, is that for an attack to succeed against a well-prepared defense, the odds must be at least 3 to 1 in favor of the attackers. The brigade was preparing to attack—on ground of the enemy's choosing—outnumbered by the NVA 3 to 2. And most ominous of all, monsoon clouds were seeping into the valleys around Dak To, threatening to remove the Air Force from the combat equation.

Said Cai as he appraised the bowl of mountains surrounding Dak To, "I never saw Dien Bien Phu, but this sure looks like the pic-tures."

General Giap may have had the same thought. He had another regiment across the Laotian border ready to pounce on the brigade if it became locked in the Twenty-fourth Regiment's bear hug. The Screaming Eagles no longer had to look for trouble; it was coming to them.

The 1/327 did not walk far from Toumorong before they found it. They advanced their companies like three fingers of a hand, moving abreast but separated. In succession, each collided with strong, entrenched forces blocking access to the valley's ridges. Jab-and-parry fighting erupted in the claustrophobic jungle, and lasted six exhausting days. Then the NVA struck with two companies against the 1/327's isolated reconnaissance platoon. The Tiger Force, as this platoon was called, fought them off, but was nearly overrun.

For the first time since An Ninh, which was an accidental battle in contrast to the professionally planned NVA defense at Dak To, the Screaming Eagles had been stopped and forced to defend against encirclement. But Pearson would not let the initiative pass to the NVA, and decided to insert the Oh-deuce far up the valley, closer to the gathering monsoon, and deep into the Twenty-fourth Regi-ment's fortified concentration.

Of course at the time he did not know exactly how the NVA were deployed or the extreme danger they posed around the Oh-deuce's tiny and scattered LZs. Luckily, the monsoon mists helped conceal the helicopter landings; the Oh-deuce landed without incident and

First Brigade, 101st Airborne Division, arrives at Cam Ranh Bay, July 1965. *(U.S. Army)*

Ben Cai Lam during an operation with
the Oh-deuce, 1965. *(101st Airborne
Division Association)*

Stay alert, stay alive: a slackman covers
the point. *(U.S. Army–Higgs)*

Vietcong (VC) stock a trench
like the ones at An Ninh.
(U.S. Army)

During the Dak To I campaign, 101st troopers cross a vine bridge built by NVA. (*U.S. Army*)

Contact on the checkerboard. (*101st Airborne Division Assocation*)

Though laden with canteens, troopers also found coconuts helpful to prevent dehydration. *(101st Airborne Division Association)*

Because of good treatment by the Oh-deuce, this wounded NVA sergeant warned them of the trap at Bu Gia Map. *(AP/Wide World–Huet)*

The Oh-deuce closes in at Bu Gia Map. *(101st Airborne Division Association)*

En route to a
hot LZ.
*(U.S. Army–
Rockoff)*

The chaos of combat: a 101st company commander reacts as fire
begins to be exchanged in the jungle about thirty meters ahead of
his command group. *(U.S. Army–McLaughlin)*

A 173d Brigade trooper calls for a medic during Dak To II.
(U.S. Army)

The price: a trooper's body is hoisted by a chopper from dense jungle near Bu Gia Map. (*AP/Wide World*)

Premier Ky decorates the First Brigade commander, B.G. Pearson, after Dak To I. Behind his shoulder, *from left,* are Lieutenant Colonel Hackworth; an unidentified officer; Major Schroeder, who commanded Task Force Schroeder, and Colonel Timothy, the original commander of the First Brigade. (*101st Airborne Division Association*)

The SDS marches in Chicago during its "Days of Rage," 1969.
(*Black Star*)

The price: a dead NVA, with his belongings strewn beside him.
(*Magnum–McCullin*)

The delta.   *(Brenda Reed Sutton)*

An ARVN officer in action in the delta. (*U.S. Army*)

NVA porters on a branch of the Ho Chi Minh Trail. (*Library of Congress–Morris*)

Supplies are parachuted into the ruins of besieged An Loc, where ARVN turned back the NVA's 1972 Easter Offensive. (*CONTACT–Burnett*)

An NVA officer reads the People's Army newspaper to his troops.
(*U.S. Army*)

Panic at Nha Trang as the NVA closes in, April 1975.   (*Gamma Liaison–
Francolon*)

As a form of terrorism, the NVA rocketed cities to show that the GVN could not protect the population, and also to punish refugees who had fled from communist control. Here, the boy on the highest stair is the only survivor in his family after a rocket attack. (*Gamma Liaison– Slyveine*)

Refugees using inner tubes to swim to the last boat leaving Nha Trang. *(SYGMA)*

April 30, 1975: on the day Saigon fell, this officer saluted the statue of
the ARVN soldier, then killed himself at its base. (*SYGMA–Pavlorsky*)

began radiating into a checkerboard designed to isolate the NVA engaged against the 1/327, which by this time had seized commanding heights and were repelling NVA counterattacks. It appeared to Hackworth, now commanding the 1/327, that the bloodied Twenty-fourth Regiment could be knocked out if struck from the rear.

For this purpose, C Company of the Oh-deuce was put under Hackworth's command (OPCON), and he ordered them into a position to block the NVA from withdrawing. C Company had only two of its three rifle platoons, and Emerson was annoyed that the entire Oh-deuce was not moved south to encircle the NVA fighting the 1/327, but the detachment of C Company was General Pearson's decision.

Cai was with B Company, which was commanded, after I left, by Lt. Lou Sill. Battling only palisades of bamboo, B Company patrolled to the north and seemed to weave around the valley like that rare pinball that slips by without setting off any flashing lights. For A and C companies, the valley went "tilt."

Murphy had left C Company, now commanded by Bill Carpenter, the "lonesome end" of West Point football fame, so named because he never entered the huddle but stood removed on a far flank where he received play signals by watching the quarterback's body language. I saw him in his last game; he had a miserable time in a thumping defeat by Navy. The super bowl at Dak To was incomparably more shattering.

As Carpenter described it to the press:

> When we came over this ridgeline we could hear them talking all around us. We went into a draw and then up a finger [a secondary ridge]. I left the Second Platoon there. Right away they got in a fight and cut down ten or twelve NVA. That must have alerted the rest.
>
> I then maneuvered straight up another finger. There were .30 and .50 caliber machine guns firing on our rear, and we just got pinned down. They started getting in amongst us. We couldn't get to our wounded.
>
> So I just called in an air strike [napalm] on top of us. It was where I thought it would do the most good.

Over the radio, with small arms popping audibly over the air, Carpenter told Emerson that the napalm would "take some of them with us." The pyric strike did more than that; it seared the edge from the NVA's attack and allowed First Sergeant Sabalauski to organize the company CP into a perimeter defense.

The only thing that saved them, Cai learned, was the bamboo. It broke up the jelly, Sabalauski surmised, and the napalm must have been old, because not all of it burned.

Carpenter feared his company was doomed, as they were separated and stuck in thickets on narrow ridges, and so advised Emerson, who brought the Oh-deuce to the rescue. A Company was closest. Abandoning caution, Brown hurried his men down a stream bed, the fastest way to travel in dense bamboo.

Every war has its unique representation of hell: bloody footprints in snow, infantry over the top into muddy no-man's land, or cavalry charging into carnage. Wars are remembered that way—by how they were at their worst. That night for C Company was as bad as Vietnam could be, a night from which nightmares were born that live in the minds of people today like reruns of a classic horror movie.

This ultimate was the climax of a cumulative ordeal. The company had been enervated by patrolling in spooky, sweat-soaking jungle for six days. Then they were ordered to climb Hill 1073, the dominant mountain in the valley, slipping behind what was at least a battalion of first-string NVA, already alerted and embattled with the 1/327. C Company's infiltration ascended through even more difficult terrain. Tension also ascended as each hour the troopers became more aware of an NVA force far larger than C Company, and as well-armed, lurking in these bamboo-choked hills that long had been their private preserve.

The C Company guys said many ridges ran up to the top of 1073, so the platoons split up to check out each ridge. Pretty soon the platoons could not see each other. All the ridges had a lot of NVA dug in. Real quick there were firefights all over the mountain.

AK-47's to their front brought a rush of adrenaline; AK's lapping the flanks, a rush of fear. Then the AK's were joined by heavy caliber machine guns firing on present azimuths. The search for the Twenty-fourth Regiment was over, and a new search began for a way to back off. Crisscrossing machine gun fire closed off the route by which C Company had arrived. From then on there was nothing but the consciousness of separation, of encirclement, the taste of the jungle floor when your face stays in it.

A firefight is a contest for dominance. Each side quickly announces what it brings to the contest. Nothing is withheld from the opening fusilade, so that both sides understand who is stronger that day, and who owns the psychological advantage. Within ten minutes C Company knew they were overmatched, and almost as soon realized they could be overrun. Artillery and air support was not blasting into the bamboo with enough impact to sway the battle, obviously a condition the NVA had foreseen. Only Carpenter's suicidal napalm forced back their first assault.

The napalm brought a temporary reprieve before darkness began to blur the hillsides where the platoons sprawled in isolated ovals no longer than fifty meters. The firefight was largely over: what Americans call mopping up was about to be done on them. Low on ammunition, they had only single shots to reply to smothering bursts as the NVA, growing more confident in their probes, felt for C Company's positions. As the NVA moved in, their supporting machine guns furrowed the ridges, chopping off chunks of bamboo like invisible buzz saws.

Clutching the ground, saving each round for a point-blank target, the troopers were silent except for the chilling groans of the wounded. They could not move. Again and again they were struck as the NVA found new angles of fire. When American machine gunners fell (they, with radio operators, were always a principal target), the nearest rifleman crawled over to keep the gun in action until its ammo or the new gunner expired.

All this was prelude to a night to make the strongest men cower—veterans who had won in hard fights like An Ninh, Con Tinh, and Bu Gia Map.

In the night, sound summons death. That was how the NVA located those wounded who could not stifle their moans. Grenades bounced beside them unseen, the fuses hissing a warning, then blasting in the darkness like depth charges.

The Twenty-fourth Regiment as well as C Company understood

the situation—that the night had arrived as the NVA's ally. They crouched and waited in their hatred, the product of decades of indoctrination and reinforced by the memory of comrades slaughtered in the Dak To campaign. A new wave of attackers called out taunts. Somewhere a bugler played taps for the Americans. With bayonets, the NVA crept closer to find the wounded.

The black sky began to flash as if the devil were playing with a light switch. Thunder boomed and resounded down the valley, the rumble of artillery puny by comparison. Then the monsoon broke like a ruptured dam.

"That first rain was so hard," said a C Company survivor, "I had to grab this bush I was in or I'd wash down to the NVA. They'd been calling to us from about ten meters away. Now the rain just drowned them out. I really thought we'd go down some stream together. Then it got real cold. I was shivering because I was so scared. Now I was shivering twice as hard.

"This was it. One magazine left. Whole night ahead. Guys on both sides of me wounded. They died about an hour apart."

The wild electrical storm cracked and bolted through the night. While the rain sluiced down, an argument seemed to rage in the sky, deciding how C Company would die.

"We're down to nothing. Every man on that hill thought he was the last one alive. I knew it was over for me. I just wanted a bullet to get me clean through the head. Hell, I even took off my pot (helmet). I just wasn't going to get captured—get a bayonet through me like I heard another guy go.

"I don't know how we kept 'em out. Wasn't much firing that night. Maybe I couldn't hear it for the storm. I got off just six rounds all night—waited till I had a big shadow moving in front of me each time I shot. I knew there weren't no troopers moving. I got curled up in these tree roots, just kept my '16 pointed out.

"Little by little I could see. First a tree. Then branches on it, then leaves on the branches. Everything slopping water. Rain's over, but patter-patter all the time. Maybe it was too slippery for the gooks to get up at us. I crawled over to see how Townsend was doing. He was cold and hard like a wet stone.

"When I saw Ski it was like coming back into the world. I still didn't think we were going to make it—the NVA could see better in the morning too—but there was fuckin' Sergeant Ski, so I knew someone was alive besides me."

The night produced a man to match it. This was First Sergeant Walter "Ski" Sabalauski, fifty-five years old but immortal. Said Keyes Beech of *Stars & Stripes*: "I have known the likes of Sabalauski before in other wars. They are the Skis of the armed forces, a vanishing breed to whom the Army or Marine Corps is home.

"There was a Ski at Tarawa in 1943, at Iwo Jima in '45. There was one in Inchon in 1950 and at the frozen Chosin reservoir. There had better be more Skis coming along."

"We kicked off about 5:30 [p.m.]," said Brown, describing the rescue, "an hour after the heavy fighting started, and pushed straight up that mountain, killing thirteen along the way. We started down toward Carpenter and could hear NVA talking on both sides. We just kept hacking and shooting till we reached C Company's perimeter.

"Carpenter said, 'It's your show, now. I don't have anything left.' At that time he thought he had lost most of his company. But survivors, some of them wounded, filtered in, and it wasn't as bad as he first thought."

But there was still an emergency. Two Oh-deuce companies were now where one had been trapped. Artillery pounded the NVA's grip around them, but within the perimeter wounded men would die until some level ground could be cleared for choppers to evacuate them. Brigade's reserves were used up. The First Cav was moving down to join the campaign and take some pressure off, but for the moment the 101st had no forces left to help Emerson evacuate his critically wounded.

Cai sensed the crisis:

B Company tried like hell to get down and help C Company, but bamboo made us very slow. I was behind Lieutenant Sill and his radio. He looked surprised when he heard Emerson talk to Major Schroeder because we thought Schroeder was back at Phan Rang, two hundred miles from here.

Maj. Don Schroeder, the Oh-deuce executive officer, had indeed been in Phan Rang. Emerson had sent him there where the base camp was about to undergo a command maintenance management inspection (CMMI), a despised relic of stateside administration some bureaucrat had imported to harass the American forces as they battled the communists.

On the coast at Phan Rang, Schroeder had learned of C Company's plight. In vivid phrases he told the CMMI inspectors they would be welcome when the war was over; meanwhile he was going to recruit a relief force for Dak To. No one told him to try it because no one thought it was possible, for he needed volunteers—real volunteers—who would go only if they really were willing.

The most difficult volunteer to get in the army is the "short-timer."

These were the only men at Phan Rang: men whose year in Vietnam was over, others about to leave for R and R. Both groups were in their khaki uniforms, waiting with happy anticipation by the Phan Rang runway when Schroeder approached them.

In 1968, Schroeder was killed in the delta, but on that hot morning in June 1966, he gave a brief, unrecorded, yet immortal speech. No one who heard him remembers exactly what he said, but the effect bears comparison with any of history's great military exhortations. Eighty-four men—every one of them about to depart Vietnam—dropped their duffel bags, packed their khakis, put on fatigues, grabbed weapons, and followed Schroeder into three Chinook helicopters.

When they landed at Dak To in a pelting rain, they regassed and took off for the high ground above C Company. In a matter of hours, Emerson had Task Force Schroeder, a reserve where the army showed none on paper.

It had daunting work to do. The choppers could find clearings large enough for only one ship at a time. With artillery and air strikes pelting the NVA around them, the volunteers landed and pushed the NVA off the ridge crest. Emerson then dropped them a chain saw to clear an LZ as A and C companies struggled uphill through slippery muck, carrying the dead and wounded to join Schroeder.

Nine of his volunteers were wounded, but C Company was rescued. Created in crisis, Task Force Schroeder disbanded after only two days, its history showing that no matter what distance or danger separates them, a trooper will go to another's aid when lives are on the line.

The Oh-deuce regrouped on a ridge opposite the one where Task Force Schroeder had extracted C Company. The 1/327 continued to push up from the south, but Pearson knew it was past time to even the odds with the big equalizer, an Arc Light.

On June 13, while morning mists and smoke from artillery barrages lifted from the disputed valley, twenty-four waves of B52's set the earth shaking all the way into Laos and Cambodia. When the Arc Light was over, so was the Twenty-fourth Regiment's role in the war (though a year later, another NVA regiment in Laos was called the Twenty-fourth—such was the benefit of a sanctuary). They left 1200 identifiable bodies—more than half their strength—and galleries of tunnels, some fifty feet deep, throughout the denuded mountains.

"This was their redoubt," Emerson explained to the press who had flocked to Dak To by the time the sixteen-day campaign concluded. "They fought for their lives—which most of them don't have anymore."

"First class, first team fighting men," Brown described the late Twenty-fourth Regiment, and no one has ever doubted that Dak To was a heavyweight championship bout. The NVA climbed out of the ring, and out of Vietnam, but from their sanctuaries they would reenter when they found their chances improved. A rematch was staged a year later at Dak To, this time against the 173d Airborne Brigade.

But the perennial nature of the border war was unforeseen as the Oh-deuce and 1/327 emerged from the smoke of the Arc Light. Congratulations and VIPs poured into Dak To while the Screaming Eagles mended their wounds and surveyed their booty.

There were many POWs to question so I was up very late. Then brigade say, get some POWs to meet Premier Ky—he comes with Westmoreland. Everybody must look sharp.

Ky, with a pearl-handled revolver thrust in his hip pocket, presented forty decorations to the men of the brigade. Westmoreland brought personal congratulations from President Johnson. Cai was impressed, but not nearly so much as by a visit from John Wayne, hero of Cai's favorite movies.

He's big, heavy guy. I turn my head up to look at him. He shakes my hand like I'm a big guy too. Even NVA prisoners like what's happening because everybody talks happy. Ky talked to them real friendly like they were just bad boys in school. Even the rain stopped that day. When the celebration was over, Westmoreland took Captain Carpenter away to be his aide. No one ever saw him again.

I did, very briefly, as he left Phan Rang and I arrived back.
"Carpenter of Toumorong!" I hailed him.
"Taylor of Hong Kong!" He grinned.

Chapter
Ten

After Dak To, as the brigade's first year in Vietnam drew to an end, so too did the tour of almost all its original members. There was time for one reprise at Tuy Hoa, where the NVA had gathered again to raid the summer rice harvest.

"Tuy Hoa II was really *déjà vu*," Emerson recalls. "Same hills, same AOs, some of the same LZs even, and a couple of the same objectives. But the Ninety-fifth NVA still hadn't learned not to mess with the Oh-deuce. What's more, I think they'd had so many replacements they weren't as familiar with the terrain as we were."

A visitor to this operation was Moshe Dayan. Within a year he would direct Israel's armed forces to victory in the Six-Days War, but in 1966 he was a journalist. Dayan was unimpressed, generally, with U.S. tactics in Vietnam, and especially critical of the strategic decision to fight on ground of the NVA's choosing at Dak To. But he had heard of the Oh-deuce's unconventional tactics, and came down for a look, spending several days with Emerson.

Dayan much approved of checkerboard, particularly its emphasis on night patrolling, and he got on famously with Emerson. Checkerboard reminded him of the Special Night Squads to which he had belonged, the Jewish counterguerrilla patrols developed in the late 1930s by the maverick British officer Orde Wingate, about whom I would write a novel.

"Dayan was a great student of warfare," Emerson recalled. "The U.S. Army comes into a war as if it were the first one ever, or else a continuation of the last. Dayan could tell you about guerrilla wars most American officers never heard of."

Back in familiar territory, the brigade undertook "civic action," the vital component of pacification, which meant winning hearts and minds of the populace for the GVN—no matter how unworthy of affection the Saigon regime might be. Victories were not easily measured in this psychological struggle, and most U.S. commanders believed, as one of them said of the uncommitted populace, "Grab 'em by the balls and their hearts and minds will follow."

The VC, of course, conducted their own version of civic action. It was cynical, simple, effective, and inimitable by the Americans. Stripped of class and nationalistic embroidery, the VC's message to their uncommitted countrypeople was, "Cooperate and we will not harm you. Cooperate with the GVN and we will harm you—and see that the Americans do too."

This second threat was easily accomplished by sniping at the Americans from a village that was not cooperating with the VC. Diplomacy was fine in its place, but when under fire only the superhuman trooper did not become a warrior—and the village a battlefield. Thus the VC achieved a twofold purpose: the uncooperative village was punished—ironically by the Americans—and pictures of dead civilians were thrown into U.S. living rooms.

Nevertheless, some peasants chose to defy the threat:

One village hid rice from the VC, so we reward it. I went with a civic action officer and a medic. For a whole day he did a lot of treatment for local people. We also brought cans of C rations that troops did not like. We brought them in a jeep trailer and gave to the village chief; then we took nice pictures with him in front of his office.

But I found out that this chief was never in the village because he is scared of VC. We told him the C rations are reward for the village, not for him. This chief smiled a lot and made a nice speech, but I found out later these villagers did not get the rations. I know this because in the market next day we saw the same cans we gave him.

With Emerson's departure, the Oh-deuce was turned over to another brilliant combat commander, Lt. Col. Frank Dietrich. Cai was now the longest serving veteran, the last of the original interpreters, after the departure of his good friend Toai.

After Tuy Hoa, Toai got married, and transferred to Cam Ranh MACV. Not too long after that we got two more interpreters, Ich and An. Poor An was always getting wounded—five or six times. Even when there was only one sniper shot, it hits An. People make jokes that they don't want to go on patrol with him. Even when we got back to Phan Rang, An was wounded again. On the strip one night he just went for a drink, and this CIDG walks into the bar to throw a grenade because he was jealous about a girl. Everybody jumps out the window but An is the only one wounded!

Though Cai was now eating only for himself and one tapeworm, he continued to lose weight and began to run a fever. Raised in IV Corps, he did not seem to have immunity to the bugs of II and III Corps, where the Oh-deuce had been operating for the past year. American doctors diagnosed him as having malaria and sent him to the major hospital in Nha Trang, where he convalesced for two months. On his next operation with the Oh-deuce, he had a chance to compare the medical facilities of the NVA.

We went back to Tuy Hoa again and hit favorite NVA spots. Where you overran that hospital in caves, we found another one and captured three wounded NVA. They were cut by artillery. The wounds smelled and had worms inside.

That was about the last operation for Hank. The Oh-deuce was very lucky that he was able to pick Colonel Dietrich to be the next commander.

Frank Dietrich was a crafty veteran of both World War II and Korea. Under his command the Oh-deuce improved on their experience, and near Tuy Hoa in 1967 even staged another "perfect" battle like Bu Gia Map.

The operation was called "Geronimo," and its stealth and patience was worthy of the legendary Apache. Contact months earlier caused Dietrich to suspect an NVA base camp on a particular mountain. Rather than chopper the battalion to the location, he landed them across the valley as if the operation would be conducted there. By night the companies slipped around the mountain, taking no resupply for three days and growing hungry, but easing carefully through a few hundred meters of jungle each day until they knew every trail on the mountain and had set up a complete picket of ambushes.

Within the loose noose, Dietrich sent two- and three-man patrols—not to fight or ambush but to determine the layout of the base camp, just as the VC did before attacking some allied stronghold. When he felt he had a good idea of what was on the mountain, he mangled it with a sudden avalanche of artillery. Then Cai was sent up in a helicopter where, with a loudspeaker, he informed the NVA that they were trapped.

I told them we got heavier artillery coming. If they don't surrender, they will get blown away.

Dietrich made good on that promise. When a thunderous bombardment concluded in the morning, Cai told the NVA on the mountain it would be repeated in the afternoon. The NVA battalion executive officer tried to get away alone, but he met two PFCs named Kick and Kelly. A reporter described their cat-and-mouse encounter:

Kick could barely make out the figure of a man crawling toward him. He held fire, not certain whether the man was friendly or enemy. Kelly, from his position, had also seen the elephant grass move, but he too held his fire.

With Kick's challenge [a password], Kelly heard the grass rustle. Someone was in a hurry. Kelly fired at the sound and motion. The fugitive turned in Kick's direction. Kick started stalking. He had moved only a few yards when the tall grass parted and a man in black pajamas stared at him through the underbrush. The man fired twice with his pistol.

"That's when I knew we had an officer!"

The officer spun on his belly and headed away. Straight toward Kelly. The enemy was between them but as elusive as a snake in tall grass. The NVA would move a short distance and lie still. He went back and forth in the thick underbrush as the two troopers closed in.

Trapped, he finally made a dash, falling in the tangle of vines and branches. The two M16's cracked simultaneously—four times. Papers on the body proved he was the battalion executive officer—comparable to an American major.

Now the NVA were believers. Just before the next promised artillery bombardment, several came down the mountain.

My broadcast said bring weapons but with the muzzles down. That's the way these guys came out. I got their names and said them on the loudspeaker. Then more NVA came down. Tell the truth, I was surprised because this never happened before.

Forty NVA surrendered. Two hundred had been killed. From the prisoners, Dietrich learned that another hundred were still hiding. He had plans for them. The Oh-deuce got on choppers and flew away to another province but left small stay-behind patrols armed with grease guns and silencers Dietrich got from the CIA.

NVA make plenty of noise when they think they're alone. That night they came out and started calling to each other. Our guys killed a couple dozen without making a sound. Then Dietrich brought back the battalion and combed the mountain again. That's it for the NVA—I think the Ninety-fifth dropped that battalion from their books.

Tuy Hoa II concluded, and the brigade moved once more into III Corps, participating in the biggest sweep of the war, Operation

Junction City, to clear the NVA's approaches toward Saigon through War Zones C and D from the Cambodian border. The Screaming Eagles were in reserve as the First, Fourth, and Twenty-fifth Infantry divisions teamed up with the Eleventh Armored Cavalry Regiment, the 196th Light Infantry Brigade, and the 173d Airborne Brigade. There were nearly as many troops (30,000) in Junction City as there were defending Europe. Cai had never seen so many troops, and remembered choppers filling the sky from horizon to horizon.

In twenty-three days (at a cost of approximately a million dollars per day), Junction City featured much searching, destroying enormous quantities of communist supplies, but no major enemy formations were cornered or brought to bay. Within a month, though it was no longer a freeway, the NVA route to Saigon was open again to infiltration. Operations like Junction City were just too big to be repeated every quarter, and Westmoreland did not try to sweep the border again with such a massive broom.

Dak To II was the next major phase of the border war that kept Westmoreland preoccupied with the exits of the Ho Chi Minh Trail from the DMZ to Tay Ninh. By holding off the NVA, the border screen was designed to allow ARVN to pacify the interior population centers. Obversely, by drawing the big U.S. units to the frontier, General Giap was trying to keep them off the backs of the VC.

The Twenty-fourth NVA Regiment was back in action, filled with replacements from the Ho Chi Minh Trail. They had been joined by two more fresh regiments.

The allies had raised the stakes as well, committing 16,000 men of the Fourth Infantry and First Air Cavalry Divisions as well as six ARVN battalions and the Screaming Eagles' friendly rivals in Vietnam, the 173d Airborne Brigade. There was a fraternal bond between the only two U.S. paratroop units in Vietnam at that time, for veterans of both brigades served with the other. In November 1967, the 173d shared the Dak To experience against the NVA, who had learned considerably from the first go around. The results of Dak To II raised grave questions as to whether the U.S. generals had learned as much.

As before, NVA strategy was to draw the Americans into densely jungled mountains where the effect of their artillery and bombs would be minimized by three layers of vegetation, called triple canopy; they also wanted to trap them in large ambushes if possible and to bear hug them to death if not. The written objective of the three regiments: to annihilate a U.S. brigade. It was bad luck for both sides that an airborne brigade once again became the target for annihilation in a replay of Dak To I.

Cai heard that the 173d was entering the same terrain around Dak To, and assumed the B52's would go in first this time rather than wait until the battle was concluding. He was right: the fight was very much in the same arena as before, but at first the B52's were withheld.

Almost as Carpenter's company had been relieved by Brown's, two companies of the 503d merged into a two hundred-man composite unit called Task Force Black.

On Veteran's Day 1967, Task Force Black probed out from a hilltop that had been planned as a fire base for an artillery battery, but when the infantry landed to secure the site, they got into a heavy firefight in bamboo mangled and tangled by air strikes.

For two years now, the NVA had prepared positions for their mortars and fortified the jumble of hills around Dak To. Wherever the 173d probed, the NVA could deploy into well dug in and masterfully camouflaged ambushes. Task Force Black was first to discover that the playing field had tilted steeply since the 101st had battled through these jungles.

In 1968, we captured some NVA who fight 173d at Dak To in 1967. They said they practiced that battle many times. First they wait to see where helicopters land. Then they have good trails they made so they can get to any hill pretty fast. Almost every hill had plenty of tunnels and trenches already dug. When 173d patrols, it's like they walked in a minefield.

I'm glad I was not there the second time! NVA was too ready. POWs say 173d was very brave but must move above the ground. The NVA was all dug in—not worried about anything except B52's, so they wait till troopers right on top of them before firing. That means 173d had to fight without B52's.

Deceptive helicopter landings—that is, swarms of choppers touching down on many hilltops without disgorging troops—would have confused the NVA as to the true U.S. objectives, but at Dak To II Major General Peers, the overall U.S. commander, did not seem much interested in ruse and guile. He was looking for a slugging match, and Task Force Black found it for him.

Probing downhill from the disputed artillery site, they were saved from annihilation by the jungle craft of their point platoon leader, Lieutenant Cecil. Brisk contact the day before, and the eerie feel of an otherwise dead jungle made him hyperalert, raising the hunch that the task force was headed into a trap.

So sure was he of a close-by NVA ambush that Cecil tried to prematurely spring it through "reconnaissance by fire." His men blazed away as if they had discovered an ambush. No doubt to the consternation of their commanders, the NVA returned fire and the hillside erupted in a barrel to barrel shootout where every bush seemed to sprout a gun. Men dropped on both sides, so close that bodies lay among each other, and when the troopers ran out of M16 ammunition they picked up AK-47's of fallen NVA.

The ambush Cecil had so skillfully and fortunately triggered (for this he earned a Distinguished Service Cross) had not been set for just his platoon. As he backed uphill, delaying the ambushers with claymore mines, the entire task force was enveloped by an NVA battalion that, though they had lost the shock of surprise, had the troopers pretty much where they wanted them—in an elliptical perimeter, 100 meters by 40, the long axis pointed downhill, with no protection but fallen trees, scrub brush, and clumps of bamboo that the NVA's heavy machine guns began to shred. It was almost time again for suicidal napalm.

NVA mortars sprinkled the perimeter, using delayed-action fuses to penetrate the layers of vegetation. Task Force Black called for the same fuses from their far away artillery. But again the NVA had learned well some lessons from Dak To I: they kept the artillery FO's head down, watching for his radio antenna.

Exposed above ground, exchanging fire with NVA invisible in spider holes, the task force was pinned down and losing a battle of attrition as the fighting flurried and lulled. Air support was frustrated by deep jungle canopies that prevented pilots from even seeing the perimeter. Only artillery was holding the NVA battalion back, for the American line was decimated as wounded troopers dragged themselves into the center of the perimeter but found themselves almost as exposed as before. Many were hit repeatedly and died from loss of blood.

By mid-afternoon there were as many men dying within the perimeter as fighting on its edge. Ammunition ran low; the troopers now fired only single shots instead of intimidating bursts. A Huey pilot braved the NVA's machine guns—his ship took thirty hits— to drop a sling load of ammo through the canopy. He radioed Task Force Black for a smoke grenade to mark the center of the perimeter. Overhearing his message, the NVA popped their own smoke, and the ammunition fell into their hands—another demonstration that they had learned more about the Americans than the Americans had learned about them.

By the time a relief force broke through to the perimeter—wisely "walking" artillery in front of them—the 200 troopers of Task Force Black had suffered twenty-five men killed or missing and a staggering 155 wounded, mostly from grazing fire from NVA they never saw. Two thirds of the dauntless 4/503d parachute battalion were casualties and out of the war. With only seventy-five NVA bodies counted, this eight-hour round of the border war went clearly to the NVA.

And the bout was not over. The U.S. strategy, successful in Dak To I, had been studied and countered by the NVA in Dak To II, which Westmoreland nevertheless described as a U.S. victory. With another victory like Task Force Black's, the NVA's objective of an- nihilating a brigade would be attained in nibbles if not in one gulp.

And by the grimmest luck, it was the 173d who went back into the ring. In the myriad of nondescript hills in General Peers' AO, almost all had to be investigated. With sixteen battalions checking out these hills, the 173d was assigned one called 875.

Remembering the buzz saw Task Force Black ran into, the troop- ers tiptoed up the hill, preceded by air and artillery preps. An Arc Light was the best way to start the investigation, but none were on call by the 173d. Two companies started up the hill in parallel lines, moving through foliage shattered by bombing. A company remained in reserve at the base of 875.

Landscaped by bunkers interconnected by tunnels, the hill was a vast catacomb. So devilish was their camouflage that the NVA shot the first trooper from five meters away.

Cai recalled how a POW he interrogated described the NVA's rehearsal on 875:

They walked up the hill to see the way the 173d can come. They did this weeks before the battle and thought just how it will happen. When the Americans came to Dak To again, the air strikes tell the NVA where the troopers will land. This time the tunnels are too deep for small bombs and napalm to hurt.

By building ingenious gutters, the NVA even neutralized grenades the troopers shoved into the bunkers' firing slits. Defying the enemy's advantages, the troopers maneuvered up the rolling slope, rooting out bunkers and raking trenches with fire. Bit by bit, portions of 875 were cleared, but through the web of tunnels the NVA slipped back in to stop the second wave of attackers. By the time they were halfway up the hill, the troopers were fighting in all directions. In effect they were nearly surrounded, so they pulled back into a defensive perimeter only twenty meters uphill from where they had started the assault.

Between them and A Company, the NVA had infiltrated a force nearly as large. Supported by fire from their bunkers, these NVA attacked C and D companies from the rear while a second company similarly blindsided A Company. The confused intermingling was better than a bear hug—it was like the coils of a python. U.S. artillery had to stand by until the situation sorted out.

The A Company commander was killed by mortars. A platoon was overrun by NVA coming up what seemed an inaccessibly steep flank, where in previous months they had carved and concealed a staircase. Finally A Company fought their way into C and D companies' perimeter. It was the story of Task Force Black repeating itself on even more difficult ground, even more to the NVA's liking.

As in Task Force Black's earlier predicament, a second battalion launched a rescue the morning after the first was trapped on 875.

Carrying extra water and ammo for their besieged comrades, they broke into the perimeter by dark. During the night, air and artillery bashed the hillside above them in preparation for an assault on the peak, for General Peers had vowed to the press that 875 would be secured by Thanksgiving. The first assault failed, but the 173d made good on Peers' promise the next day after the NVA had decamped, beginning a withdrawal toward the border and sanctuary.

The "score" of Dak To II was really not found in numbers. Giap must have taken satisfaction in the nearly 300 American dead, most from the 173d, which left the border at less than a third of its original strength. Westmoreland could point to 1400 NVA bodies and the fact that of Giap's three regiments engaged at Dak To, only one was available three months later for the climactic Tet Offensive. Moreover, said Westmoreland, there was no diminution in pacification campaigns elsewhere in the country.

What was not measured by these numbers were the learning curves of the respective generals. Clearly the NVA were better prepared for the 173d than they had been for the 101st the preceding year. There was little to choose in the fighting qualities of the two paratroop units; the comparisons must be drawn in how they were committed by multistarred generals.

The 173d was committed as if the experience of the 101st had never happened, or as if what worked in 1966 would work equally well in 1967. Tactical lessons and jungle craft had been handed down, mostly from sergeant to sergeant, but at high command levels the capture of terrain seemed to validate an ill-considered strategy. Terrain like Hill 875 became symbolic in two ways: for U.S. generals they were tangible objectives, welcome reminders of conventional warfare that they dearly missed. For the troopers, such intrinsically irrelevant objectives began to symbolize the indeterminancy of the war.

At Phan Rang, where they were standing by in reserve for the border campaign, the 101st heard the stories that seeped out of Dak To II:

Americans are not like any other soldiers. They have to under-stand why they do things. NVA are put into positions and just told to stay there and get killed. GIs do that once but not every time. If they find out that tactics are no good, they say that to their officers. If the same thing keeps happening, they say "fuck it" and just take care of each other.

After Dak To I it was evident, or certainly should have been to General Westmoreland, that the place to fight the NVA was not on the border, which was Giap's home field, but a bit farther in the interior where the terrain was not so disadvantageous to the Americans, and where the NVA could not scamper to sanctuary when cornered. From captured documents, MACV knew an oversize NVA division would penetrate into Kontum province. They could not carry bunkers and tunnels with them. MACV should have sucked them in rather than accepting Dak To II.

In the Oh-deuce, everyone felt very sad for the 173d at Dak To. No one wanted that to happen to us.

So Dak To II was the first crack in the troopers' morale. It was widened by the commander who brought the rest of the 101st Airborne Division to Vietnam in December 1967. Major General Barsanti was as indifferent to casualties as General Giap but not half as shrewd. In Vietnam, the paratroops were both the leaven and barometer of morale. All-volunteer units like the 173d and 101st were seen as bellwethers of attitudes and standards. When the elite have cause for resentment, the average soldiers see reason for revolt.

At first I was so happy because the division rear base is at Bien Hoa near Saigon where my parents live. There were plenty of interpreters to go to the field, so I worked at Headquarters for Military Intelligence because of my experience. I saw troops around Saigon that were no good, smoking pot, and going AWOL. One day I surprised my captain and said, "If things happen like this we are going to lose the war, then I got to follow the enemy." The captain looked at me coldly and said, "This is your country. You can't stand behind us."

The Division moved up to Hue in I Corps. I got this job riding all day long with convoys to Tam Ky. I ride in an open jeep and wave at people sometimes to show friendship, but I have to talk to them if they hold up traffic. All the new 101st guys are cherries and plenty nervous. I tell them not to worry, but while I ride along a sniper shoots and the bullet misses me but hits the radio antenna. I asked for a helmet after that because before I had a soft cap!

By January 1968 Cai was stationed at division headquarters called Camp Eagle. He was glad to be back from the convoys, immersed in the dull but safe work of translating myriad captured documents. Among them were functional battle plans that the communists routinely interlarded with revolutionary exhortations and hackneyed propaganda. Thus, Cai did not find the text of an Order of the Day particularly striking except that it came from "Headquarters, All South Vietnam Liberation Armed Forces."

To all cadres and combatants,

Move forward to achieve final victory. This Tet greeting of Chairman Ho is a combat order for our entire army and population.

To fulfill the attack ordered by the Presidium, Central Committee, South Vietnam Liberation Front, all cadres and combatants should advance in direct attacks on all headquarters of the enemy, to disrupt the United States imperialists' will of aggression and to smash the puppet government and puppet army, the lackeys of the United States, restore power to the people, completely liberate the people of South Vietnam, and establish democracy throughout the country.

It will be our task to fight the greatest battle in our long history that will bring forth worldwide change but also require many sacrifices. It will decide the fate and survival of our fatherland and shake the world and cause bitter failure for the imperialist ringleaders.

Comrades! We see that the American aggressors are losing. This is the order for their final defeat. The central highlands and the Mekong River are moving. You should act as heroes with spirit and pride so final victory will be ours!

Cai completed the translation and sent the Order of the Day over to the intelligence section with a note that identical documents had been captured at several locations near Hue. He was asked to comment because the order seemed to suggest a general offensive might be imminent—a very desirable circumstance for the division, for it meant the VC and NVA would be easy to find and consequently destroy.

On the translation, Cai commented that the communists always talked to each other in such language. No one should worry too much until the Tet new year's truce was over because the communists appreciated the break in the war more than anyone. Then, to celebrate Tet himself, Cai went out to buy some firecrackers.

Chapter Eleven

I was sad to leave Saigon before the 1968 Tet holidays, but I must report to Camp Eagle. Before I go I heard a strange rumor from Vietnamese. They said U.S. and North Vietnam will soon agree there should be coalition between GVN and VC. I told them that is a crazy story, but they said it must be true because police caught a VC agent going to the U.S. Embassy. The American press reported it too.

Most Vietnamese never trust the U.S. They trusted American individuals but not the U.S. government. That is hard for Americans to understand because you did so much for us. Vietnamese cannot understand that U.S. forces were here just to fight communism. They think you must be like the French and wanted to dominate. They said, "In election only one vote count—the vote of U.S. Ambassador." They did not know why, but Vietnamese feel the U.S. wants the war to go on and on. Maybe it is because there is profit for American companies. That make sense because many Vietnamese businessmen make big profit from war, and do not want it to end. All Vietnamese know the U.S. could end the war if they used their power, power of strongest nation in the world, so they did not believe it when Americans say they just want to make South Vietnam independent. That's why there were so many rumors about U.S. policy.

I forgot about stuff like that when I got to Camp Eagle. Americans are all on alert, but 50 percent of ARVN was on leave for holidays. That's why the communists plan the big attack for that time.

Camp Eagle was hit with big 122-mm rockets. Two interpreters wounded by sapper attack at First Brigade HQ. Then division got ready to go to Hue, where there is the biggest fight. All the cherries got lots of action and everything goes pretty good except we got hit by 122's every evening.

I told Major Parker that we should clean up the damage because civilian workers come into Camp Eagle every day. Some of them for sure are VC who want to see where the shells hit so their gunners can change the range a little bit. Parker agreed, so the damage is cleaned up every morning before civilians come into the camp.

Parker did a smart thing. He told me to tell all the people in the district near Hue that 101st will pay for the ammunition that civilians find. Villagers bring in lots of it because there has been much fighting. They get paid and the VC could not pick up old ammo to use again.

When I worked with villagers I heard another rumor like the one in Saigon: People think there is an agreement between the U.S. and Hanoi. Hanoi wants big publicity for attacking all province capitals. U.S. agrees because the attack will test the loyalty of the Vietnamese people. Also, this is the chance to get VC infrastructure because they come out into the open.

At first I think maybe there is a plot too because communists seem to make big attacks against ARVN camps—not much against places where U.S. troops are. I asked American friends about that. They said GIs are on alert and ready for attack but ARVN are mostly on holidays—so communists go to easiest targets.

The easiest one of all was Hue, the ancient capital of all Vietnam and the travel poster symbol of the country. The imperial court at the heart of Hue was modeled on the "Forbidden City" of Peking with its ramparts, turrets, and perimeter wall within a moat draped with lotus. The Citadel, as the court was called, was at the heart of

the city but separated from it by the Perfume River, a name sug-
gesting Hue's haunting charm.

Built as an eighteenth-century stronghold, the Citadel was as
formidable as it was picturesque. Once it was occupied by the NVA
they were able to hold it against U.S. fire power for twenty-five
days, the longest single battle of the war and the most publicized.

Two battalions of NVA, aided and guided by VC cadres, swept
into the city around 4:00 a.m. on the first morning of Tet, January
31, 1968. It had been a short march down from the nearby hills,
which in the previous weeks had rarely been patrolled, so safe did
ARVN feel within the walls and with the Tet truce so imminent.
Their sentries were cut down in a few bursts. Fighting continued
only at the encircled U.S. advisers' compound across the river and
at the headquarters of the First ARVN Division within the Citadel.
Throughout the rest of the city, the government had changed overnight.

*Hue showed what happens when communists are in control.
They start killing right away. VC had lists and addresses of
everyone who did not support them. Anyone at the address was
executed. The whole family.*

*I saw the carts taking bodies to dump in the river. The dead
floated to sea for many days after Tet.*

The NVA established their headquarters and directed the pogrom from the Palace of Perfect Peace, where during February the
Vietcong flag flew from perhaps the most photographed and televised
pole in history. The reconquest of Hue by the allies was the story
the press had been waiting for: Marines attacking (the climax of
Stanley Kubrick's memorable film *Full Metal Jacket*), NVA defending, and the outcome emblemized like some parody of Old Glory
at Fort McHenry.

*The rest of the world watched the end of the battle when the
U.S. and ARVN wins, but nobody saw what happens while com-*

munists were in control of that city. I had to talk to many people afterward, but they are scared to tell, even when the communists are all dead. They told us where to look for bodies of people VC punish. Usually they used shell holes but also buried wherever the ground was soft like in parks and gardens. One place where strawberries grow, all the earth was turned over like it was farmed. Bodies were in layers there—like stacks of artillery ammunition. First the VC put lots of dirt over, then less and less, I think because they must hurry when Americans start attacking.

Many more people missing. No one knows what happen to them except that VC took them back into the hills.

We found out about two years later. Two NVA came over to the 101st in Ashau valley. When we interrogated them, they said they were at Hue in Tet offensive. They were young guys, and felt sad about what they did. They thought people in Hue would greet and support them. Their commander told them the battle was for final victory without much killing. But later they felt guilty. They took us back about fifteen kilometers into the hills southwest from Hue, up a river bed. Bones all over like elephant cemetery. Hundreds and hundreds of skulls, arms, and legs— everything white because the river washed them for so long. There were so many skeletons we could not take them away so we called Chinooks. Skulls all broken because VC hit them very hard. They did not waste bullets after Tet.

Even troopers are sort of scared by this place because it is cursed. They call it Death Valley and want to leave.

Though positive identification was possible for only a few of the victims, most of those slaughtered in Death Valley were probably the Catholics herded into Phu Cam Cathedral, some 400 males, from teenage to old age, who were marched away never to be seen again. The communists had a special vendetta for Catholic priests, who were symbols of the ideological allegiance from whom their parishioners must be pried. Even in 1988, Hanoi protested to Rome when the Pope canonized a number of Vietnamese martyrs from earlier centuries.

When the Tet fighting erupted, Vietnamese Catholics flocked by thousands to what they hoped would be refuge in the monasteries. This pleased the communists, who were provided a huge audience for the exemplary punishment of live burial.

This was the fate of Benedictine Father Urbain, a French priest on good terms with the local VC, who for years had effectively controlled the territory of his parish in the suburbs of Hue. The VC exhorted his flock to denounce him and demand his punishment, but when none did, ten were shot and Father Urbain was bound and thrown on top of the bodies. His other parishioners were forced to bury him as he gave them his blessing.

Father Dong, of another nearby village, was probably the most popular in the province. During an earlier truce, Cai recalled how the pastor brought government troops and VC together for a holiday dinner.

He also delivered mail for both sides, because it sometimes happen that one brother fought for the VC and one for ARVN, and parents loved both kids. In his room was a picture of Ho Chi Minh. He prayed for this communist and told other Catholics to pray too.

When VC overran Hue, many people asked them to spare Father Dong. At first that happened, but then the communists were angry that he is so popular, and they buried him alive.

As it had been a symbol of so much of Vietnam's centuries of war-torn history, the battle for Hue encapsulated the unmitigated misery of the present war. For any subjective claim of victory by either side, the other had a counterclaim. What was won was Pyrrhic; what was lost was as irreplaceable as life itself, and made a mockery of numbers.

The numbers, however, were large enough to compare to famous battles of World War II. Eleven NVA and VC battalions were ground up at a rate of 320 dead for every day of the twenty-five they ruled. The body count of 8000 was indisputable this time because at the end, allied encirclement of the battleground was complete. Nearly a thousand ARVN and Americans from eighteen battalions died in the muddy rubble of a city 80 percent destroyed, 100 percent gutted of its pricelessly historic buildings.

Even the staggering civilian losses—5800 dead and missing; 116,000 homeless—were not as abysmal as the extermination of the city's spirit, the transmogrification of its identity that defied its physical restoration. For underneath its new buildings, Hue was a sprawling cemetery, as if grief was all that could be preserved.

People in Hue did not take bodies to one place. They buried them where they died. So many Catholics were executed that there were crosses everywhere, like at street corners, many in parks, bunches on the riverbank. Every house with a yard had crosses or Buddhist graves. When the wind blows, the streamers fly, and I saw people cry while they walked.

There was a finality about Hue that would have made it a fitting end to the maddening war, but of course it was not, only the end of a climactic phase. The slaughter of the innocents, the burning of the temple around themselves as the VC ended their reign of terror, is reminiscent of Hitler in his Berlin bunker willing the German people to die with him. Ho and Hanoi were equally disappointed in their countrypeople for not rising up against the GVN in the wake of the great offensive. Great propagandists, the communists became victims of their own lies by believing them.

The American fighting man was victimized by a reverse outcome. Where the Vietnamese people in Tet demonstrated their nonsupport for the communist war, the American people demonstrated their disbelief in the war as it was being fought by the allies. The question in the States was, "If we've been winning as General Westmoreland says we have, how could something like Hue have happened?" At Camp Eagle, Cai did not hear such talk until replacements began arriving:

Everyone felt good about how we kicked ass during Tet. VC and NVA lay low and did not fight much after that. When division was changed to air cavalry, guys started coming in who are not volunteers anymore. Most draftees are good soldiers but they came over after Tet and said in the States that important people called Tet a U.S. defeat.

NVA were not around to protect VC anymore. That's when the Phoenix program started to find the communist infrastructure. It worked pretty good around Hue because people were so glad to get rid of the communists who made atrocities in the city. So many people arrested, there was not enough room in the prison camps.

Thanh worked for me and begged for help when his brother was arrested with some students. I could not do much except get his brother a job sweeping the prison hallway so he does not have to sit in one place all the time. Before Tet, students in Hue made many demonstrations against GVN. They thought communists will bring democracy but they only bring death. Thanh knew this too but his brother learns too late. But later he got a pardon, and when communists took over Hue again in 1975, he fought them very hard, and maybe he still does.

The devastating turmoil from the Tet battles fought in South Vietnam's cities generated 600,000 refugees. Cai had no way of knowing who among his family might be among them, or who indeed was still alive. Near Camp Eagle was his youngest brother, Toan, interpreter with an American combat engineer battalion at Tam Ky. Cai found him unscathed, but now a veteran after three weeks of fighting. Together they tried to contact their parents in Saigon, but phone service was disrupted and overloaded. It was not until Cai escorted the casket of an interpreter to Saigon that he learned how the rest of the family had fared.

All were alive and lucky. The VC infrastructure had been weak in the Chinese community of Cholon, a relatively affluent quarter of Saigon. Most of the communist sympathizers lived in the poorer quarters; it was there that VC troops were harbored and where intense house-to-house fighting broke out.

In Saigon I went by one cemetery and saw every grave open. I asked "What happen to all the bodies?" People told me that for many months the VC had taken bodies away at night to put weapons and ammo in the caskets. Just before Tet they dug up the cache to use.

My reason to be in Saigon at that time was to bring Ngo Van Long back to his parents. He got killed with the Second Brigade during Tet—first interpreter to die with 101st. I could not believe that his family was so rich. They lived on one of the nicest boulevards and had a very expensive funeral. His mother cried very much and said, "I thought American unit was safe for my son but now he is dead."

Cai's parents were troubled for the same reason. With two sons as interpreters with the Americans and two more elsewhere in the armed forces, they felt the family was bearing a disproportionate burden. To the elder Lams, the war was an incomprehensible evil. Though they understood communism, having fled from it in China, the allied effort to defeat it in Vietnam seemed an enormous paradox. Sons of generals continued leisurely studies in France while peasants filled the ranks of ARVN. Civil service was a career coveted for its access to corruption. No one understood why the American gravy train had rolled into Vietnam, but everyone wanted to get aboard while it was at their station.

Jolted by the Tet offensive, MACV began to see that American idealism was quite misunderstood by the South Vietnamese. Westmoreland demanded that the country be put on a full war footing. Aid began to go where it was most needed, to ARVN, which for the most part was still armed with World War II weapons. The widely ignored draft became at last a dragnet for military-age males, swelling ARVN to over a million troops. U.S. strength too was reaching its peak of 500,000.

*   *   *

Back at Camp Eagle, Cai was put in charge of all the division's 120 interpreters, surely the largest group of men ever commanded by a sergeant in ARVN, or in any other army for that matter.

The sergeant major of 101st told me I got the world's biggest squad! I didn't see them much because division AO is so big. This job gets me a nice office with telephone near division staff, and I saw important people all the time. I got to hear rumors first, and when I went out to see old buddies in the Oh-deuce, they always asked me what's going on. They also tell me how nice my uniform looks because I don't have to hump the hills anymore. Maybe they think I got no more problems but there were plenty of them:

New CG wanted good pacification around Hue. Lot of nights I had to go out for "cordon" operations. The way they worked was that during the daytime, the troopers hung around the villages and played a lot with the children. Each family was observed so all members are counted. At night we closed up the village and did a new count. We caught many VC that way when they show up to be with their women.

Another thing I did was cut paperwork for Vietnamese decorations to Americans. The regular channel was for ARVN liaison officer to report good U.S. officers to MACV. They send it over to First ARVN Division, who writes up citation for medal, then send it back over to their liaison officer. That system never worked very good because the liaison officer was not in the field with U.S. troops much. So Colonel Dong said to me, "Cai, I will give you a box of medals with citations already signed by General Truong." That was a good system because I found out who did a good job in the field, and the adjutant always made the awards I recommend.

Most of my problems were not about the war. One time there was conflict about a woman, and the interpreter Ngoc killed a U.S. sergeant in the 2/327. They both dated her and had many quarrels. Inside a bunker the sergeant pulled his machete and hit Ngoc on the neck, shoulder, and back. He grabbed an M16 and shot three times into the air to warn, but the sergeant kept swinging at Ngoc so he finally shot him in the stomach.

A big investigation then, and I worked on it for a month. I had to interrogate Ngoc, the witnesses, and the woman involved. What Ngoc said was proved and the Americans decided he is okay because of self-defense, but ARVN said he must face another judge. He was many months in prison waiting for trial, then released to go to another U.S. unit.

I also had to interpret for two court martials. First one, a PFC tried to rape a twelve-year-old girl. He said he was lonely and towns were off limits and no strips around either. He got three years in Leavenworth prison.

Another trial was about a mess sergeant who hit a Vietnamese worker with a pan. He had to pay the worker for injury. The Vietnamese were very surprised that soldiers can be punished. Some false claims were made when people hear they can get money.

Another interpreter got involved with an elementary school teacher. She wanted to get married but he did not, so he asked me for transfer. I sent him to another brigade but on the way his helicopter crashed. He was the third interpreter to get killed with division. I told my parents this is very few—much less than in ARVN.

The division was pushing into valleys toward the border of Laos at this time. Sergeant Major Sabalauski was still with Oh-deuce, and he told me it is like dogs chasing cats. Many POWs collected at division, and I had the job of asking them how they fight us. All told me they had orders to avoid contact with Americans because we have so much fire power. An NVA company commander said that they fear M79's very much, and always try to capture one. He had been fighting U.S. Marines for one year, then after Tet he was in 101st's AO. He got wounded by both U.S. troops, each time by M79. I reported what he said, then an officer from G3 told me to ask this NVA captain what was the difference between the 101st and the Marines. We have many more helicopters, he said; we make lots of small ambushes and like to fight with artillery. Marines wear flak jackets that makes them move slow but gives protection too. Larger units go on Marine patrols but not so many patrols as 101st. Marines use more air strikes than artillery. I asked him which troops are better. He thinks first, then says Marines are better in defense but 101st are better in attack. I laughed because it sounded like he did not want to make anybody mad at him.

We worked with First ARVN Division a lot around Hue so they sent us three liaison officers. Two of them no good at all. Lieutenant Thuy tried to make money through laundry women in Camp Eagle. Lieutenant Yee sold empty artillery boxes to local people for making furniture. I told these officers not to get involved in these affairs but they did not listen to me because I am just a sergeant. I reported what they do to division and they were sent back to ARVN.

After the war was lost, I met Yee again when we were both prisoners of the communists. He was not angry with me but very sad that he did not do his duty so that the communists could be defeated.

Also assigned at Camp Eagle was Lieutenant Nga from the ARVN Military Intelligence. He brought with him Sergeant Coc, who became my good friend. He told me to watch for the pretty girlfriend that Nga brings into camp sometimes. She came in his jeep and looked all over the place. She was very interested in everything that is going on. Coc told some people in the Phoenix campaign about her. She was arrested, and turns out she was a member of the connection cadre between Hue and Danang. Lieutenant Nga had a shock and must go back to Saigon.

Lot more communists surrendered than before Tet. One VC told me he was sleeping in his bunker when a U.S. bulldozer buried it. The troopers did not know the VC was in there, and did not see him. When he dug himself out, his rifle was full of dirt. He was afraid his squad leader will make him dig another bunker and punish him for the dirty rifle, so he just walked into district Chieu Hoi center and surrendered.

Air Force dropped millions of Chieu Hoi leaflets in the jungle, and we shot artillery shells that have leaflets in them too. They are good for "safe conduct" pass if a man surrenders. He gets a bonus if he brings his weapon. Bigger weapon, bigger bonus.

Each leaflet had a number so when it is turned in MI will know where NVA was when he found it. This helped locate where NVA units are.

A couple of guys surrendered because they were afraid of sickness called black death. They heard that we were giving shots to thousands of Vietnamese for this disease. This was true, but NVA did not know that no one had the disease yet. Our PSYOP unit did a smart thing to make them worry. They dropped leaflets that looked like they were for civilians. It said "Watch out for dead rats because many will be drowned in big rains of the monsoon. These rats have fleas with black death disease. When rats die, fleas must find new place to live, on humans."

When PSYOP heard how some NVA are worried about black death, they had us interpreters work on a message that looks like it was written by NVA headquarters. It said there are very few shots available, so NVA officers should come and get them but not tell the soldiers. This made the soldiers angry at officers!

PSYOP worked good when NVA morale was low. When some surrender we made tape records, and broadcast them from airplanes. Some ralliers called to their buddies and used real names telling them to come in. We also gave TV sets and generators to villages and showed news programs every night. More than two hundred VC and NVA were Chieu Hois in September 1968. I liked this kind of work because it is smarter to make them surrender than to kill them in battle.

Best job was when PSYOP people asked me to help with a new leaflet. They think if it has a pretty girl's picture, NVA will show it to others and maybe more will read the message and surrender. I thought about this and said if picture is real good, NVA soldier will want to keep it for himself. They said, no problem, there will be plenty of leaflets, enough for whole North Vietnamese Army. If this is true, I think maybe girl pictures are a good idea because soldiers will start looking for these leaflets. PSYOP people were glad I agree, and asked me what is the best picture because they must choose Asian or Western girl. I think it should be Western girl because NVA never see that kind. The decision was for German woman named Elke Sommer. She wore a bikini suit because the NVA had not seen that either.

Chapter
Twelve

Ralliers from the NVA were so abundant in 1968 (the equivalent of nearly three divisions of VC and NVA had defected by that time) that some were selected to serve with U.S. forces much the way Cai did, fully trusted and uniquely valuable. These former NVA were called "Kit Carson Scouts" (KCS), so named for their similarity to the once hostile Indians recruited by explorers of the old west. As the 101st began the second year of their drive from Hue on the coast to the NVA's mountain redoubts on the Laotian border, KCS joined them at the fighting level. No longer did a company commander have to speculate what the NVA in the jungle were up to; with a KCS beside him he could ask an authority.

They were valuable in other ways. A particular prize was Lieutenant Minh, former commander of a sapper company. In some armies, even western ones, sapper means "pioneer," though American military parlance equates the term to "combat engineer." More descriptive is "kamikaze engineer," for the job of the sapper is to penetrate solid defenses and deliver explosives by hand. NVA sappers were all volunteers, some of the bravest and highest skilled soldiers on either side.

As the 101st rolled toward the Ashau valley, the NVA used sappers regularly for their devastating hit-and-run night attacks. NVA infantry was too depleted and demoralized to do more than badger the U.S. offensive. Sapper attacks became their most feared and frequent tactic, especially against fire bases.

*D*ivision *Chief of Staff Colonel McDonald asked Minh to demonstrate how sappers can sneak through any barbed wire and mines that the 101st use. Minh said okay, and McDonald told our infantry to set up the best barbed wire and trip flares so troops can watch how sappers do it. But McDonald also said use only dummy mines because he did not want Minh to blow up. Minh ask that real mines be used so troops can see how good sappers are. McDonald was very worried, but finally he said okay.*

Troops watched from behind sandbags. Minh first took off his clothes so his skin can feel everything. He wore a blindfold so he can not see, just like at nighttime. He lay down and took a blade of grass to feel all around him as he crawled into the wire on his belly. This way he can feel strings of trip flares but not pull them. He moved very slowly—probed the ground lightly to find mines.

Minh knew all U.S. mines and how to unarm them in the dark. Next he snipped the barbed wire—each time he carefully tied cut ends to rods he pushed into the ground so there was no release of tight wire.

It took him more than three hours to work through one roll of triple concertina [a pyramid of spiral barbed wire]. Then he backed out, tying everything so it looks just like before. When he was NVA he came back many nights till job was done, sometimes weeks till he had a lane to get into perimeter.

The troops watched for only a few hours. It was very hot and they must wear helmets, but all watched careful and nobody talked. At the end of the demonstration, some people clap because of what Minh did, but other guys told me later how scared they are and didn't sleep that night.

Though not considered so at the time, the KCS program was a preliminary step in the "Vietnamization" of the war that the American public found too long and too costly to fight to the end. Since 1961, when the first American adviser was cut down in a VC ambush, U.S. killed in action had grown to 16,000 by 1967, and nearly doubled in 1968. The material cost in the seven-year period averaged twenty billion dollars annually. In June 1968, Vietnam also became the longest war in American history. One way or another, the U.S. was leaving, and the preeminent questions in Washington and Saigon were when and how.

A new American high command would do the extraction. Secretary of Defense McNamara resigned and his "systems analysis" approach to the war was discarded. General Westmoreland was kicked upstairs to become chief of staff of the army, and his successor at MACV, General Abrams, was told to come up with a way to do better without more troops.

But the most stunning psychological impact of Tet was manifested by the commander in chief himself. In March 1968, President Johnson took himself out of consideration for reelection with the vow to devote the rest of his term to "the search for peace." His gesture was no salve to the antiwar rabble, who created new opportunities for frenzy at the Democratic national convention, and found soft targets for disruption on many college campuses. The nation suffered additional convulsions with the assassinations of Martin Luther King and Robert Kennedy.

Internally torn and bleeding, it was apparent the U.S. was in no mood to continue the role of Uncle Sam for Nephew Thieu and his GVN. American doves ridiculed (hawks could only shake their heads) that it took Tet to convince Thieu to order general mobilization of the country—after ten years in a war where its survival was at stake. Under paper banners of reform, revitalization, unity, and anticorruption, Thieu managed to eliminate much legitimate political opposition and consolidate his personal hold on the government. Though uniting South Vietnam in a loathing of communism, the ordeal of Tet neither galvanized the people nor attracted their allegiance to Thieu's regime.

Why should it when, as a U.S. Senate subcommittee reported, "rampant and inconceivable corruption" diverted half the American medical aid sent for refugees. Equally unconscionable but condoned graft plundered every form of relief donated by the free world to the victims of Tet. Indifferent to the obligations of sovereignty, contemptuous of any social contract with its citizens, the GVN masqueraded as a nation while it remained at core a feudal system.

Nevertheless, the U.S. would continue to fight for South Vietnam's preservation. Throughout the war the Americans were accused of impatience, but their forbearance toward the GVN was enough to make Buddha proud.

ARVN was filling with draftees at one end and emptying at the other from desertions at the rate of 12,000 men per month. These were not defectors to the VC—life was too hard as a guerrilla—but simply men who were abandoning an army that neither returned loyalty nor represented a higher cause.

Resisting invasion was such a cause for which thousands of ARVN fought and died with bravery that went largely unnoticed. The communists' barbarity during Tet amply demonstrated how dark and perpetual would be the evil if they won. But to make the sacrifices required by combat against a ferociously implacable enemy, an army must believe in what it is defending as well as what it is defending against. These are not always complementary motivations; they can be reciprocal forces, like push and pull. Both cause motion but do not necessarily reinforce each other.

Too much of ARVN was not defending the South Vietnamese people, but rather the interests of favored South Vietnamese. An army adopts the values of its commanders. For the most part, the ARVN high command valued only personal advancement and parochial advantage. Thus the troops took that same attitude toward the civilians in their AOs. They appropriated the peasants' livestock, for they had watched their own supplies appropriated and sold by their commanders on the black market.

A peasant told me in 1968 that he did not care who wins. If communists run his village then the people don't have anything, but everyone has the same. His family is the only important thing, and maybe have better chance for grandchildren with no war, even if communists rule.

With scant respect for ARVN, with contempt for the GVN, American troops had abundant reasons to wonder what they were fighting for. By the middle of 1968 they, like ARVN, were fighting for themselves but only to show they could win. They were intimately involved in the ultimate contest, literally a life-or-death contest, though they did not know or much care what its origins were or how it would end as a war. Except as careerism created a riptide among U.S. officers, they had little personal stake in the outcome. But everything was at stake in the brotherhood of combat—the unmentioned bond with the guy next to you on the chopper, with your point man on a patrol—your teammates in the deadly, personal contest uninfluenced by political context. In short, the troopers were fighting to keep faith with each other.

They would have to fight superbly, for until the 101st returned to the United States three years later, its missions would focus on the Ashau valley—the strongest, most valuable, and best protected NVA base in South Vietnam—the arsenal of communism.

"The Ashau" meant a trunk valley and a complex of tributaries sprawling through thirty miles of rugged mountains veiled in variform jungle as if this were the arboretum of Southeast Asia. Trees and brushwood of all kinds marbled the terrain in every tint of green. Along the watercourses were most of the bushes, scrub growth and grasses, including the seven-foot-high, saber-sharp elephant grass for which the border highlands were famous.

Cherries asked about elephant grass a lot. They wanted to see it, but old guys had jokes for them. One patrol went out in elephant grass and almost fell in a B52 crater. An old guy told a cherry, "that is the footprint of an elephant!"

Another time a cherry couldn't sleep in a hammock so he took his air mattress to Ashau. He lay down at night and felt a snake beside him. He thinks this is a bamboo viper because there are a lot of them in the jungle here. He has to lie there for a long time till another guy woke him to pull guard. Cherry said, "There's a snake with me under my poncho liner! I can't pull guard right now." Other guy said, "Okay, buddy. I pull it for you. We'll be back in the morning and see what kind of snake you sleep with."

But the cherry got no sleep at all. When it is finally light, his squad came back with a medic ready to take care of snake bite. They stood around him with M16's. They said, "We pull off your poncho liner, then you roll away fast as you can."

He does that super fast. Rolls all the way down this hill. He does not hear M16's shoot the snake. What he hear is his buddies laughing. All night he has been with a big lizard!

Elevations tiered down from 6000 feet on the border to the coastal plain and cities like Hue and Danang. In their offensives, it was these cities that the 101st would protect from onslaughts like Tet. The Ashau was the major offshoot in I Corps from the Ho Chi Minh Trail, which by now the NVA had improved until much of it was negotiable by vehicles. With this protected supply line, with three years of uninterrupted occupancy, 10,000 NVA in the Ashau were prepared (if not anxious) to fight. The Screaming Eagles and First Cav first came at them in strength in April of 1968 in a month-long operation called "Delaware."

Preceded by six days of B52 strikes, the First Cav flew into the northern Ashau through swirling clouds and thunderstorms, while two battalions of the 101st penetrated overland. It was safer on the ground, for the NVA revealed an unexpected strength from well-sited antiaircraft batteries that downed sixty helicopters in three weeks.

Thirteen of the guns were captured during Delaware, as were over 2400 weapons of all kinds, enough to arm a regiment. Sobering evidence of the NVA's improved supply system was found in the capture of a tank, three tracked vehicles, and seventy-five trucks.

Recon patrol from 327th saw this mound and think maybe it is a grave for NVA. But just below ground they dig up two new tires. Then the patrol leader thought there must be a vehicle around and they looked for a long time till they came to a little clearing where there are two French trucks in camouflage. One was torn up by the NVA to give parts to the other.

Patrol is happy because they think now maybe they can ride and not have to carry rucksacks on their backs. They found a

*fifty-five gallon drum of gasoline but cannot get the truck started
and have to blow it up and keep walking.*

The NVA were now so well supplied from Laos that they could
afford the loss of war material if that meant conserving men. Only
850 were killed in Delaware, a poor ratio for the 139 American body
bags.

Though still infiltrating an average of 15,000 men per month into
South Vietnam, the NVA was quiescent in the middle of the year
as Hanoi's diplomats bickered with their American counterparts at
the peace talks in Paris (much of the discussion was about the shape
of the conference table). Asked about the lull in fighting, General
Abrams told the President that if the NVA could be kept bottled up
in their marches as they were in the Ashau, it might be possible to
bring home some troops in 1969.

Though this announcement encouraged the folks at home, it was
hardly incentive for the troops in the field to press on into the Ashau.
Where "short-timer" had been a sobriquet for fortunate individuals,
now perhaps a whole division was "short." No one knew which units
might be withdrawn first, but until it was determined everyone
agreed with Abrams that "one more casualty is too many."

It may have been the 101st commander's (Major General Zais's)
nervousness about a pervasive short-timer's attitude in his division
that resulted in a bloody assault in the upper Ashau on Ap Bia
Mountain, an obscure 3000-foot elevation that became known to the
world as Hamburger Hill.

Operation Apache Snow, in mid-May 1969, was the sixth visit
by the 101st to the Ashau. Joined by 1800 ARVN and U.S. Marines,
the forces choppered into LZs on the northern and western fringes
of the valley in order to avoid the NVA antiaircraft batteries that
had so riddled the First Cav during Delaware. The western landings
were a particularly daring maneuver, placing two battalions of the
101st as close as 300 meters to Laos.

Snug on the border, the troopers hoped to cut off the NVA's
usual escape route. This purpose even attracted the attention of
Radio Hanoi, which broadcast that "guerrillas' blows will answer the
tricky plots and stubborn acts of the Americans."

"Guerrillas" was Hanoi's euphemism for its own troops, the NVA, who, according to their version of the war, never once entered South Vietnam. Many U.S. politicians also found it convenient to endorse that fantasy.

The early action in Apache Snow went well for the Americans as they killed about a hundred NVA per day and lost less than ten themselves. Then at night, two sapper companies hit a Marine fire base, broke through the perimeter wire, and destroyed a howitzer and killed twenty-five artillerymen. The next morning the 101st started up the slopes of Ap Bia Mountain, which at the time looked like just another hill to explore. It would take ten days and fifty-five dead to seize the top.

One of those who made it, SP4 Bob Rocklen, described the first assault:

"When we first started up, we were in pretty heavy vegetation, but all of a sudden that thinned out to absolutely nothing because of the artillery and air strikes.

"It looked like there was about 100 meters of open area with no cover. Except for some large bomb craters, there was nothing. Actually, that first day we got two squads to the top but they were too exposed. NVA must have got up there through tunnels. They drove us off. Then more air and artillery came in. Seemed they blasted the mountain down to bedrock."

SP5 Bob Borders described the next day's assault: "The air is laced with flashing green and blue streaks of NVA tracers [U.S. tracers were red] and the smell of cordite hangs over the hillside. The troopers are faced with concentric rows of solidly built, well-concealed bunkers around the hillmass. The bunkers dominate avenues of approach up the mountain."

The NVA were not going to give it up because the mountain fortress was headquarters for the Twenty-ninth Regiment. Nine hundred of them were burrowed in, awaiting attack by the same number of paratroopers. Even after the first assault was driven back, General Zais did not bring in B52's to better the odds. "Real victories don't come easy," he told the press.

Colonel Conmy, commander of the assaulting brigade, had a more specific reason for withholding Arc Light. He believed, correctly, that the NVA had been tipped off. From many previous experiences, it seemed the NVA got last minute warning before the B52's arrived. Truong Nhu Tang explained how:

B52's flying out of Okinawa and Guam would be picked up by Soviet intelligence trawlers plying the South China Sea. The planes' heading and speed would be computed and relayed to COSVN headquarters, which would then order forces in the anticipated target zones to move away perpendicularly to the attack trajectory. Flights originating from the U.S. Thai bases were monitored both on radar and visually by our intelligence nets there and the information similarly relayed.

The press began to wonder about the absence of B52's as the eighth day of the assault unfolded.

David Lamb, of UPI, recalls:

By mid-afternoon a misty drizzle had become a bone-chilling downpour that soaked the fallen paratroopers, splashing off their ponchos in torrents. The wounded men were stretched out on the ground head to toe, along a trail at the base of Hamburger Hill. Drugged with morphine, most felt only numbness and the cold. Some shivered but said nothing.

A negro medic as black as the jungle night cradled the pale, white face of a badly wounded trooper, filling his ears with words of comfort.

Thick clouds settled over the tiny clearing, casting a ghostlike appearance over the blank expressions of other wounded who had stumbled off the mountain in tattered fatigues. Medics worked over the prostrate forms, cutting, carving, bandaging, cleaning, soothing. The rasps of labored breathing grew louder, the rain stronger.

Jay Sharbutt, of AP, described the eleventh and final assault:

Before the attack, artillery worked over the mountain. The crest resembled a huge, shell-pocked sand dune with scorched trees dotting its slopes.

"The artillery has lifted, the tubes are clear. Go!" radioed Lt. Col. Weldon Honeycutt, commander of the 3/187, which had borne the brunt of the fighting. In a light observation helicopter, he was keeping watch on the battlefield below.

It was 10 a.m. The paratroopers, wearing flak jackets and each carrying 1200 bullets for his M16, moved up the ridgeline at the word "Go!"

They came under heavy small arms fire: rocket-propelled grenades and hand grenades from the bunkers. The mountaintop crackled with gunfire.

Honeycutt, watching from the air, snorted and fumed as the men in one of his companies began clustering together as they came under heavy fire. "There's no security in togetherness," he radioed the company commander. "Get those people spread out!"

He sounds brutal and hard as hell, but he gets them mad at him and it stops them from feeling sorry for themselves. "It keeps them moving," said a ground officer.

The 3/187 and a combined force of three battalions kept moving and rooting until they emptied the catacombs of Hamburger Hill. More than 2000 bunkers and other structures were destroyed. For 600 NVA the mountain was a tomb, but only General Zais had much to celebrate. As Cai recalled,

Zais was promoted to lieutenant general after this battle. When interpreter Phuong came back from Ap Bia, I sincerely asked him if he wants to transfer to division headquarters but he said he will stay with 3/187. Men have lots of respect for him because he stay, after so much killing.

When another interpreter was killed on this mountain I flew over to get his body. I could not believe that we lost so many men to take the strong defenses. To me, factories could produce the bomb or airplane in days or months, but it takes seventeen years to raise a man. My opinion was that if we spot enemy positions we should use the best of our weapons to destroy it. I was sure the 101st commander wanted to prove to the press and whole world that his men were airborne, and the best outfit in the war, even though they had to pay a high price for that.

It was a price too high for many in Congress, including Senator Ted Kennedy, who asked the Pentagon, publicly, how such storming of NVA fortifications was leading to conclusion of the war. This was a Clausewitzian question, not easily answered. So long as the NVA could lurk undisturbed in their sanctuaries, they would accept battle only when and where they chose. It followed, consequently, that General Giap was prepared to accept NVA losses as heavy as those on Hamburger Hill. It was evident from the outcry that the American public was not.

Nixon was now commander in chief. His successful campaign for the presidency included a secret plan to end the war. Though that sounded somewhat odd, the secrecy was necessary so as not to tip his hand to Hanoi. The visible aspect of the strategy was to begin Vietnamization in earnest.

The U.S. troop drawdown began by pulling the Marines out of I Corps. In national defense doctrine, Marines are equipped for sixty days of combat. By October 1969 they had been fighting for more than four years. They were withdrawn from along the DMZ and replaced by the U.S. Fifth Division and the 101st. Nixon announced that 35,000 more men, most from the Third Marine Division, would be brought home by Christmas.

Smarting from criticism of Hamburger Hill, the 101st strategy along the DMZ was defensive and featured mostly small reconnaissance patrols. Typical was the work of Jones Platoon, described by Steve Warsh of *Stars & Stripes*:

These days the war below the DMZ is one of no large battles and few incidents of sustained contact with the enemy. It is fought by units like the twenty-four men of D Troop led by Lt. Jon Jones.

Jones Platoon responds to reports of enemy activity supplied by light observation helicopters. Monday afternoon the platoon got the call to check out a pocket of thick underbrush nine miles below the DMZ where a lone NVA had been sighted.

Hacking, brushing aside tentaclelike vines, shoulder-high elephant grass, and sharp bamboo stalks, Jones Platoon weaved its way down the steep, slippery banks of a ravine. Once on the floor, they spread out in three squads to search the thick vegetation.

Most reconnaissance patrols were what the troops called "walks in the woods"—searches that found nothing. This one was different.

The riflemen chanced upon what appeared to be an enemy R and R site. A well-concealed hooch yielded a cache of corn, rice and dried roots neatly stored in American-made sandbags. An American gas mask, a typewriter, fifteen pounds of reading material, binoculars, a bamboo fish trap, a battered harmonica, and tattered socks came out of another camouflaged hut. Elsewhere, bamboo picnic tables and jungle beds were uncovered by the roving paratroopers.

Such poking around is presently the name of the game below the DMZ.

The troop withdrawals, the sitzkrieg for the troops remaining—their idleness that diffused common purpose and nurtured drug use and racial tension—these were the memories of the war imprinted in 1969. Worst of all was the revelation of the My Lai atrocity. Committed by U.S. Army troops the previous year, it had been covered up until a combat photographer present, Ronald Haeberle, went public with the shocking pictures of women and babies slain for being Vietnamese in Vietcong territory.

Major General Koster commanded the Americal Division of which the battalion responsible for My Lai was a part. When the story broke in 1969, he was Superintendent of the United States Military Academy at West Point. Under investigation, he asked to be relieved.

At Camp Eagle, when we hear Koster resigned, we know something serious happen. Many, many villages like My Lai got searched in the war. ARVN took lots of things from people when they go through, but U.S. troops usually leave alone—not much they want in villages. My Lai was very hard for me to believe because VC did not shoot from there.

It was even more difficult for General Westmoreland, who reluctantly became convinced that there had been "a kind of diabolical, slow-motion nightmare that went on for the better part of a day, with a cold-blooded break for lunch." When the darkest day in the Army's history ended, hundreds of villagers—almost all women, children, and old men—lay dead in grotesque heaps.

Communists do things like that to teach lessons with fear. The world says, "Well okay, that's too bad, but they are communists." Village of Duc Duc was burned with all people in it and nobody remembers. Same with Hue at Tet—I read that political killing is not atrocity. How come? Hundred times more people murdered in Hue than My Lai. Different feeling when Americans murder —it is the big crime of whole war. Crime should be crime for everybody, but many Americans do not believe that.

We went to the DMZ when Marines leave. I thought the war must be going pretty good like it is with 101st. We can read what Nixon wants to do—make ARVN real strong so it can stop NVA, then maybe guerrillas stop fighting because they are so weak and need NVA for replacements.

101st worked a lot with First ARVN Division in the Ashau. They were pretty good when U.S. fire power was available, sometimes better than Americans. Very good team, First ARVN and 101st. That made me think Vietnamization can work like Nixon say.

Vietnamese like him because he was not afraid to bomb North Vietnam more. They shot big rockets into South Vietnam cities so we were glad when Nixon bomb them back. Best thing he did is support Operation Toan Thang in Kampuchea.

Translated, the operation meant "Total Victory," better known as the Cambodian Incursion when it exploded on the American home front. It was this raid into the NVA's sanctuary that caused the wild demonstration at Kent State University, where four students were shot and killed by the Ohio National Guard after the ROTC building was burned.

About a half million Cambodians lived in South Vietnam. They were some of GVN's best fighters, like French Foreign Legion. Also, just about as many Vietnamese lived in Cambodia. They were not treated well by Prince Sihanouk. He pretends he is neutral in war but he let NVA stay there as much as they want.

Sihanouk also permitted the North Vietnamese to discharge millions of tons of war cargo at Cambodia's principal port, Sihanoukville, for transshipment to the front. Ethnic hatred seethed in Cambodia's border provinces until, in March 1970 while Sihanouk was in France, he was unseated by Lon Nol, a pro-western general, who demanded that Hanoi get its troops out of the country. With its Khmer Rouge allies, the NVA responded by attacking Cambodian army outposts. In retaliation, the Phnom Penh government imposed curfews and quarantine on their Vietnamese citizens, measures that burst into a pogrom. Though many of these Vietnamese had originally come from South Vietnam, for Hanoi they amounted to a convenient pretense for full warfare against Lon Nol, so the NVA overtly consolidated their control of the Cambodian border provinces.

Lon Nol appealed to the U.S. and GVN to expel the communists. The possibility of stanching an infiltration route, second in importance to only the Ho Chi Minh Trail, was an opportunity Nixon was bold enough to seize. President Thieu and General Abrams were particularly delighted to clean out the "Parrot's Beak," a tongue of Cambodian territory that protruded to within fifty kilometers of Saigon.

The equivalent of three and a half divisions pounced onto the NVA base camps overflowing with supply dumps, hospitals, underground command centers, mess halls, barracks, and transshipment hubs. This sweep kicked off while Nixon announced the incursion on April 30, stating that U.S. forces would pull out of Cambodia in sixty days.

With that notice, the NVA faded deeper into Cambodia, taking with them their headquarters, called Central Office for South Vietnam (COSVN) which was their field directorate for much of the war effort. The NVA pulled back to fight another day but lost logistic stocks that retarded future offensives by about six months.

The incursion introduced a new demolition device for make-your-own LZs.

We heard about this bomb called "daisy cutter." I don't know this flower but I found out the bomb makes the jungle flat for three choppers. A 15,000 pound bomb! I saw a picture—it is bigger than a truck.

The allied booty was by far the largest of the war, rivaling even that captured in the wake of the crumbling German army in World War II. After COSVN fled, a three-square-kilometer complex yielded up hundreds of surface and subterranean buildings, eighteen mess halls, two well-stocked hospitals, a huge training facility, arsenals with thousands of weapons, so many tons of ammunition and rations they could not be counted, uniforms to clothe several regiments, over 300 vehicles, and even a military farm with hundreds of livestock and a swimming pool for cadre recreation.

In May, the U.S. Navy, in a hundred-ship flotilla, moved up the Mekong into Cambodia. They were to clear the banks, rescue Vietnamese refugees, and help bring back NVA war material. All told, by the end of the incursion, over 13,000 NVA were dead or prisoners, and double that number of weapons were captured. The sixty-day raid was the allies' finest hour.

Vietnamese newspapers and radio were very proud. When the communists lost the Cambodia sanctuary, it was a hard blow for them, and III Corps was quiet for a long time. All roads were clear and people could drive even at night just like peacetime.

Chapter
Thirteen

The success in Cambodia encouraged the allies to cut the last and principal NVA supply line, the infamous Ho Chi Minh Trail. If this could be accomplished, South Vietnam would finally be insulated from future communist infiltration. Its coast was now patrolled by the U.S. Navy, which effectively blocked significant communist re-supply by sea. With the Lon Nol government controlling Cambodia's ports, that country was no longer an avenue for infiltration. Indeed, the Cambodian region still dominated by the NVA now had to be provisioned by lengthening the Ho Chi Minh Trail.

By 1970 the trail was a 3600-kilometer ganglion of roads and paths, staffed and maintained by 150,000 service troops. The NVA infantry trekked down the trail, usually in battalion size (vehicles used parallel routes), progressing through a chain of way stations about a day's march apart. They were harassed by bombing and U.S.-instigated guerrilla attacks, but they suffered most from diseases of the jungle, principally malaria, which decimated battalion after battalion.

Depending on destination, a journey down the trail in its early days could take from three to six months. Typically, newly trained battalions assembled near Dong Hoi and received a week's supply of trail rations (jerky, salt, sugar, tea) to supplement rice provided at the way stations. When on the road, they marched at night to avoid air strikes. Periodically they would rest for several days in prepared cantonments where they dropped off casualties and picked up stragglers.

The route followed natural land corridors, but where mountains had to be climbed, support troops carved out stairs or constructed ladders with bamboo. Streams were negotiated with rope or vine bridges that could be swung into place for a crossing, then swung back out of sight from reconnaissance aircraft. Motor vehicles used log ferries or sometimes bridges built below the water surface, but the prime wheeled transports were bicycles, pushed rather than ridden down the trail.

When in deep jungle, marches shifted from night to day. The NVA began two hours before dawn and continued until midday, breaking for food and sleep, then resuming until an hour before dark. Like the U.S. Army, there was a ten-minute break in every hour's march. With weapons, their loads were about forty pounds. One of the early trailblazers described the trek in his diary:

> We marched all day bent under the weight of our packs. In the heat and humidity we are forced to stop often for rest and to get our breath back. In the evening, utterly exhausted, we hang our hammocks and mosquito nets from the trees and sleep under the stars. At times we have to search far from the trail for a waterfall or spring where we can drink and fill canteens. There are tigers in the jungle, and we knew about attacks on stragglers and people who have become separated.
>
> We climb mountain faces of over a thousand meters, pulling head-bands down over our eyes to filter the sun's rays. From the summit a spectacle of splendor and magnificence offers itself to us. It is like a countryside of fairy tales.
>
> Those who get sick we leave at the next way post. The group continues to march. We must have faith in our struggle, in our leaders, to endure these tests of suffering and pain when we can no longer distinguish the line between life and death.

Truong Nhu Tang, some ten years later, described the trip after the route became the Ho Chi Minh Turnpike:

> The route had become an interlocking system of two-lane roads, their hard-packed dirt beds surfaced with crushed stone. At approximately

every hundred kilometers was what amounted to a village for soldiers and work battalions that protected the lifeline, a largely self-sustaining force that in early 1974 numbered close to 100,000. Barracks, armories, storage and shop facilities, farms, dispensaries, guest houses, fueling stations—everything imaginable for defense, repair, and transportation was available in these places and in smaller depots and camps that marked the road between them.

Some of the veritable army of workers had lived on the road from eight to ten years without seeing their homes. Several of the volunteer youth I talked to had arrived as teenagers and were now in their early thirties. Over the years [they created] a web of bypasses and cutoffs which made the system practically invulnerable to air attack.

We drove along this marvel of construction at a constant speed of about thirty kilometers an hour. Each night an eerie and beautiful spectacle would emerge before our eyes, an endless stream of flickering headlights tracing curved patterns against the black wilderness as far in both directions as the eye could see.

There were antiaircraft positions strung through the mountains, but the most effective defense was camouflage and tunneling. Even when B52's were free to bomb the trail, the infiltration rate had been reduced by only about a quarter.

Therefore, an overland strike to sever the trail, even temporarily, had long been an allied ambition. President Johnson had never permitted it because of his insistence not "to broaden the war" (as if NVA use of Laos did not make it part of the war zone already). The success of the Cambodian incursion convinced Nixon that the NVA could not defend their Laotian sanctuary any better than their Cambodian one but, because of domestic outcry and congressional strictures, he could permit only U.S. air support for the ARVN raid on the trail. Nevertheless, Lam Son 719, as ARVN called this operation, would be the touchstone for Vietnamization of the war.

Thieu decided to send the best units into Laos—Airborne Division, Marine Division, First ARVN Division, and many ranger battalions. Huynh Van Trong was national security adviser for Thieu. But he was also a top spy for the communists. After Lam Son 719, when Huynh was arrested, he admits he informed NVA about this operation. That is why many of our best troops were killed.

The combination of treachery and inability in the South Vietnamese high command doomed the ambitious operation. The objective of the drive into Laos was the trail terminus and supply dump near the former village of Tchepone on Route 9, some forty kilometers west of the international border. A division of NVA regulars and one of support troops were believed to be in the vicinity. The attack had to be short and shocking, for within two weeks as many as three more NVA divisions could join the battle and no doubt would because of the high stakes. To prevent these reserves from converging on Tchepone, the U.S. Navy, with a complement of Marines, steamed about near Vinh on the North Vietnamese coast as if they would launch an amphibious invasion. This deception worked very well, and for a week it kept two NVA divisions from moving against Lam Son 719.

I worked a lot with First ARVN Division while Lam Son 719 is going on. Colonel Dong was chief of staff for General Truong, division commander. Mostly I have to get American gin and cigarettes for Truong—he smoked Pall Mall, more than a pack each day. For this Colonel Dong gave me SKS rifles that First Division captured from VC. Americans wanted these very much because they are semiautomatic rifles that GIs can take back to U.S. for souvenirs. SKS rifles were never captured by 101st because they always fight NVA, who have only automatic AK-47's.

Just before Lam Son 719, Colonel McDonald told me about this secret operation. I was told because I must round up all the interpreters so they can ride in 101st choppers that will carry ARVN into Laos. I cannot tell the interpreters where they're going; just have to say they have a mission. After the operation they told me what happened. They were very happy to get back with 101st because General Lam screwed up so bad. He was in charge but was too worried about what President Thieu thinks in Saigon. Lam did not take responsibility on his own; he always waited for Thieu to make decisions.

Lam's aide was Captain Duc. I got the word he wanted to see me in Dong Ha, the CP for Lam Son 719. I went there and he was very nice—thanked me for the work of the interpreters. I told him Colonel McDonald said 101st gives all the support it can, and we wish General Lam lots of luck because the war may change if he is successful. Duc said, could I get Lam a pair of new jungle boots? And he would also like an aluminum cot and American sleeping bag so he can be comfortable at night. That's all he was worried about. When I was in re-education camp, another prisoner told me Lam made general only because he was big buddy of President Thieu. A lot of dead men would agree with that. General Truong should have been in charge of Lam Son 719, but he was not good enough at politics.

Truong was counting on a speedy brigade of tanks rolling down Route 9, supported by artillery choppered into fire bases on adjoining hilltops, to reach Tchepone in a matter of days and hold off counterattacks. There would be massive U.S. air support, including American-piloted choppers.

Except in the air, Lam Son 719 was an all-ARVN show. Eleven B52 strikes hit suspected NVA concentrations just before dawn, and the tank column jumped off. With scattered LZs secured ahead of them, the armor still advanced only ten kilometers by nightfall. Route 9 was cratered and mined—as if the NVA had been forewarned. For the next two days, heavy rain flooded the road, holding the armor to a crawl. As Saigon vacillated whether to continue the drive, General Abrams (one of Patton's favorite tankers) steamed at Thieu's indecision, while the NVA gathered their forces.

A five-day lull cancelled any advantages of surprise, and the NVA struck back with their own tanks. Defended by hard-fighting rangers, the northern LZs met the brunt of the counterattack; Saigon delayed a further armor advance up Route 9 until the situation with the rangers cleared up. Bad weather hampered air support, and one by one their LZs were overrun in spite of 10 to 1 losses inflicted on the NVA, mostly by artillery and B52's, for whom weather was no problem.

The remaining rangers, depleted by half, were withdrawn; then the other LZs began to fall like dominos, and for most purposes Lam Son 719 became a battle to extract GVN forces from Laos. Twenty-eight ARVN tanks were lost to twenty-three of the NVA's in one of the very few armor engagements of the war.

Guys who got back told me the NVA had their artillery dug into mountain caves like they knew what the battle would be like. B52's cannot destroy those caves. NVA also captured Colonel Thau, the Airborne Brigade commander, so they knew all the secrets about ARVN plans. Our troops fight hard but there was too much against them.

The tally sheet for the seven-week Laotian incursion was of course approximate but also respectable—13,000 NVA killed or captured to 1300 of GVN's forces—but the blow to South Vietnamese (and vicariously, to American) morale was devastating. Unless proficiency in combat replaced political connections as the touchstone for promotion, Thieu's generals would remain unworthy of the gritty willingness of ARVN soldiers to take on the NVA, now as modern and mechanized as any army in the communist bloc.

In several ways, Lam Son 719 was the Gettysburg of the Vietnamese war. It was the high water mark of the south, carrying the battle to the north, which won the campaign through superior generalship. Thereafter, the initiative passed back to the north and remained there until the end.

All this was not evident at the time, and Lam Son 719 meant little to the 101st troopers, who with wry pride dubbed themselves "boonie rats," boonies being a contraction of "boondocks," itself a slang expression for wilderness. After Lam Son 719 ended in March 1971, the war largely went on hold as its center of gravity revolved less around military than diplomatic maneuvers. General Abrams's holding strategy shifted the diminishing number of U.S. divisions into defensive arcs around clusters of cities. The NVA strategy was one of stand-off terrorism—hit-and-run rocket and sapper attacks to demonstrate that the population could not be protected. Hue, still symbolically important, and, since Tet 68, a focus of world attention, was a prize target. The 101st was to keep NVA away from the prize.

Everything was in the Ashau valley. Six, seven big operations up there from Tet 68 till 101st left Vietnam in '72. Like a private war with the NVA. They never give up trying to attack Hue; 101 never stopped pushing them back.

One of those big operations, Texas Star, in August 1970, was the basis for John Del Vecchio's landmark novel *The 13th Valley*, the boonie rats' book on Vietnam. It describes a two-week search-and-destroy operation in the Ashau by a company of the Oh-deuce. Del Vecchio regularly attends Oh-deuce reunions, and in 1988 got reacquainted with Cai at the dedication of a memorial to our 450 troopers who were killed in the war.

Everyone wanted to cry because we remember things like in 13th Valley. Your speech made me think about Ashau valley, when everybody knew 101st will soon go home. It was wonderful that men fight so hard at that time.

I gave a speech at that reunion, and asked if it would be cold blooded or blood thirsty to imagine a similar monument counting the enemy we had killed. Fighter pilots paint flags for the number of their kills, and warships do the same. For us, considering the tragic outcome, our losses seemed a waste of the best men America produced.

"But war," I continued, "is an individual as well as collective experience. Would the men whose names we read in granite wish to reclaim their lives if the choice they made could be repeated? We would wish to do so for them, but at that time they made individual choices to be where they were, where the jungle was thick and the bullets were flying.

"Why? Because combat is, for better and for worse, a peak experience in life. An experience worth risking death. A sublime experience made so by the combined grip of fear and faith.

"The fear is easily imagined. The faith is an unspoken spiritual unity with those around you. That faith came easy in the Oh-deuce. It was there in famous battles like Bastogne. It was there in unknown battles like Bu Gia Map, and in unlikely places like the 13th Valley."

Del Vecchio's 13th Valley (the number designating one of a sequence in the ranges between Laos and the sea) was the AO for demonstrations of the boonie rats' faith in each other. There was nothing else to fight for except unit pride and the compulsion of warriors to do their best in the worst of circumstances.

These later campaigns in the Ashau were jungle warfare at its most developed and sophisticated level. Each side knew the other well, having surged back and forth in the same arena since Tet 68. The Ashau resembles some valley debouching from the high foothills of the Cascades. The upper slopes are smoothly ribbed, densely forested, and dabbed by shifting mists in the transition between monsoon and dry seasons, when the hardest battles were fought. Before reaching the wrinkled valley floor, these lush swells slope down into a choppy piedmont of long, bare ridges, spotted on their flanks and in saddles with clumps of trees.

"You feel the mystique of the valley when you first see it, either from the air or on the ground," said Maj. Richard Horvath, an officer who worked near Cai at Division Headquarters in 1969. "Newspapermen jump at the chance to go into the Ashau if for nothing more than to fly over it and gaze upon what has been called 'Marlboro Country.' It's a very green valley that looks as if it should be in Oregon, yet once on the floor, visitors encounter elephant grass fifteen feet high, bomb craters as big as backyard swimming pools, tigers, and elephants. It's thirty-five miles of another world. The mystique is there—no doubt about it."

Ashau operations in the 1970s, such as Del Vecchio described, were jungle games of hide-and-go-kill. Certain rules applied. The Americans owned the air, the NVA ruled underground, and the jungle was neutral. The game's preconditions were that the NVA could always leave the contest and scamper into Laos, but if they did, the 101st was free to pick up everything left behind, and that meant the NVA would have to wait one round before they accumulated enough supplies from the Ho Chi Minh Trail to come back into the valley and the game.

If the NVA wanted to play, the first move was the Americans'. From long-range patrols, various detection devices (e.g., "people sniffers," heat and motion sensors), captured documents, intercepted radio signals, ralliers, POWs, indigenous Montagnard tribesmen—from any sources at all—the division high command selected a promising area in which to search for the NVA and destroy them or their supplies. The 13th Valley was a tributary of the Ashau. Intelligence sources indicated it hid the headquarters of an NVA transportation battalion, an infantry regiment, and the highest communist headquarters in the Ashau, that of an NVA front. These targets were hardly pinpointed. If they were in the AO at all, it was somewhere in or around a watershed some 100 square kilometers in size.

If the 13th Valley was a bad guess by the Americans, the NVA won the game at the end of the first move because the Americans wasted scarce resources (approximately a third of the 101st's fighting strength when a brigade was committed as it was in Texas Star) as well as limited campaigning weather. To find out if the 13th Valley was a "dry hole," the troopers began patrolling as soon as they jumped from their choppers.

Hide-and-go-kill then moved from the strategic to the tactical level.

Burdened by equipment and the requirement of aerial resupply, the Americans were tied to LZs, and these were quickly sought by scouts of the NVA, who could pepper them with mortars and sneak attacks, inflicting casualties on the Americans while minimizing their own. Thus the Americans tried to deceive the NVA by prepping bogus LZs and touching down choppers that did not disgorge troops. Visibility was so limited in the jungle that unless the choppers happened to land atop the NVA, it was difficult to determine which LZs were actual and which were feints.

In the first days of an operation, both sides slinked through the jungle looking for each other. Chance encounters between searching patrols were the first contacts from which opposing commanders tried to determine the size and intentions of the other. The Americans got away from their LZs as quickly as possible, sometimes leaving ambushes for investigating NVA patrols. From their intimate knowledge of the local trail network, the NVA could usually track platoon and larger size American units, especially when they had to stop at night. That is when the mortaring began, answered by U.S. artillery from far-off fire bases carved from hilltops. In turn, these stationary fire bases became targets for sapper attacks.

Advantage and initiative remained with the NVA until the Americans began to learn the terrain and the secrets in its web of trails. Depending on the nature and frequency of contacts, U.S. commanders had to decide how to parcel their companies into patrols. Small patrols meant more chance of locating the NVA headquarters, but if too small they risked annihilation by ambush.

For apart from harassing mortar fire and sapper raids, the NVA's principal tactic was the ambush. A glancing encounter could lure the Americans into a trap, and the NVA were quite willing to sacrifice some men to lure incautious pursuit. Unless many landings were feinted, resupply LZs gave away the Americans' jungle bases, and the NVA commanders could plan attacks to draw attention away from what they wanted to protect, i.e., war materials, headquarters, underground hospitals, and rice caches.

If the AO was a dry hole or if the NVA conceded use of it, the forces slipped past each other, and the game resumed later at some other corner of the Ashau. But if under orders to fight, the NVA did so like the Japanese of World War II. At Hamburger Hill, some had messages on their shirts like "Hurl them down!" and "No retreat!"

When they had a vital installation to protect, the NVA invariably sited it in the best available terrain for defense, dug in, and camouflaged it superbly, using dense jungle or bamboo to funnel the Americans naturally into close quarters where their air and artillery support would do them the least good. When the NVA accepted the gauntlet, battle blazed like spontaneous combustion.

When it seemed the NVA might be brought to bay, American point men armed with M16's were reinforced by a "thumper"—a man with an M79 grenade launcher—plus a machine gunner, who together penetrated the jungle like the slithering head of a krait ready to strike with sudden impact.

The relative volume of fire in the first exchange very much predicted the outcome of the action. If an ambush was quickly neutralized, the ambushers lost more than surprise. The NVA weapons were heavier caliber (but also heavier to carry with bulkier ammunition), while the American arms fired faster with lighter ammo. Sudden engagements in the jungle hinged on psychological as much as ballistic impact. If the Americans put out an intimidating base of fire, they could maneuver in short, crawling rushes, bring squads on line, and call in artillery and air support. But if the NVA's first fire pinned them down, the paralysis was often infectious.

Targets on both sides were fleeting if not invisible; reactions were instinctive and instantaneous, resulting in moments that recur in dreams, as in this account by Del Vecchio:

> The platoons move into a mix of brush and bamboo and grass. Nahele moves to the far right flank. He moves easily, cautiously. His machine gun seems to pull at his finger as if the weapon wants to be fired, wants to fire . . . On the knoll First Platoon reaches the midpoint of their ascent. Every step has been quiet, yet they feel a presence, are oppressed with apprehension. Cherry looks left, right . . . Suddenly pure white flashes cut across his world. He whirls, squeezing his M16, firing at the sight before the sound registers, before he knows he is firing. Bursts from AK-47's flashing from the right, then the sound erupts in his ears. There is firing to the left, explosions, the crackcrackcrack M16's returning fire, his own M16 barking.

Unless surprised, the NVA always fought until dark. That was the time they could either break away or probe around a stalled American attack. The night brings the high-tech reinforcements from air and fire bases. Transports with gatling guns spurting tens of thousands of bullets per minute in a luminous stream churn the jungle canopy into lawn mower cuttings. The longer the battle continues, the more the jungle is stripped away, the more the NVA must retreat into the ground. The top of Hamburger Hill was blasted bald, the remaining earth as loose as potting soil. If the NVA still have fight in them, the Americans must probe for them in their tunnels and underground bunkers. Underground is the NVA's element, just as the air belongs to the Americans.

Morning brings droves of helicopters: gun ships on call for targets and to watch for escape; medevacs, for there are always wounded; resupply choppers to bring in food, water, and ammo, and remove the dead and prisoners; C&C ships carrying senior commanders for a look-see, to converse with the captains on the ground and determine what to do next. Sometimes the morning choppers bring reporters, chaplains, and mail.

Rarely can the NVA withstand a third day under intense assault. They have lost either their lives or their elusiveness. The survivors crawl away dragging their wounded through quaking tunnels as the Americans obliterate the battlefield above like wrathful gods. The NVA do not count their losses in men but in units. This company is no more, that battalion is gone. The NVA's toll is recounted by the frozen faced survivors who reach Laos, where new units await orders to enter the Ashau. These NVA are stoic, grim, resigned but unflinching. The human side of their psyche can be expressed only in poems they send back up the trail to North Vietnam. One wrote: "My pieces will be part of the jungle that continues to live, so I will not have to die again."

After grubbing around for booty, the Americans leave—are extracted by chopper, return to far-away bases, and there collapse from exhaustion, and into memories. This is the aftermath of hide-and-go-kill, repeated in many Ashau sequels until the end of the war. It was war as apolitical as the jungle in which it was fought. It was the boonie rats' saga, known only to themselves but relived in the combined grip of fear and faith.

Chapter
Fourteen

Despite the cheap success of the Cambodian incursion, General Abrams was not allowed to clean out the more important Laotian sanctuary, so the U.S. troop withdrawal only confirmed that the war was unwinnable. Shredding NVA in the Ashau amounted to no more than clipping weeds—more would grow from the undamaged root system. A MACV study concluded that at the projected rate of attribution, it would take thirteen years to drain the NVA's man-power pool. In 1970, U.S. ground forces had about thirteen months left in Vietnam. Until then, both the generals and the GIs had an agreed policy: hold down American casualties.

Casualties now came more from an absent enemy. Mines and booby traps accounted for 50 percent of all wounds in 1966; by 1970 that percentage was up to 80.

Even Screaming Eagles were not steeled for that kind of war in that day and age. A squad leader patrolling southeast of Hue was ordered to comb a hill recently mined and booby-trapped by the VC. "It just wasn't necessary. Some of my men might have been killed." He searched another hill and returned with his patrol. He was consequently demoted, but ambiguously. "One general told me it was a disgrace for me to refuse an order in combat. The second general told me I did the right thing."

The "right thing" became immensely subjective. Another trooper who refused an order during an operation was court martialed, but his sentence was suspended. At the end, Cai saw a new generation of troopers:

1971 *was the last year for the 101st but also the worst one, even though not so many guys get killed. Lot of short-timers came in from other units that went home. They are not like guys who came to 101st before. New guys wear eagle patch but that's all.*

I am so happy to see men who came back to 101st for second tour, like Colonel Dietrich. He was back to command First Brigade. Sergeant Major Sabalauski came back too—two times, two more years—I cannot believe it. He always wanted to be with the Oh-deuce. Very tough for him because there were not many NCOs to help him. Maybe just half of how many there should be. Too young. No experience. Platoons have lieutenants right out of OCS. Sergeants same age, just twenty years old some of them.

Without respect, troops call Sabalauski a "lifer." That should be because he saved so many of their lives by tough training and discipline in the field. But some of the drug guys that came from Fourth Division, he is too tough for them. There is a boxing tournament and he was the best. More than fifty years old and he still knocked young GIs down! That made some of the kids mad. When he was at fire base one time, they try to burn down his hooch. I met him when he got back. He showed me his money, all of it burned.

Vietnamese were mad that Americans were leaving, so not so good relations as before. Sergeant Nelson was with Oh-deuce first tour and he came back for assignment to division headquarters. He asked me if there can be Christmas party in Hue. Town was off limits but I arrange for him to have party at sport club next to Perfume River. Very nice party with barbecue and cold beer. It lasts all day, and next day beer is to be brought back for other troopers. Sergeant Nelson locked up the beer but when he came back to the sport club much is gone.

I asked the club manager what happened because he is re-

sponsible. He said there is still beer but Sergeant Nelson told him half is gone. In a loud voice he said, "We liberate this town for you and now you steal our beer." I felt ashamed about how the people of Hue are. Never grateful for anything. They think this is America's war. I think they miss Americans very much after 1975 and maybe that serves them right.

One interpreter I never saw is like that too—he just thinks Americans are here to give him money. This guy's name was Hien. He reported to First Brigade when it was down at Bien Hoa. Nobody's ever seen him since that time—eighteen months —I can't believe it!

I got his address and wrote him to report. He wrote back and said he cannot come because he needs a travel order. I fixed him right up. Pretty soon he walked into Camp Eagle and want to talk with me. According to him, when division moved up to I Corps, he stayed behind because he thought they would come back. Every month he went into Bien Hoa to draw his pay. Nobody knew the difference!

Hien did not want to lose this good deal. He asked me if I know where he lived in Saigon. It is address right next to U.S. Ambassador's residence. That way he let me know he is from very wealthy family. I could get a big bribe if I let him go home again. But I tell him his next address is in Ashau valley. When he saw that I was serious, Hien disappeared. MPs checked with Air Vietnam and found out he used a ticket back to Saigon. We reported him as deserter. Never saw Hien again.

Phan was another interpreter who wrote a monthly bulletin for me. This was a paper for all interpreters in the division to express their thoughts about families, friends, units, the war, and all complaints or suggestions. They can say anything they want. It helped me very much to know their problems.

One month in this bulletin, Phan announced he is getting married and interpreters are invited. He was at Second Brigade. I called him and said I had a wedding gift for him but he must come to Danang and get it. I had a secret with his brigade commander that he will be gone for about three days.

When I met him in Danang, I took him out to the hospital ship Repose. Phan is cross-eyed ever since he was born. He cannot believe it when Navy doctors look at his eyes closely. They put him to sleep and when he wakes up his eye is normal. I cannot describe how happy he is when he looked at himself in the mirror before wedding day.

Another good memory is Bob Hope show at Christmas. With him was Neil Armstrong, the first man to be on the moon. Division commander had the Christmas show in the field to let reporters know that area is secure and NVA are gone. But there was one infiltrator. He pretends to be civilian interpreter. MPs all over the place and capture him. He had a good story, and said, "Look, I did not bring a weapon. I just wanted to see tall girls in short dresses who come with the show." They let him defect and told Bob Hope he gets credit for one VC rallier.

For two years I tried to do everything I can for 101st interpreters. I think the Buddhists are right that when a man does good things for others, they will repay him if they can. When I was an outlaw from the communists, there were times that some of these interpreters helped me very much. Only one rejected me.

By 1971, it was as clear to Cai as to most Vietnamese that the American train was chugging away, leaving a very empty station behind. This was more than a troop withdrawal, it was the departure of an entire artificial economy amounting, by some respectable calculations, to nearly a half of the South Vietnamese gross national product. With the U.S. driving the war effort, spending $450 million annually on it, the South Vietnamese had become accustomed to living beyond their means, relying on a single-client service industry that did nothing but soak up the carefree spending of the GIs. (When Russian advisers settled in Ho Chi Minh City, the South Vietnamese called them "Americans without money.")

In 1971, the good old days of the GI economy were rapidly concluding. Approximately 125,000 Vietnamese depended directly on the American war effort—people like Cai. Probably double that number were significantly affected—bar girls, shoe shine boys, pickpockets, and landlords for the huge American community that worked in cities like Saigon and rented recreational apartments. As

U.S. bases closed down, tens of thousands of their economic dependents became inhabitants of ghost towns.

I can see all that changed. Beer can hooches along the strip are torn down. Girls go back to Saigon. Don't think they find much work there either. I think I have done good job for Americans and want to stay with them. I get very good letters from division, so I ask to go to OCS at Fort Benning, Georgia, in the States. Some ARVN officers have done that. I also wrote Hank Emerson and he said he will look into this for me.

U.S. Army says it will be fine if I go to their OCS but I need ARVN to send me. This does not happen because I did not have good connections in Saigon. I thought about what I must do. I can stay till 101st goes home, but then I will get any job that ARVN assign me. I think it is more better to get best job I can in ARVN while I still have some influence from Americans.

My parents wanted me to come home and help with business. All their boys are in the military. They think one should be with family like Chinese tradition. I agreed with this. I had served six years, but in ARVN I am still a sergeant. They will probably not let me go because ARVN will have to do more fighting because Americans go home.

I talked a lot about this with 101st officers. They said I should get a better deal. Finally, I learned I can get commission as lieutenant in ARVN. Also, they will let me go to Intelligence School, and that can get me the best job.

So I must leave 101st. So many new people there, I do not know many because they went home so fast. There was a little party for me and a sign that said "Oldest Eagle." I asked what that means. Someone told me that I have served longer in the 101st than anybody, anybody in history of the division. This is very strange. I am a Chinese-Vietnamese, not even an American, but I am Screaming Eagle longer than anybody. It is a very fine division, the best ever, I think. I don't think anybody is more proud of what it did in Vietnam. I saw it all. From beginning to end. Beginning was better I think. Troopers win every time and have high morale. Later it is different. Still winning, but people in States did not support these good men. They beat very tough VC and NVA who have been here all their life. But Americans will not stay here long enough. I don't blame them. South Vietnamese did not do enough for themselves. I decided I must do everything I can, even if other Vietnamese do not, or the communists will rule, and everything I have will be lost, even freedom.

Neither Cai's sense of urgency or patriotism was echoed in Saigon, where he went on leave before reporting to ARVN. With fast dwindling foreign credits, Thieu chose to continue importing luxury items rather than gear up the economy for long-range self-sufficiency. "I do not ask the U.S. troops to stay here for 100 years," he pleaded. "I only ask the Americans to have the courage and clear sight to remain here until we nationalists have enough military, economic, and political strength." Apparently seven years was not long enough.

As the gravy train pulled out, anti-Americanism became fashionable, especially among the Saigon elite. An editorial cartoon showed Johnson and Nixon literally raping South Vietnam. A university art exhibit in 1972 featured a mural showing Americans as predators stalking the countryside. MACV found it necessary to warn the few remaining troops not to travel alone on the streets of Saigon. The surly fretting of the GVN was matched obversely by the joy of homebound Americans, only too willing to let the South Vietnamese "restore their culture and dignity," as Ky put it, but doubtful they could ever take responsibility for themselves.

The ultimate irony of the GVN's hypocrisy is well personified in Premier Nguyen Cao Ky, who as they departed denounced what he called the Americans' "colonial slavery," blaming South Vietnam's insecure situation on "unreasonable meddling by unwelcome masters. Let the cowards run away with the Americans," he exhorted a crowd of supporters in the last hours of his regime, for he himself would stay to battle in the last defense of the capital. At least for a few hours. Shortly he commandeered a helicopter and flew to the *USS Midway* to become one of Vietnam's original boat people. Ky settled in Garden Grove, California, to run a liquor store.

Undoubtedly, though unintentionally, the Americans had contributed to the shattering of an ancient culture by their indifference to it. The family-centered peasantry had been whipsawed by the fighting until vast numbers became refugees in the cities. There they found a relatively easy life in the GI service economy. For the young, there was no getting them back on the farm after they had seen the Paris of the Orient. The patriarchal culture of their elders was ruptured, and later would disintegrate under the communists' policies to atomize all families.

In exchange for the culture shock they had blindly inflicted on South Vietnam, the Americans left behind a world-class transportation network and communications system, an electrical grid throughout the countryside, as well as a score of endemic diseases eradicated, plus modernized agriculture with miracle crops that were the envy of the third world. And at the same time they produced huge gains in literacy and universal schooling, while raising a shield and scaffold within which a representative democracy could be built. The local architects just never appeared.

"I don't know why God is pissed off at Vietnam," a departing officer told Cai. "Maybe it's because the Vietnamese are so ungrateful. Look at the beautiful land He gave them. They expected everything—they got it—but that's all they're going to get."

What the ARVN high command got was a quick test of the independence Ky had been calling for. This came in a go-for-broke conventional invasion, called the Easter Offensive, by the NVA in March 1972, by which time Cai was a lieutenant in the delta.

Not many NVA where we were, but in Easter Offensive the VC make high activity. Sometimes we made four, five helicopter landings in one day to look for them.

One time we landed in wrong location. It was by mistake because everything in the delta looks the same from the air. Two of my best men were wounded together. Chom was hit in the stomach while he tried to get Den. But Den died anyway. We watched him but cannot get close till darkness. Then a good man crawled out with rope and tied it on Den's leg to drag back. I thought how different this was than with 101st: we were taking our wounded out like the VC.

Chom was brought back to hospital at Can Tho. His intestines had been broken off in many places. Lots of wounded to be treated at this time. Busy doctors sewed him up and say go home for thirty days. While he was home his stomach swelled up and hurt him badly so he cannot even eat. Doctors operated again to see what's wrong. They found a big bandage in Chom's stomach, all infected. That's it for him. He got a medical discharge.

Easter Offensive was even bigger than Tet 68. Fifteen NVA divisions hit ARVN in I, II, and III Corps. I think this is everything NVA had, even 500 tanks. Very heavy fighting for six months, but we stop them.

At first there was no stopping the all-out onslaught. The recently formed Third ARVN Division crumbled south of the DMZ, losing such famous U.S. Marine bastions as Camp Carroll and The Rockpile. Within weeks the entire province of Quang Tri and its capital of 800,000 fell. The NVA next rushed through the Ashau, overrunning fire bases Bastogne and Veghel, which the 101st had named from their World War II history. With no U.S. Marines or paratroopers to protect it, Hue was threatened once again.

But in front of Hue, the tide began to turn. Having chosen to assault like a conventional army, the NVA were relatively massed and vulnerable to U.S. air attacks. These came with vengeance. ARVN stiffened and regrouped on the Perfume River under the command of General Truong, a proven battle leader, displacing one of Thieu's political cronies because the need at last had become obvious. "Truong is the only Vietnamese I would trust to command an American division," General Westmoreland told me at a 101st reunion in 1988. "He was that good."

Though outnumbered two to one, the ARVN divisions Truong committed at Hue were the best: First ARVN, First Marine, and the Airborne Division. Under swarms of B52's and tactical fighter-bombers, they thrust back into the outskirts of Quang Tri City. By early September, they drove the NVA out.

I think this was the biggest victory for ARVN in the whole war. Cambodia invasion was very good but NVA did not fight much there. In Quang Tri, they gave ARVN their hardest blows. It was not good enough against best ARVN and super air support. NVA are not always smart. It takes them time to learn from mistakes, so they tried again in II Corps while battle for Quang Tri was still going on.

In II Corps the NVA, staging from Laos, had more room for maneuvering than along the narrow coastal corridor between Quang Tri and Hue. Their plan was to cut through the vast and sparsely populated central highlands to seize Qui Nhon, on the coast, and thereby cut South Vietnam in half. It was to prevent this very plan that the 101st had been committed at An Khe in 1965.

Once again Dak To was a major battleground; this time the NVA took the town, with it the headquarters of the Twenty-second Division, and killed the commanding general. After this defeat, Kontum, the linchpin of the highlands, became exposed and endangered. Soon an ARVN division was surrounded there by two divisions of NVA.

Once again it was the B52's that saved the day and the town. Massed to besiege Kontum, the NVA died by the thousands. After the first B52 strike, they poured reinforcements into the crater fields. After the second, they had no one left. Their tanks were tossed around the landscape like childrens' toys.

It was like they do not care how many men they lost. They just want to see if they can grab the country now that U.S. troops were gone. They made one more test. This one was very important because it is closest to Saigon. NVA came across from Cambodia with three very good divisions. They tried to capture An Loc and make it the capital for a government they say is for all South Vietnam.

Wisely, the III Corps commander ordered his border outposts drawn in before many of them were overrun. Behind scores of tanks, the NVA Fifth Division seized Loc Ninh. Coincidentally, they were opposed by the ARVN Fifth Division, which became cut off in An

Loc. When they lost the airfield, the town was besieged and could be supplied only by parachute and risky helicopter forays.

The NVA brought in another division and hurried the battle to its climax while B52's were busy elsewhere. They captured half the town in raging house-to-house fighting. On May 11 the defenders were compressed into the last third of what was left of An Loc. Their situation was desperate enough to call in B52's so close that ARVN foxholes were within a grenade throw of the craters.

Thirty B52 strikes rolled over the outskirts of An Loc. Ten thousand NVA became smoke. A third division tried to make up the losses. They too were obliterated by the unseen rain from the sky. The deafened defenders crawled out to retake the bomb-plowed airstrip. ARVN had held under the last protection they would receive from the U.S. Air Force.

U.S. air also hit the north very hard during this time. Mines were put in the water at Haiphong. For a while there was worry that the Chinese or Russians would do something about this but I don't think they cared much. Chinese were having a hard time with NVA in Cambodia at this time. I never knew that before till I heard it at ARVN intelligence school.

Le Duc Tho, representing North Vietnam, and Henry Kissinger had long been in negotiations over a means to end U.S. involvement in the war. In the fall of 1972, the decisive contribution of the U.S. Air Force in destroying the Easter Offensive (and 100,000 NVA) gave Kissinger strong cards to play, and a cease-fire agreement shaped up with these main features: no further seizure of territory in South Vietnam by either Hanoi or Saigon, return of American POWs (mostly downed pilots) concurrent with U.S. evacuation of their air bases, no further infiltration of NVA into the south, and a multibillion dollar reconstruction program in which the north could share.

For the two parties, the guts of the agreement was the exchange of U.S. POWs for removal of U.S. air bases in Vietnam, but for the GVN the prospect of a standstill cease-fire was a red flag.

Thieu was afraid this is going to happen so he started operations right away to get as much land back as he can before there is cease-fire. We go out to fight VC much more than before.

VC now have a tough time. Before, they could just control villages at night. But before peace agreement is signed, they must show their control all the time so they can say the land belongs to them. That means they stand and fight like they did in Tet 68. Even without U.S. troops we chewed them up.

We see this captured COSVN document that tells guerrillas to capture hundreds of villages and gives the names. They are supposed to put political cadre there before cease-fire. I heard maybe 10,000 villages like that. So we knew just where to look for them. I think we got about half.

That happened after I was with Twenty-first Division for a while. When I first got there they do not do much fighting, not even patrolling. They were not a good outfit, but I liked that assignment because it was near my family in Saigon.

The Twenty-first Division Headquarters was at Bac Lieu, in a coastal province tucked in the southeast corner of the delta. Its importance in the war was only as a huge rice bin for whichever side controlled it. The local population was very much anticommunist. Rice rich, the land holdings were large and profitable for trade with the GVN, who resold the rice to less fortunate regions of the country.

When I got down to the Thirty-third Regiment, rich families invited me to dinners and parties because they want to show they are happy that we will protect their rice from VC. Very big houses, fancy as the best in Saigon. Servants and everything. I think this is how the French lived when they ran the country.

Things here were not like in most of South Vietnam. The Twenty-first Division did not move around fighting all over like airborne, marines, rangers, or First Division. I knew things were different in other parts of the country, but down here they looked pretty good.

In all the other parts of the country, devouring inflation pushed corruption into the lowest levels of society. Never well paid, soldiers could no longer live on their salaries—when they received it, which was irregularly, as it became common practice for officers to invest their men's pay to draw private interest.

The GIs' dollars were gone, and with them much of the value of the piaster. The Vietnamese consumer price index rose 40 percent in 1972 and 65 percent in 1973, largely due to the doubling price of rice, which, fortunately for Cai, was cheap and abundant. "Those who suffered most," wrote Colonel Le Gro, Intelligence Officer in the U.S. Attaché's office, "were those upon whose strength and constancy the country's survival depended: the soldiers, airmen, and sailors."

The suffering of the fighting men was never much of a concern for the GVN. Military salaries were raised, but at less than a third of the inflation rate. Alone, a man could barely live on his pay; with his family he could not. A colonel with twenty years service received the equivalent of $80 per month. It took at least half that amount to feed a typical family of ten.

ARVN had always been notorious for living off the countryside, i.e., confiscating edibles from villages they liberated. This was so common that U.S. advisers rarely commented when troops returned from operations with ducks and pigs under their arms. During Tet 68 in Saigon, ARVN seemed as intent on looting shops as they were on clearing the city of NVA.

But after 1971, looting was no longer just opportune, it was the core of subsistence. As Le Gro reported, venality could be grotesque:

> There were a few documented cases wherein officers and soldiers sold weapons, ammunition, and other military equipment and supplies for cash, knowing full well that they were trading with the enemy. But the most despicable of all cases of venality—and reports of these were widespread and persistent enough to deserve credence—were the demands of VNAF helicopter crews for payment from ground troops for the evacuation of casualties. This is not to say that this practice was the rule, but that it happened at all was a vivid commentary on a pernicious flaw and the conditions which spawned it.

*I*n MI school I met Phuoc, whose father was regimental commander in the Twenty-first Division. He told me, "Come on down to the delta because you have already seen the rest of the country." So I did. I think it was real lucky for me because there was a lot better chance of getting killed somewhere else.

It was easy to find Phuoc's house in Bac Lieu, it is so big and looks nice. Servant told me Phuoc is now payroll officer for his father's regiment. I was assigned to another regiment, so I reported there. Phuoc had told me I could get "a good function" if I want to. I did not understand this till I go see an old soldier named Bao, who is regimental sergeant major. I think I should report to the adjutant, but Bao told me he is busy and I should wait for him in officers' club. First drink is with his compliment. I did not finish this drink when Bao came in and said the adjutant will be busy all day, so come back tomorrow please.

Next morning, there is still only Bao around. He closed the door and said even though I graduate from intelligence school I got to go to line unit unless I qualify for staff work. I said that's fine, I want to do some fighting in the delta. Bao said, "I guess you don't understand—a lot of lieutenants get killed out there." For 200,000 piasters he will make sure I get assigned to regimental S2. Bao said this is a special deal just for today. Already enlisted men pay 100,000 and NCOs 150,000 piasters for staff jobs. He said I only have one night to think it over.

At BOQ I got a call from Phuoc. He asked me to have breakfast with him so he can give advice. At breakfast I told him if I want to be safe I could join the navy. He smiled and said, "Smart people use their money to protect their life. Dumb people use their life to protect their money." I said "Maybe I'm dumb, but if we lose the war to the north, we lose money and lives too." Phuoc shook his head and say I make a mistake. Because I am tall and speak good English, I could be general's aide someday.

When I got back to Bao's office I told him respectfully that I like to spend a little time in the field so I can learn what is going on. He looked like he is sorry for me and say to report to regimental XO, Lieutenant Colonel Ba.

I cannot believe Lieutenant Colonel Ba is so fat. He cannot even get out of his armchair. He said, "Welcome to the Sunrise Division. Follow orders. Do your duty." That's all.

Later on I found out he has very good business with his father near Bien Hoa. They made coffins for dead soldiers. About 1000 were killed every month in III Corps. Government offers contract to make these coffins. They must be sold to the dead soldier's family for 1250 piasters. Many businessmen are invited to bid for coffin contract. Ba's father, Duc, always gets it. He said he will make a coffin for the government that cost them just 1000 piasters. Nobody else can make them that cheap. They wondered every year why he wants this contract that loses money. Duc said it is just to show respect for dead soldiers' families.

But he made good money every year from coffin business! Before family comes for body of son, government gives them flag and 10,000 piaster death benefit. Duc is very smart. He had nice car to pick up family when it comes to Bien Hoa. Takes them for good meal and showed lot of respect. Duc had picture of dead son by altar with incense. Then he showed them the government coffin. Right beside it is luxury coffin he made. He say to family, "This one cost 5000 piaster but for you only 4000 because I will buy the government coffin from you for what it cost me—1000 piaster."

Families always buy luxury coffin to show more love for their dead son. It was important because they take the body home for burial and everyone in the home town will look at the coffin. Just cheap GI coffin makes family lose face. Duc also knew that there is strong tradition of Confucius—never take money from a dead person. He makes a suggestion that the government death benefit is like that—it belongs to the soldier—right thing to do is spend it on him.

His contract say he must have 1000 coffins available every month. He does. But he does not have to make that many because most families left their GI coffin with him.

PART III

"Phantom soldiers, flower soldiers"

Chapter
Fifteen

As a fitting assignment for a lieutenant recently graduated from ARVN intelligence school and looking for action, Cai was named to lead a platoon in the reconnaissance company of the Thirty-third Regiment. His job was to find out what the VC were doing, and how they were getting their rice.

Delta is where the VC try to get most of their rice for IV Corps and III Corps too. First they "requisition" rice from peasants and pay them with communist money. Then they take it to many caches—tunnels, storage bunkers, places like that, most of them underground or dug into canal banks. A little bit at a time, they move this rice to caches nearer to Cambodia. Then it goes up the Ho Chi Minh Trail to main NVA forces that invade III Corps. I hear they use delta rice in II Corps too. What we try to do is block VC rice from going out of the delta.

VC try other little things to get rice, like sending women and kids to buy it in markets. Some NVA even raise rice most of the time! We captured one and he said rice farming is better than fighting.

Captain Thanh was recon company commander. Lieutenant Sanh is executive officer. Quite a few Cambodians in this company. Sanh told me they are the best fighters, and loyal.

Right away I find out patrols are very tough in the delta due to rivers and canals. I had a hard time in the field for the first few weeks: the water, the mud, mosquitos, and leeches bother me all the time. I never had on a dry uniform. Whenever we have an enemy contact we must lie in the muddy water.

I spread my platoon out a lot so we cover more ground on patrols. We have more contacts but not as many captured weapons as other three platoons. I can't figure out why because my men work harder and patrol better. Thanh told me trophies are most important so I better get busy to capture VC weapons.

Finally it looks like my platoon gets a big chance. We are on night ambush at a river bank. About 11 p.m. three VC in a sampan start across. I radio this information to Thanh and he said blow them away right now.

I think it is better to see if more come across. We can handle just three with knives.

But Thanh said, don't wait, blow away these three and make sure you get their weapons. So we shoot two in the boat, the other jumped into the water and we threw grenades and get him too, but cannot find his weapon because water is too deep and dark. Two AKs are my first trophies. Thanh said that was pretty good job but I am still way behind the other platoons.

Soon there was another late evening. Only my platoon is on ambush but Thanh stays with another platoon with his CP about 300 meters away. A young woman came rowing a sampan. She keeps rowing in same area of river. First I think she is fishing because she does not use motor on sampan. Then I looked at her closely with binoculars. She is not fishing at all, and it seems to me she is waiting for someone. Very careful, I moved my men one by one down the bank till we can see her better.

It was pretty late then. I reported to Thanh what my platoon was doing. He doesn't think it is anything so he said just keep him informed, he's not going to come up and look.

She just drifted close to the other bank till the moon goes down and I cannot see much even with binoculars. But I heard some noise on the other bank and an anchor goes splash. Then there was sound like something being loaded in sampan. Pretty soon light flashes on and off like signal.

I reported this to Thanh. He is sleepy, so he said do whatever I want. I told my platoon to get all M72 rockets ready. We fired seven of them in one volley, and other side of bank lights up bright. In the flashes we see many enemy over there. We opened fire and they do too at the same time, just fifty meters apart, river in between.

But the reeds burn in back of them and they cannot see us. It is like shooting at targets in basic training. The explosions wake Thanh up. He called me but I cannot answer in the firefight. I called for big artillery flares. They help us cover the area on the other side so enemy has more trouble to get away. Then they surprised us with a machine gun. They really wanted what was in the boat, but, it sunk already.

Before the sun comes up, Thanh told me to swim a squad across the river so the VC cannot take bodies and weapons away. It takes a few hours to find them because rockets and artillery tore up the area. With twenty captured weapons Thanh is real happy: one machine gun, two rocket launchers, and the rest AKs. Couple of wounded enemies too, including the young woman who rowed the sampan. Thanh reported all the trophies to regimental commander, who said, "Good job—I come out right away." Thanh is really excited then because he will maybe get a medal.

I went over to interrogate wounded prisoners. Thanh said, "Hurry up. I want them part of body count."

That's the way it was with the recon company. We are not to carry prisoners. I tried to tell Thanh about how important prisoners can be. Told him about the guy the Oh-deuce captured at Bu Gia Map. What we learned from him stopped an ambush and turned the operation into big victory.

Thanh did not care. He is just eager for bodies and weapons so he can get promoted. If he makes major, maybe I will move up to company commander and then I can have different policy. But if that does not happen, I am to follow his policy: question POWs and then "convert" them. That is the code word to use on the radio. My men laughed when they heard it; they say it means convert prisoners into fertilizer.

Under South Vietnamese law, Cai would have been court mar-tialed, possibly executed, for disobeying Thanh's orders regarding prisoners.

When we checked the woman's boat, there were thirty big bags of rice, each weighs 100 kilos. Thanh told regimental commander we captured it for him, but he is nice and said we can have it. The troops all shake hands with each other because they can bring it back to their families. Thanh said, ten bags for families, extra ten for my platoon, and other ten for company fund. I stopped a civilian boat and told the owner to deliver this rice to our rear area. He better not go off with it because I take down his name and boat license number.

After this good action at the river, it looks like I can be considered to command recon company. Lieutenant Sanh was ahead of me; he is the XO. Sanh is a good man but he's afraid to fight. He is willing to let me run the company when Thanh is not there. Sanh told me his family was very unlucky—that is why he is so worried about himself. Three of his brothers were killed and two of them were officers when they died. I never saw Sanh smile because he worried so much about his fate.

The day comes when Thanh is gone for a meeting at CP of regiment. Call comes in that RF outpost is being attacked. Company goes to check it out. All platoons in straight line horizon with company CP behind mine. We find one thatch hut out in a grass plain, then start taking a little fire from a canal. My platoon moved out—I don't know what happened behind me, but Sanh and his RTO went into this hut. Nobody can see them, but a sniper round came right through the thatch and hit Sanh in the neck. He died very quick. I didn't know this till his RTO called me and said I am in charge of the company.

In this action we cleared VC from around a canal. Suddenly a mortar round hit about twelve meters in front of me. A fragment got Xuong, who carried my sleeping gear and was also my body-guard. The medic came over to help him but Xuong was dead. That shook me up a lot. His wife had just had his baby, and I promised him a pass after this little operation was over, but now he was gone. I called the rear to give his wife some money. I have to check that was done because sometimes widow is given only official death benefit of 500 piasters ($25).

Hen is my new bodyguard. It was near Tet holiday then. We think there is maybe a new offensive. Company gets order to check out faraway village where there may be lot of VC around. We went to this village, and I asked the biggest landlord for permission to have company CP in front of his terrace.

He introduced himself and said he was also owner of a little cement plant in the village. He also invited me to stay in his house. I say it is better if we just use his terrace and he said that's fine.

On New Year's Eve the landlord told Hen, please ask me to have holiday dinner with him. I think it is better to eat with my troops but he asked me again and I change my mind.

He had fantastic food, best I ever tasted since I worked at Club Nautique as a boy. For this dinner he had a case of cognac, twelve bottles, worth a year of my pay. His two sons stood near the table to serve me. I think this must be the way French officers felt when they run the country. I also think this guy must be friends with VC or he could not live so great in an unsecure area like this.

In this village was Ba Hai, an old lady with no teeth. She was a midwife who lived here all her life. Her husband was killed when he fought against the French. She had three sons. To revenge their father, two of them follow the Viet Minh. They were killed too, so she lived with her youngest son and his wife. One day this couple was working in a rice field when they explode an old mine. Both were seriously wounded. Due to lack of medical treatment they both died.

They left behind a twelve-year-old boy that Ba Hai raised. When he grew up, she is very worried about him, her only grandson. Sure enough, he became a local guerrilla. He wanted to revenge his family but also stay near his grandmother. He was like many guerrillas all over the country—they are in the field a lot of time but come into the village at night for visits.

By 1972, Ba Hai thinks VC will lose because so many have been killed. She tried to persuade her grandson to give up so he can stay all the time with her. He will not do this but he dug a secret hideout in her house so he can be with her more.

When I was at the village, Ba Hai came to me in private. She told me she does not trust police but maybe because I am army officer and treat peasants good, she can tell me about her grandson. She asked if he can be rallier if she turn him in to me. I say that's fine, but if he surrenders to my troops they got to turn him over to police. Nothing I can do about that. I told her I won't tell anybody—the decision is up to her.

She decided it is safer for him if she told police that he is hiding under her kitchen. They surround her house and tell him on loudspeaker to surrender. She goes in and pleads with him too.

Finally, he gives up. When he came out from under kitchen, his hand is holding an AK-47. First policeman who see that shot him to death. The boy is dead right in front of his grandmother.

I never saw her after that painful incident. A few days later she disappeared from the village. Old as she is, she joined the guerrillas.

This war had gone on for so long, longer than I have been living. So many VC killed that most are real old people like Ba Hai, or teenagers like her grandson. When we left her village, we went through this rice field where there was a bunker falling apart from the French days. An old homemade grenade came out—just a coke can with gunpowder and scrap metal in it. The fuse burned a long time so my men got out of the way. They laughed while they wait for this funny thing to go off, then they shot up the bunker. Inside was this old man. He got no rifle, just some of these grenades. My medic started to bandage him but the old man was dead in a couple of minutes.

Sometimes strange things like that happen. It was like there is nothing left to do in such a long war except killing back and forth. In the dry seasons we went out with helicopters and chase VC till we kill them. When the rains came, the VC moved back closer, bringing kids who never fought before.

One monsoon season, we were in a night camp on Cape Camau, a long way from any place. No civilians around because this is a free fire zone. Due to the rain, I set up company CP in *a hut by a small river. This was just a little shelter where rice workers rest from the sun during the dry season. Nothing but spider webs in it for a long time, and the thatch was falling apart.*

It was raining hard outside in the middle of the night. Then a grenade goes off right by the hut. First I thought VC threw it from other side of the river. Hen, my bodyguard, checked the area and chewed out the men on security. Two of them were wounded and I was real mad. We found no tracks, nobody in the area for miles around.

Next night this grenade attack happens again. This time Hen said maybe he saw someone around the little hut. I am very nervous and said search this hut if you have to tear it down.

What he found is a secret hideout under the place where rice workers built cooking fire for barbecues. We threw in tear gas and a man and woman came out. Hen beat them hard, but they would not say how they got way out there where no one was living. I reported we have two prisoners but higher headquarters said to convert them. My men whispered to each other, then told these two they can go free. When they walked away, M79 grenades hit them, then they were dumped in the river. This is the third time we had to shoot prisoners because of orders from Thanh.

In 1973, after the Paris Peace Talks, both sides make one exchange of POWs. How stupid it was to kill the ones we captured. We could have gotten some more of our men back. During this time there was a group from four countries [the International Control Commission, ICC, composed of Hungary, Canada, Iran, and Indonesia, to monitor the widely ignored cease-fire]. They flew around in white choppers, and checked to see which side controlled the territory. VC had a joke about what letters "ICC" mean. In Vietnamese they say it stands for "sit and wait." Whenever ICC team came to an area, the enemy attacked to place their flag. We lost a lot of outposts because of that.

Recon company went in to relieve one of these outposts. We surprised the enemy force and made a circle around them. I lost four KIA and eleven wounded but we fought through this unit that was NVA and VC working together. After all day of fighting, we have their antiaircraft machine gun, seven AKs and one B41. We were almost through when we found a bunker with an enemy inside.

First he did not want to come out, so we threw tear gas to him. Then he said he will surrender. He raised his hands and came out coughing. No weapon, but when we searched the bunker there is K54 pistol and a map. I made a quick interrogation: this guy is Lieutenant Sinh, NVA company commander. I knew he is from the north because of his accent.

I think Sinh is an important POW who should be questioned by higher headquarters. When Thanh sent choppers to pick up captured weapons, I urged him to take Sinh back too. He said, "Get all the information you can, report it on radio, then convert Sinh and all prisoners." We got three others who were wounded.

Sinh is wounded too, in the leg. My men used a wheelbarrow for moving him into a open field. He thinks he was taken there for medevac. Because he must be shot, I lined up a squad to do this. That way no one knows which bullet killed him. All have same responsibility, including me. We must share the same memory.

In the field, Sinh now knew what we must do. He tried to stand up from the wheelbarrow. He raised his arms and say, he is a married man and we are all Vietnamese who should not kill each other. He would be very good Chieu Hoi for making propaganda to other NVA, but I must carry out Thanh's order and convert Sinh with no more talk.

For the weapons we captured in that battle, the company was rewarded 10,000 piasters. I give 6000 to families of killed and wounded soldiers. The rest is for party with drinking. We celebrated with village chief. I ate supper with him that night so Hen does not have to do my cooking, and he went to party with the troops. Everyone say Hen was outstanding soldier, brave and honest. Only problem was he raised hell when he drinks.

Rice wine in that village is very strong. My men had no wine to drink during the long operation. When it got dark, Hen staggered back to my CP. He ran into a policeman and teased him because he was a REMF (rear echelon motherfucker). Hen said,

"Let me see your pistol," and came toward him. The cop pulled his pistol, then fired three shots, two in the air and one in Hen's chest.

I heard about this right away. In a rage I told my company to surround the police station and tell this cop to come out. Everyone in the village cleared out, shut doors, and closed their shops. My company aims their M72's like police station is a bunker. My men want to knock it flat.

Tears came while I kneel beside Hen's body. I am very sure I get a court martial if I attack this police station. I think police chief knows that too because he did not come out. Village chief, who I just had happy dinner with, came to me and begged that I stay calm. I screamed at him, "What should I do when asshole-REMF-cop kills the best man in my company? Tell him to come out and say why he did this!"

The cop was too much of a coward. We waited an hour and my men got madder. Finally, a good sergeant whispered to me, "Sir, give me a few men and some days off. We come back here and get this guy. Make it look like VC."

I really wanted to kill this cop right now, but my sergeant had a better idea. I lifted Hen on my shoulder and left the village. The company followed in tears of anger. After many hours of marching, a man said we had this incident because we killed Lieutenant Sinh. I don't know. The enemy killed their prisoners; we killed ours. I don't think that is as bad as when police kill soldiers who protect them.

Vietnamization and the phase-out of U.S. units was complete by the time Cai commanded the recon company. As his narrative indicates, he was unusually aggressive in fighting the otherwise sluggish war in the delta; so from the start he was bewildered as to why the other platoons of Thanh's company captured more weapons, while killing fewer VC and taking lighter losses than his platoon.

When *I first got to Twenty-first Division Headquarters, there were still U.S. advisers. The U.S. colonel had a 101st patch on* *his right shoulder. I saluted him and said, "Airborne!" He was glad to meet me and we talk about 101st, then I showed him a letter Hank Emerson wrote for me to get in OCS. This colonel said, "Oh, yes, I know Hank from the Korean War. Anything you need, you just let me know."*

I did not ask for anything because I was brand new in Twenty-first Division, but he told me radio frequency for air support if I need it. Everyone else have to go through ARVN to get bombers or Cobras. I thanked him very much.

Cai had joined what Colonel Le Gro described as the division which deservedly had the worst reputation for discipline and effectiveness in the delta. The Thirty-third Regiment had few contacts with the enemy other than receiving attacks by fire. The division was no more than marginally combat effective.

When *I first met Captain Thanh I think he must be a good man because he has many medals and I was told his unit captures weapons whenever they have contact with VC. At that time I thought his record means he did not lie about body counts because he has weapons to prove he killed communist soldiers.*

He showed me places on the map where he thinks VC are controlling canals and shipping rice on them. "Go out and watch these canals," he said, "and see if it is true."

Pretty soon I took my recon platoon out to see how good they are. I saw some great platoons in the 101st so I know what they should do.

My platoon was not too bad. Moving across flat delta land, enemy can see us coming, so we learned to do this at night. One time we see some activity after curfew, probably VC. Our job is not to fight, just to report intelligence like this. I call Thanh but he did not send the reaction platoon.

We came into his fire base in the morning and I see Thanh going out with another platoon. I told him the VC already left this canal we were watching but he said not to worry, he can find them. I think to myself, if he can do that, he's a real stud!

The radio was on while I got ready to sleep. I also heard firing far away. Sounds like it might come from around canal where we were. Then there is Thanh on the radio. Firing is near his mike. He says he has contact with VC, and they are having pretty big fight but he is doing okay. I think he must be real airborne guy—likes to fight and kill Cong by himself. He does not even call for artillery.

I was asleep when he came in but later I see he got three AK-47's with blood on them. Also ten body count, but he said he buried them.

Biggest surprise of my life when I learn how he got those weapons. From criminals! I learned this after more patrols where some of my guys got hit. Recon company never had many casualties before. Then I took troops where enemies want to stay, and we get into firefights. We got some weapons—one time a heavy antiaircraft machine gun—but my men are not too happy because of our casualties.

One of them said to me, "Lieutenant, we should be like Captain Thanh's other platoons: buy enemy weapons and not take risk to capture them." I did not know what he meant. He said Thanh took the machine gun we captured and traded it on black market for many AK-47's. Then Thanh went out and said he captured them in the firefight I heard on radio.

I asked Thanh about this and he said that's right. He wants to be major, then he can become a district chief. The way to make major is have good body counts, but more better, get weapons. ARVN gives medals for weapons captured. Enough medals and a guy can get promoted. When he is promoted to major, he can be chosen to be district chief.

If he make district chief, he got it made. For safe district, a rich officer is willing to pay 3–5 million piasters. They get that money back real quick. Under him he got village chiefs who can tax the peasants; also government contractors pay him bribes for building bridges and things like that. District chief can also run the rice cartel. Troop units in the district are under him too. About once a month he has a meeting with all these important people and tells them how much money they must pay him under the table. If they do not do that he can get them fired. He also tells stores the kind of things he likes and they give it to him on his birthday or for his wife.

If he can not get 5 million piasters to buy a district himself, he can find a rich civilian sponsor to lend him money. That's what Thanh wants to do when he makes major. He got a sponsor all lined up. The loan will be paid from contracts, from percent of flower soldiers' pay, and from all rice in the district that is ready for market. Sponsor also will run the only whorehouse for troops, and a casino, make illegal wine, and take money from canal checkpoints.

Sometimes a district chief gets too greedy. Then all those people who pay him off get together and bribe the province chief to get him fired. They call that "buy him away." Sometimes they pay VC to assassinate him.

Thanh could get job of chief in a VC district real easy. If he did a good job there, he could make lieutenant colonel. But that's too risky—VC kill a district chief if he gives them a hard time. So Thanh rather make major by trading weapons; then his sponsor will buy him a safe district.

So one thing he did is report something like M60 machine gun is "combat loss." That means one of his M60's was destroyed from enemy fire. But Thanh just hides it away someplace. Couple of months later he say he captured an M60 from the enemy. He must change serial number but he has a friend who can do that. Another thing he did was steal M16's, sometimes from his own men. He can trade these on black market for AKs and say he captured them.

I asked him about the firefight I heard. I was surprised that VC stayed around that canal in daytime. He said the battle was just his troops. Some of them fired their own weapons and some fired communist weapons to make a show on the radio. Then he thanks me for the machine gun I captured. Now that I know what's going on, he said we will be friends and he will help me with rice business.

I know this is good business because I have already started a little of my own. When peasants plant rice, I loan them money.

I pay in advance for rice they will grow. They are glad because they do not have money till rice harvest.

When that time comes, I have a couple trucks of rice. It is legal to sell to the government or to middleman who gets a better price somewhere else, maybe in II Corps where rice is not grown. This is good money for me, much more than I get from the army.

Super rice is planted in delta. This is the kind Americans brought to Vietnam. It can give two crops in each growing season but needs lots more fertilizer than old rice. Many officers make fertilizer from explosives they get from Army Engineers and sell to peasants.

I only buy and sell a little bit of rice, but local businessmen do not like that. They have a cartel and want to keep rice price the same everywhere in the province. They offered me money to leave my business but I said no thanks. There is not much they can do about that because I have troops with me.

After a while the cartel made an offer of more money to peasants than I can. The cartel lost money on these deals but they knew I am out of business if peasants do not sell to me.

I mention to Thanh what is happening about my business but he did not want to help unless his sponsor agreed. My problem was that his sponsor was also big man in the cartel. Then some good luck happened.

One day recon company came in from a long patrol while the security battalion was just sitting around. Securing the fire base was not our job, so that night we slept because we had completed our mission. The security battalion slept too. They should have patrols out but they didn't.

Middle of the night we are hit by NVA company. Sappers came too and get in the barbed wire. Security battalion was plenty scared and just fired wild. I was going to get killed because of them, so I had to try something. I got out the card the 101st colonel gave me. I turned my radio on that frequency and called for the forward air controller in English. Told him what is happening. The American colonel got on the radio and tells me to stand by. In just a few minutes three Cobras fly over the fire base. I got the security battalion to shoot mortar flares.

When the flares burn, the Cobras see NVA all around the wire. Miniguns, rockets, everything is fired down on them. Cobras flew around and around till there were no more targets. The American colonel called me and asked if I need more air support. I say, no, that was enough—thanks very much, they save my ass.

Next morning we policed the wire and drag fifty NVA into a pile. They are all shot up. Pile looked like it was painted red. Guts are all over the place. We decided to dump everything in a pond so the stink is not so bad.

But before we do, VIP choppers arrive. Division commander, General Truong, has come with the American colonel. Captain Thanh comes and was happy too. We had some wounded from the security battalion. I watched every stretcher, how it is used to hide a NVA weapon that goes out with the wounded guys. Thanh saw me watch and winked.

General Truong gave me a medal that is the Vietnamese Silver Star. The American colonel says he will give me American Bronze Star too. They left, then Thanh came up to me very happy. He said thanks for the weapons, and if I let him have the Bronze Star he will make everything okay for me in the rice cartel. This is a good deal so I gave him my Bronze Star.

After that I have only to buy shares in cartel, and don't have to handle rice myself. I just get some profit from the cartel at harvest time. Everything is legal because in the Vietnamese army soldiers can be businessmen too. With some of this money I set up a little tailor shop because my wife wanted a business too. She mends uniforms and made little dresses for peasants. Then she wanted to get more expensive material for dresses for ladies of rich families. But she does not do a very good job, and did not make any money from this.

Thanh knew everything that is going on about people's business. He said, too bad about my wife's shop—maybe I should look harder for weapons. I said my guys are the only ones who really capture weapons, and he agreed, but if I get more, he will send some rich ladies to my wife's shop. I thought about this. I do my job because I want to stop the enemy. I saw what happen in Hue; nobody here in the delta saw that. I turn over captured weapons to Thanh and do not ask for reward. What he does with them is not for my conscience. I told him that if he sends ladies to my wife, I appreciate that, but I will keep on doing my job like before. He said that's fine, but maybe I should be more aggressive in the field, then there will be better weapons count. I laughed because he knows already that I am the most aggressive lieutenant in the regiment. Okay he said, but not everybody likes you, and if you lose more casualties, headquarters will expect more weapons. For a while I don't understand what he means.

In 1972 it was business as usual in the delta. All the big towns were secure, and mutually profitable relations prevailed between ARVN and the populace, who were grateful to have their rice protected for the national market. They gave food to Twenty-first Division soldiers, while elsewhere in South Vietnam ARVN confiscated it. The communists too were on short rations, and Cai marveled at how skinny his prisoners were. Both sides committed all their resources in the Easter Offensive, which for I Corps did not conclude for six months. Cai could sense that the delta was a sideshow, and the future of the war was being shaped elsewhere.

We know things are not so good in the rest of Vietnam. After Easter Offensive, some ranger and airborne officers are transferred to Twenty-first Division. They need a rest from very long and hard fighting. Some were still shook up and drank too much.

I talked to one ranger captain. He was wounded three times. One in Lam Son 719, one in Quang Tri province, and last time at An Loc. His ears not too good because of B52's. He was very good fighter, but he told his ranger battalion commander he must desert so he can be black market man to support his family. They are at Phu My but he can never see them because he was always fighting in I and II Corps. One of his kids died from not enough nutrition. His wife told him she will not let another of her children die, that she will be a prostitute first. He cannot stand this, so he told his battalion commander he must go AWOL.

I felt very bad for this officer and loaned him some money to start in the cartel. He was very grateful to me. With this little money he brought his family to a hut in a town near here. He was also grateful that his ranger battalion commander transferred him to Twenty-first Division. That commander told him, "I don't blame you. If this government cannot pay enough for you to live, why should you die for it? If you cannot support your family in Twenty-first Division just call me. I will say you were KIA, then you don't have to worry about being reported as deserter. Go out and do black market or anything you want."

This ranger captain said he was very lucky man now for being in Twenty-first Division. The ranger troops, he say, have it even worse than him. They came to him in I Corps and asked to attack where they think NVA have a big rice cache. To get there they must get through strong defenses—whole NVA battalion. No helicopters available but they want to do it anyway. This captain said, okay, the attack will be called a recon patrol, then province chief will allow it.

These men are very brave because if they do not get NVA rice, there is none for their families. One platoon infiltrated through NVA battalion at night. Kill only with knives. Never heard about such a thing, even in 101st. Whole U.S. platoon would get medal of honor if they did that!

A company of NVA supply troops were surprised in the attack. Rangers killed them and the rest run away. Rangers called on radio that they have big cache, tons of rice. In that case helicopters come. NVA came too and there was big fight, but most of that platoon got out with the rice.

Most of the rice goes to helicopter crews. Ranger platoon gets only as much as they carry in rucksacks. For men who were killed, their share is given to their families. At that time I cannot believe that men volunteered to die for a few kilos of rice, but I believed this ranger captain. When we have to surrender in 1975, he said "No way." I never saw him again but while I am outlaw I heard he got out to Australia.

When I let him in cartel some people were angry. They want to keep it very small. They didn't say anything to me but some funny things happen: Three times I went on patrol with the company and my bodyguard was killed. This is the soldier who cooks rice for me in the field, digs my foxhole, and is close beside me all the time. I know this is dangerous assignment because VC always look for radios that are with leaders.

One time a sniper got my bodyguard. Next time it was a mine. Third time the CP group is mortared. After that no one wants the job anymore till I get Hen, who was shot by the cop.

I cannot believe VC are so smart to get my bodyguards this way, but it is also unbelievable that the cartel could tell them things that would make this happen. My company is getting other casualties too. They start to say I am unlucky. Regimental CO told me maybe I am too aggressive. I tell him that is what I learned with the Oh-deuce. After a while aggressive units have fewer casualties because enemy stays out of their way. That is what I told my men before we go on operations, but not many support me after our losses. I start to think about what Thanh said. I am not surprised if he has relations with the VC. Because I rejected his offer to bring him more weapons, I have to watch out for my own security.

Always I am worried about VC in my company. Most of my men grew up in this region. Some families have sons in ARVN and VC both. There is pressure on men who are in families like that. They give secret support for VC. I made sure to rotate everybody's time on night guard. Nobody knows when he will be on duty; that way the VC do not know when to attack.

I think a lot of people were trying to get me transferred. If I go away the cartel does not have to pay me. They probably kick out the ranger captain too, even though he is the best officer against communists.

One day chief of staff asked me to come in for a talk. He

said there is a slot open for captain in G2. I can have that job and not have to go to the field anymore. Good chance to get promoted too. If I am interested, I only have to pay him the difference between lieutenant's and captain's pay. I said thanks, but I will stay with recon company.

I do not know who was against me, I only have ideas. My wife thought I should buy the promotion to captain. But I remembered what the MI officer told me after Tet 68: that Vietnam was my country. If I don't help save it, who will?

It turned out that I didn't change my mind soon enough.

An exhibit in the SRV's "War Crimes Museum." The cross is formed by pictures of American POWs. *(Brenda Lee Sutton)*

In this picture, staged by the SRV, a prisoner of re-education eats rice from a bowl that contains more than twice his daily ration. (*Amnesty International*)

A survivor's sketch of a windowless barrack in Ham Tan re-education camp. The drum in the foreground is the toilet for fifty men.   (*Amnesty International*)

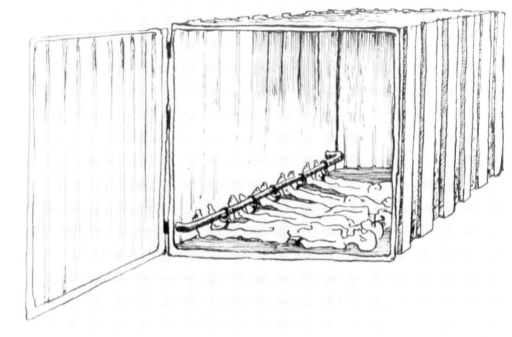

A conex container used for a punishment cell. *(Amnesty International)*

A disabled ARVN veteran begs on the streets of Ho Chi Minh City. He is carried by his son. (*AP/Wide World*)

Ben's Cai Lam's mother, Christmas 1983. *(Ben Cai Lam)*

Ben's Cai Lam's father. *(Ben Cai Lam)*

A river ferry like the one used in Ben Cai Lam's escape attempt.
(*Brenda Reed Sutton*)

Boat people shipwrecked on the Malaysian coast.
(*UN High Commission for Refugees [UNHCR]*)

Malaysian marines watch a refugee boat *(top left)* pull in.
(SYGMA–Dejean)

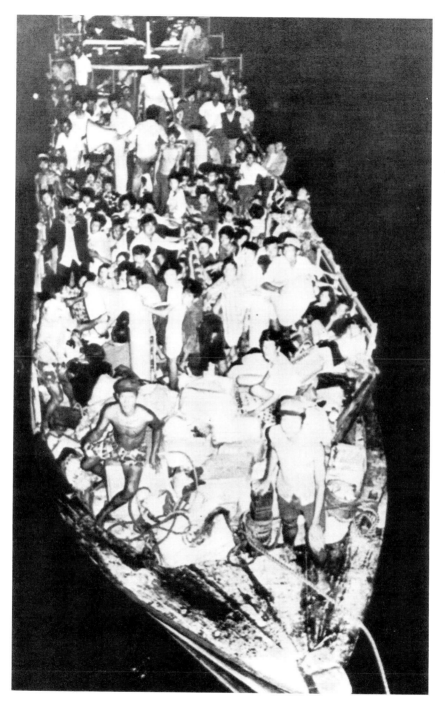

A refugee boat arrives. *(UNHCR)*

A street on Pulau Bidong.   (*Black Star–Kokojan*)

Ben Cai Lam on his first day in the U.S.A., already a Montana cowboy, with Hank Emerson. *(Ben Cai Lam)*

Ben's son, Dat, and daughter, Van, in Dillon, Montana. His other daughter, Huyen, is still in the SRV with his wife, Lena.
(*Ben Cai Lam*)

The Oh-deuce authors, Del Vecchio *(left)* and Taylor.   *(Ben Cai Lam)*

Ben with retired Sergeant Major "Ski" Sabalouski, the hero of Dak To I, at the Oh-deuce reunion.   *(Ben Cai Lam)*

Ben, with his son and daughter, at his graduation from Western Montana College, May 1989. *(Ben Cai Lam)*

Chapter
Sixteen

In 1972 we have plenty of ammo, artillery, and air support because Americans left everything for us. A lot got used up in Easter Offensive and before cease-fire when GVN tried to control as much land as possible. When 1973 comes, things are not so good. Lucky for us there is not much fighting in Twenty-first Division AO. Worst thing is that there are not many medevac choppers, so wounded must be carried out. If we want medevac, we must first go to chopper unit and make agreement with them—5,000 piasters for medevac from a cold LZ. If we call for medevac without paying, chopper comes out and says he can not land because of enemy fire.

This makes me think that maybe old-time officers are right. When they told me I am too aggressive they always say war is not for months of fighting but will last for years. Already I have been in war for eight years. Maybe they are right. U.S. troops at the end said this war was not worth dying in. At that time I thought they just talk like that because they are short-timers. But without good support, soldiers should be more careful. I did not want to get wounded if medevac can not come get me.

Because of medical shortages, I got very interested in what the VC used for their wounded—maybe I have to use it myself. I know the way to find it is to watch each village pharmacy.

District I'm in is very quiet so I know VC are using it to get supplies. I think they bought the district chief. I have a stakeout to watch who buys tetracycline—VC need this for their wounds. I also learn who pays off the guy who does loading at the rice factory. These men are followed. When a man who buys from pharmacy and one who visits the rice factory leave town together, we went after them with a patrol.

Couple of days later, patrol radios to me—they caught the guys and found a cache. They need helicopters to carry it away. I went to the regiment's aviation company. They said they will fly if I give them a box of M79 grenades. They want this to go deer hunting. They can sell the meat in district market.

The supply system pinched even tighter in 1974. Because of cutbacks in promised U.S. aid, and the insatiable siphon of corruption, Colonel Le Gro reported:

Stocks of supplies, many of which were in the lifesaving category, were seriously depleted, such as blood collection bags, intravenous fluids, antibiotics, and surgical dressings. The onset of the monsoon brought with it the scourge of falciparum malaria in the northern provinces, but the supply of insect repellent for the troops was exhausted. Roughly half the items on stockage lists were not there, and shipments into depots had fallen off dramatically: from about 24,000 metric tons received in March to less than 8000 in May.

Draconian measures were applied. Only 55 percent of available transportation could be fueled, and tactical movement required the approval of the corps commander. Bandages and surgical dressings were washed and reused, as were hypodermic syringes and needles, intravenous sets and rubber gloves. In the Air Force, squadrons were reduced from 66 to 56; no replacements were ordered for 162 destroyed aircraft; flying hours and supply levels were further reduced; and 224 aircraft were placed in storage, among them all 61 remaining A-1 bombers, all 52 C-7 cargo airplanes, 34 gunships and observation planes as well as 31 Hueys.

Without American largesse to exploit, the Vietnamese government turned their genius for corruption on their own country. Smug-

gling became the favored career. Strategically positioned civilian
and military officials ensured abundant importation of whiskey, cigarettes, and toiletries for the black market, where sales resulted in
private profits rather than desperately needed government reve-
nues. Outbound contraband included $17 million worth of scrap
metal. The Quang Ngai province chief swapped tons of war supplies
with the communists for cinnamon he exported at a huge profit. The
GVN was literally selling its country out at the same time it was
crying betrayal by the U.S.

*I know things are getting pretty bad when the army starts fight-
ing the navy for fuel to sell on black market. Division AO has
An Xuyen province on south coast. One day we heard the VC
have sunk a navy boat there. But it turns out that RF troops of
the army sunk it!*

*There was this little port where the navy came every week.
Big fuel tank is buried in the ground there. The RF watch the
sailors pump diesel fuel from this tank and sell it to fishermen.
RF asked sailors for share of profit but they were told money
must go to navy headquarters in Saigon. Next time navy boat
came to that port, RF asked them again to share profit. Sailors
say no, then RF shot up the boat till it sunk. After that, the RF
got some of the money.*

*Another thing that happen around that time was "phantom
soldiers" and "flower soldiers." When guys are killed, this was
not reported. Commanders kept getting army pay for these dead
men. If wife is near by, she was paid off by commander and she
goes away. These dead men are phantom soldiers.*

*Flower soldiers are men who pay their commander and stay
in the rear to do private business. Commander gives them a pass
so they are okay if MP stop them for check. Some battalion
commanders made quarter million piasters every month from
flower soldiers. Some of this goes to regimental commander,
division CG—right up the line. Every Vietnamese general wants
troop command even if he did not want to fight the enemy.*

*One thing he can do is get pay for AWOL soldiers. About
half of the men who go on leave never came back. Corrupt officers*

report them AWOL till pay day, then collect the money. Next morning, they are reported AWOL or deserter. That way if inspector come, the officer says, "See, the men who are not here have been reported."

I had a Honda motor scooter that I bought from rice business. There is a very good mechanic in the town. Nhut fixed my scooter whenever I want—takes it first even when other people are waiting. When I paid him he charges me very little, like just for the parts. I never knew why Nhut is so good to me.

Then one day I got a surprise when Nhut came to my home. He told me he is a flower soldier, that he is supposed to be in my company. I don't know this because I never saw his name on company roster. To make me believe him, he showed me a letter signed by my CO to excuse Nhut from training. I'd never seen that letter. He did not know why, but maybe because he made his deal with regiment and they want to cut me out—but now Nhut has big problem. Because on paper he has been in the army so long, he is to be promoted to sergeant. That means he must go to NCO school for a couple of months. If Nhut did that, he must leave his mechanic business and lose lots of money. He wanted me to hold up his promotion. I told him, no problem, I make sure he does not get promoted.

In the idyllic delta, Cai was only vaguely aware of the political-military situation that was going through a sea change elsewhere in the beleaguered country. Devastated by losses in the 1972 Easter Offensive, the communists had been reequipping and reorganizing their forces, still the fourth largest in the world. 1973 was a year of ARVN counteroffensive, the "land grab" by both sides to seize maximum territory before boundaries were drawn by the Paris peace accords. Cai called this the "war of flags." In the delta and everywhere, villagers were ordered to fly GVN flags to show their allegiance. The VC did the same with their flag.

By 1974, however, the pinch of reduced U.S. aid began to tell, and the communists were right to declare that their position was stronger than at any time since 1954. The Ho Chi Minh Trail doubled its capacity after development of the Truong Son corridor, a modern supply system sufficient to support a modern half-million-man army in the south with seven divisions in strategic reserve. They called their new strategy, "war in peace," meaning that they would exploit the fiction of a cease-fire while maneuvering their forces into position for the decisive blow. Stretched over a 1000-mile front, ARVN did not know where the blow would strike. Thieu did not have the political will to narrow the front, for this would cede territory to the communists.

So he had to lose it, at first bit by bit as remote outposts along the border were overrun. Astoundingly, at the same time he decided to reduce the size of his million-man army by nearly 200,000. Oil had been discovered on the continental shelf. A new petroleum economy, he apparently believed, would need the manpower, though there was still double-digit unemployment from the loss of the GI service industry.

ARVN was also thinned by a desertion rate that monthly took 2 percent of its total strength. As Gen. Cao Van Vien, the last chairman of the Vietnamese joint chiefs of staff, described the situation:

> Recruits intended to make up for the deficit never filled the projected quotas due to extensive draft dodging. Very few deserters or draft dodgers chose to go over to the other side in spite of the enemy's propaganda efforts. Most simply vanished into the cities [as] fugitives or returned to live in their villages with the connivance and help of friends or relatives. Some simply got tired of hiding, so they reenlisted in a different unit under a new name.

Cai saw such draft dodging become a business:

*E*very province had a quota. At that time in the war, everybody male 18 to 42 was supposed to go to basic training. Army didn't care about names, just numbers. So when a man did not want to go he can hire someone else. There were plenty of guys who will do this for them. The man who is hired makes up a name and reports. He takes basic training and asks for assignment somewhere else in country. No problem with that if he asks for *a unit that does a lot of fighting like in II or III Corps. Then this guy goes AWOL. He comes back and gets hired by another guy when the next quota came down. Some guys who did this for a job went through basic training four, five times!*

Aware of such decay, the NVA, like a cautious python, began their final squeeze. Their principal worry was the return of the dreaded U.S. Air Force, still based nearby in Thailand, but prohibited by the U.S. Congress from intervening. The NVA verified the U.S. policy by seizing a border province capital, Song Be, seventy-five air miles north of Saigon. With the U.S. Air Force vanished from the skies, the NVA attacked in daylight. An ARVN survivor of the battle described it this way:

> The NVA were not so good and so courageous as we might have thought. There were simply too many of them. The enemy's artillery was fierce and many times more accurate than it had been during the battle of An Loc (an ARVN victory in the 1972 Easter Offensive). Our air support was not very effective. The planes had to fly too high to avoid all the antiaircraft guns the NVA brought this time. If only we could have had B52's as we did at An Loc!

In March 1975 the NVA surprised ARVN and struck at Ban Me Thuot in the heart of II Corps. With its loss, the overextended front crumbled fast. Thieu decided I and II Corps had to be abandoned. The withdrawal was mismanaged and engulfed in refugees. ARVN troops disappeared by the thousands to rejoin their families.

As the situation grew desperate, a U.S. congressional delegation rushed to Saigon to appraise what, if anything, should be done. Nothing Thieu said could persuade them to increase U.S. support, but the communists convinced all but Bella Abzug that the alternative to the GVN was mortifying.

The delegation was able to meet with high-ranking PRG and NVA officials. The Americans' concerns were principally the hundreds of U.S. MIAs that the communists had made no effort to account for, and return of the remains of scores of U.S. servicemen.

Instead of remains, the communists had brought scores of news reporters to listen to the PRV's lectures on U.S. imperialism. After this intended humiliation, the PRV general refused to discuss the MIAs and walked out.

They could afford to be haughty. In ten days 75 percent of ARVN in II Corps had been lost. This was in March. At the current level of U.S. aid, the South Vietnamese armed forces would run out of essential supplies by June. As the front collapsed, so too did the morale and credibility of the GVN. Mobs of demonstrators surged through the cities, denouncing the U.S. and demanding Thieu to go. South Vietnam's days were numbered under fifty.

It was in February 1975 that Twenty-first Division got its biggest battles. My recon company started the first one. There is a point in the delta where three provinces come together. Regional forces can not do much because each must stay in one province. VC knew this so they operate around this point. Recon company was sent to see if VC have built up a base there.

Delta fighting is very different than in terrain like Ashau. Everything is wide open so I must spread troops out. In jungle, most fire hits trees. In delta, one RPG [rocket propelled grenade] can get three or four men. So I kept my troops far away from each other. That means not too many of them near to me. That got me in big trouble in this battle.

We choppered in and moved out toward where this VC base may be. Reaction battalion commander is in C&C ship so he can watch what happens. First thing, a big round went off about hundred meters behind me. I took radio and say, "Hey, I didn't ask for artillery. That almost hit my men!"

He said, "Cai, that's not our guns. You got incoming."

Then I knew this is not a little bunch of guerrillas out there. I called him and said he should get his battalion ready because we have probably run into NVA. He said, maybe, but spread out my company more and keep looking. I asked, how much more you want us to find? There's too much already.

He gave me our objective: a little RF outpost that the enemy surrounded. Soon as we got a little closer, 82-mm mortars start coming in. My men hit the ground and I cannot see them. Next, a .51 caliber machine gun opened up on my command group. My RTO was killed—I knew him very well, and his family.

It made me sad and angry that we must push into enemy fire like this. I took the radio from his dead hand and called the C&C ship. I said okay, we find this force for you, bring in reaction battalion because they are too heavy for us. He said, not yet: try to break through to the RF outpost. Reaction battalion is just for very important targets.

We got a little closer. Red smoke signal went off, and the NVA came out of the ground. Just like that—can't even see where they come from. They and my men shoot at each other from just ten meters. Like western movie—never seen hand-to-hand combat like that in Vietnam. Coconut tree beside me broke up in pieces when enemy machine gun shot at me. My bodyguard's head explodes.

I just carried pistol, so I have to run. NVA saw my radio I think. A squad of them took off after me. This is when I was most scared in my life, diving over paddy dike, crawling so fast I think I am running. They want to capture me and get bonus. Looked like they will.

Whenever one popped up, I jump into another paddy and crawl some more. Paddies are very dry in this season, rice was already harvest, just short brown grass left. I cannot hide.

I was moving back through some of my men but they are far apart because mortars still coming in. My men fired back and forth with the NVA. Shooting was going in all directions. I cannot hide, so I played dead. Lucky for me two things happen. One is I had blood of RTO on me. Other thing is NVA started shooting at each other because everything is so mixed up.

Like a dead man, I kept my eyes almost closed, but then I saw one of my platoon leaders. Fire keeps digging up the paddy so I think I better get over to him. He might have some men with him and we can get all-around defense. So I stayed low but rush toward him.

That's when a German machine gun opened up. I never heard

that sound before. I heard it before the bullet hit me, and I am knocked flat. The round struck my shoulder and went into the chest. I remembered very well the slap sound from my first action at An Ninh.

But I fell over the dike and the platoon leader got to me. I told him to call the C&C ship, call him to get me out. Then I lost blood, and consciousness. The chopper landed and took me away—that's all I remember.

When I woke up I am in Soc Trang hospital. First, I think I have died because there is a man from my past beside me. He is Hoanh, one of my interpreters from the 101st. But he is really there. Just from luck he was assigned as a medic in that hospital, and he saw me come in on the stretcher. He told me I was unconscious for twenty-four hours.

There was bad news from the battle. Before they pulled out, recon company lost twenty-eight men. The regimental commander wants to court martial me for that, maybe put me in jail during the investigation. I was still not thinking very good but I told the investigator that we ran into an NVA battalion at least. I am right because battle goes on for ten more days. ARVN finally surrounded the battalion that surrounded the RF. There was much hard fighting but the NVA were destroyed. Then there is a big victory celebration in regiment and I am put in for promotion. I got it on the last day of the war, the day South Vietnam surrender! Maybe if I just stayed a lieutenant, the communists would not have treated me so bad.

Cai was hospitalized throughout March. In April he was put on light duty in charge of a small sector of the delta. Here he was in daily touch with his brothers on a hot line to Saigon, where they were able to keep him informed about the deteriorating situation in III Corps. Everyone in the government with any connections was leaving the country. The only hope for those remaining was miraculous intervention by the Americans.

Cai's brothers begged him to deal with the realities. They offered to send a chopper for him and his family. But he could not bring himself to desert his country.

All the bad news was so hard to believe. In the delta we were short of supplies but we were still doing all right. When I heard an American B52 bombed the NVA at Xuan Loc, I told everyone, "The U.S. will not let Vietnam fall!"

What happened at Xuan Loc was that the U.S. Air Force delivered a few daisy cutters to Saigon from Thailand. The Vietnamese Air Force loaded one of these awesome 15,000 pound bombs in a C130 transport and dropped it on an NVA division headquarters with devastating effect. The local communist propaganda radio went off the air, a sign of hope for the hope-starved ARVN. Consequently, the GVN had no incentive to quash the rumor that B52's were back.

But there were Cai's brothers, well informed of the portending debacle, telling him that "Anyplace better than Vietnam now." Mr. McGill, in the office of the U.S. attaché, told him the same thing. Cai can not explain exactly why their entreaties did not persuade him. Truong Nhu Tang, the PRG foreign minister, offers a reason why the Americans were expected to save the day, even at the eleventh hour:

> One contributing factor to this Vietnamese propensity to place trust in persons comes from the culture's ingrained Confucianism. Of the basic ethical principles in this philosophical tradition, the fifth is *tin* ("faithfulness"). Foregoing *tin*, a person becomes devoid of honor, of face. He loses his essential humanity. Among the very deepest feelings of one raised in a Confucian society is the inhibition against betraying those with whom one enjoys a relationship of trust.

Cai was simply disbelieving that in their darkest hour the Vietnamese could not rely on American *tin* to prevail over all other considerations. He remembered too many American lives that lengthened the ledger on the side of *tin*.

I did not know how to stop believing, but the war was over for America. The communist cause won there. I did not know that.

There was like divorce between our countries. Everything that had been together between us was forgotten.

No more U.S. aid because GVN is so corrupt. I understand that now. We put up with corruption too long. There should have been a coup to stop it. But probably there will be a new corrupt government. Very few at the top can be willing to sacrifice their own interests. While Americans were here, there was enough money for everybody so no one care very much. We saw this too late. Not right to blame Americans. They should make their own self-criticism. We were the ones responsible. We could not make sacrifices like VC. Only the ARVN troops did that, and they do it in many battles while rich people did not care.

On April 30 we learned we must surrender. Nobody knew what to do; they did not believe this could be. People cry in front of others. Me too. I saw Thanh come toward me; he was drinking. He ask me if I can call a U.S. chopper to pick us up. I shook my head. He said, have a glass with him because he has made major. I asked him, now the war is over, "Why did you always tell me to kill prisoners?" He said, "Cai, some of them trade weapons to me. I don't want them to be interrogated and say that."

After nine years, Cai's life and mine intersected again in this last week of April 1975. My wife, Pamela, is a Pan Am stewardess. All the while there were U.S. combat troops in the war, she had taken them to R and R sites from Saigon, Cam Ranh, Danang, and Pleiku. Her flight records show she spent more days (one day being a take-off or landing) in Vietnam than I had. So when Pan Am prepared for the fall of South Vietnam, they asked Pam to volunteer for the last commercial flight from Tan Son Nhut, Saigon's airport.

In event of capture, she had a military ID card temporarily commissioning her as a lieutenant in the U.S. Air Force. This entitled her to the protection of the Geneva Conventions regarding treatment of prisoners of war.

Other volunteers on the crew were her friends, Gudren Meisner

(German), Valerie Chalk (British), and Tra Dong, a Vietnamese desperate to get her family out. In 1987 the crew reached agreement with a producer to have their story depicted in an NBC miniseries called *Last Plane from Saigon.*

They brought in the next to last plane (Flight 841) on Tuesday, April 24, when the NVA were still nine miles from the airport, barely outside artillery range. The 747 carried eighteen passengers into Tan Son Nhut. A full plane of 300 was expected for the flight back to Manila.

During the two hours inbound to Saigon, the crew and passengers got to talking. Most were Americans, some servicemen returning to pick up wives and children. One was an ARVN colonel hoping to retrieve his five-year-old son. He was resigned to staying with his wife and four young daughters. He and Tra struck a deal:

She had three sisters whom she hoped to smuggle aboard and stow away in the lavatory. But first they had to get through the fence bordering Tan Son Nhut and be spirited into the cargo hangar where she could arrange to pick them up. For his part, the colonel could get access into the airport but had no way to slip his boy through immigration or onto the plane. Tra would take care of that if the colonel would pick up her sisters at their Saigon address and get them inside Tan Son Nhut.

It would take two days for Tra and the colonel to accomplish what they had to do, but this flight on which they met would be on the ground in Tan Son Nhut for only two hours, then return to Manila. So they agreed that the flight on Thursday, April 26, would be the escape plane.

To avoid antiaircraft fire, the 747 came in like it was flying down a spiral staircase. As they touched down, South Vietnamese fighters were taking off constantly, laden with bombs and rockets. So close were the NVA that the planes returned within a few minutes while the resounding explosions from their bombs still thundered across the runway.

Because of the frantic refugees thronged at the terminal, the 747 was not allowed to park nearby as it always had. Instead, the debarking passengers and crew had a half-mile walk before reaching the gates and ticket counters. Vietnamese of every age were massed there. Thousands more were visible through the glass terminal doors, jammed against the security fence. Holding submachine guns, immigration guards watched the one passenger entrance for the flight to Manila.

The stewardesses' uniforms allowed them to move anywhere in the cavernous terminal. From a crowded corner, Pam and Gudren saw Valerie waving. A Vietnamese woman was whispering, tugging her sleeve.

"She wants me to take her child out!" Valerie told Pam. "Let's try."

For a moment the mother knelt over her four-year-old girl, murmured something, kissed her, and with a gentle shove pushed her daughter between Valerie and Gudren—and into another life. The stewardesses took the girl's hands. They cut through the crowd and swept by immigrations, the tot concealed by the women's skirts. If the guard had stopped them they would tell him the girl (whom Valerie renamed Laura) was an unescorted minor, and her ticket was already on board.

Nearby, an American who looked as though he had worked in Vietnam for years, observed the little escape. He sat on a sagging suitcase watching Pam, then sent his Vietnamese wife over.

"We have son," she said hurriedly. "No visa. Can you take?" Then she pointed to a skinny boy standing silently by his parents' baggage.

"The rest of you on this flight?" Pam asked.

"Yes, two children with us. We don't have visa for him. Too much money to pay. We bring to airport—hope somebody get him out."

"How old is he—ten?"

"Fourteen. He's good boy."

Pam felt the boy was being offered like some nice but excess pet, an unwanted mixed breed. He now became a project for her and Gudren. They tried to bluff him by immigration. The guard looked at the boy uncertainly.

"He's a passenger," said Gudren.

"Momma, Poppa already on plane," Pam added, and pulled out an empty boarding pass. It didn't work. They were turned away.

But there was still the cargo connection, the second access to the plane. Working with the Pan Am baggage personnel, they were able to reach the cargo hangar and make a dash for the plane. It was far off and they were spotted. A jeep with armed soldiers turned them back. The boy was lucky not to be arrested.

Back in the terminal, Pam took him aside. "English?" she asked. He nodded slightly. "Thursday. Day after tomorrow, we come back. You be here?" He nodded hopefully. "We have to go now but we come back on Thursday, the 26th. You be here, okay?" He nodded again but his narrow shoulders sagged.

Pam and Gudren caught the crew van back to the plane and soon all the legitimate passengers were aboard. There were only 191 of them, a tragically small number, just a little more than half of the jumbo jet's capacity. It was apparent that in spite of its imminent downfall, the GVN would exploit its citizens to the end. That meant no bribe, no exit visa; no exit visa, no plane ticket.

Just before the doors were to close, the Vietnamese ground hostess who had escorted the passengers from the terminal whispered she was staying aboard. She held an infant in her arms and a toddler hid behind her skirt. The children were hers though she appeared to have brought them for departing passengers. Her children were seated with families while she hid in the lavatory. Before immigration made a check of the plane, the pilot ordered the doors closed and started the engines.

Like so many of the refugees, the ground hostess was both grateful and heartbroken. Her escape had been so hurried and secret that she had not even been able to say goodbye to her parents. Her husband was a soldier still fighting on Saigon's outskirts; there was no way to get word to him that his family was gone.

Valerie was overcome by the situation. She resolved to adopt Laura, and see her through to the United States, even though this meant going AWOL temporarily from Pan Am. One passenger, a Frenchman with the UN, took it upon himself to scold her for getting involved.

The crew resolved to really get involved on the next and final flight. From what they had seen, a Pan Am uniform would be a sure ticket for refugees they would try to get out on Thursday. One way or another, there would be no empty seats on the last Pan Am plane from Saigon. Back in Manila, they borrowed extra uniforms from Pan Am crews who were laying over from other flights.

Valerie proceeded to Guam, then Honolulu, with Laura. There, U.S. immigration stopped her. Laura of course had no visa, and was consequently refused entry into America. In spite of prolonged efforts, Valerie was denied custody; however, Laura was soon adopted by a family in Hawaii.

On Thursday morning, before Flight 841 could depart for the last time to Saigon, the FAA declared that Tan Son Nhut was too dangerous a destination for any commercial aircraft. The U.S. State Department, Air Force, and Pan Am negotiated an alternative, and the commercial flight was redesignated an Air Force charter, officially a humanitarian mission. Their tote bags bulging with Pan Am uniforms, shoes, wigs, and dark glasses, the crew took the last 747 back into the war zone.

All safety requirements of a commercial flight were suspended. There would be no limit in numbers for infants in arms or small children in laps, and the pilot could load as many seated and standing passengers as he thought the plane would hold. He decided that would be 550. Weight would be no problem because there would be practically no baggage or cargo.

The 747 again flew a corkscrew glide path down to the last usable runway. The rest of the tarmac was laced by intermittent cross fire. Amazingly, there were fewer people in the terminal than there had been two days before. GVN roadblocks had stopped most of the refugees short of the airport.

The abandoned American-Vietnamese boy did not make his rendezvous. Pam searched the terminal, but if he had left Tan Son Nhut on Tuesday he hardly could have returned. The security was too tight. The ARVN were running things as if they were occupying their own country—what was left of it.

The ARVN colonel had made good: hiding in the cargo hangar were Tra's sisters. They also had a message—the colonel's little boy had already made it out with the rest of the family by sea.

Hiding with Tra's sisters were six Pan Am ticket agents. Their boss had developed a plan to get almost all his employees out. First, those working in the control tower would infiltrate onto the passenger buses. Second, vans from the cargo hangar were to take women disguised as stewardesses to the plane, where they would appear to be escorting passengers up the ramp. Finally, if the immigration checkpoint at the foot of the ramp could be bribed, the vans might return to the cargo hangar for members of the employees' families. In effect, Pan Am was leaving Vietnam on its last plane. All the ground personnel necessary for the scheduled departure—ticket agents, mechanics, caterers, operation controllers—were themselves backing on to this last flight.

The stewardesses did what they could to cover for the escapees. Gudren staffed the ticket counter, Pan Am's last representative to leave the terminal. A nonchalant American strolled up as if this was a scheduled flight from Chicago, and asked if it was delayed.

"Nope," said Gudren. "Follow me and you'll be the last aboard."

Pam was at the door, herding in passengers as if the plane were a Japanese subway. Two sweating Americans approached, each lugging huge suitcases. She gestured for them to toss their baggage into the cargo bay.

They were CIA men who had closed down the Saigon station. "Lady, these are full of money," they protested.

"Yeah. How much?"

"Four million—in green."

The suitcases still went in the belly.

Only the last phase of Pan Am's plan remained—escape for the undisguised relatives waiting in the cargo hangar. The van sped away to get them and it soon returned overflowing. It went back again and again, each time bringing loads of siblings, uncles, aunts, grandparents, cousins, lovers, relatives at the fringes of the extended family. In clusters they stood at the foot of the ramp, stopped by a single armed soldier.

All pretenses were dropped now; he could either turn these hundreds back or let them on, knowing they had no documentation. But they had some money, now worthless piasters. A garbage bag came out of the plane. This the refugees filled at his feet as he let them pass. Inside the stewardesses shook down the legitimate passengers, filling pillow cases passed out to this guard, who was rapidly becoming the richest enlisted man in ARVN. GVN's authority and the bureaucracy ended with him, but in the end he was a human being, and stood aside as the last group of Pan Am's refugees surged up the ramp.

The red beacon above the cockpit was whirling. The 747 slowly pivoted and rolled ahead toward take-off. Like all large planes moving into position, it was led by a man on the ground wearing the noise suppressors that look like earmuffs. This last guide pointed his wands toward the departure runway, then raced under the taxiing plane and jumped onto the landing gear. The 747 lurched to a stop. The pilot waited as the man scrambled up the wheel well and climbed into the cabin through a floor panel.

PART IV

"A meticulous and long-range process"

Chapter
Seventeen

We surrendered to a radio! I cannot believe what happen. Big Minh just said that there was change of government so we must turn in weapons and wear civilian clothes from now on.

Twenty-first Division had not much fighting. Not even any VC around for us to give our weapons. ARVN chain of command broke down pretty quick. I don't know what happen to division staff. They just disappeared. Same thing with regimental commander and staff. Battalion commander asked me what we should do. I said why not just go into town and pile up weapons and uniforms there. He did not say anything but that is what we do.

People very mixed up about how they feel. War is over. Most of us were born during the war. For the first time there is no more war. No more artillery, no more choppers, no more wounded screams. Soldiers start taking it easy. Happy to get through and still alive. But good NCOs are mad too. Nobody beat us. We did not lose battles to communists. But we must quit now—war is over. Maybe there is peace to rebuild our country.

We make jokes about President Thieu. He lost the war, not us. "Wonder where he is?" everybody asked.

In prison I met two of Thieu's bodyguards, Hieu and Nguyen. They had been with him about ten years. Every day they checked his office and palace. Only time they didn't watch Thieu is when he went to the bathroom or sleep with women.

When he took off for Taiwan, Hieu and Nguyen guarded him at Tan Son Nhut. When he got on the plane, he handed them just 5000 piasters, not enough to even buy a bicycle.

In his tearful televised resignation a week earlier, Thieu had promised to stay on as "a fervent fighter" defending his country to the end. Meanwhile, his C118 was warming its engines. So loaded with fifteen tons of gold and presidential relatives that it needed extra runway, the U.S. Air Force transport flew him to Taiwan, where the next day he excoriated America's betrayal of the GVN.

Betrayal it had been, and Thieu had reason to be shocked. The shock should have come years earlier, administered by a U.S. president who could clearly enunciate that America's commitment was to South Vietnam's freedom, not to a regime steeped in corruption. Uncle Sam was finally rid of his spoiled nephew, a disgrace to them both, a disgrace punished by the tortures of a new Dark Age but suffered in brunt by the innocent masses, not Thieu's ruling class, which had been coddled by three U.S. administrations. It is difficult to apportion the disgrace between the GVN elite and the one-eyed U.S. Congress that could see no evil in the north.

My battalion dumped all equipment and weapons in a big market. Then we took off our uniforms. I remembered when I first put it on. I was a teenager, going to the 101st. Many things in my mind when I took it off for the last time: I never thought I will ever be a soldier for so long, but that is what I've done most of my life. Many, many memories from all over the country and ten years—with this mess at the end. I shouted at the air, and men looked at me but I could not stop. They must have thought I was crazy because not very many were so bitter. A lot of them just write addresses for each other and say they will get together after a while. They asked me what I think. I told them to forget about me—I was in Hue in 1968.

Soldiers left on all roads from the town. While I was still there, a few young kids sneaked around. I never saw them before and I'm pretty sure they are VC. They don't say anything and look like they're still scared of us. But they have been told by the VC that all weapons must be collected. They worry that people will pick up guns and maybe become resistance. A kid said to lock our weapons in a building. I told him to get out of the way, that's not my problem.

The district chief just disappeared. Nobody knew where he went, but probably he has his own boat to reach U.S. Navy. I saw another man go with some guys with AKs. He goes to district chief's office and started taking stuff out—real nice desk, expensive things that show district chief is so rich. This man ordered office workers around—says he's leader of VC. People believed him till real VC came to town. Then this guy is gone! He stole everything in district headquarters.

I am so angry at everything. I knew I made the biggest mistake of my life. I should have got out with my brothers. I tell my family [wife, two infant daughters, a ten-year-old son] we got to go, maybe there is still a chance.

The roads toward Saigon teemed with refugees desperate for the chance to escape the liberation Hanoi promised them. With his motor scooter loaded with all they owned, Cai and his family tried to bypass the shuffling mob on the road. He knew the country well. Using dikes and trails, Cai made relatively good time to the Mekong. But there the VC were already in control of the ferry.

At ferry I tried to make my first bribe. All the time before, people try to bribe me, when I was ARVN officer and with 101st. Too many people at the ferry. Cannot get close to VC honcho. All spaces already full. He got very rich I think on that first day.

We have to go back, but I think maybe later there will be a way to get out if the communists are like GVN and take bribes.

But my wife was very upset and the kids catch that from her. We did not know what to do. I decide to get away from the crowded ferry so I can think better. I tried to stay calm so my family will be. We must think what to do next.

That's very tough. My wife had a tailor shop where my bat-

talion was. We can stay there and see what happen. I thought maybe I can still use the telephone and call McGill. I don't know that he already left. Phones don't work. Everybody is gone.

McGill's departure was part of the infamous scene at the U.S. Embassy where Marines had to beat away people from the last American choppers to fly in Vietnam. Many would ditch in the South China Sea and their passengers would be picked up by U.S. warships.

When *we got back to her shop, we were very tired and hungry after a hundred miles on the scooter. We looked for food but I can only buy two bananas. Someone went through the shop while we were gone, took everything valuable. That made my wife cry but I knew we lose that anyway. We closed the door but it is broken and I must tie it with string so no one else breaks in while we sleep. We lie on the floor. My son is scared by dreams, but I was too tired to hear him. We woke very early because a loudspeaker is making announcements from the market.*

A VC woman spoke. Nice calm voice like airport announcements. She said peasants should go back to work on land. Shopkeepers must report to market so new government can count them and make a list. ARVN soldiers are to go to bus station, and officers to district chief's office. I thought about this, that maybe it is better to go with soldiers, but someone will probably know me and say I was an officer. I did not want to register at all, just pretend to be a peasant, but I have to worry about my family if I get caught.

So I go to register. That was best thing to do so I can see what's up.

Everything not organized. People go around and not know what to do. I think communists were not ready for such a fast victory and GVN surrender. VC kids took our names and say just stay a little time in jail. Okay to go get food before I report back.

The jail is hot and small. I knew I don't want to stay there very long. I talked to my wife through the bars, told her I will try again to get to Saigon. I go alone this time, find out how to get out of the country, and come back for her and the kids. I think this will not be too big a deal because so much is screwed up here and probably the same thing everyplace. I learned at E&E school that best time to get away is right after capture.

Indeed, confusion reigned throughout the south. Caught unprepared by their sudden victory, the north rapidly dispersed their cadres into the conquered territory with two aims in mind: first to consolidate power, and, second, to disguise the blood bath that the world press predicted. Thus, "reconciliation" and "concord" were the themes for broadcasts such as Cai heard.

F or a few days, I watch the way the jail works. I'm very careful how I talk but I found some good men that are prisoners. Some of them and I took a good chance to leave because there were only a few guards. They don't know what to do, and every time the head count is screwed up.

I stole one of their motorcycles. We head for Saigon but the road is more jammed than before. Two days just to get to the ferry. One of the guys with me knew where to get a truck on the other side. I must leave the motorcycle because we get across at night on sampan.

This guy Tat has been to Saigon already and came back for his family. He said there is awful refugee situation there, but he can get through crowds because he parked an M48 tank in Cholon. He just found it when ARVN broke up. Tat knew how to drive tank because he worked with Eleventh Cav as interpreter. He put a red banner on the antenna so people will think the tank belongs to NVA.

When we got to Cholon, the tank was there and all ready to go but it needs gas.

Tat said, "You know Cholon. Where is the closest gas station?" I say Shell station is about a mile away. We get in. I have never been in a tank before but Tat told me to stand where commander should be, in the turret. He sat with his head out as driver.

But we don't look like soldiers anymore—no uniforms—so I said maybe we should close the hatches for this drive. He said okay, because he did not want NVA to see us.

We go pretty fast because all people get off the street for us, and cars too. One big truck was loading stuff from a house. He was in our way. Tat told me on intercom to move handle so turret points its cannon at this truck. It dropped a lot of furniture, runs up on sidewalk, and got out of the way.

I am looking through this little slit in the turret like a bunker. I saw a VC with weapon at Shell station. Lot of people around with little cans for fuel. Looks like they want gas for cooking. Pretty sure they offer bribes to VC because he told some to go in back of station, and I see them go away with heavy cans.

Tat said, "Shoot a burst in the air." He told me how to do that with the machine gun next to the cannon. People ran like hell. VC looked scared when Tat drove up. Tat opened his hatch and shot this guy with a pistol, four, five times. "I just want to get one more VC," he said, then told me to fill up the tank. I just pump a few gallons because I'm afraid more troops come. It is enough to get us where we want to go. Then we both got out and shake hands, wished each other good luck. I'm pretty sure Tat is with the resistance now.

I went to my parents. They told me radio said low-rank officers have to report for ten days of re-education. Soldiers only three. Many are already out. I knew how communists work so I don't believe this. So I went to Vung Tau to see if I can steal a boat. Rumors are U.S. Navy is off the shore. All I need is a little boat for my family, but I cannot find one.

VC were checking everybody's ID because so many people got away from Vung Tau. I hid in the brush in daytime and try to see what is going on at boat docks. There are guards around all boats. Right in front of district headquarters VC let one man hang from a pole till he die. He had a sign on his chest that he tried to escape with a boat. That night I spent in a whorehouse because nobody check ID there. Next morning he was still dying.

So I went back to Saigon, and my parents told me again that

I should take ten days of re-education. But I must register soon the radio say, or be a criminal. This is a lie, I'm pretty sure, that ten days is bullshit—if I give myself up I will be prisoner for a long time. My parents said why didn't I think about this before and leave with my brothers? I had no answer, so I went back again to my family to decide.

The decision like Cai's was being mulled by not only the hundreds of thousands of former GVN servicemen and police but also all journalists, government and municipal workers, elected officials from village to national level, every employee of the judiciary from clerks to Supreme Court justices, teachers throughout the school and university system, and members of the Red Cross. Broadcasts and leaflets exhorted that registration would lead them to "reform themselves and cleanse their wrongs in order to quickly become honest citizens, loving the fatherland and peace, and return to the nation with quick progress." All told, a million Vietnamese—"puppet personnel," the new state newspaper called them—were ordered to turn themselves in under "a policy imbued with Vietnamese humanitarianism."

It was a policy displayed for Western media consumption, whose reports conveyed the impression of forgiveness and leniency, just as the communists intended. To reinforce the impression, most low-ranking soldiers were indeed released after the promised three days of thought reform. But there were unpublicized exceptions, tens of thousands of them, for enlisted men who had served in intelligence with marine, airborne, or ranger units.

R*ight after biggest mistake I ever made, I made the second biggest: I reported for registration.*

Announcements say bring clothes, mosquito net, and food enough for ten days. Also plenty of paper and a pen. In intelligence school, I learned what writing is for. Communists always make prisoners write their life stories.

For a long time I thought about a good story. If I tell them my real story, it is over for me. I cannot say about working with

101st or about intelligence school. I must think what sounds good to communists. First thing I decide is that I was drafted. I learned a little English in school so I was assigned to work with U.S. adviser. I don't want to be but they make me an officer. Twenty-first Division is bad unit and I went AWOL a lot. Never liked the war. I was promoted to captain because officers in unit are bad leaders—me too, but I can talk with U.S. adviser so that makes me look good. I also need money and take promotion. First battle I'm in I run away. Second one I get wounded and don't fight anymore. If war go on I would be in court martial. I imagined all this, every date and place. I also remembered how brave VC are when we fight them. I will tell them that with great respect, like I am very scared of them. They will think I am weak person and not respect me, but maybe they will not think about me after that. Before I report, I wrote all this down and went over it just like it was true. I remembered a very lousy officer I knew in Twenty-first Division. I thought about him and act that way.

I told my wife this story too in case they ask her. Then I took my son and daughters and hold them a long time. I knew my life will change very much. I argued with myself that I am believing the communists and that is as dumb as I can be. But everyone was going along with what they say. I let my hope be my guide that they are right. Maybe the end of the war change the communists. Everyone wanted to think that. Just before I report I want to turn away in front of the communists' office, but I went in like it is something I must do.

Cai was quickly processed. Nothing was asked of him except name, rank, birth data, unit, and duration of service. All he was told was that he was going to a re-education camp. Trucks left hourly loaded with ex-ARVN. He waited all day until enough officers (2d lieutenant through captain) were assembled to fill a Russian cargo truck. Officers went to different camps than enlisted men. Cai had reported early so he could see where he was taken, but it wasn't until dusk that his truck rumbled off to the west.

The only guard in the truck sat by the driver, so in the cargo bed the prisoners could speculate where they were going. In a few hours they all knew where they were: in Tay Ninh province close to the Cambodian border. One of the prisoners recognized even more when they arrived at a ramshackle camp sprawled over ten acres of hardpan. It was Trang Long, where the Twenty-fifth ARVN Division had been based in the latter years of the war.

The truckload was split up into different barracks. From the start, the prison cadre separated potential friends. Except for "lecturers," the cadre was all twenty-year-olds, arrogant and irritable in the chaotic influx of prisoners. There were several head counts before the prisoners were shut in for the night. They provided a bucket for a toilet, along with a gallon of dust-covered water for the twenty cellmates in Cai's barrack. The mosquitos arrived with the darkness. The sweating men rolled out straw pads on the floor and looked for places to attach mosquito nets. A few nails and numerous splinters protruding from the plywood walls held the irregular drape of nets; then the men whispered to each other, and a few ate from the food they had brought. Cai wasn't hungry. His mouth was dry from fear of the future.

Some of the guys talk tough. Made fun of the VC and said they do not know what they are doing. I didn't say anything. I think maybe VC agent is in that room and try to find out our thoughts. Some of the other guys talked a little bit about what they will do after ten days are over. That made us feel a little better. We all want to think VC will let us go then.

A fragile faith pervaded the society that had finally come out of civil war. If there was ever a time for clemency, the early months of the PRG was when it would be born. Families had been divided, one of them that of Truong Nhu Tang, the justice minister of the PRG, a founding father of the VC, and one of its ambassadors. Obedient to the PRG's re-education policy, he drove his two brothers in his own car to their re-education camps. One had worked in a bank, the other in a GVN hospital. In these categories, they were scheduled for thirty days of detention. Months later,

Truong, because of his official importance, was allowed to visit their camp:

> We were received by the camp commander with chilly politeness. He would arrange a car to drive us around the area, he said, but we would not be permitted to stop or talk with either our relatives or anyone else. So we were chauffeured through the camp, trying hard to make out our loved ones among the clumps of dazed-looking prisoners. As we drove by one group I saw my brothers walking together. Even now their faces haunt me: pale, thin, frightened, their eyes fixed in a glazed stare. For a moment we glimpsed each other. I can't even imagine what they must have thought, seeing me in the back seat of a government car driving around that ghastly place.

Cai hoarded the food he had brought. From the first full day in camp, he suspected what the principal control measure would be: not the barbed wire fences or the guard posts, but hunger.

As expected, every prisoner's first duty was to write an autobiography. Cai did so quickly; it amounted to only a few pages in contrast to the hours and sheaves of history produced by other prisoners. His first interrogator looked at it skeptically. It was unsatisfactory. Cai would have to do it over in more detail after group instruction and discussion of the first point in the re-education curriculum, called "errors."

We sat on the floor in the barrack. It was very hot and we sweat with no water. But the cadre kid did not sweat even though he is excited. He looked at each of us very close, and spoke like he knew me for a long time. He said things like this, over and over:

"You are criminals against the people. But we do not try you. No punishment. We know you will be sorry when you learn the crimes you have done. You worked against the fatherland and helped the ruling class. You owe much blood to good people who fought against GVN. Each one of you stand up and say your crimes."

He started with me because I wrote such a short history. I looked very sincere and said that I killed some VC, though I did not want to. That is not enough, he said, but I am to sit down and think of more while others confess.

When a guy gives a big confession, like how he was in an operation that burned a village, cadreman says that man is honest and others must think of things like that. So we all told things about combat. Okay, he said, but what we think is more important. We must tell how our thoughts helped American imperialists and GVN puppets.

When that is through, after all morning, we have thirty minutes for lunch. Just half a bowl of rice in water—swill is what Americans call it. Nobody was very hungry but we needed that rice for work in the afternoon. Near camp is a big old airfield. Concrete has many cracks, but it must be all broken up and taken away so we can grow vegetables for the cadre.

No hats or anything. For work we just have sharp sticks. Some of us were told to twist metal rods that stick out of the concrete. If we do that we can use the rods to break up the concrete easier. We were not strong enough to bend and twist steel that way. But six of us tried for a while, then another six. Cadre said other groups have broken rods and we must try harder or our group will be criticized. We worked like that all afternoon. Each six pushed and pulled on the steel rods, then went back to work with sticks. Not much concrete got moved. Cadre said we have bad spirit.

After thirty minutes for swill, same as lunch, cadreman told us to criticize our work on the airfield. One prisoner said very polite that we can do much better with pick or hoe. Maybe our group can make these tools. No, bad spirit. We are too soft from not being in working class. More spirit tomorrow. Now each of us must tell about bad spirit of others and himself.

We all do about the same, so we all said that we are too weak. Cadreman said we are a very bad group. Next morning they split us up, but no group was any better; nobody can work well with no tools. About a month later, cadre took a blowtorch and cut the rods. They gave each of us one and we used it on the concrete. Just kept hitting it with rods in fist like children do in games. Knuckles bleed but cadre says that is good for us.

That night we were very hungry because we worked so much.

I ate a little food I brought—the fish sauce because I need salt after so much sweat. In a couple of days, all the food we brought was gone. Cadre says, too bad, the fatherland does not have enough to give us more. We are parasites—they started calling us that—people who need charity from the government. To do better, we must work harder.

Now food was very important for us. The swill came in a big bucket. We must dish it out in each bowl. Every man watched very carefully that he got as much as the others. When we had arguments, the cadre just walked away. They wanted us to fight and be angry with each other.

After ten days, no one said anything about leaving. The guys who said we would get out were crying at night. Daytimes they bowed their heads and said nothing or cry to themself. One guy tried to kill himself but just made a lot of blood on his head. Cadre took him away.

People were taken away all the time. Nobody knew where. Maybe a couple of times each week we heard shots outside the perimeter. That could be executions. We don't know. Probably the cadre wanted us to think people are shot. Keeps us scared. But cadre also made us think some guys who were taken away are let go. That keeps our hope up—if we do what the cadre says, maybe we can go home.

All this time we must stay up late at night for lessons and confessions. First lesson was about our errors during the war. Always we have to talk about our errors in camp. This was called self-criticism. That is the last thing at night so we can think about it before we sleep.

Other lessons were about American and GVN crimes. Mostly we just had to listen. VC are smart to make us so hungry we cannot nap with eyes open. All around me I heard prisoners' stomachs make noise while we listen. I was so tired but cannot rest while I listen because I think of food all during lesson. At night in the dark, everybody dreamed about food. Once I woke up and heard all these teeth click like they have chopsticks in the mouth. It was the guys dreaming about eating.

I just let my mind go out of the camp, but VC knew that trick too. They asked us questions about lessons so we must listen so we can remember. One guy said the wrong thing about ARVN atrocity we are suppose to learn. Cadre said he was not paying attention so he got no swill next morning. He cried all night.

The weeks passed, and prisoners began to break in different ways:

Trang Long looked like big construction site when Americans built the port at Cam Ranh. But no big machines. Just guys beating at the ground. Many groups worked to dig up runway. Other groups worked outside the wire pulling up brush and stuff. No clouds till monsoon. Sun filled up the sky. Not much got done, but a lot of work for nothing.

At the other end of the airfield I heard shouts. Everybody looked up to see. Sweat was in my eyes and I cannot make them dry because my hands have lots of concrete dust on them. But I heard this prisoner far away. He shouted like he want everybody to hear. He said, "Okay! Shoot!" and he walked away from the guard. Guards jumped on him but he kept shouting. Before they get his hands together for hand cuffs, he dived at their knees. I can't believe he got away for a minute. He ran toward us, then he stops and turns and shout again, "Okay, shoot me!" VC get around him but he had a rock and he threw it very hard at guard. NCO came up and they all shoot like they been waiting for that order.

He goes down—lots of bullets hit him but some burst on concrete near us. I wasn't scared. I thought that guy was brave and lucky. Everybody rather be dead than here.

The Trang Long experience was being repeated elsewhere as an archipelago of bamboo gulags sprouted all over the country (some 200 camps by 1981). Trang Long was run by the PRG, but military governors of the NVA were free to set up their own systems of imprisonment so long as they did not attract foreign notice.

The official re-education policy was tacitly and infinitely broadened so that anyone was subject to indefinite detention. It took no more of a pretense than that the suspect was South Vietnamese. Eleven years under the GVN was reason *ipso facto* to assume that a person needed his mind purged. Ingeniously, the communists were able to display such indeterminate sentences as manifestations of liberal leniency. Thus, in response to inquiries by Amnesty International, the PRG replied:

> Re-education without judiciary condemnation [i.e., without trial] is an extremely humanitarian system which is very advantageous to the detainees, compared with the usual system of trial before a court. In Vietnamese psychology, the absence of judiciary condemnation spares the person concerned a tarnished record which may adversely influence his whole life and that of his children.

Slowly the captors were able to sift through their million captives, comparing autobiographies with external evidence, which was obtained mostly from informers.

After a few months, everybody got individual interrogations. Always they try to make you say more things about the past. They knew we will be prisoners for many years. They did not say that, but they know more records will come in because they keep making us write about ourself and others. I kept saying I do not remember more because then they cannot catch me if I say something different.

They said I have bad spirit because I cannot remember. Only way to be better is if I remember things about other prisoners. I said prisoners move around too fast. I do not know anybody for that reason. They did not like that answer either. They asked me names. Most I do not know. Some I knew from Twenty-first Division. I tried to help those guys and said they were bad soldiers, sometimes get in trouble because they were not good in operations.

Then the cadre tried something else. They rounded up officers from one division, like the Twenty-first, put us together, and made us read confessions. I looked around when I read mine. Some guys smiled like they knew I was lying.

When I'm finished, cadreman say, "Anyone like to help Cai remember more?"

Nobody said anything, but I think someone informed on me in private.

At first all prisoners around me were lieutenants and captains. Higher-ranking officers were in other camps. Then a few were brought into our camp. I don't know why. One of them was a famous airborne officer, Major Dan. He was a gangster when the French ran Vietnam. His sister married a French officer; with his good connection, Dan became a French officer too, then a major in ARVN. Thanks to his street gangster background, Dan was one of the bravest officers on the battlefield, and he had more medals than anyone else. According to his friend in prison, Dan liked to pin his highest medal on the skin of his breast and walk in the street while he was bleeding.

His friend was like his servant in prison. Dan could take anybody's food when he was hungry. If there was a complaint, he and his servant beat up the guy. Cadre just let that happen. Lucky for me I was not in his barrack.

We dug three wells inside the prison for 1000 POWs. All water was full of mud, but one well must be saved for cooking. Prisoners were always around the other two wells to wash. When Dan took a bath, he wanted no one around, and everyone had to leave.

But after a while another group of prisoners came to that camp. In this group was another big gangster, named Lieu. He was also a major in airborne. From his time as a gangster he was Dan's master. When Lieu took a bath at the well, Dan must scrub his back.

Cadre let things like that happen. Never stopped us when we fight or dominate. Cadre just watched, then a long time later moved some people around. They wanted to know who was strong and who was weak. They always tried to make us think they are on our side, that they want us to reform and leave.

They say, "We are military men like you. We understand about the war. We fought you because that was our job. You fought us because it was your job. Now our job is to teach you correct thoughts. Your job is to learn. We got nothing against you. It is the people who have sent you here. We just report to them. Please cooperate so we can tell the people you are ready to join them to build socialism."

Someone must have informed on me. I think the cadre took my background [autobiography] to some other prisoners and see if it was right.

I always said I don't know or cover for guys when VC read me their background. Somebody did not do that for me. Someone wanted extra food or easy work and traded that for denouncing me.

Chapter
Eighteen

I must roll up my mosquito net and leave it. That's what happen when guys are taken away. Other prisoners turned their eyes to look somewhere else. If I am denounced, no one wants to say they knew me.

The guard did not know why he was taking me away. The cadre was busy working on other individuals so nobody interrogated me for a long time.

Out where ARVN division motor pool used to be was a long row of conex containers [hollow metal cubes] from U.S. Army. One of the first things the cadre did when they open the camp was drill holes and run a pipe through the conexes. The guard locked my feet to that and put handcuffs on behind my back. The sun was on the conex all day. Hot as an oven, so I pass out in the heat. No hole for air except where light bulb hangs on wire. When generator starts at night that light came on. No way to sleep.

I did not know what day it is. Because I am not working, there was no food in the morning—my first swill was at night when the light goes on. Nothing for toilet. I knew other prisoners had been here because lice get in my hair. It itched so much I hit my head on the conex. When it was so hot, I heard myself breathe like a dog after running.

I begged for water, but the guard that brings swill never said anything.

Maybe after a week I got my first interrogation. I must stand at attention but my legs bend and I cannot help it because they were very weak. When that happen the guard pulled up my handcuffs in back till I scream. Then I must apologize for that.

Interrogator stayed behind his desk because I stink so much. He went over my background, but I memorized it so he can find nothing wrong. The guard poked me under the heart when the interrogator gave a signal. It made me gulp with pain. I learned later this is a karate blow—does not have to be hard to make great pain. I thought I will have heart attack if he keeps poking me. Each time it hurt deeper and made pain in my war wound too.

I got these pokes when I did not give long answers. The interrogator said, "Come on, Cai. We have your record now. We know everything you did." When I don't start confession, the guard's fingers strike into my heart.

I was moaning when he said, "Okay, just tell me about the Americans." I tried to think what I can say because the guard will not poke me while I talk. So I said lots of words I learned in my lessons about American crimes. Interrogator nods while I talk. I talked slower so I get more time between punishment. There were not so many pokes because I talked a lot. I think they just wanted me to talk about anything. They took me back to the conex. My heart was sore for many days, and the war wound swelled.

Some months later, Cai saw how hot those conexes were. He was close to a work party standing by the row of metal boxes. One of the prisoners felt a huge spider in his hair, probably one that had dropped on him while the work party was clearing jungle. The spider started to scurry for shade under the man's shirt. He screamed and swatted the spider away. It landed on the corrugated surface of the conex and started bouncing like a grasshopper until its legs smoked; then it died in a shriveled ball.

It was night. I didn't hear anything but the generator. I tried to bend my back over the handcuffs to find a way to sleep. I woke up quick when metal struck the conex. My sweat went out very fast—I felt it suddenly. The conex roared like a bell.

The guard was angry. I think someone woke him up to get me. It was about three a.m.—that is when interrogation is hardest on prisoner because everything in him is weak then. So I thought this must be important interrogation. All the time I wondered what they really want to find out from me.

The interrogation went like this:

"Your record arrived, Cai. You better tell us the truth now."

"Yes."

"Okay, tell me." The cadreman made ready to scrawl on his pad, an ever-present record of all interrogations.

"I was born in Hainan, China. I have two dates of birth—"

"No, about the Americans."

"I worked with Captain Slaughter [a name Cai invented], imperialist adviser, from April 1967 till—"

"You speak English much better than what you wrote in the confession."

"I learned a little in school. I learned more while I was lackey for Captain Slaughter."

"Better than that. You helped them with plans."

"Yes, I have written that." Cai was trying to imagine what might have been entered in his record, trying to anticipate what an informer could have said about him. His suspicion was that he had been denounced by some fellow officer from the Twenty-first Division. "It was a crime for me," he added abjectly.

"Yes. Where did you see American plans? Not just with Twenty-first Division, Cai."

"Nowhere else, sir."

"No, you were in TTH. How many years? Which American unit?" TTH was the Tri-Thien-Hue Military Region, the NVA jurisdiction that included much of I Corps, where the 101st operated during their last years in Vietnam.

"Never been there." Cai gulped. "Twenty-first Division was always in delta."

"No, you used words from TTH. Tell the truth now or your lies will be punished."

Cai's mind scrambled to recall some slang he may have picked up in I Corps. His denial cost him a tightening of his handcuffs.

"Only my brother served in ARVN I Corps!"

The interrogator leaned forward at the desk. "Who did not give up their arms?"

"Everyone I know surrendered."

"No. There are counterrevolutionaries. Did Captain Slaughter stay with them?" The NVA believed that 25,000 plainclothes American military men had remained in Vietnam.

"No, he went home."

"What plans did imperialist Slaughter tell you about U.S. infantry coming back to help counterrevolutionaries?"

"I know no plans."

"Where did the other lackeys hide their arms?"

"I don't know."

"Where was the best region for caches?"

"Do you ask me to guess?"

"Tell us or you will be punished."

"Hobo Forest." This was a mysterious region penetrated by the 101st during Operation Checkerboard in 1965. From the tightened handcuffs, Cai knew he would have to give the interrogator some location; the Hobo Forest seemed as good as any.

"When were you there?"

"I go near the forest on leave from Twenty-first Division."

"Was Captain Slaughter with you?"

"No, sir."

"What did the Americans tell you about Hobo Forest?"

"Nothing. I just guess that is a good place to hide things."

"When are the Americans coming back?"

"I do not think they will come back."

"You speak English so they will contact you. How would they do this? Be truthful. You can not be reformed until you tell the complete truth about American plans." The guard emphasized the point with a wrench on the handcuffs.

"They never come back!" he cried, expressing two forms of pain.

The interrogation about suspected American plans lasted until morning. More prisoners had been condemned to the conex, and Cai was to remain isolated.

They took me blindfolded. I think it was a little way from camp because this new place was an old jail built by the French. Very tiny cell—walls so close my shoulders touched them—it was like sitting in a file cabinet. Thick walls, so nothing to hear from the other cells. They locked both my legs to a big log. During my time there I cannot tell day or night because a bare light bulb shined twenty-four hours.

I learned to tell time by bells the guards used. First bell means morning swill is coming. Second bell was for evening swill. My stomach had pain all the time from hunger, but then a new pain started in my intestines. I had a can for toilet but used it only a couple of times a week. Rice just got hard in my stomach. I can feel it with my fingers, a hard thing like a dry sausage. I thought it must be from sitting week after week, and not having water.

I tried to not think too much. Turned away from thoughts. They were the same worries over and over again about how I can ever be free, and how is my family. These things I can do nothing about while I am so weak, so I stopped worrying about them. But I worried about things that are happening to my body. There is a terrible rash where pants have rotted away. My hands shake when I go to touch it. If I tried to scratch the itch I must dig deep and rub till the skin was raw, then the new pain is better than itch, but the next time itching came back stronger. Crabs lice were on me too. Everything got worse when the cell heats up in daytime. It was a funny thing: I hated the French more for building this cell, hated them even more than the communists who put me in it.

Not so many interrogations. I guess the communists were not so worried anymore that Americans come back to kick out PRG. Because I was by myself, no re-education classes. Only one more time do I have to write long confessions, all about old stuff that I already told them. When I finish, the interrogator looked like he's satisfied. He smiled and said, "This is enough to keep you here for twenty years."

Stung by some critical foreign reaction to their re-education system, the PRG had begun to use the prisoners' forced confessions as the retroactive basis for long sentences. When asked why prisoners were originally told to bring only thirty days of personal supplies to the camps, the PRG president, Huynh Tan Phat, replied blithely, "We never said the term would be limited to thirty days. All we said was that they should report with thirty days worth of food and clothing."

They left me alone for a while—I think many months—then interrogations started again. This time they want to know about my family, everybody back to great-grandparents. I didn't know what this was for, but then they asked many questions about what every one of my relatives own.

They want to know even how many cameras my father had in his business, how many ducks he killed for his restaurant. The cadreman wrote all this stuff down like I am reporting as my father's accountant. I almost laughed and said, I have not seen my family for a year so I don't know what they got anymore. Cadreman said that does not matter.

He had one more question. I didn't know what the right answer should be. He asked, "Do you believe Americans went to the moon?"

I said I saw pictures of that. He said they were false. Americans were never on the moon because the Russians were not there yet.

My last confession made my background about twenty pages. I had so much practice I can remember it all. Every interrogator tried new tricks and punishment to get more information. But everything in my story fit because I had so much time in the cell to go over it in my head. That was the only good thing about my future: if they let me back into the camp I will just be another prisoner with no special attention.

Then sometimes I sobbed to myself, that I am forgotten, even by the communists. They had put me alone for a year and can just leave me here in the tiny cell till I die. I often hoped that I die soon, like that guy who told the guards to shoot him. These thoughts controlled me like fever that comes and goes. Never knew when they come; I just started shaking and sobbing, but no reason. Best way to keep myself together was to know that the communists wanted me to suffer and know all the ways how. Just like beating and starving, they know what it is like for me and want it to happen. When I told myself that, it helped me believe I was not forgotten.

Cai's experience was part of the PRG's nationwide program and pogrom. Suffering was indeed the intended objective of re-education. Whether the prisoner suffered communally or in isolation was a judgment by the prison cadre as to the fastest, most efficient route to total control. Their process was like AIDS, overcoming a person's resistance in manifold ways. The NVA journal (People's Army Publication, June 1975) described what needed to be done:

Re-education is a meticulous and long-range process. Management must be tight, continuous, comprehensive, and specific. We must manage each person. We must manage their thoughts and actions, words and deeds, philosophy of life and ways of livelihood, as well as social relationships. We must closely combine management and education with interrogation and punishment of every degree.

After a year of being chained in the cell, they cannot get anything else from me so they sent me out for hard labor. First I had to confess that I was a parasite and promise to make up for it with extra hard work.

To tell the truth I was plenty scared in the middle of the night when they dragged me out of that cell and threw me in a big truck. There were about thirty POWs with me. We cannot see anything because the door was locked. We talked in the dark. Some said the VC take us away for execution. I was so miserable I don't care. One guy was crazy from prison and said we should be happy because now we go home.

It took a long drive to get to the new camp. When we got out I think I'd seen this place before. It was in Tay Ninh Province. I think maybe the 101st was around here during Operation Junction City.

It was a big camp called Catum. About 10,000 prisoners. Barracks same as Trang Long but everything was more rundown because PRG never cared about maintenance. Only thing new was more towers and barbed wire. Prisoners put that up. I have now seen pictures of concentration camps from World War II. Catum looked like that. I think all re-education camps should be called concentration camps because that is what they are.

When I was first put in prison, we must wear uniforms like American POWs in Hanoi Hilton—gray material with wide red stripes up and down. "Dangerous" prisoners had shaved heads so guards can see them easy. Those first uniforms wore out. At Catum there was nothing to wear but sandbags. We pulled them apart and shaped them like the body; put back together with strings. In the rain and sweat they fell apart, and all the time they rub the skin. One man wore his wife's underwear for this.

Guards never went in this camp except if there is trouble. Only cadre in there. Guards patrolled outside the wire and checked the moat. This is a very good security system. Guards just watch the water. If it is moving, they know someone has gotten through the wire.

Each barrack had about forty-five prisoners, fifteen groups of three with leader for each group. VC called these leaders "progressives." That means they had good brainwashing. We called them "point men" because they point to other prisoners for denouncing. Because of my year in solitary, I was way behind in re-education, and my leader told me I must catch up so his group will not be criticized.

There was another guy like me. He was crazy from his solitary—yell and scream all the time, and talked to his father, who was dead. Made people scared of him because he is insane.

He was very weak and stumbled a lot, but people still scared of him because of his eyes, and what he said so loud is like he was not in this life anymore.

There was an ARVN doctor in our barrack. He told cadre that he can help this insane man. Doctor thought there is a cheap medicine that can help but he is not allowed to. This man should be in hospital but cadre kept him around us, for example I think.

We all sleep on the ground. When Catum opened, there was a wooden floor but it was torn up to make something for the cadre, so we were down on the dirt and broken concrete. Cadre woke us at 5:00 a.m. six days a week. One hour for singing songs and exercises. We did them like very old men. No breakfast in Catum because food must go to prisoners rebuilding factories. We were told our prisoner leaders volunteered to donate this food for socialism.

By this time in 1976, Hanoi had dissolved the PRG, and the north and south had "reunified" into the Socialist Republic of Vietnam (SRV). The VC were shoved out of the new government, and many ended in prison identified as "dangerous elements."

First thing in morning there was a short lecture that say how good labor is for us. Each day a different prisoner has to say something like that. Then we went out and did it. One half hour break at midday. Pot of swill is brought for forty-five men. We must be very fast to get it out into our little bowls. This was hard, and there were fights because everyone is so hungry. Guards let us fight. It was policy to divide us. They also said we must learn how valuable food is for working people. I just think they liked to see former officers fight with each other.

For labor, usually groups were assigned duty one night before. Some cut trees with old ARVN bayonets, not sharp at all. We sort of beat trees to death. Nobody knew why trees are cut. I think it was just to clear ground and make escape hard. Some groups moved huge rocks, then tried to knock them smaller. Any working tools must be made by individual. Best we can do is to tie long sticks with vines and try to sharpen them. Worst job was clearing old minefields.

Mine clearing is a practice expressly forbidden by the Geneva Convention, the universally accepted standard of humane treatment for POWs. The SRV had three excuses for ignoring it: first, as a newly declared nation, they were not signatories to the Geneva Convention; second, mine clearing was not being performed by POWs but rather "volunteers," and third, the volunteers may have planted the mines in the first place so they were responsible for removing them. This last excuse assumed that all prisoners were former military men, whereas many were women, clerks, and other types of noncombatants including doctors, nurses, and Red Cross workers.

Guards gave us metal rods, put us in a line, then stood far away.

Accidents happen because a prisoner was so scared when his rod touches a mine he did not know what to do. Others were not allowed to help him. We must keep crawling forward and search for more mines or our group did not get enough for quota.

Thing to do is take rod out and brush dirt away till you can see the top of the mine. Not many booby trapped, but it is a good idea to feel under the mine for wire. I knew U.S. mines, how to put the cap in safe position. Most prisoners did not know. Guards just told them to lift mine and carry it to edge of the jungle. Guys shook so much when they lift them. Every day prisoners were killed like that when they do not handle mines right. Always the explosion injured prisoners around him too. Not even bandages for wounds. Only thing to do is pack dust in wound. They tried to stop blood by pressing the wound but when they got weak, their hands let go. The rows just kept going. We pretend not to hear the wounded men cry in their pain. At first we went to help, but one man got bayoneted for that.

At 5:00 p.m., time for second swill bowl. Never any meat at all. Guards ate peanuts all day long but we did not get any.

From six till midnight everyone must present himself in front of his barrack group to say what he did during the day. We hate the "progressives" at these times because they decide if each group did enough. They decided if a group must do extra work on Sunday, which is our one day off. Cadre gave leaders quotas—so many trees or rocks in one week—so leaders must do the quotas or lose their favors like a few peanuts. Leaders pretend we made the decisions for extra work ourselves because we must all vote for leaders' recommendations. Only one time I saw a POW not vote. He was taken away.

Criticism and self-criticism were not just about labor but also about what we said to each other. Sometimes we were with POWs from other barracks so our stories can be checked. A man can make points with cadre if he said something the man he talked to did not report. If there is difference in the stories, both men must meet with cadre and write about the incident. I got in serious trouble one time like that and lost half of my food ration for four days.

I knew from assignment the night before that our group is to clear mines. I wanted everyone in the row to know what to do so nobody gets hurt. At morning bowl I told a few guys around me how to disarm the mine we find most often. Three guys thanked me, but one did not say anything. That day, no explosions on my row. That night at criticism, the guy who did not answer stood up and denounced me for wrong thoughts. Everybody hated him already. He was biggest coward in the barrack.

Cadre likes what he said. They asked him to tell how my thoughts were wrong. He said I want to do things different from socialism. Cadreman said that's right—the best way is how we were told to pick up mines and take them to jungle. This cadreman said I try to change things for "individualism."

I was told to criticize myself, and I must be coward too because I asked for leniency and said that I just tried to protect socialist manpower. The barrack must vote if I should accept the correction the cadre asked for. Everyone raised their hands and said yes, even me. So I got half food ration for four days.

That made me very weak because a full ration is two small bowls of swill. Now I had just one, less than a coffee cup, mostly warm water. When my group went out to level ground for plant-

ing, I was behind from weakness. Every group tried to do better than the others; every man tried to work faster than man beside him, because they want the cadre to recommend them to go home. To tell the truth, cadre did not know who will be sent home. Maybe 100 guys out of 5000 were released about every six months. I find out later the names got picked in Hanoi, maybe like a lottery. Really didn't matter how hard you work, but prisoners don't know that.

I got behind. The guard came over and said go over to the shit detail. This is the worst job in the camp. Every day fifty-five-gallon drums of prisoners' shit must be spread on the ground where vegetables will grow for cadre. This was the nastiest job but dangerous too because of infection. There were prisoners who died the same day they get shit in cuts. I showed the guard a cut on my hand. He told me to go anyway. He chambered a round like he's ready to shoot me, and told me to kneel.

Good thing a cadreman came out. He heard the guard shout at me. The cadreman ordered me to go back and write self-criticism. I must also go to shit drum and stir it for spreading. My clothes stunk for a long time.

Funny thing happen a couple of months later. I was on a row with this point man who denounced me. He touched a mine and gets real scared. He keeps looking at his hand and at me. It is against the rules but I looked over at what he found. Then I got scared too because it is a "bouncing betty" mine, most dangerous kind that jumps up before it explodes. Frags go in big circle like air burst. If this guy set it off, it gets a lot of us, maybe the guard too.

So I respectfully asked the guard for permission to help my comrade. He said okay. I crawled over and told this guy he is on a mine that is like a grenade. I said he has five seconds after he lifts mine to throw it in the jungle or it gets him. I told him the quickest way is for him to throw it to me. I can get halfway to the jungle and will throw it the rest of the way.

The guard lets the other guys move away because this is such a dangerous mine.

I went halfway to the jungle and called, "Okay, friend, I'm ready." He was still very scared and I had to urge him more, *but he just sat there shaking. After a couple of minutes, our group leader said we must get back to work so this point man should hurry and throw the mine.*

He did not want to be denounced. Real quick he picked up the mine and falls to the ground when he throws it. It blew him up so bad we can not even use his clothes.

That night I criticized myself for not knowing the kind of mine he found. Some guys laughed, but the cadreman did not punish them.

While Cai was in solitary confinement, the SRV found it necessary to create a showcase camp (Hay Tay) for guided tours by selected western journalists. This is what Tiziano Terzani saw:

The detention cells are clean; flowers bloom in the garden; the food is excellent; the guards smile. . . . In a classroom, a prisoners' orchestra plays a waltz. Twenty-four former generals, colonels, and judges of the Supreme Court under the Thieu regime rise up and applaud when the camp commander examines them in turn and explains that one or the other man has made great progress but that, alas, there are still inmates who have not yet written a full and frank report on their misdeeds.

Cai's camps were in an intermediate band between the SRV's facade for the press and the ghoulish sites for wholesale revenge, where the death rate purged the prison population almost annually. Where the Nazis had considered mass extermination as an exercise in efficiency (e.g., gas chamber processing), the SRV's gulag seemed modeled on Stalin's Siberian policy of death by indifference.

That way the stain of a bloodbath was faded, and attrition was attributed to natural hardships. After all, the SRV was a poor country struggling up from the ashes of high-tech destruction. Life was hard for all—Ho Chi Minh had said it would be until pure communism reigned—so no one should be surprised if soft imperialist lackeys succumbed to Spartan conditions.

Where Stalin let the arctic do his work, the SRV relied on the jungle, and starvation was the common instrument. Disease, the handmaid of starvation, offered a host of allies. Outlying camps (more than a hundred) seemed selected for their unhealthy environments. Bu Gia Map, for example, where the Oh-deuce had lost more men to malaria than to the NVA, became an infamous camp. Prisoners shivered in the monsoon and were allowed neither blankets nor mosquito nets. In constructing their camp, they were digging their own graves.

With nothing but their hands, they were first forced to clear jungle and plant the posts for barbed wire. Once these fences were erected, they were allowed to raise bamboo huts on floors that alternated seasonally between dust and mud. According to Amnesty International, their diet deteriorated from even two small bowls of rice per day. Soon they were given only locally grown root crops like starchy manioc. The total amount of food for each prisoner was about 200 to 300 grams (approximately 8 ounces; i.e., two-thirds of a beer can) per day—much of it spoiled. There is virtually no protein except on rare occasions such as Ho Chi Minh's birthday when the diet is supplemented by a few tiny morsels of meat.

The sickest prisoner I ever saw came from Bu Gia Map. He was not in my camp long because he died. But he was very good at catching lizards and crickets when we went out to clear jungle. He said that was the only way they lived at Bu Gia Map. One night during lectures, a big moth flew into the barrack because light is on so late. This guy sneaked around till he caught it. I saw him put it right in his mouth and it made a crunch sound.

I learned about eating wild things from him. Food like that was not allowed because the cadre said we had enough already, and if we try to get more it shows we are not grateful to the SRV. But this guy from Bu Gia Map did not care about criticism because he was so low in life he knew he will soon die.

He told me what to do with rats, worms, snakes—also poisonous kind—grasshoppers and crickets. If you can make a little fire, all these things can be eaten. If no fire, you may get sick the first time but it still good for a starving body to eat these things.

I think he died with malaria because he was shivering and yellow. He said that was why they sent him down from Bu Gia

Map. Guards there were afraid he can cough that sickness at them. But I think they sent him to die in Catum to show us there is a worse camp if we didn't like it here.

I almost made a mistake when I talked to him. I asked him something about Bu Gia Map because Oh-deuce won a big battle there. I should not say I was there—Twenty-first Division never in that area—but this guy did not say anything to cadre about me. He didn't care about them anymore. He just wanted to hurry up and die.

Few have escaped to tell about conditions at Bu Gia Map or camps like it, which were overtly devoted to extermination, and sprinkled through the wilderness. The handful of visitors have been from communist countries, and even they have not been able to observe realities. The Red Cross and Amnesty International have been turned away completely. There has been only one published first-hand account, that of Nguyen Cong Hoan, a one-time legislator in the SRV who fled the country in 1977:

Taking advantage of my position as a congressman and also of my acquaintance with Lieutenant Colonel Xuan, a camp commander, I asked permission to visit his camp. However, I was allowed to come and observe only some showcase areas and to make contact with just a few prisoners who, I know for sure, were not so stupid as to tell me the truth about their prison—that is, if they did not want to die.

The party leaders themselves have told me that they are very proud of their talent for deceiving world opinion. "We've been worse than Pol Pot," they joke, "but the outside world knows nothing."

Chapter
Nineteen

We wondered why the cadre is smiling. At morning songs they sang real loud, like church people in U.S.—born again people. Then there was an announcement before we went to labor: we will be allowed to receive a gift from home. We looked at each other, eyes asking if this is true and what it means.

Progressives are given first chance to write to their relatives. They can ask for food. Guys who are group leaders can get one kilo [2.2 lbs]. Cadremen went around to each barrack to tell that news. SRV is giving us too much kindness, he said—some prisoners don't deserve it. He is angry that we drag ass during labor. We must have new spirit to show we appreciate what SRV is giving us.

What are they giving us? I asked myself—nothing but permission to beg food from our relatives. A package is wonderful even if it is small, but I was more glad that I can inform my family where I am. For eighteen months I have disappeared.

Right away I thought about escape. As soon as family knows I'm here there is a chance I think, but I didn't know how.

Progressives got their packages but keep everything for themselves. We went up to them and said, "We thought you like communism a lot. How about sharing with the people?" They walked away. Only one guy answered back. He said, "I must keep my food so I can be stronger to lead others on the right path."

I saw these packages that had some dried fish, so when I am allowed to write to my wife I ask for fish, salt, and sugar. Cadre says to put a special number on the letter. That is the camp address. They looked at the letters carefully to make sure we do not complain about the camp.

One secret we have from them is yoga. I don't know who first did it, but the word got around. At night we tried to escape from hunger with yoga. We don't do it with our bodies but in the mind. Best thing is to lie on your back for good concentration. For us, yoga was all in the mind; no body movement like in the States. Stomach can talk, but that can be forgotten if concentration is good. Yoga is the best time we had in prison.

A couple of weeks later a brown paper package arrived from my wife. It was opened and the fish was taken out. I think the reason cadre let us write for food is so they can get some for themselves. I remembered this so if we can get more packages I just ask for things the cadre has already.

In a couple of more months, we were told our family can visit us if we show good spirit. We must write thanks to our camp commander for being so nice to us and promise to work extra hard for SRV.

To tell the truth, I worried very much before my wife and children came. I was afraid they will think I am dying. If they think that, maybe I do.

From the way his pants bagged at the waist, his shirt hung on him like a scarecrow, and the skeletal appearance of his fellow prisoners, Cai knew he was emaciated. Later he was able to confirm that his weight had dropped from about 150 pounds to below 100. What there was left of him was "rice fat," a puffiness caused by a solely starch diet. His hair had coppered, his teeth were loose in their gums.

The time came but I don't want to go out in front of my family. There was a little room, only big as a bus, with many families coming for a visit. Little groups squat with each prisoner. We talked soft because guard is there walking up and down.

I see my wife and little children. They looked like it is hard to tell if it is me. My baby girls did not want to touch me, and my boy was shy like he did not remember me good. I cannot say a word, not even hello, but start weeping and cannot stop.

Visits to prisoners in Cai's camp were genteel compared to those with which Legislator Nguyen Cong Hoan became familiar—at camps like Bu Gia Map:

During the New Year holiday (Tet) I came to visit a cousin at Ngan Dien Camp. I personally witnessed a scene in which an old mother who had brought a bottle of fish sauce for her son was viciously insulted before everyone and then denied permission to see him. The old woman went down on her knees, but her plea was ignored. When the prisoners were allowed to line up to receive their packages, the cadre loudly asked them, "Do you need fish sauce here?" All the prisoners shouted back, "No, we have quite enough fish sauce here!" The truth was that far from having any fish sauce, they didn't even have salt.

Other camps in Hoan's district were so deep in the jungle that visitors had to stay overnight. They were restricted to a hut divided into cubicles.

During the night, prisoners who had been informants for the camp authorities were given official permission to force themselves on the women visitors sleeping in the hut. This privilege, the camp cadre made known, was a reward for progress in re-education.

There was a lesson from these visits for the family as well as for the prisoner: the conditions they glimpsed were an immediate reminder of what could await them if they were tempted to join the resistance that was beginning to emerge in mid-1977.

This first visit with families made everyone more lonely. Right after that Lieutenant Nghia tried his escape. Don't know how he did it, but he got an NVA uniform. Maybe his family bribed someone so they could bring it to him that first visit, or maybe he received gold sewn in the string of his package, and he bribed a guard himself. I wish I knew because I thought all the time about how I could do something like that. I found out what he did later:

When night time came he threw the NVA uniform across the moat. He cut the wire like a sapper—must have studied it for a long time. Then he got in the water really slow and careful so waves go away. Nghia swam under water to the other side—breathed through a straw to come up slow. He waited a long time to get out so the water never moves much. Then he put on NVA uniform. He was on the road but must go by gate guard.

The guard challenged Nghia. He did not know the password. First thing we heard is a grenade when he blew the guard away. Next morning he was caught after five miles of running.

For execution, three prisoners from each barrack must come and watch. Guards tied Nghia up and blindfolded him. Cadre made big speech about how he must be an American spy. Cadre was asking us about rumor that U.S. would come back with sea invasion like they did in Korea. They said Nghia was a U.S. agent who was going down to the coast to signal them.

We think he did a great job but at the end he begged not to be shot. That's too bad because he was our hero till then. We still named the road he escaped on "Nghia Road" so prisoners will remember a brave try.

The communists are smart. They knew that to see our family made us more lonely and sad. A long time later I found out another big reason for visits and packages. Top guys in SRV wanted to know which prisoners belong to rich families. They knew something from the backgrounds we wrote but visits show that family is interested in their prisoner and maybe how rich they are too.

One or two times, prisoners get released. Very sick ones with disease like cholera that the cadre can catch are let go, and on communist holidays SRV made big thing called "amnesty and clemency," but that's only for progressives.

Releases are done so high guys in SRV government can have a game to make money. Before communist holidays, they went around to rich families and say, "I try to get your boy out but can't be sure. So I don't charge you anything if he is not released. But if he comes home, you pay me five leaves of gold." Families are very glad to agree.

When amnesty list comes out, SRV guy checked it and went to the families and got paid—but he did not do anything to get the prisoner released.

I think it was 1977. We still did labor on the same things. It was dry again after big monsoon. When it rained, we were sent into rice fields far away. We must pull plows with ten men, five on each side. We took off clothes in early morning and tied rags around us like Montagnards. Water buffalos watch us do their work. Long rows must be kept straight for planting, but we staggered too much, and one side pulled more than the other. Every two hours five new men replaced. This was hardest work of all—from five a.m. to five p.m., with just two little bowls of rice swill. I was so tired, every place I step I thought my feet will not come back out of the mud. My nose was wet all the time. At night my body was too tired to sleep.

So we were very glad the dry season is back. I was moved to another barrack with all new people because too many men in my group were sick from overwork. Disease got them then, and cadre must keep men like me from getting it or else we will not be able to do more work. Also, it was policy for prisoners to move like that all the time so nobody can make friends. Everyone can be a cadre informer. Nobody knows who, and there was no trust.

In my new group, we were clearing mines again. On the other side of camp, about a mile away, we heard a big boom. I looked up. First I thought someone had set off a mine, but the sound was like what I heard at Camp Eagle at start of Tet offensive. It is a 122-mm rocket! We all looked around. Boom-crash many more times. Dirt flying up near the cadre buildings. The 122's stop, but far away we heard artillery and infantry weapons.

Cadre plenty scared and ran around like panic. This was a

good time to escape but I am too weak. I think a couple of guys did get away that time. Guards were very angry, and some prisoners were punished for nothing.

We were brought back to the barrack and did not have to work for the rest of the day. Some guys I almost trust. We sat together away from progressives and decided what we will say if they report us. Then we asked each other what the firing can be. Someone said it was the Khmer Rouge. That is possible because Cambodia is so close. Someone else said it is Americans coming back; it could also be ex-ARVN who were hiding in the mountains.

This is the first I heard about ARVN. I found out it is true some are out there. I decided I must try to join them. I didn't like ARVN much before but now they are like the greatest people in the world for me.

In the military-political kaleidoscope that churned Indochina after the fall of South Vietnam, unlikely allies and opponents fought in a vicious round robin. Laos was a cockpit, but could not compare to the cauldron on the Vietnamese-Cambodian border near Cai's camp at Catum. To the north, a Montagnard irredenta resisted the SRV as it had the GVN. Formerly armed and trained by U.S. Special Forces, these hill tribesmen replaced the VC as the new guerrillas of South Vietnam.

The NVA was too preoccupied to do much about them. Unbelievably, the SRV's erstwhile communist allies, the Khmer Rouge, began slashing across the border, massacring in Vietnam as if they had run out of victims among their fellow Cambodians. Within two years the SRV would use Pol Pot's madness as the excuse to counterinvade Cambodia and overrun it, treating the world to a clash of evils not seen since Hitler double-crossed Stalin. But in 1977 the NVA was bent upon extermination of ARVN die-hards whose strength and intentions are still a mystery in the west.

Nobody knew anything, but there were many rumors. We started talking about how there must be plenty of ammo and weapons left over from the war. Most prisoners thought that some rangers, marines, and airborne troops maybe stayed together and did not surrender. They were smart because SRV had special camps for these units and almost all died who are in special camps.

Prisoners who served in ARVN around Loc Ninh got interrogated again, so we thought this was where ex-ARVN is strongest. That area is near Cambodia too, so this could be how ARVN and Khmer Rouge got together. When they attacked around Catum, this was the best news we ever had. I don't think they tried to liberate the camp, only just a raid. It really shook up the NVA. The cadre said: "We were not worried about that little raid. Why should we? We have defeated the strongest nations in the world—France, Japan, U.S. There is no worry from little groups of bandits. We get them. We got plenty of time."

That's what they said, but they were plenty worried. They sent lots of prisoners to camps far from the border. I am one of the first they moved.

No one ever knew where they are to be moved. In the truck I can tell it is east, and I was glad because that will be closer to home. I peeked out the back and saw things that I knew. We went a little north of Saigon. I saw fences and gates from my past, then a big airfield but most buildings around it are destroyed. Doors hang sideways and inside was dark and empty.

There is a big fence, miles long, a very big base. I knew where it is—Bien Hoa. I was here in 1965. The more I see, the more is remembered. We went toward barracks near the end of the airfield. The old USAF officers club is still there. Laundry is hanging from it. Cadre made it their headquarters. Then there are barracks I knew and the mess hall. This was where the Oh-deuce came from Phan Rang for first operation in III Corps— Checkerboard. It was here I first went to look for Lena, my dearest sweetheart.

NVA told us to get off the truck and go to the barrack. But I cannot move and tears are in my mouth. My new prison is the same building where I lived with the Oh-deuce. I thought of Lieutenant Johnson, who gave me a pass to go look for Lena.

My mind was so crazy from surprise memories, I thought he will come out and greet me and say the Oh-deuce is back. But then I knew how cruel that thought is, and that I am still a prisoner, and one who can not live much longer.

Other prisoners saw how sad I am. I was trembling like with malaria. I hope that is what NVA thinks because they may suspect me. Over the floor I put up my mosquito net ten feet from where my bunk was twelve years ago. It is the saddest day I had in prison. I thought my luck must be very bad to have this happen to me, and this is special punishment. Everyone I knew from that time was enjoying freedom, but I had come back to die like a slave.

This bitter irony at least remained Cai's secret. Fate had returned him to Bien Hoa, but the cadre's reason was probably his demonstrated proficiency in removing mines. The Americans had ringed the airbase with deep and elaborate minefields. Cai found himself on the row with other ARVN infantry veterans who, if anyone, could survive ten hours a day hunched over an iron prod.

Prisoners called this camp Suoi Mau. This name means "stream of blood." In Tet 68, U.S. troops surrounded an NVA battalion here. NVA counterattacked across this stream, but all were killed. For many days their blood mixed in the stream. We liked the secret name because we hate the NVA so much.

We were much better mine clearers than the rows at Catum, but every day there was at least one explosion around the camp. Guys are too weak, cannot concentrate because of poor food and so much heat.

No progressives here. No point men, no competition to work hardest. Everyone knew competition was just another communist trick to control and divide us. Some guys went to sleep while they listen to lectures at night. Cadre told them to stand up, but then they fall over. This stops lectures too much, so cadre did not say anything about sleeping if guys do not snore. I think even cadre got tired of lectures—same ones for about three years.

Only thing new was movie called 55 Days about how the NVA won the 1975 invasion.

Prisoners pretty sure they will be here till they die. Life was very hard so they think it is better to end it soon. No more hope from America, not much hope in ARVN guerrillas, and communists have lied about letting us go. Guys decided to try escape or let mine blow them up.

Two men made up their mind that this is the best way. One was ready to die. The other will take a chance, and if he dies, okay. They tried to work every day around same area of the fence where the minefield is not so wide and jungle comes close by. It takes maybe a month but they were able to find where barbed wire is loose. They knew things that sappers do, like holding wire back with thread, and they used stiff grass to saw at a piece of wire till it will break easy.

This took a very long time. They were able to use grass on wire for maybe a few seconds each day. When cadre found out what they did, they were the most mad I ever saw, but we were very proud.

Each row these two men work, they remembered how the mines were laid. They tried to understand what Americans were thinking when they laid the mines. I didn't know they are trying for escape, but they asked me like it was not important if I knew anything about how Americans make minefields. At first I did not answer, but after I think about it I believe they are not informers. I trust them in my heart because they are tough and did not take more than their share of swill. I also thought that maybe they are thinking about escape, and their victory can be like one for me.

So I told one of the men what I know, but it is not good news. Americans tried to make every row different, so the enemy cannot learn how to take them out. That made it hard but it is also true, I told him, that the same number of mines go in every field. He asked does that mean if he takes out so many mines of one kind, there are not any left? I thought that is about true. There are maybe three or four different types, more one kind, less another kind, with total for each field about the same. I don't think this information helped him much but they went ahead.

They chose a very rainy night in a big monsoon storm. It was easy to get out of the barrack. Guards were only at posts at corners of the fence. The two men went in a straight line to the place where they had worked on the wire. They were far from the fence corners, and rain was so heavy they cannot be seen.

We do not know they had gone. Nobody noticed because if he saw their empty mosquito nets it can be that these two guys just went to crap in the can. And everybody was so tired at night, nobody stayed awake.

The two walked so the man who was ready to die went first, the other a little way behind him. We saw their footprints in the morning. I looked very close when I go by. The mud showed how they feel for mines with their toes. Their line was very straight, like with a compass, so they met fewest mines.

They got to the first fence and through the wire where they had worked. That was a big surprise when we saw that. But the last fence is double wire, one fence in front of the other, and the first man did not make it. He got his foot blown off—I think M28 mine. Then the second guy must crawl from him and find mines like we did every day. He made it to the double fence and put much blood on it but he got through, so he is at the edge of jungle and can get away.

I do not know why but he stopped and waited for the other man. That man was dying back in the minefield but he waited for him like he is coming, but that man was ready to die anyway so it does not make sense. For the rest of the time I am at Suoi Mau I cry when I see that place in the fence where the man got through and was free to escape.

But morning came and he is still there. Because of rain and thunder, I don't think guards heard the mine go off, but they saw this prisoner sitting outside the fence. When he called to the dead man, guards started shooting. One bullet hit him, then cadre went out and killed him with bayonets.

His body was brought back and must stay with us while it rots. For the other man, we must clear mines to get him. We can see how he lay there after his foot was blown off. He threw a lot of mud at the fence till there was a big scoop in the ground.

I am sure he did this to get the other man to leave him. It was much worse that one could not escape—that was the good plan—but I think they loved each other so much they cannot separate.

During this time we got the cadreman Ai. He was very dedicated communist, more than any of the others, who are stupid kids. Except for Ai, the guards and cadre were the worst soldiers in the NVA. That was different from the first camp, where they used their best people to break us. After two, three years I don't think they cared what happens to us. They just wanted to work and starve us to death.

That was why we didn't have hope anymore. Before they really tried to brainwash us. Now they just let us die. For mine wounds they just told us to put dirt on it to stop the bleeding. If a man was too weak to work, they beat him harder every day till he died. Guys die from disease with no treatment, not even aspirin. Guys die from just hunger. For something like not standing at attention when cadre calls, punishment is half ration for one day. That is enough to kill some very weak men, just that little bit of rice they don't get for one day made it so they never survive.

Ai worked very hard to make us work harder. It was like he wants every one of us to be communist like him. After the escape attempt he lectured us very sternly. I hated this man but I respect him too. I think that he must be like Ho Chi Minh, a man who believed so strong that he can get a few men to believe like him, and only this few can make victory in revolution. It is too bad the GVN did not have some people like him. If the ARVN officers knew what the country is like after SRV takeover, I think they might be dedicated like Ai.

After escape attempt, he said to me, "Why do you think those parasites killed themselves?" I said I don't know because I will not say what I feel.

"They did not have to escape," Ai said. "We did not want them here. You either. We want to release you. You are a drain to the SRV here. The people have to feed you. You are doing nothing for the country. You are a parasite.

"*You can leave tomorrow. We are trying to push you out but you are so stubborn. Do you want to stay here in the minefields, Cai, or do you want to go out and contribute to the fatherland? It's up to you. Just show us that you are sincerely a good citizen. That's all. Show us you have reformed. Show us by criticism and self-criticism. I will listen to you any time. Work a little harder. Raise your quota. You can be group leader if you are sincere in what you say and do.*"

One man, named Lung, was a prisoner who believed Ai. I am surprised that he is not at a special camp because he was very important man in GVN, the number-one political interrogator for Saigon police. His job was to interrogate the highest communist defectors and captured agents. One man he questioned was Huynh Van Trong, President Thieu's national security adviser, who betrayed operation Lam Son 719.

Lung was such an important guy in GVN that he shot himself when Saigon fell. He used a .25 caliber pistol that just made a scar in his head. I joked with him that he should have got a .45 caliber from U.S. attaché.

Three years after his re-education begins, Lung still wrote every day about his interrogations for GVN. Cadre treated him with respect because he gave them more and more information. He had many talks with Ai that he did not tell us about. Lung liked to talk very much, and sometimes I talked with him. He had many stories about important communists who were double agents for GVN. Once he told me about a big honcho in SRV who worked secretly for GVN.

I did not think that is good information for me to know. This person became very powerful. She will not want anyone to know she was double agent. Pretty soon, I thought, she will find out about what Lung knows and get rid of him. He will be interrogated and made to say who he told. If he said he told me, then she will get rid of me too.

I got very worried about this. I was pretty sure that when Lung does not have any more information he will be taken away to be killed.

Lung was very lonely, but I cannot speak with him again because I did not want to hear any more things about important

communists. I cannot tell him my reason for not listening to him.
I hope he understands my difficulty.

One day he said to me, "I am afraid that when I stop writing
I will stop living. I will only leave this place when they take me
away."

That's what happen, I think. He had too much information
about important people in SRV. One day Lung was gone and
nobody sees him again.

Many were the prisoners who disappeared. So many that "disappear" was used as a verb by the prisoners and cadre. There is no
way of knowing how many were taken away for execution rather
than just shuffled in the random rotations between camps.

*E*verybody feared if his name was heard on the loudspeaker.
When it came on, all prisoners stopped like statues. Usually the
loudspeaker just played awful communist music that is supposed
to help us work harder, but if the music did not start then
someone's name is to be read. This man must report to camp
headquarters at night. If he came back later he was shaking, but
most did not come back.

Where the U.S. forces had mauled the NVA, as the 101st did
for years at Tuy Hoa, there seemed to be a particular vendetta against
the local population and inmates of re-education camps. Two incidents as recorded by Nguyen Van Canh hint at the consequences
of removal from camps, and how punishment extends even beyond
death to the families of victims.

The commander of a camp near Tuy Hoa ordered all 1500 prisoners to line up. Names of over two hundred were read. Unchar-
acteristically, their fate was announced: they were to be sent to the
city for specialized re-education. Segregated in a corner of the camp,
they were bound together in groups of nine. As night fell, they were
marched away. Two hours later, the remaining inmates heard the
sputter of AK-47's from a jungle-choked valley.

For five days local villagers were too fearful to approach the valley, now declared off limits by the camp commander. Then some relatives had to venture in, guided by birds of carrion. The putrifying corpses were still in rows bound together. All were shot in the face. They had burst from internal gases, and could be identified only by their names written on the undersides of their sandals.

Because sandal marking was not a practice in the camp, the victims themselves must have done it, obeying the last order from their executioners. Thus the communists subjected the devastated relatives to a dilemmatic torture: if they recovered the remains, the communists would note which corpses were missing and punish the families who trespassed into the valley, but to abandon the unburied to scavengers is an eternal horror in the Buddhist faith. Most families chose to brave the retribution of the camp commander and recovered their loved ones. For this their huts and crops were confiscated and they were consigned to re-education camps themselves.

Also near Tuy Hoa, a former ARVN militiaman never reported for re-education. Instead he lived as a fugitive under a river bridge. One night he saw NVA approaching with thirty prisoners from the camp, tied together in three groups like a chain gang towed behind communists riding motorcycles. Above him on the bridge the procession stopped. He heard heavy metallic bumping: the groups were being attached to massive angle irons. On these anchors, the prisoners were toppled into the river. Their cries were brief, drowned instantly in three dark fountains that subsided in the night.

The communists never intended that these bodies be recovered. Their families were left with the anguish of eternal uncertainty. As Nguyen Van Canh put it, "The extreme barbarity of these killings were part of the communists' plan to terrorize the population. Beheading, stabbing, denial of proper burial—such practices, reminiscent of those of ancient emperors, were no more lethal than others, but they did serve to outrage and humiliate the victims' families. When the communists, as they sometimes did, beheaded the corpses of those they had just massacred, they knew that any relative who came for the bodies would view such a death as particularly shameful, and that the memory of it would remain with those families for generations."

To hear one's name on the camp loudspeaker was to contemplate such a ghastly fate, not only for oneself but for the family name forever. Thus there was unspeakable relief when the summons to camp headquarters resulted in only an intercamp rotation. Cai was numb with fear when Ai called for him. It took him days to recover even though he was only moved next door to an annex of Bien Hoa. He found himself on the floor next to a man named Huong. The rains were back, and they huddled together in the cold, whispering of the past. Huong had been in the navy.

Chapter
Twenty

It is something I thought about more than anything else: How
do I get out of Vietnam if I can escape from camp? No good just
to escape if I got caught again. If that happen, there is no more
chance because they kill me for sure.

So I thought about two kinds of escape. All the time I looked
for a way out of Soui Mau. Probably best chance is when we do
labor outside the camp. Most mines are cleared so sometimes we
were sent into the area around camp to beat up bushes and little
trees. We cannot use things for cutting because they might also
be weapons for us. Bushes we cannot pull down we must dig up
with no gloves or anything. Hands were bleeding every day.

One day after I have fever, I passed out from heat. Skin got
very dry. Guards did not even allow water. One prisoner fanned
me with hand till guards made him get back to work. Lucky for
me it was near time for midday swill. Then prisoners can stand
near me to give shade.

I can not eat swill even though I die from hunger. I just drank
water around the rice. I left that in the bowl. I said to another
prisoner, "Give me water from your swill and you can have my
rice." He agreed. Another very good man let me have his water.
I told him I pay him back. Guard then stuck me with bayonet
and told me it is time to labor again.

I know I have to do this. I did not know how, so I pray that

I can. Prisoners helped me back to brush where we are working. I was breathing very loud like a dog. Maybe guard thought that it was from work I do, so he let me alone. I was not working, just trying to keep from falling. Prisoners let me lean against them while we are squatting.

But I fell anyway. I felt the painful branches and heard my heart going so fast. I was sure it is time for dying and I watched myself like I was someone else. I thought about my parents, who bring me to this world by birth. Over and over I passed out. Heard voices far away. One is guard, I think, but other voices were talking to him and he did not bother me.

I felt pain in my wrist. I looked at it. I bit myself to make blood that I sucked into my mouth. If there was no water, I must do that. Stomach was very hard like I hold muscles tight. I asked myself, Cai why do you do that, use muscles like exercise when you are so weak? I cannot stop it.

Dirt is little bit cooler than my skin. I pushed it on my face like powder. Guard's face was now over me. He was not saying anything. Nobody is talking. I knew he watched to see if I die. I want to know that too.

Body was living by itself. Very strange feeling. So very dry. Nowhere can I feel sweat or spit. By itself my body was working very hard to stay alive. I can do nothing.

At five p.m. Cai was carried back to camp with the crew when they ended their labor. The camp's water was hauled by the prisoners from a muddy stream. They made an extra trip for Cai, pouring water by wringing rags over him. Death by heat was a normal monthly event in the dry season. The prisoners knew what little they could do to prevent it. The life or death test was whether Cai could keep down the evening swill. In every case where the victim's stomach rejected it, he weakened beyond recovery. Cai watched himself slowly slurp the swill, and waited.

After the swill, I was put on the floor with wet rags all over. Guys stood around to see how I am doing. I saw them up there like I am in a clearing in the forest. Their heads are the treetops.

While this happen I felt very calm and smart. I thought about the day that is over, the times I passed out. I knew I was in the brush a long time, just lying there. I thought about how long.

I looked up at the guys and heard my stomach make noise. Everything moving in there. I'm afraid I will throw up. I am on my back and the vomit will not get out of my throat. I wanted to tell them, please, don't let me choke, but I cannot say anything.

I thought again about how many minutes I was down in the brush. The guard cannot see me there. I saw myself escape that way. Big bright flash like now I know everything important. I must work close to the ground all the time now, always make guard think I am down there. That is the way to escape.

Not so many heads way above me now. I did not vomit and lose water. Guys knew I made it so they went away to rest. They saved my life.

But I stayed just like I was on the floor, thinking. I saw myself out in the jungle. What do I do now? My thoughts were very clear. There was nothing I felt except the thoughts in my head. I am the smartest man in the world. I followed just what I should do like someone is showing me.

The guards will think I will go south fast as I can to Saigon. No, I don't do that. Go little southeast by Song Nha River. Do not use bridge, stay in swamp and swim at night to two islands I know. Then there is smaller river that goes right, west to Saigon.

I saw myself in clothes I steal. Good black pajamas, right size for me. Parents are talking to me. I look awful but know what to do. I wait to see what I do next but there is only the sea, nothing else. I must be on a boat but cannot see it or other passengers. I waited more, but then I start to feel my body on the floor in this camp. It pained very much. I felt it tell me "Do not let this happen again." Only one more strange thing happens. That is I know I know enough. I must escape by sea.

I cannot wait much time. My body was not strong enough to survive longer in camp. Four years is too long for any more.

Cai's struggling recovery had several setbacks, and he received a pro forma beating for not working up to standards, but a resolution now possessed him. It was as if his delirium confirmed that he had escaped, not that he would. With that apparently accomplished, it was only the escape from Vietnam that he had to ensure. Reflecting on his nautical vision, it dawned on him that the key figure in his plans was Huong, the ex-navy man sleeping next to him.

Huong did not hope anymore for getting out of Vietnam. I asked him a lot about it. He said all good boats left very soon after communist takeover. Navy personnel all gone too. He had very bad morale about this. I told him, "Keep thinking about escape." It is possible from this camp, and he was lucky because after that he knows what to do at sea.

He was like me, very weak, and did not think he will be released, and cannot escape either. He was radar operator in navy, with no hardship experience. He was too scared to try escape from camp.

But he did tell me what he knew about the sea. If I want to try getting picked up by foreign ships, little boat is enough. I must take plenty of water and some food because I must wait a long time before someone finds me. Chances not too good for that, he said. Easy to drift away from where ships travel. Big storms can also sink my boat.

I told him I must take my wife and kids with me. He asked how old is smallest kid? I said, just a baby. Then I cannot stay out in sea very long or baby will die. Better that I take bigger boat—at least twenty feet—that may be big enough to get to another country.

Navigation is easy he said. Just keep steering into afternoon sun and there will be land in a week. He also told me the best time for west winds, how to use a rudder and sea anchor at night, how to keep away from the coast guard, and how to put the right lights on the boat. He told me I should paint "SOS" on the side of the boat; also what radio frequency is used for weather reports and ships talking to other ships.

This was very good information for me. I tried to remember. I did not think about it in the camp, but when I am outlaw, organizers think maybe I was a navy man.

About the time Cai was sent to his first prison camp, the communists evicted his parents from their home in Saigon. North Vietnamese cadres swarmed into the south to run the country. Dazzled by the contrast between Saigon and Hanoi, they quickly confiscated what they coveted and that included most sizable dwellings.

Through a credit system honored within the Lam clan, Cai's parents were able to acquire a storehouse the size of a garage across the street from their former home. They lived there and began a small system of barter in commodities, principally poultry that they raised on the roof of the storehouse.

Before 1978, most prison guards and cadre were NVA. After that, the police ran the camps. This is because there was trouble with China and Cambodia. Army must use all their people for these problems.

Police had a new policy: about every two months, families can visit with food packages. That saves SRV money. Without these packages, I die for sure. Cadre controlled me that way. I must be a model prisoner so I can have these visits and packages. Best thing was eggs my parents bring. I always gave one to cadre. They liked it very much so they let me keep getting packages.

His parents' street became something of a black market mall. With all cars confiscated or immobilized for lack of fuel, there was no vehicular traffic, and the street was a convenient pedestrian thoroughfare, a floating crap game of illicit transactions and whispered conversations.

Frequently passersby would ask the Lams for water. It seemed wise to keep on good terms with the black marketeers, so glasses of cool water were complimentary, but the Lams' hospitable reputation began to be an imposition as more people came to the door.

In their merchant tradition, the Lams saw opportunity in imposition. They began to sell ice tea (they were fortunate enough to have a refrigerator) for one *dong*—about 3 cents—a glass, and this service became a popular amenity for the black marketeers. A few rickety chairs and tiny tables came out on the sidewalk, and soon glasses of ice tea sealed many deals at this extemporized outdoor cafe.

The facility also became a surveillance point for secret police. They were easy to spot. Sipping ice water, they sat observing for hours and spoke with no one.

I saw a movie once about Africa. It showed the alligator with birds moving on his head. That was like these secret police. They are just quiet like that while action is around them. Watch everything going on. Dealers knew who they are but are not worried much. Everything was illegal at that time. People cannot live if they do not do illegal things. Only reason farmers brought food to the city is to sell on black market. If they sell to the government they go broke. Police knew this. They let it happen. They just want to know who is dealing. Then they can step up quiet and demand a bribe.

One secret policeman began to be a regular ice tea customer. The Lams knew he was important because when he first arrived several police were already occupying the tables and rose immediately when he sought a seat. Over the weeks he spent more and more time sipping and watching. In time he exchanged pleasantries with Mrs. Lam and drew her husband into conversation.

They were convinced he was snooping, probably appraising the taxes the Lams should pay for the tea business. Mr. Lam was punctilious in reporting his earnings to the neighborhood cadreman.

But the policeman's interest was elsewhere. Eventually he disclosed his name, Major Sau. Apparently he was sure that his introduction would impress the Lams, induce them into more sensitive topics than the weather, but his name meant nothing to the couple.

Finally he came out forthright. Major Sau was an assistant to Cao Dinh Chin, the deputy police chief of the SRV administration in Ho Chi Minh City. This was a boggling revelation for the Lams, who cowered at night when they contemplated the man's power. It amazed them that Sau had so much time to spend idling in front of their nondescript storehouse.

Cao had been a legendary figure in the communist underground.

Cai had studied his case in the ARVN Intelligence School. Now about eighty years old, Cao had organized the original assassination/sabotage rings against the French occupation. The Americans had become aware of his work when Cao's forces bombed the principal quarters for American advisers in 1964 and the famous My Canh floating restaurant in 1965. GVN counterterrorists had named Cao public enemy number one but could never get a photograph of him.

The underlying reason for Cao's interest in the Lams remains veiled in communist mores, but an understandable reason was profit. Cao was aware, of course, that Cai was being re-educated: all paperwork on the thousands of prisoners flowed through the police system. No doubt Cao, through Major Sau, had worked the shell game scam on other parents of prisoners; i.e., asking for payment only if a prisoner was released, never knowing who would be. It could be that the scam was over-exploited, that there were too many SRV officials going around with the same "no money till release" proposition, so that exploitable families were deluged with such offers to the point that they were meaningless. The Lams had been approached in this way by several communist small fry.

Major Sau's approach was somewhat different. He frankly admitted Cai would never be released. Not even a man in Cao's position could arrange that. Suspicion still hovered over Cai—that he had worked extensively for the Americans. Several prisoners had denounced him on that count. His biography (because of its simplicity) had withstood meticulous and intense interrogation, but nevertheless the suspicion was ingrained. Eventually some cadre zealot like Ai would find a crack in Cai's story and he would break. One way or another, Cai would slip up. That was inevitable, or otherwise he would die in the struggle for his mind. His sentence was open-ended, and his interrogators, successions of them, would never relent. That's how they advanced in their hierarchy—by breaking tough cases.

So Cai was doomed; Major Sau convinced his parents of that. The only way out was to escape from the camp. It would be costly, but Sau could provide that chance.

About a month after I had the heat attack it was time for another visit from my parents. It was cancelled because of an uprising in camp at Christmas. What happen is men in another barrack started singing Christmas songs. Many of them are the same as in America but with Vietnamese words. Police did not know what to do. Pretty soon we started banging on cooking pots and conex cells. People inside them started singing too. Then someone jumped a point man and everyone beat those guys up. Cadre must call guards to come into camp. Some prisoners were shot but there is great spirit for us. When it is over I was punished with many others.

I was looking the worst ever when my father came for a visit, but he said to me my eyes are wild like a warrior. This was true because I know I must escape.

He gave me a package and said it has twenty-two peanuts. I wished he use the room for something else because shells have weight, but he said in Chinese, "Eat one each day. Start tomorrow. On the day of last peanut, you must escape."

My chin began to shake. It was like my dream is coming true! My father did not know how I will escape but I knew where I will start. It must be from labor detail. I didn't know how but the guard must know too. I guess somebody will pay him off. Or maybe pay off cadre who will punish the guard but then pay him off too. I just sat and looked at my father. I cannot say anything. He must make all the talk till it was time for his leaving. I did not even feel my legs when I walked away.

I was very careful to be model prisoner. Each day I ate a peanut. Each day it was like a step away from this awful camp. I did not pray for myself. I prayed for all the suffering prisoners who must stay here. But one I do not like. Chat was always denouncing others for sleeping in lectures. Now I spent lots of time talking with him. When I escape he will be suspected and maybe punished in interrogation. That serves him right.

Five peanuts left when the loudspeaker called for me. That made me shake, but then I think maybe Ai will tell me something about how to escape. I must go to him at midnight. Terrible thought came that maybe I will be moved to another camp.

"Who are your friends?" he asked.

"Everyone who is reforming himself is a friend."

He smiled a little bit. I think he asked me something else with his question.

"Is Chat a new friend for you?"

"Yes."

"Why?"

"Chat makes good progress."

"You want to be like him?"

"I try."

"Good. What does Chat say to you?"

I must be careful because Ai will ask Chat too.

"He says if we work hard—get rid of old thoughts—we will be welcome in SRV."

"Why do you believe him?"

"He is a good man. Wants to be a good citizen."

"I tell you the same thing. Why do you believe only when Chat says that?"

"Oh, I believe you."

"I give you very lenient treatment. More attention than others. You are not grateful."

"Please, I am very grateful. You teach me first but I still have old thoughts. You teach Chat too. Now my mind is ready. He teaches me what you teach him."

"Is he your lover?"

"Oh, no!" *Four years in prison, but I did not know how SRV feels about homosexuals. Some of that was going in barracks, but secret.*

"You like a lover?"

"I never do that. I forget about love."

"You have disease from love?"

"Yes! I'm afraid I do." *I thought it was a good idea to lie.*

"That was not in your confessions."

"I was ashamed."

"You will not be punished. You were not asked about it."

"Thank you."

"I can get drugs for sex disease. Do you know the name?"

"Girl was prostitute for Americans. Very bad stuff. Everybody catch it if there is contact."

"What is the name?"

"*Imperialists call it, 'gone-to-Korea.'* "

"*Health in our camp is important. You should have reported this disease. See that you keep it to yourself. I will get you the right drug.*"

"*Thank you.*"

"*Everything is based on trust, Cai. The people trust the leaders. There can be no secrets. I am always making trust. There are rewards when trust is returned to me. If you trust me with things you have not yet confessed, there can be trust between us. Then we will be true comrades. Together for the people, together for everything. Are my words clear?*"

"*Always.*"

"*You must give true reports about what is done for you here.*"

"*I will.*"

"*I have been like your father, overlooking and pardoning your misdeeds.*"

"*I am grateful.*"

"*You should be. You were very corrupt. I have saved you. That should be known.*"

"*I will tell them what you have done.*"

"*Good. A father must be stern to help the child grow. Be grateful for that too.*"

"*You and my father have taught me more than anyone.*"

"*He has not been the influence I have. Remember that. Return to your barrack, Cai, and think about what I have said.*"

A dozen prisoners slouched behind the guard. They had to walk a long way to the gate, then turn outside the fence to the area near where the two men had been killed escaping. The jungle had been cleared so it was not as close as in those days. Concertina wire had been sprawled onto the minefield, the only additional measure to prevent another attempt over the same route.

Cai peered at the spot where the first man had lost his foot. It may have been his imagination but he thought there was still an indentation where the prisoner had scooped mud and flung it at his eternal companion.

Without a signal, work began on the brush. As always since his heat stroke, Cai crouched low to the ground. Rooting and pulling the tough vegetation, he glanced at the guard as often as he could without being noticed.

The guard was relatively new, a misfit from the NVA, a couple of months out of combat in Cambodia, where someone said he lugged a mortar baseplate. He looked as though that job would have been a mental challenge. Slack-jawed, he hunkered by a tree, the underbrush nearly concealing him as he gazed with reptilian eyes over the scattered prisoners inching along in their perpetual work.

He seemed to be worshipping boredom. Insects alighted and left him without notice. He was either the best or the worst possible creature for a part in the escape scheme: Cai could not tell if the guard was watching everything or nothing.

*T*his guy did not move for hours. Only one time he got up to *pee. He looked like he thought about that for long time. Then he went back to where he was till midday swill come.*

When we break up to go back to work, someone told a dirty joke. We laughed but he did not look like he understands Vietnamese. Never heard him say a word. After while I went off to pee. Usually we just stand up and do it but I wanted to see if he noticed me go off under a tree. He never moved, even his eyes. Maybe was he stoned, like I saw some GIs. That's when I decided to cut out during the day. Safer way is to hide when work is over, then it will be dark when they look for me. But I think it is more better with this dumb guy that I leave early and get a good head start. This is the day because I have eaten the last peanut.

I moved a little bit more into the higher brush that we were clearing. I kept low, just eyes over the leaves. He was still looking away from the sun. In the morning he looked one way, now he was looking the other, so he always had shade. I ducked my head and I'm gone.

I never moved so fast in jungle before. Like a deer I have so much energy. I don't break any branches so no one can know I was there.

It's dark when I got out of jungle. Went around little villages so dogs do not bark. I looked for separate farm where there is rice. It is not cooked, just a pile of it in big basket. I filled my hands and ate this hard stuff as I ran.

Morning came; I am miles away. Heard roosters by coconut trees. Took a look but stayed in the jungle edge. A family had clothes drying on a laundry line. I knew this is the place for my dream. I took down black pajama before anybody woke up. It was nice and soft and fit like my own clothes. Threw my prison clothes into a stream. Stopped and watch it float till it sank. Very happy feeling when prison clothes are gone under water.

With clothes like everybody else, I jumped on back of bus to Saigon without paying.

Trembling and weeping, the parents held their son until Mrs. Lam became quite aware that Cai needed a bath, and assisted him through it as if he were a child again. Then it was time to eat; steaming, aromatic bowls of rice at first, then garnished with bits of fish and pork. As the day's black market activities began, Cai climbed up to his parents' loft and slept like a gorged animal. At midday, she brought him another rice dish but said nothing about Major Sau's presence outside, so Cai went back to sleep.

The payoff was in gold leaves, five of them worth about $2000, a sizable Vietnamese fortune. Sau offered congratulations, then announced the bad news.

He told my father my name and picture will soon be sent to all police. I am big outlaw in SRV now. They want me back very much because I know about terrible revenge camps. If I get out of the country the world may find out. So police will start looking for me right away. Their orders are what Americans call "shoot to kill"—doesn't matter if they capture me or not because they just want to make sure I don't leave Vietnam.

But it is possible that Cao Dinh Chin wanted me to get away for good. That is because he was Vietcong, not northerner. He may want world to know how Hanoi is doing atrocities in the south and not letting southerners have any power. I don't know.

That is my guess why he told Major Sau to give me advice about getting out. He said grow a beard and find an organizer. I can be in international waters in a couple of days.

Cao may also want very much that I do not get caught. If I am interrogated I could say how he arranged escape for me from revenge camp. Cao is so powerful he can tell police to shoot me without questioning. He is pretty safe if either thing happen— if I am killed I can not accuse him. If I get away from Vietnam, then maybe my story helps southerners in SRV. I do not know what he thinks will happen if my story shows he helped my escape. That's his problem.

Anyway, Major Sau told my parents the first place police will look is here at their home. I should also tell my wife that they will come to her place in Phan Rang. I got to get going. "Good luck," he said to my father, and he put the gold in his shoe.

Chapter
Twenty-one

I got away from prison on February 11, 1980. Now after one day I have to get away again. I asked my mother where I can meet Nho, my wife. Mother spoke very slowly and quiet: Nho lives in my house at Phan Rang. She lives there with my jeep driver from Twenty-first Division and had a baby by him.

This news hurt me badly. I was still hungry but I cannot eat.

I shouted my anger that she did this. My mother thought it was wrong too, but tried to explain for Nho. She said Nho did not like being poor. She had no money from me. I can accept that if she just told me. It is even okay if she got married again, but what she did makes me rage because my mother say Nho just lives with my driver right out in the open. This brings shame on the family, so my mother never allowed her to come into our house since she started living with this guy.

I was so sad and angry, I want to divorce her. My mother told me other things about Nho. When I was in Soc Trang hospital with machine gun wound she did not take care of our kids so they must be brought to Saigon to my parents. Always Nho wanted to make money but she costs so much with her businesses and never made any. She had opened a bar in Hue when I was at Camp Eagle but ARVN troops busted it up all the time so I decided to close and move her to Saigon. I thought maybe my parents can look after her a little bit if Nho was close to them.

In Saigon she wanted to learn clerk-typist work and be a pretty receptionist, so I paid for her vocational school. After that she changed her mind and wants to be a tailor. That's what she did when I was in Twenty-first Division.

Worse than her money spending is the way she was with our kids. When she was in her bar one time, she cut meat with a long knife. Dat was a baby. He ran to her and she turned with knife in her hand. It stuck him in his right eye. I was in a panic and drove through town to all doctors. Horrible blood was on me, worse than all my combat.

Every Vietnamese doctor said Dat must lose his eye. I jumped into my jeep and drove fast as it will go to 101st dispensary at Phu Bai. Medics got me on a helicopter to hospital ship Repose *in Danang. They did two operations, but in six months it turned out poor Dat will be blind in that eye because the cut was right in the middle.*

When Saigon fell, Nho took all my properties and fooled around with every guy who said she is pretty. Now I had to get my children from her. I didn't care if I must go to communist peoples' committee for divorce.

I sent her a message from my father to come to Saigon with my daughters. She came, maybe because she thought my parents can give her some money, but she did not know I was there. She had a big surprise to see me and when my parents did not allow her to step into their house, I talked to her outside. I said she can have my houses in Phan Rang and Bac Lieu but she must give me my children.

She said she now has no more money and please forgive her. I said no, we must get divorce, because she slept with guys I know in the army and lives with my driver. Next morning we stood in front of peoples' committee. They said I have been fair with her so I get my three children. We were divorced before they found out that I am an escaped prisoner.

My sadness became more heavy every year. First I lost in war, then I lost my country. I lost my wife, then give up my daughter so she might escape with my sister. Now I must leave

my boy with his grandparents. Alone I went to cousin Lam Kho,
who used to own the Club Nautique, where I worked as a boy.

Cai gave up his youngest daughter within a few days of his divorce. At this same time, his sister Hoang had found an organizer whose boat had room for another child. Cai's parents had been pondering what to do, who should go, even before he broke free. In contrast to all his siblings, no one of Cai's blood had escaped Vietnam. His parents felt that to preserve his lineage, one of his offspring should take the gamble of going with Hoang. When Cai learned of the chance he agreed, and he chose Van. With one son and two daughters, a grim logic nominated one of the girls.

Cai's father brought out an ancient camera to photograph Hoang and Van so an image would mark their grave even if they perished at sea. This was very likely because their boat was too small to cross open water. Instead, its destination was the international sea lanes near Vietnam, where they would drift until rescued by a passing vessel. The average longevity of such an overcrowded boat was about a week. If they were not picked up by then, they would succumb either to storms or thirst.

With this forewarning, Cai wrapped the tiny girl in his arms, prayed with her in the vocabulary of childhood, and watched her depart. She looked over her shoulder at him as she held her aunt's hand. Then Cai had to begin his own flight into the city, his own reliance on relatives.

Kho *said he will help me—he asked what I think is the best*
thing to do. I told him I am hating the communist more now: I
like to join ex-ARVN resistance forces. Kho's wife had a shock
from what I said. Resistance fighters are the most dangerous
people to be with in Vietnam. If I am one, then Kho and his
family can all be sent to prison and receive torture.

She talked to Kho privately. He came back and said he heard
some ARVN are in the seven mountains region. People say some-
time they saw RVN flag out there. Somebody told her they got
parachute drops back in the hills—maybe CIA airplanes. Kho

said communist soldiers are still being buried so maybe there is
fighting. I decided I should take a bus to that region and see
what is going on.

Before I left there was a message from my mother. She met
a woman in the black market. This woman said she knows about
a fishing boat in Vung Tau. I can go on it with my children but
it does not have diesel fuel. Mother will pay two gold leaves for
diesel. I must wait with Kho till I get the word to go to Vung
Tau.

The wait would have to be short because Lam Kho lived in a
ward intimately inspected by local communist cadre and their
agents. It was difficult to avoid them on the street at any hour.
Children, particularly, had been recruited as unwitting informers.
Potentially, this included Kho's sons and daughters.

All families had been "invited" to send their children to the ward
day care (i.e., indoctrination) center. Even if parents declined (this
was enough to draw suspicion on them), all children in the neighborhood were organized into "Vanguard" groups (also called "Assault
Youth"). Membership was compulsory, and meetings were held
weekly. Parents could not attend and only learned of Vanguard
activities by asking their children, a curiosity the communists ordered the children to report.

Vanguard cadres introduced the children to the practices of criticism and self-criticism. They learned to denounce each other for
missing meetings, talking while they stood in military formation,
removing their red scarves while "off duty," and other signs of in-
sincere commitment. Vanguard meetings also devoted much time
to talking about the children's parents, siblings, living conditions,
activities, and—especially—any visitors. An innocent word from an
eight-year-old could give Cai away.

Even though I had just come from prison, I cannot believe how
the communists' noses were in everything. There was a loud-
speaker on corners just like at prison. On Sundays, around 4:00
a.m., it started getting people up for kids PT (gymnastics) classes.

*Three times every day it played revolutionary songs, talked lies,
and made speeches about the great New Economic Zones—tried
to get people to go there because too much population in cities.*

New Economic Zones (NEZs) were multipurpose concentration
camps, strewn about the wilderness. NEZs were convenient dump
sites for South Vietnamese who did not fit any of the communists'
original categories for re-education: families of GVN members, small
businessmen, schoolteachers whose subjects had been condemned
(e.g., history), Buddhist monks, unproductive workers (like those
incapacitated by industrial injuries or war wounds), vagrants (i.e.,
anyone dispossessed—that category included a third of the population), and owners of property coveted by cadre. For example, Cai's
parents had been "urged" to relocate to an NEZ in order to facilitate
the confiscation of their home. They avoided that fate by bribery.

Other measures to encourage relocation to NEZs included withholding ration cards, which prevented purchase of rice except on
the black market, denial of children's education, and the alternative
of a re-education camp. In spite of such coercion, NEZ candidates
had to be dragooned. Most were taken from their homes at night
by security troops.

*Many outlaws I meet escaped from NEZ. It is like re-education
camp except no guards, just jungle to keep people in.*

According to Che Viet Tan, vice-chairman of the SRV's State
Planning Commission, NEZs will eventually require the relocation
of about ten million people in the overpopulated areas.

Ostensibly, NEZs were to be self-sufficient, yet nothing was
provided for that purpose. Instead, the locations seemed selected
for expeditious elimination of their inmates. One visitor, Pham Anh
Hai, described what he saw:

In Vam Co Dong NEZ live 3,000 people who came from a section west
of Saigon. They are housed in 400 thatched huts they built themselves
from jungle material, along a drainage canal. It took them 30 days to

dig through the surrounding jungle that abounds in poisonous snakes, mosquitos, and clouds of insects.

A member of the farm told us that within the first week of clearing bushes, seven people died by snake bite. Others, later, of malaria. Because the water in this area is brackish, the only crop that can be grown there is pineapples.

For the first few months, the SRV "supports" an NEZ with the same quality and quantity of rations as re-education camps of similar size. After that, there must be self-sufficiency (though no NEZ has sustained it), and farm income, in the unlikely event there is any, is allocated as follows: Thirty percent used to pay government taxes. Twenty-five percent of the communal crop sold to the government at official (deflated) price. Fifteen percent reserved to pay salaries of cadres managing the NEZ. The remaining thirty percent divided among workers based on the work points earned by each.

The workers mentioned by Hai, like the vast majority of NEZ inmates, were people from the cities with no previous agricultural experience.

There was a joke I heard on the streets about NEZ and a slogan of communism. "From each person 100 percent work, to each person 30 percent crop." Best thing about NEZ is that it is easy to escape. If not, many million Vietnamese are dead.

I must hide in Kho's attic most all the time. Everywhere in the city it was like this. Security soldiers came into any house, not even knocking. This is because the army call itself "children of the people." That means children of family can come in anytime just like they live there.

Kho must belong to an association of workers like him. His wife too was forced to be member of the women's association. At night they must listen to lectures and make reports about themselves—what they are doing, how children are in school, how association can make better work for socialism. Then when they come home, there are ward meetings with more lectures and reports. Kho and wife had very little time to sleep and see children. Sunday is only day off. They were very tired from working for nothing and being watched all the time.

I asked them how the communists get so many informers. In

*five houses around us were two informers for ward. They looked
like people like Kho, not communists. Kho told me they are controlled by blackmail. Sooner or later, everyone slips up. Get
caught listening to foreign radio, making joke about government,
owning extra pair of shoes, throwing away paper without using
both sides—very little stuff like that, but enough that ward communist requests that they volunteer for NEZ.*

*Then these poor people are afraid. So ward communist say,
"Well okay, I give you another chance, but you must tell me
everything Mr. Nguyen do." That way communists get informers
everywhere. That was not a surprise for me; that is just the way
they do it in prison camps.*

The Vung Tau escape boat was a fraud. The gold Cai's mother
paid for diesel fuel disappeared with the woman who was to have
bought it.

My *father was real mad. He found out that this woman moved
to another town to live with her boyfriend. Father said, "There
is no respect in this country for people who trust."*

*I had to move from Kho's house. His wife was too worried
that informers can see me. I went out on the street and looked
for friends from my past.*

*It was just luck if I find them because there were more than
five million people in Saigon and no one lived where they did
any more after the cadre from the north took over so many
houses. But I remembered addresses of school friends and interpreters from 101st. I must be careful how I find them because
they may be watched. For a week I cannot find anybody I know
and must stay at An Dong bus terminal, the biggest one in Saigon.
Not much chance anyone notices me there because there are five,
six hundred people always around. I also grew a beard for disguise.*

*Every week I made contact with my parents. It hurt me very
much not to see them and my children but I must stay away—
just leave messages for each other.*

Soon my parents found some organizers around Vinh Binh.

One told them he can get me out for three gold leaves. My parents must pay half now, other half when I let them know I am on board boat. We used a family code for this. My father cut a piece of money in two and gave half to me. When I am on board, I will give the organizer my half and he takes it to my parents, who give him the rest of the gold.

This organizer picked me up at night in Saigon. He was angry because I do not have any ID if we are stopped. I told him I'm working on it. It takes half a day to get to Vinh Binh. When we got there, he put me with a safe family. I will be picked up the next night. That night came but nothing happen. Next night organizer rushed in and said I must go back to Saigon—the guy with the diesel got caught. When everything is ready again the organizer will tell my parents. But that never happen and we lost one and a half leaves of gold.

In Saigon I am outlaw again. First thing I did was go to black market and get blank ID cards. SRV does not require photos— maybe because they shut down all photo stores. When I found a friend where I can stay, I put his name and legal address on the card. In case I get stopped, I pull out a card from another part of Saigon. If cop checks official list of addresses, he finds one like the name of my friend on my card.

At first there was only one friend, Thien, an interpreter in the 101st who I helped when the cops tried to frame him for adultery in 1970. One night each week I can stay with him in poor neighborhood where there was not so many informers because people there drift around a lot. Other nights I must find a place to sleep outside someplace. Curfew is from midnight to 4:00 a.m. and I have to be hiding in those hours. Tell the truth, I did not sleep at all except sitting up. I must always be on alert in case I need to run away. Night is the time communists always make arrests. When I get sleep it is in daytime in the park.

That is my life—like a wild dog. One place it is okay to be at night is bus terminal. Communists do not arrest here because hundreds of people wait all night to buy bus tickets. These lines are five or six blocks long. Everybody sleeps on broken pavement while they are in line. Many of these poor people made their living waiting in line for other people who do not have time.

That's what I found out when I tried to get ticket to seven

mountains region, where I heard there are maybe ARVN resis-
tance fighters. I waited all day in hot sun but the tickets were
all sold before me. Then a VC veteran with one leg said he will
wait for me, cost just a few dong. He will use this to add with
other little money he makes, and buy ticket with it. He didn't
want to go anyplace but he can resell bus ticket for ten times
more.

Communist cadre have special line, no waiting. Big shots have
official cars with driver—don't have to take bus at all. One time
I met this person who was servant for cadre. He was an old man
who served the French. He told me that experience got him job
for cadre. They interview him and said he is just the right man.
They wanted servant and easy life just like French. So cadre told
him to do whatever he did for the French landlord he worked
for. But during the war this old servant was taught by the com-
munists that the Frenchman exploited him. Cadre said his work
for them was different: he was saving them time so they could
serve socialism better.

Two escape scams, and Cai's parents were three gold leaves
poorer. But the spring monsoon moved inexorably toward the coast.
The storms it brought would make the seas more hazardous for
months, a period that daily exposed Cai to recapture. His parents
threw in with one more organization before the monsoon churned
the seas.

The son of a Lam relative was also going to chance this escape.
His side of the family had checked out the organization and were
optimistic. Embarkation would be at night from a riverbank near
My Tho. Cai and his young cousin took a bus there.

We had to kill a lot of time so we went to the movie in My Tho.
Good place to hide because it is dark inside. I'm surprised there
are not more people buying tickets because poster showed that
this will be exciting western movie. I asked a local guy about this
and he told me the communists lie again: the movie is from
Bulgaria about farmers who love a tractor. If we go in we must

watch it all the way through because we will be reported if we leave. I told him that's okay—I need to sleep.

We are to be at a park at 8:00 p.m. for pickup by organizer. But that did not happen, so we are almost picked up by the cops because we hung around till midnight, when the park closed for curfew. We were the only two people left. Cops started walking around. My cousin did not want to go, but I told him we must get out of here. Tell the truth, we stayed too long already because last bus left for Saigon. So we tried to get a ride on a truck. One stopped and it cost us a lot of money for just a fifty-mile trip.

I told my cousin to tell my parents what happen. I was afraid that we lost another gold leaf. I went back to Saigon bus terminal and mixed with all the homeless people. I began to think I will die with them because many are sick, and everything is made filthy by them. Two or three toilets for hundreds of people. Everything stinks from urine and droppings. I felt myself getting sick because I thought I would be on the sea by this time.

His parents were not dejected for long because they learned of another escape that would be unaffected by stormy seas. Indeed, once Cai was aboard he was as good as in Singapore. All wards in Saigon had lectured their subjects vividly about the certain doom of escapes, relating stories (for once true) of frequent drownings, death by thirst, starvation and exposure, and the perils of pirates on the high seas. This fourth attempt at escape looked as though it would steam right through all these hazards. It would be a sure thing, and it was priced accordingly—four leaves of gold—two in advance and two when Cai confirmed he was aboard. Privately he told his parents that when they received his half of a calendar he divided with them, that meant he was on his way.

I got excited when I saw this big ocean ship with "Singapore" written on the back. It was unloading at the Saigon pier where U.S. ships used to bring tons of ammo. This is high security area for communists; every dock worker must have uniform and pass to go in there. Organizer had these for me. He said, "Go in and look like you know what you're doing. Work hard and wait for our man to put you with cargo that goes into ship with big forklift. Ship will leave in two days."

I did what he told me, but no one contacted me and the ship did not leave. At night I must take off dock worker uniform and hide around waterfront. Not much to eat, and I was getting worried. Next day after work, organizer met me at gate and took me to a good hiding place. He wanted to make sure I did not contact my parents because he had gone to them and said the ship left. It did not leave for three more days and I can never get on board. Armed guards were all over just like they knew people try to escape. The big forklift was taken away from the ship the day before.

When the organizer told my parents the ship was gone, they were very happy. Organizer asked for two gold leaves but my father asked him for something from me to prove I left. Organizer said, "What was it? Cai gave me some things but did not say they were for you." My father told him it was half of a calendar. Real quick the organizer came back with half a calendar but not the right one. Soon after that I contacted my parents and say we were cheated again, but we saved two gold leaves because of the calendar.

According to the Vietnamese equivalent of the farmer's almanac, the monsoon season of 1980 should have had ten major storms. There was a period of two or three weeks during July and August that the sea was predicted to be relatively calm. For several months Cai's parents checked the underground for organizers who would try to go through this weather window. He urged his parents to let him check the escape plan before they invested again. Finally, a plan appeared that he became convinced had a good chance to work. The boat was much overpriced—five leaves of gold. With so much at stake, the Lams decided to insist on partnership with the organizer, thereby recouping some of their investment by taking a cut of the escape fees paid by other passengers. There would be twenty of them, plus Cai and his two children.

Escape will start from Vinh Binh. In secret we bought a river ferry from its owner. He will say it was stolen after we escape. Not a very big boat—maybe thirty feet. It makes runs up and down the river like a bus: picks up, drops off passengers all day. I listened on the radio for international weather reports. They are in English so I am the only one who knew if sea will be okay. All escape passengers must be ready for signal I give. When they get the word, they go down to the dock and get on with regular passengers. They can get on anyplace the ferry stops.

Regular passengers get off where they want. Each time they do, a few escape passengers will sneak into closets at bottom of boat. End of the day, it will look like the ferry is empty and ready to go back to Vinh Binh for the night. Then the engine will make funny noises because the captain will thin the fuel. He pretend to try to fix it, but while he does the boat drift down on the tide. When he gets near the sea he must stop before police checkpoint. He throws out anchor there and gets in a little boat to row over and see the cops. He will tell them what happen, and say he must spend the night on shore, try to fix engine in the morning.

When it is dark, he swims back to the ferry. Night guard at checkpoint was already paid off. When boat leaves for the sea, he pretends he doesn't hear anything.

That was the plan. We started making it work when the radio said the east part in Gulf of Siam will be clear for a few days. This was good enough I thought—only good weather news in a week. A kid on his bike rode around to the towns to tell escape passengers now is the time to catch the ferry. Everyone was ready. Things look good.

The ferry made its last stop. Last regular passengers got off. I helped unload cargo there. One escaper was a teenage girl. She was worried about stories she heard how refugee boats run out of water. She had strict orders to stay in closet, but got out and went ashore to buy soft drinks.

She was a pretty girl. A few young guys started to flirt with her, and said they will buy her beer if she stays awhile. I heard a little of what they say while I am unloading cargo. I freezed up with sweat because one of the young guys acts like a plain-

clothes cop. I tried to attract her eyes when he starts to talk to her. I can tell he is asking about her home. Suddenly he arrests her because she is from faraway district.

When they took her away I grabbed the organizer. We are under the deck. I tell him we got to start in the boat right now. Couple of hours it will be dark. Coast guard will have tough time to catch us at night. He said no—first checkpoint will shoot at us if the bribed cop is not yet on duty. I said we got to take the chance because the girl will betray us very soon. Besides, we smuggled an M16 on board to shoot fish, birds, and pirates. I can take care of cops at the checkpoint because their hooch is just bamboo.

Organizer thought the police will let this girl go after questioning so we should wait for her. I raged at him how stupid that was, because when they search her they will find hidden gold. Sure enough, I see cops coming back to the boat. For sure they will search it and find everybody.

I was back on the shore when they came. Next to me was boat owner's daughter. She was an escaper. I whispered to her, "Put your arm around me and we go for a little walk like nothing is happening. Act like we are local young people, boyfriend and girlfriend." But she was so scared, and cannot even walk. I had to drag her.

I think the cops noticed that. They waved for us to stop. She begged me to help her but she cannot move.

I had to take off. Even though my children were still on the boat. If I am caught I can never help them. I started running for high reeds. Cops saw me and shot a couple of rounds.

Two cops followed me into the reeds. I thought I should run down toward the sea. I knew VC trick of taking hollow reed and breathe through it when lying under water.

Two hundred meters and there is this field where some corn is cut. Next to it is a field with thick corn growing. The cops are running along the dike. That takes them away before they come back toward me. I must decide quick where to hide. I dive into cut field and cover myself with corn.

A few minutes later I heard cops talking out of breath. They started searching in the thick corn field. I wait till I didn't hear them anymore, then took a look. If I run during daylight it is easy to see me, so I stayed put. After a while the two cops came back. I heard them crash around, but finally they went away.

I stay still till it is about midnight and there is no moon. Then I started slow crawl to riverbank. I went through very heavy mud and too many mosquitos.

Once with Twenty-first Division I was on an operation in this area so I know where I am. To get away, first I must go around a little farm. It was hidden by coconut trees. I can only tell I am near it when a dog barked. That scared me to the other direction. In about one hour I was on the riverbank. I must cross it, then cross about a mile of reeds to the highway. I can follow the highway ten miles to Vinh Binh. I hoped parents of organizer can help me there.

I made a ranger roll out of my clothes, put it around my neck, and went off the riverbank in undershorts. The tide was running out to sea. I let it take me while I struggled for the other bank. I am only a fair swimmer. I thought I was moving pretty fast but didn't get much closer to other bank. The river is wide, more than hundred meters. I got so tired I decide to drop my sandals.

Still only halfway, and now I think I won't make it. Never so much exercise since prison. It is a surprise how weak I am. It is time for drowning, I'm afraid.

My head stayed down longer. When it came up I tried a few more strokes. Down again, then a few more strokes. I think that's it for me. I was standing almost straight in the water, not going anywhere except drifting to sea. I thought, this is how Dat looked when he first learn to swim. He was scared when the water come to his mouth. Now the water is to my nose.

But my feet hit something even when the riverbank is still far away. It was mud under the water. For a minute I can stop swimming, get my head up for air—but the current dragged me slowly over this mud bank.

I was out in deep water again but now I think I have a chance to make it. After a long time I can reach a root that is under water. Above me was the bank. I almost came too far, almost got lost in the sea.

For a long time I walked up the bank. I changed my plan. With no sandals, and body covered with mud, I cannot go to highway and walk to Vinh Binh. I must find a little boat to go up this river that also goes to Vinh Binh. If I do not find a boat, I will be walking when daylight comes and people who see me will tell the cops. If daylight comes I must hide in reeds all day.

Two, three miles very hard walking on bank. Everywhere it is up and down, many roots and snags that made me fall and bleed. Never saw any boat. Very hard to see anyway without moonlight.

Then I heard snoring. I froze and decide to go back in other direction because this was maybe a guerrilla sleeping at his post. I listened for a while and think this sound comes from the river.

I looked real close. There is a boat near the bank with three mosquito nets. I climbed down and used a branch to pull the boat in. If they are VC I will try to throw them in the water to kill them. Snoring stopped for a minute. I decided these are fishermen and woke one of them up.

He was surprised that I am here. I talked tough, told him I am a guerrilla who was looking for a fugitive. Slipped in the river and lost my weapon. I told him to calm down, I need his help.

He complained that he is just a fisherman and I should find someone else. I said, look here, I have two rings of gold for him if he gets me up to Vinh Binh before morning. This is a big reward for him so he woke the other two guys.

They decided they know where there is a sampan to steal. One stayed with the boat, the other two helped me paddle the sampan. We worked very hard against the tide. After hours one of them said, "You can get off at next curve in the river. Guerrilla patrol goes by there every morning." I said "No thank you," and then they both laughed because they know I am a fugitive, not a communist.

Chapter
Twenty-two

Caked with mud, Cai burst into the organizer's house. He washed as he panted out his story, and he told the parents how to contact the Lams for money to arrange his children's release. Because of the seriousness of their capture at the ferry, that would take some weeks and bribes. So too for the organizer.

His family had a emergency plan for being caught. They got money to the police right away before the paper work is started. When he was caught on the ferry boat it cost them three leaves of gold. That's one of the reasons why other passengers have to pay so much—to pay off police in case organizer is caught. Vietnamese say at that time, "Spider's web catch the flies but cannot hold a bird." That means small people who are caught escaping go for years to bad prison or NEZ, but organizers get out pretty quick. This guy had to spend only three months in jail—other passengers got six years. My kids were let go after three weeks and my parents took them back to Saigon.

The next escape opportunity would be around Tet, the one time of year when people could travel all over the country with few restrictions. The Tet holidays (two of only three days off allowed by the SRV, the other being Ho Chi Minh's birthday) were the last vestige of earlier times, a brief interlude of hopeful feeling, which the SRV considered sentimental and quasireligious but tolerated as a transitional indulgence in the relentless march to socialism.

Travel at all other times of the year was tightly controlled. Passes were required for intercity buses, and since there were no private cars (or any fuel for them if there were), hitchhiking was the only alternative transportation, and far from being free, the hitchhiker had to wave a wad of piasters.

The SRV's hope and purpose was to hamstring the population's mobility. The communist ward system worked best when the people it controlled stayed close to home. Strangers could be watched more closely when there were few of them.

Though confined to the city by controls and scarcities, within Saigon the dispossessed freely milled in misery. In the five years since RVN's fall, South Vietnam's economy had sunk from the level of a developing country right behind Taiwan into the abyss next to Bangladesh. Within the flow of the impoverished and the illegal, Cai could drift in relative safety.

*M*any *times I had no place to stay so I rode the city bus all day. It is not allowed to sleep on buses, but I can if I take a seat way in the back. So crowded nobody notice. I kept paper money in the crotch so pickpockets cannot get it when I sleep this way.*

Once I felt a hand there. I grabbed for my money. It was a woman who wants to wake me for love. She was very skinny but still beautiful. She said I should get off with her, she was daughter of high GVN official. This could be true because many people who were rich before communism now must pedal passenger bicycle, or do some other low job, and the women must be prostitutes.

Round the big An Dong bus station there were many former rich people, poor people from the NEZs, prostitutes, and also young guys who gave themselves to drugs.

If they had no home it is not so easy for them to get drafted into the army. In 1979 NVA had a hard fight with Chinese army on the north border. NVA was also fighting in Cambodia. A new generation of South Vietnamese tried to get out of this by being street people and using drugs so much that they lost their health and couldn't be soldiers. Many former rich people got drugged too, then they forget what happen to them. Sometimes they died after drugs. I think they wanted that to happen. No street cleaners, so bodies lie on pavement like they are asleep till dogs eat pieces of them.

Not so much marijuana as with U.S. GIs. Smoking dope makes the stomach hungry and there is not much to eat in SRV. Heroin is more popular, but opium is cheaper and is better for accepting hard conditions.

It was a good idea for me to stay near heroin people because they watched out for each other. Whenever a cop flashed his light on them they pass the word and go off in many directions. They sort of rotated around the city to different bus stations so authorities cannot keep track of them. That's what I wanted to do too. Never good to be around one place too long.

But sometimes late at night I wish cops were near because drug people act crazy. They got around a candle and shared a needle, then some of them scratched themselves and scream. One told me that their body can "overfly" [levitate] but I'm afraid of their violence. One night I heard a pistol, because a cop shot one dead.

Mostly cops at night just wanted to find a nice prostitute to take to sub-sector police station where everyone can enjoy her. We joked with these women, "Go ahead, it is warm there and maybe you get some food," but usually they didn't want to go because no pay. I remember one night the local cop looked around and said, "You come."

She said, "Damn, I got twenty-eight tickets today [customers often paid with bus tickets], now I got to serve the SRV for free."

Finally Tet is coming. I was with another organizer, and he announced a big wedding party for New Year's Day. He knew passengers can get permission to come from many places far away. Also there is reason to tell local authorities why so many people stay overnight.

The nice wedding party is to be next to the river, so nobody is to be stopped when many guests come in sampans. Most guests go home when party goes into late night, but passengers sneak into sampans and go to escape boat. That was the plan for Tet 1982.

This was the attempt that ended on the mud bank. Once more, Cai's children were imprisoned, fortunately not in the district of their first arrest. The communists never were able to create central records for criminals, nor did they know how to fingerprint, and lateral transmission of police information between districts was uncommon.

When I got back to Saigon, I do not know how long my kids will be in jail. This is horrible for a father, and I felt I brought them only bad luck. I thought that way and started to drink too much.

The way this started is because I must act drunk when I stay at friend's place. Then if ward inspector came around after curfew my friend can say I had little bit too much to drink and should not go home because of criminals. Drinking was not fun. No beer can be bought anymore. People must make home brew wine from fruit peels and banana skin.

There were six different places I can sometimes stay. Three of them were with old friends from childhood. Another was with Nguyen Van Huynh, who did the black market with NVA at Long Binh. Other places I can stay once a month.

Nguyen was the only one I can tell about my true situation. He is the only friend who knew I escaped from re-education camp. With others I acted like I was just working in the black market. These people I stay with I knew for many years, but no one can trust completely in SRV. There is too much pressure. When children are hungry, informing can be only way to feed them. That is why whenever I go to stay someplace I brought food from black market.

When communist VIPs came to town from the north and other countries, security forces made sweeps to get beggars, whores, and drugheads out of sight. That is when it was hardest for me to find places to stay. Couple of times I ask Thien, another interpreter, to let me come in for the night. He is a good man, but he did not understand the danger.

Because he learned agriculture in New Zealand, communists gave him a job for the government. He made just a few dollars per month, not enough to buy a pack of imported cigarettes, but he accepted that because his children can stay home and help him and not have to be Vanguards or learn communist bullshit. He was very poor, but he looked around at other people and thought he had it made.

One time when there was a sweep of the city, I asked to sleep on the floor near his back door. If an inspector knocks, I can leave quick, but if there is inspector at back door too, I must get into the ceiling. So I asked Thien, please let me have time if he hears knocking at night. I almost got caught that time because he did not remember what I told him. After that, I only ask to stay if I had no place else.

A guy I trusted more is Pham Quang Tam. He was an artillery battery commander in Twenty-first Division. Once I saw him in re-education camp in Catum. His father was a customs officer in GVN. I never ask Tam, but everybody knew customs job is great place to make corrupt money. His father had nice three-floor house in 3d District of Saigon, but when the communists took over he decided to commit suicide. He left his family with some money and they were able to bribe cadre not to take over that house.

3d District is called Ban Co because it had so many funny alleys that if people look down from above, the area looks like a chess table. Not many street lights in Ban Co. It is a good place to stay away from security forces, so while I am outlaw I liked to visit Tam.

His story is better than most families in Ho Chi Minh City. His mother was killed in an NVA rocket attack in 1968. He had five brothers; all of them were in same artillery unit. Also two sisters. One worked in the black market selling dead flashlight batteries that she made look like new. Before she sold these batteries, she heat them up so they make light. Little while later they are all dead again, but she sold them in other parts of the city and hoped nobody sees her more than one time.

The brothers spent everything to bribe their way out of re-education camp, and had no money left. Tam pedaled a cab. Duc's leg was very bad from camp torture so he can only be a beggar. The other three did not tell me what they do. Sometime they came in with pieces of machines from waterfront. They can sell them because everybody wants to make motors for escape boats.

The youngest brother got TB while he was in prison. His job is to watch out for other brothers while they steal parts. But he was coughing too much, no good for security. Brothers told him it is sad but he cannot work with them anymore. Unfortunately he must become a beggar like his other brother. These two eat mostly rice that bounces out of trucks. Usually they brought home only a couple of handfuls.

It is a very hard struggle for their families. Because they were in re-education camps, they are not citizens and do not have ration cards or passes to travel. Children of ex-ARVN cannot go to school either. They have no future except in NEZ.

Twenty-nine people, men, women, children, lived on these three floors. Just three rooms, one tiny kitchen and bathroom. Not as much space as in Chinook helicopter. After while I got lice from there because everybody sleeps so close. When it rains, it came in because the roof is rotted. Dirt is up there for growing vegetables. They must be watered and that rots the roof and makes wood worms too.

Tam's family was better off than most families in the neighborhood. Another reason I like to stay with him is that his ward cop was a good man. Most cops were northerners but this one was ex-VC who did something very brave at Xuan Loc and got this job for reward. He sympathized with poor people of Saigon because VC got screwed by NVA too. SRV wall posters all over town say, "If you love Vietnam you love socialism." That means VC must accept the way northerners run the country.

Tam's mother-in-law lived a couple of blocks away. She was successful running a gambling place for blackjack, mah-jongg, and lottery. The only people who can afford gambling are families who got gold from overseas. People who have escaped in boats send money back to Vietnam. Government takes cut at post office but let families come and get what is left. Communists do this so money keeps coming in.

Tam was worried if our good cop will let the gambling place stay open. He asked if I will get some imported cigarettes for our cop. I did that but he does not take it. He does not believe in corruption.

This is too bad for us and too bad for him, because he was fired for not making enough bribe money for his police station. New cop came in. He is a northerner and checked up on every-thing. He found out about drug making in the ward, gambling, daytime whorehouse, and draft dodging. He made everyone pay him so all this can go on. It is very expensive. When he went on leave to North Vietnam, all ward people must collect money to buy him a bicycle and "two window, no pilot" watch (i.e., a Timex automatic digital). These things are big luxuries in North Vietnam. I cannot believe that things are harder up there than in Saigon, but it is true.

People in Tam's house were even more poor now that this new cop is watching them. The brother with TB had a big fight with the others. He was eating more than he can get begging, and he needs a little medicine but cannot buy from the govern-ment because he is ex-ARVN, so black market is the only place. Black market medicine is too expensive. He must admit this and it made him like an insane man because he has no hope. Finally, he let himself get caught stealing. He said he would rather be in jail than be starving and make his family starve too.

This situation made me so sad and angry I cried without control. I did not like to remember Tam's brother, so I moved away from there.

After he moved out, Cai became the navigator for the escape that sailed halfway across the Gulf of Siam before being turned back by the storm.

He had the reputation of a skilled navigator and was in demand by organizers. Many now operated out of Vung Tau, and Cai was called there for several attempts that were aborted at the last minute because the organizations had been infiltrated by government agents.

There were many checkpoints in the country, but most for tax collection except on the roads into Vung Tau. All people who arrived here must stop for cops, who looked them over very carefully. To tell the truth, I was most afraid to go in here. In Saigon, most cops were young guys with no brains, but at Vung Tau they were old and mean looking. When the bus stopped at the checkpoint, they slowly walk around and observed each passenger. When they look at me I held my breath and boldly looked direct at their eyes like I was ex-VC.

One time when bus started again, I saw this guy ride by on a Lambretta motorcycle. I knew him. He is Thien, the interpreter for 2/327 who was AWOL. I saved him from hard labor at deserters' camp. I saw where he stops. It is at Water Department building. A good contact in Vung Tau is a big help for escape, so I took a chance and went to him when he is alone. If he is communist now, I had a knife to kill him.

Thien looked at me with surprise, then said he is glad to see me. He invited me to his house, a nice place. I didn't tell him what I am doing but asked for a pass to travel around the district like I work for Water Department. He said, sure thing—he will fix me up with pass for fifteen days—charge is 2000 piasters! He saw the look I give him and said money is not for him, only for his supervisor. I paid because this pass will get me around without worry about tough cops. Thien asked if I need a place to stay for night. I answered, "Sorry, I can't afford your place," and walked out.

Escape had become an industry second only to fishing in Vung Tau. Indeed, so many trawlers had disappeared on escapes, the remaining fishermen were doubling their catches. Like the resort it had once been, Vung Tau now made cash from transients. Beach homes now were valuable as safe houses.

An organizer, usually from out of town, reserved enough houses to hide his passengers, who infiltrated from all over South Vietnam. Typically the organizer arranged to pick them up in Saigon, then dropped them off near Vung Tau, where a local confederate led them to the safe house for a two-day stay before the escape. A local rowed them out to the escape boat that put to sea at night. When escapes were postponed—as they often were for weather, mechanical, or security reasons—the procedure reversed and the passengers dispersed to points outside Vung Tau until the organizer was ready to bring them in again.

Over the years the local authorities had been bought off so that a Vung Tau departure was a selling point for an organizer. But the SRV, getting wind of a good thing, started shifting new cadremen into Vung Tau, and new bribery rates put arrangements in flux. Consequently, Cai had to make several trips in and out of Vung Tau because negotiations between authorities and organizers often fell through.

*O*rganizer said everything was okay now. He will not make much money because there was a new guy to bribe, but I should go down and look over the boat because we would leave the next night.

I was to go where fishing boats are tied up together. This area, called Ben Dinh, is very dangerous because cops want to keep watch on boats. Organizer said, no problem, there is a new guy in charge and he is paid off.

But when I got to this boat area, the old cop was watching. He was looking with binoculars I think. Suddenly I heard his motor scooter stop behind me. He looked at me and knew I was a stranger. He pulled his pistol and put it at my head. He said, "Who organized for escape tonight?"

I said I did not know really. I was poor and hoped to hide on board. He looked at my money and saw I have just 20 piasters, so maybe he believed me. Then he introduced himself. He is Mat, the cop who has been in charge of Ben Dinh for years. He was angry because he thinks organizers do not deal with him anymore because of the new cop in charge. He told me to go to a bar later in the night and he will get me in an escape.

I learned from the organizer that Mat was very rich because of payoffs. SRV put other cops in to get some of this action. Organizers liked Mat more better because he kept his promises. New guys, they do not know. Mat asked me how many people are going on escape so he can get fair share. New guy will not say what he wants. I do not like the new setup and told the organizer to get another navigator. I am right because next time a boat tried to go out, everyone was busted and so is organizer.

Lot of organizers want me after I got halfway to Malaysia. I decided that I will not work with any who use Vung Tau because it is now too dangerous. Nine times I went there for escapes but all go nowhere.

Afraid of Vung Tau, and depressed by Ho Chi Minh City, Cai drifted back to the delta to contact organizers there. Now a rural rather than urban fugitive, he had to adopt a new persona:

Toughest thing I got to learn is how to use the right speech. In the countryside, I always wore plastic sandals. These are only issued to army officers and SRV officials, but I buy on black market. Young guerrillas will not usually ask questions to a man in plastic sandals.

But if I go down around water, better to look like worker and have forged worker pass. They go around with no shirts lot of the time and roll up pajama pants from mud, and wear no shoes. When I had to do that I must watch out for bad sunburn. Also wear cone hat like Chinese. Hard to learn workers' words because they do not open mouths or speak loud.

It was not easy to find organizers in the delta. I had been away for a while. Some organizers I knew have escaped. New ones think Vung Tau is better so business down here not so good.

And the cops got smarter. They let fewer people into fishing villages. They looked over strangers careful. Organizers more careful too because cops learned how to penetrate their organizations. Cops pretend to be outlaws like me. They pay to get in escape plan, but just before boat leaves they come in and arrest everybody. Then secret cop gets bonus.

I had to ask questions to find an organizer in Ba Tri. There is one guy I should suspect because he was so well known and he is not very careful. He told me I must see his number-two man, who will take me for boat ride to see if I am good navigator. Turns out this guy is a secret cop. Later I found out he blackmailed the organizer. He said to him, "You just keep organizing big escape. I will get all the names of passengers. When they are arrested you get good reward and can move away."

For sure I don't know about this plot when I met number-two guy. He acted friendly, said his name is Vo [a surname]. Most guys in organizations use only first names. When Vo took me out on the boat, he asked a lot of questions about my background. If I am escaped prisoner from re-education camp, he will get bigger bonus. I told him I was enlisted man and was released. He made many criticisms about SRV and asked if I agree. This made me suspect him. Everybody knew how bad SRV is but don't talk about it.

On the boat ride I made many mistakes about navigation— ran the boat on a mud bank. I thought that if this is real escape, Vo will say I cannot be navigator. But he did not care much. Laughed at my mistakes. I asked if I will be okay. He said, sure—just pay gold leaf and I will get the job.

I wanted to get away, so I told him I got to go back to Saigon for gold. Vo was surprised that I am not ready to pay. I guess he was making a plan to keep me around, and make sure I am arrested. Last bus for Saigon is eight p.m. He said maybe I should stay tonight and try navigation with him on dark river. I thought it is not a good idea to refuse.

The river is a mouth of Mekong, the Ham Luong, very wide. When it got dark, we went out in a row boat. Nobody is supposed to be out there except fishermen, but Vo is not worried. Then I am pretty sure he is an agent.

I sat in front with a compass while he rowed. I did an azimuth for him but got it wrong. I said, very sorry—if he keeps rowing I will get it right. We rowed way out where there are no lights and we cannot see the shore. I did the azimuth right, then said, sorry I make him row so long—I will row back.

Vo was tired and let me have oars. I said, please step over me and sit in front, I need him to guide so we will get to shore at the right place.

We went along quiet but the oars are squeaking. I made them do that because I have a plan to get rid of him. While I row along, I whispered to him, "Vo, I make so much noise with oars I'm afraid patrol can hear us."

"Don't worry," he said.

I row more quiet but then we didn't make progress, and the tide is moving us. I said, "Excuse me, but we can go fast and be quiet if we paddle, not row. Please paddle with oar at front and I will paddle in the back."

Vo did not think we need to do this, but he reached back for oar. I took it out for him. His head was turned, and in the dark he cannot see me swing the oar. It made a rushing sound in the air. It hit and I heard his skull break.

I hit him so hard I almost fell out of boat. I saw his dark shape sitting like a rice sack. I swung the oar again, down like an ax this time. It hit the same side of his head. He made one moan, then I felt him to see if he is still alive. Blood was coming from his nose. I washed that off my hand very careful.

Air from the nose made bubbles in his blood. I thought he was pretty dead. I put the oar back and began rowing. Tide was moving quicker. I thought I'd better choke him till he is dead for sure, but I changed my mind because even if he is still alive he cannot swim back a mile in the hard tide. I pushed Vo over and he floats away in darkness.

Boat is lighter now. When I got close to shore I had to hit the planks very hard to make them break. Then the boat is sinking. When it does not come back, people will think we both had accident and drown.

So no one must see me in Ba Tri. Under the moon I walked to find the highway. I took off wet clothes and lay in a field but did not sleep because of mosquitos. Next morning I cannot take a chance on the bus to Saigon so I paid a truck driver lots of money to take me there.

Chapter
Twenty-three

*T*he truck broke down before we got to Saigon. That was because there is only one lane; the other was torn up from the work of a road repair crew. Long line of trucks had stopped, some of them from the army. My driver shut off the engine but must start again because line moves on about twenty meters. Start and stop. This happens again many times. Just before we get to a cop, this truck's generator is dead.

I was watching this cop check if taxes are paid by drivers. Looked like passengers must pay too. I didn't have any more money except gold in my underwear, so this cop could give me a hard time.

Other thing this cop did is keep people away from the road crew. He had two soldiers with rifles for this. While my driver was working on the generator, I walked up close to the cop. There I can see road crew. They had pretty good equipment, and knew what they were doing.

Some of them look like Americans, but they wore caps with a red star. Vietnamese are not allowed ever to get close to foreigners, but I tried to hear their language. I thought it is Spanish like I heard some GIs talk in the Oh-deuce. Turns out the road crew are Cubans, Cuban communists.

I thought, what is the best thing to do? Traffic was one-way,

*changes every few minutes. A bus came from the other direction.
It must stop for inspection and to pay travel tax. Sign says it
goes to Vinh Long. I knew an address there. When bus went by,
I hopped on.*

All addresses came from Cai's memory. In Vinh Long, a delta
town of about 50,000, he could remember only a street. During the
war an interpreter from the 101st, Le Van Rang, had his home there.

When *I asked about the name Le on that street people looked
at me funny. They told me that is the name of elementary school
teacher, a woman who is also the ward security chief.*

*I must find out more about her. Turns out she is Rang's wife!
She was not a cop, but cadre from north got her elected ward
representative. That means the cadre trusts her, not that people
want her. Whoever cadre selects people must elect.*

*I left a note for Rang to look for me in the market. If he is
informer, there is always big crowd in market and I can get
away. When he showed up, he is glad to see me because he
remember good things I did for interpreters in 101st.*

*My story is that I am in Vinh Long to do some black market
deals. Also I was model prisoner in re-education camp so I got
out in Tet amnesty first year. He asked me if I told camp cadre
I was interpreter. I said, to tell the truth, no. Rang laugh and
said, me neither. Lucky for him he never was officer in ARVN,
so he got out of re-education camp with enlisted men after just
few days.*

*I didn't say anything about his wife but he told me anyway.
He got it made: he can sell imported cigarettes and not worry
because if security cops want to search anyplace in his ward
they come to his wife, who goes with them. His cigarettes are
safe. He also got a deal with Cubans: he trades them heroin
and opium for good strong cigarettes. I told him about Cuban
road crew I saw and he say, yeah that's them. They send the
dope to Cuba and make good money, maybe sell it to America
he thinks.*

Rang invited me for overnight stay. I'm kind of worried because of his wife. I think he knew that but he said, come on, it's okay.

She is a very smart woman. She heard about interpreters from Rang and welcomed me. She said she is saving money for escape! She asked me if I knew any good organizations but I said no, I have accepted SRV and will work here rest of my life. She laughed and asked about getting to U.S. I told her that might be tough if she is communist official.

She knew a lot about the SRV, how it is set up and everything. I can't figure her out: she talked just like hard-core communist but she also is saving for escape.

One day it is her job to make a public trial. She said come on down to city square and watch. At the city square there are some soldiers who arrested a man who was caught for stealing gasoline. He had a needle syringe, like in hospitals. He gets the gas by sticking the needle in fuel lines and sucking it out. Very little comes each time. It takes him all night to get just half a liter. In daytime he worked full time moving rocks for a government dike. One night when stealing, he was so tired he fell asleep under the army truck and is caught.

Rang's wife name is To. It is her job to use loudspeaker and get crowd to hear this case and order punishment for the gas thief. People at town square have to stop and listen because a squad of NVA don't let them leave.

To did a good job denouncing this thief. She said his crime is extra bad because he took gas from SRV vehicles. To tell the truth, no place else to get it except from civilian motor scooters. People put stuff in their gas to make it last longer but it messes up motors, so now there were not many scooters working.

To went on about how thief is class enemy. He has ruling class background because during the war he owned a fish stall. He was also a "false soldier" because he was in RF. Thief didn't say anything but I think everybody felt sorry for him because he is so skinny and has very bow legs from carrying rocks on a pole across the shoulders.

To demanded that the crowd say if he is guilty and what punishment he should get. Nobody said anything. Soldiers went around and said softly that people must stay in the square under the sun till they say something.

One brave guy yelled, "Let him go! SRV sucks!" He said that where there are many other people so soldiers do not know who say it. Tell the truth, some of the soldiers smiled. Finally, To sent for a cadre person and he made a speech about how lenient SRV is so this thief will be able to reform himself in NEZ. People clapped so they can leave and finish their business.

That night at Rang's house I didn't mention the trial, but To said it wasted her time. People do not understand that there must be hardship before communism makes everything all right. If people starve it is a good example that the old class system must be destroyed. People must not think so much about making money either and not try to do things private. Everybody must have same thoughts. It took everybody working together to unify Vietnam—that showed thought unity is possible. The party knows this will be resisted but in one more generation everyone will think the same. Old people with old thoughts got to go.

I can't believe she talked like this and also gets ready for escape. Rang sort of had to agree with her, but he also understood what I am thinking. He said what a good time it was when war was over. For about one week everyone so glad that there is no more killing, bombs, mines, and fighting. Then so many people got taken away for re-education. To didn't say anything, but I think she remembered too.

It was a perfect place to stay, but To told me she must have part of my black market profit. She wants to know what I do. I cannot tell her so I said I go back to Saigon to bring my business to Vinh Long. I don't come back because I'm afraid of To and cannot afford the high price she demand. Last thing she said to me, "You Chinese, right? You better watch out because SRV getting rid of them."

She was right. As a result of the 1978 rupture with China, the SRV rounded up 300,000 of its million ethnic Chinese, loaded them in small boats, towed them to Chinese waters and literally cut them adrift. The SRV also took this opportunity to rid its prisons of violent criminals, adding a few to each boat, where they robbed and raped until landing.

I didn't know about this. Now I'm even more scared because I am Chinese. I can be picked up just for that. I asked my parents about the deportation program and they said, yes, they had to pay big bribes to stay. They did not tell me because they thought I had enough problems: I was already a fugitive and cannot hide more than I was.

Cai returned to Ho Chi Minh City, doubly wary. It was 1982; for two years he had struggled to escape, had been involved in nine attempts to some degree, and spent twenty gold leaves in the effort. At most, once a month he was able to see his children in clandestine rendezvouses. His parents were becoming discouraged and reproachful as Cai drained their savings. He felt very much that he was still in prison, the inescapable prison bounded by the shores of Vietnam.

I started to think crazy thoughts. I believed maybe I should turn myself in for voluntary deportation to China. If I can get to Hainan island, maybe relatives there can get me boat for escape to Hong Kong. My father did not think that is a good idea. He said, "Easier to get out of communist country you know."

In mid-1982, Cai's father got him a message that a man named Chinh was looking for him. Chinh said he was a veteran of the Twenty-first Division. Cai's father was inclined to believe him but said no more than that his son was in the city.

I was going through the market looking for a good deal for matches. Almost time to close. I needed matches so I can have

*a candle at night. Not much street light anymore, and lot of times
I need a candle to find hiding place to rest.*

*Like a dream, I heard a voice say, "Oh-nine, this is one-one,
over." This made me jump because in Twenty-first Division my
radio call sign was oh-nine. I turned around and there is this
guy, Chinh, making big smile. We shook hands and hold our
shoulders hard. I didn't remember Chinh too good but he was
assistant operations officer with the Thirty-third Regiment. He
helped get reinforcements for the battle where I was wounded.*

*Chinh said, "Let's walk over to the zoo." All animals there
were eaten, but it is still like a park and we can talk in the dark.
He knew a good place where we can see in every direction.*

*He asked how I was doing. I am honest with him, and said
things are pretty bad. I'm lucky because my parents give me
money, but I never made an escape and worry all the time about
being robbed or killed by criminals and captured by security
cops. Now I'm worried about being Chinese. Very few people I
can trust, so I'm real glad to see him. Then I asked Chinh how
he's doing.*

*Chinh smiled and said he got all those problems too except
he didn't worry about being robbed because he got no money.
Tell the truth, he looked like a beggar, and I said that. Chinh
laughed: he wears rags in the city only. In the country he has
old ARVN uniform. Out there he eats pretty good because he
got friends in the countryside. In fact, he got a lot of friends.
Do I know what that means? I told him, no.*

*He talks quieter but I listened real good. Chinh is with re-
sistance forces. When he said that, I say please have one of my
Cuban cigarettes. He said thanks, but he will not smoke it here.*

*I told him I tried to find out about the resistance. He said,
okay, he will tell me about his group but he cannot say too much
because of security. I understand.*

*This group did not have a name. He will not tell me how
many are in it but there is less than a battalion [fewer than 500
men]. Some are ex-rangers and airborne but most came from
Ninth ARVN Division that fought NVA in western delta. They
hide around a place called "seven mountains" near the Cambodian border. Lot of them fought the First NVA Division there*

in 1973. They wiped out that division; they found all the NVA's tunnel complexes and a big underground spring. After war these good men think seven mountains is a good place to hide. Couple of times NVA ran operations at them but they are able to get away because they know the seven mountains well.

There are also a few ex-VC in this group. It operates like guerrillas. Peasants in that region do not mind giving them rice because the group knocks off communist cadres. Killed so many that cadre must go around with troops and cannot stay in countryside at night. When resistance kills a tax collector, they give the money back to the peasants.

Food is not a big problem; plenty of weapons, but not much medicine, and group is worried that they will run out of ammo if they have to fight more. I told him about the time that Catum re-education camp was attacked. Rumor was that force was ex-ARVN and Khmer Rouge. They had 122-mm rockets then. He said, that's right—there was plenty of ammo, but every year it is harder to get. He asked me if I was at Bien Hoa when resistance force broke into Long Binh ammo dump. This was biggest one when U.S. Army was in country; NVA never moved out the ammo. The attack was by resistance force from around Gia Ray, he said.

He was not sure but Chinh thought the force got plenty of ammo from Long Binh, but when they left there was a firefight. To help get away, they blew up an artillery dump. Then explosions went everywhere—everything in Long Binh was destroyed. I told him, yeah, my parents heard a big noise like a battle in 1977. All of Saigon heard it. People thought new revolution had come. Cadres even hid for a while.

Everything he said sounds very good to me. I was so glad someone is still fighting the communists. I asked him how he found out about me. It was six years since I saw him. He said the ranger captain I help get in rice business was in this group. Chinh looked for me whenever he came to Saigon. Now he said I can help.

His group needs help from outside—medicine and ammo. I worked a long time with Americans. Maybe I can get them to drop some supplies with parachutes.

I didn't know what to say. The reason I was prisoner and outlaw was because I believed the Americans will come back and stop NVA invasion in 1975. That did not happen. I don't know anything about U.S. forces for six years.

I wanted to believe like Chinh that U.S. will help again. I think this is still possible. I asked him what he suggest. He said his group maybe can help get me out. They work with Khmer Rouge a little bit, not much now as before NVA took over Cambodia, but still some contacts. It's maybe possible for me to walk across Cambodia to Thailand. If that works I can talk to the Americans there. Chinh will tell me the radio frequency Americans can contact his group with. They can talk on radio and arrange a parachute drop. Maybe some U.S. special forces come too. They will be very welcomed.

Everything Chinh told me is very good news. I wanted to help resistance forces more than anything else. I was ready to go with him to seven mountains and escape through Cambodia. We shook hands for a long time.

But right now he did not want me to go with him. He had some other business in Saigon he cannot tell me about. I'm pretty sure he had to assassinate somebody in the communist intelligence office because he asked me about a part of the city where they live. He said he will have to leave town quick and not be back for a while. He will meet me here at this place in the zoo on Ho Chi Minh's birthday at evening time. I gave him some gold and said, "Take care of yourself."

Buoyed by his prospects, Cai prepared to become a guerrilla. He would need hard-wearing clothes for life in the field, and stout shoes for the trek across Cambodia. With searching, such items were still available on the black market—old ARVN fatigues and American-made jungle boots.

Though the buses were running irregularly, they could get him to the seven mountains region. Since Chinh used the buses, there was probably no guerrilla transportation net. But bus travel with military gear would be perilous, considering all the government checkpoints and roadside tax collectors (at least one per province).

Cai determined he would be safer with his own transportation. A motor scooter might even be helpful in Cambodia. With his gold, he could buy undiluted gas. Using dirt roads, he could avoid checkpoints. So for a leaf of gold he bought a three-wheel Lambretta.

Cai also tried to learn some Cambodian, but he found that impossible. There were no longer any language textbooks. In 1975, the communists burned every book in the libraries of Saigon. Nothing was published except by the SRV. Worn, torn pre-SRV paperbacks of any kind were a durable black market item, appreciating in value every year even as they physically deteriorated.

I got my gear ready. Made it into a little pack and hid it in the hole I found in a wall. I went to a propaganda office and asked for a poster. It say "Labor is glory"—something like that. I told communists it is for my ward. Posters all over the place but I told them we need more. They were glad to give it to me. At night I put the poster over the hole and my gear is safe.

Month after I meet Chinh, I was feeling pretty good about helping my country. So I decided one night to go to a little coffee house I heard about. After curfew they do some dancing to western music there. Western tapes are very illegal—can get you one year of prison if caught with one, even listening—but I decided to take a chance just one time and go there.

It was run like an underground gambling place. It had thick walls so no sound got out. There was a trapdoor like VC used to get away if cops come. Blankets over windows and tent had been put up for the night inside the room where people listen to music. We were very close together, everyone. Not much room for dancing. That was not what people wanted this night because music is on tape from a guy who escaped to U.S. His singing was very nice but it made all people cry.

Pretty soon after that I was down in the big market to look for a good knife. It was crowded so I had to get off the Lambretta and push it. I always looked around for security. This time I saw this woman looking at me. She looked away, then back again. I looked at her too because she is so pretty and I had many memories.

We cannot say anything. Finally she said, "Cai?"
"Lena?"

Sixteen years! I looked for her so long. Whole war happen while I was looking. I took her hand. It was formal like Chinese. We were standing there with the crowd all around us. We didn't know where to go, what to do.

I forgot about my Lambretta when we begin to talk. Then she saw it might be stolen. I pushed it with her, and we got outside the crowd.

Miracles are few in Vietnam, but this chance reunion certainly qualified. Lena's parents had taken her away on that distant afternoon in 1965, shamed by her pregnancy, which ended in miscarriage. They had gone to another part of Saigon, and Lena through her twenties grew close to her family, eventually marrying a Chinese-Vietnamese who managed to elude military service as the war thundered through its phases and crashed like a seventh wave in disaster.

Her marriage led to a daughter and divorce. After a year she remarried the same man and had another daughter before divorcing him again. During the war she had gone to a school for beauticians, and prospered serving the high-living GVN circle. Now she worked for a pittance in her one-room apartment, dressing hair and applying homegrown cosmetics.

First she worked for beauty shop that took care of women of communist officials. They don't have anything like that in north, so this shop was very popular. But the owner gave workers only 30 percent of what they earn. This is like bad capitalism but the communists didn't care.

So Lena quit this shop. A few customers came to her apartment for beauty work. Most were women who got money from overseas, but Lena did not make much from them. Biggest problem is that electricity turned off four days every week so some street lights can be on at night. That happens all over Ho Chi Minh City. Tough for her to make nice hair with no electric tools.

I met her two daughters, who are real nice like her. Just little kids, but sometimes they sold a few penny flowers to customers that came for hair. They are very polite, like Chinese kids.

They were also potential informers. First thing at school every morning, children had to stand up and recite what happened at home since the previous day. Nothing was too trivial to report: food at the evening meal, parents' conversation, any purchases, any sales, anything heard on the radio, and most important, any visitors. For information about a visitor, the teacher awarded a fruit tart sprinkled with precious sugar. The teacher worked up her class by asking, "Who will win a tart this morning?" If only routine visits by relatives were reported, the tart was withheld for another day.

The only greater reward was for a child who reported anything the parents said not to mention. This child would be given candy for a week, move from the bench to the "progressive" chair, and be allowed to color a book of heroic war scenes while classmates wrote lessons about loyalty to their late Uncle Ho. Meanwhile the parents would be "invited" to the ward police station for an interrogation from which they might never return.

At first I saw Lena only in the daytime, because of the children. We went to some meals together. She told her daughters that a cousin will soon visit—that's me—so then she introduced me to them. It's still not a good idea to be around too much so I never stayed with Lena except maybe one time each month when we got her daughters to visit with their grandparents.

At first her daughters did not like me much. That was because I never can be noticed around Lena's place. It was in an apartment building—twelve families in twelve rooms on each floor—people and kids in the hall all the time. Because I didn't want to be seen, I had to ask her daughters to do all these little things: get fish from the market, deliver letter, buy candle, lots of small stuff like that. They had no time for play and didn't like to do errands for me. They thought I'm real lazy. One time the oldest daughter said, "What's wrong with you?" but I cannot tell her my true situation.

When I got to know them better, I found out they waste time at school. Nothing is taught there except loyalty to officials and what Marx wrote. They learned how to write so they can make reports about people, but there is no math or knowledge that helps with life. Nobody can go above high school except those with good communist parents—maybe 10 percent of kids. Rest of them just go out on the street.

Only one college was left in the south. It is for cadre and indoctrination. I heard some communists are given degrees like they had college but this is just to make propaganda to the world that there is higher education. The official in charge of electric power had "people's degree for electrical engineering." That's why lights do not work in Ho Chi Minh City.

Lena and I wanted to get married. This is done by going to people's committee that is in charge of marriage and divorce. It is too dangerous for me to go. She went and said I volunteered for NEZ. That is where she said I was, so I cannot be at the committee. Lena showed them my false papers that say I was released from re-education camp. It was good for the committee to have a couple volunteer for NEZ, so they said okay and we were officially married.

Now I had Lena, her two kids, and my two. I had to think about Cambodia again. My plan after I met Chinh was to get out alone. Overseas I can make some money for my parents to pay officials to let my kids go legal. That costs a lot but it is possible for kids. The government was always glad to sell American-Vietnamese kids that way. They are lowest young people in Vietnam. I feel sorry for them and wish their fathers in the States do something for them. Even though my kids are not Amerasian, the SRV will let them out for enough money. People in Vietnam called kids their "export crop."

The coincidence of meeting Chinh and Lena in the same month confused Cai's already battered plans. His many rebuffs to escape by sea caused the trans-Cambodian route to look appealing: he would not be at the mercy of crooked organizers but rather in the company of resistance fighters he admired and hoped to support; moreover, he felt more confident with the prospect of navigating through the jungle than on the high seas.

But Lena's miraculous reappearance in his life made him reassess the risks of land versus sea escape. With the right boat and organization, the Gulf of Siam seemed, on balance, somewhat less perilous. That Cai had not yet found that combination did not mean it was not possible. And if it was, he could insist, as a highly valued navigator, that his new wife and family go with him—all of them, none left behind to be bought out of Vietnam in the uncertain years ahead. What meant most in his decision was the very fact that Lena had reappeared. He took that as an omen that his luck would ascend. To leave her for the resistance would amount to abandoning the omen. The sequence of the meetings also seemed important. First had come Chinh with new and cheering prospects, followed by Lena and the hint of even larger fulfillment. To escape with her and the children also enabled the possibility of helping the resistance once Cai made contact again with the Americans. That was the perfect outcome, the only outcome that could compensate for his seven-year ordeal.

I must be responsible for five people now, not just myself. It was hard for me that I cannot help Chinh like he wants. I will contact the Americans as soon as I escape but I must go back to the sea plan now. I had to tell Chinh. I went to the zoo on Ho Chi Minh's birthday and waited a long time. He did not come.

PART V

"Wherever snow falls"

Chapter
Twenty-four

In order to be with Lena, Cai tapped into the escape organizations that operated in Ho Chi Minh City. By keeping his focus local, he could better appraise their reliability.

I never knew anything about the organizers in Vung Tau and the delta. Eight times my parents were cheated. Nine other times I was almost caught. More better that I am patient and really check out the plan before I risk Lena and four kids.

As a proven navigator, Cai was much welcomed by the organizers he contacted. During the eight years since boat people began their exodus, over a half million had fled, taking with them almost everyone with nautical ability. Thus, Cai was no longer another refugee to be ripped off, but a prize to be won over.

In April 1983 two organizers are trying to get my help. One said he has everything ready in Vung Tau but I heard that story before, so I tell him no thanks. Other guy had pretty good plan. He got about a hundred passengers who pay three gold leaves in advance. They all want to meet me, the navigator, because this escape is so expensive. I agreed to do this if organizer will give me good place to stay. He said, "Sure—anything you want." He also made sure I have good food, and he provides transportation for meetings. Passengers liked me—they thought I was a navy captain, and I didn't say anything about that. But I said they must accept me as boss on the boat. They were glad to hear me say that because passengers cannot trust each other and wanted someone in charge.

Two policemen were going out. Organizer said he has good blackmail on them in case they are secret agents. He also said there will be his own agent with silencer gun to take care of them if they try to betray this escape.

There is also police uniform for me because he said we take government fishing boat, so there will be no worry about starting out in daytime. Another good thing: we start from the Rach Ong bridge, right in Saigon. I like these bold things the organizer did. It seems to me he has the best plan I heard about for a long time.

Only the night before did I tell Lena what we will do. We talked about escape for months, that she and the girls must be ready all the time, but for security I cannot tell her that we go till the night before. Organizer will pick her up at Saigon zoo.

From there and other collection points, the passengers would have to infiltrate to a point far downstream, between the mouth of the Saigon River and the sea, where sampans would bring them to the escape boat by night.

Organizer told me we have government fishing boat. That's the first lie I find out about when I got on this boat. Cop who is escaping with us smiled and offered me liquor. "Have a drink," he said. "We got a little work to do."

Then he took a metal sign with the name of the boat on it. I helped him nail it on. The boat is pretty new—just been built.

He took off sticky tape and there is license number of a government boat. He also had SRV flag for the back.

The escape boat was a homemade, three cylinder, thirty-three-footer, identical to a government fishing vessel (donated by the North Koreans) that at the moment was in service far upstream around Bien Hoa. The organizer's plan to reach the sea was for Cai's boat to impersonate the actual government boat. Now it was for Cai to find out if the plan he had up to this point been unaware of would work. If it did not, he, but not the organizer, would be captured.

The escaping cop handed Cai the boat's log for study. It was detailed but entirely forged.

I got to memorize this real fast. If we are stopped at floating checkpoint, river cops will ask for this log.

I am mad with anger about how the organizer set me up. I can still get off and be fugitive again but this is no good for my family. If they are missing tomorrow, cadre will move into their place. They will be fugitives too and have no place to go. Organizer figured this all out. His friendship was just to win me over.

I told this to the cop. He said, "Take it easy. We not going to have any trouble. See, I go along, so everything must be okay. Have a drink."

The cop was also the river pilot. Before they reached the pickup point for passengers, there were thirty miles of sand bars, mud banks, shoals, and fishing stakes to avoid. The communists had removed all channel markings for the very purpose of grounding escapes. Many had ended that way.

I had nothing to do but walk around the deck. I told this guy we got to have a story. Why does he steer if I am the captain? Why do I have a cop's uniform anyway? I should look like gov-

ernment fisherman or something like that. He just said, don't worry, have a drink, and let him talk to anybody who ask questions.

Cai cast off; his last chance to flee into the waterfront disappeared in a widening span of chocolate water. The pilot tried to reassure him:

He said, "Look we are not loaded at all. Boat is high in water so river patrols know we have no passengers. Not much fuel either—they cannot think we go very far into the ocean."

I was very nervous so I took his drink. I made myself busy reading the log. Then I thought if a cop sees me do that he wonder why. So I just try to look like I been on this boat for years.

This river pilot is very good. Sometime in the middle of river he turned to one side because he knew about shallow water. I see masts of some boats that are sunk. One place, pilot said, "That is false wreck. Communists put mast there to make boats go on mud at other side."

We came to the first floating checkpoint. We went real close, cut the engine back so there is no wave to piss off cops. I was really scared here because if we are regular government boat, we will have friends at the checkpoint, and they will want us to chat with them. But no one is on this thing. Pilot said a lot of them are like scarecrow—anybody who tries to escape thinks there are cops here but sometimes there is nobody.

On the shore there were checkpoints with real cops. We must go as close to them as across a room. Some looked once and go back to sleep. Couple of times we waved a little bit but they are not interested in us.

One place on shore is a big cemetery, mostly for Buddhist. We were going slow, and I can't believe what I see. People are digging up bodies! Didn't look like laborers doing this, it looks like families. The pilot said that's true: government decided more land must be for farming. Families can come get bodies of ances-

tors if they want them, then cemetery will be planted. Other places, relatives must pay for bodies. I was filled with hate for this SRV. They are cruel to people all their life; now they find ways to be cruel to the dead.

Since committing to this escape, Cai had been very conscious of signs of luck, especially numbers. Eighteen checkpoints slipped by one by one, exactly the number of his attempts, and he was buoyed.

No one stopped us. We hit the pickup point right on time, just at dark. Now I was feeling better. Sampans bumped against us. People climbed on real quiet and under control. They brought on plenty of water and some food. Diesel drums were loaded. A dinghy was tied to the back. It had a small motor but he does not use it now. This is the coast pilot who watches out for patrol boats.

What he will do is go way out in front of us into the sea. There he can see where patrol boats are. If one go south, he flash signal with light to me and I go north, or other way around. When the coast pilot thinks we are past patrol boats, he will signal me, then he comes back to his home.

With the motor dinghy scouting ahead, Cai took the wheel and handled the throttle. The three-cylinder marine engine gave a reassuring throb, sounding far more seaworthy than the puny motor that had floundered in the storm four years before. A mechanic shared the cabin with him. He said he had been in the navy and had not seen an engine this good since the war.

All the refugees were below deck. Cai asked for a head count, and the mechanic went below to get it. The total was 101. Cai smiled and thought that number to be another good omen.

"Send my family up, please," he ordered, and the mechanic went down the ladder again. Only Dat appeared. Lena and the daughters had been left behind. . . .

I spin the wheel right around. Boat tips on its side. Real quick, organizer's father climbs up and looked at me because he knew something is wrong. "Where is my family?" I shout, and called him names. He was shaking but he did not know.

I was crying with rage. His son is nothing but an evil man. Okay, then I take everybody back up the river. I can take Dat, jump on shore, and get away like I did before. I don't care. I have not worked to escape for four years to be used like this. I hope the cops catch his father and all his family. Then he will know what I feel. I have a good idea what the organizer did: my family paid no gold so he dump them. He thought only my son is important to me. He used the space for people who are profit for him.

Cai's curses and the lurch of the boat reversing brought several fathers on deck. Horrified, they watched the dim coast of Vietnam reappear. Cai slammed the cabin door in their faces but they beseeched him from the deck and more refugees poured out to join their wailing.

No use for them to argue. I am going back. They cried, "Please, please, no, no—we will get prison." I don't care I was so raged. No one is honest. Nobody care except about himself. We lost the war for that. Now this organizer family can lose their freedom. If he don't care, I don't either.

The river mouth opened again. Cai told everyone to shut up or they would be caught before he put them ashore. Then Dat began telling Cai what had happened at the Saigon zoo.

After being collected, the passengers were separated into three groups: men, boys, women and children. No one knew the reason for the segregation, and the organizer did not say. All Dat knew was that he was concealed under the tarpaulin of a rice truck, and after a long ride he got out by the river bank where sampans were waiting.

Then other families on the boat spoke up. Some of their women and girls were missing too. Not many—the boat could not have held ten more passengers—but apparently one truck from Saigon had not reached the river rendezvous. The refugees prevailed on him that the unlucky truck had been lost to the inherent hazards of such escapes, not as a result of perfidy.

I slowed the engine down. Many innocent lives are depending on me. Some people said they know how I feel, but that my life is not over yet and there is still a chance for reunion with my wife and children. Please, they said, go on. Leave communist Vietnam behind and take chance with new life—it must be better with hope.

These hundred people have no chance now without me. No more money, no homes, not even food. They prayed to me not to take them back to that. I said, "Get back and be quiet, we are near the shore." When they were below again, I turned the boat to sea, but with tears moving on my face.

A year later Cai learned that Lena and her girls, as well as his daughter, had never been picked up at the zoo. Luckily they were able to get back to their homes before their absence was discovered, but Cai's original opinion of the organizer was correct—he had dumped them for paying passengers.

The coast pilot did not see the boat turn back to the river. When Cai returned to sea there was no signal light to guide him. One, maybe two coast guard launches were known to patrol this stretch of the estuary. Both were armed with .51 caliber machine guns, searchlights, and flares.

I went very slow to keep engine noise down. I also listen for their engines. When my engine goes this slow it made clanking sound. I told the mechanic to do something about it. But he stayed in the cabin. I said, "What is this? Fix it." He said he don't know how. I asked, "You really a navy guy?" He said, yes, he was a captain in the navy but he just had a desk job. Never been out on a boat. I said, great, me neither—I was in the army.

Suddenly machine gun tracers arched through the darkness. Their trajectory was parallel to Cai's course. From army instinct, he counted the seconds between the sound and the muzzle flashes. The interval meant a coast guard launch was a couple of miles away. What the firing meant to him was that another refugee boat might be using the moonless night for an escape. The other boat's distress was Cai's opportunity. He gunned the engine and a bow wave formed white in the sea. The boat surged straight away from the coast, full speed ahead. Behind him a red flare popped in the sky, its glow descending on a small parachute.

I just go like hell. In a hour, we cannot hear .50 caliber anymore and flares went out. Another hour and the moon is up about a quarter. It helped me look for Con Son island.

It came up far away. To me it looked like a monster lying on the water at end of horizon. I told the mechanic to watch it real close with binoculars. I got to pass it on the left.

Con Son slowly disappear. I thought about how there must be so many prisoners on that island, dying slowly. It was like Vietnam's last curse for me. I did not want to look back at that island.

Boat is fast and drove through water like it doesn't matter which way the sea goes. After Con Son I headed way north, almost past Phan Thiet, then out farther to sea before I start south. With that course I'm sure we are far away from Cape Camau and patrol boats.

Daytime came and the sea was open all around. People climb up from below and look happy. I brought Dat into the cabin because I was so sad. He is the only family I can take with me.

Nothing to see anywhere, even though this is big shipping lane around Vietnam between Japan and Singapore. But nothing that day. Mechanic told me story about how little boats just came out to this part of the ocean and hope a ship comes by that will pick them up. I said, yeah, I know; this is where my sister and daughter went on their escape.

Before evening we saw something in the water that maybe comes from sunk boat. This was a piece of plank, white paint almost all gone. A water jug was floating too. We did not pick it up because that could be unlucky thing, but I thought about my daughter while it drifts away, and prayed that she made it to safety.

We started our second night on the ocean, then I turned right to 210 degrees. I let the mechanic steer a little bit while I sleep. He said he knew how to keep boat pointed with compass.

When I woke up it is 10:00 p.m. and a storm had come. Sky opened and closed with clouds—bright stars for a minute then all is black again. I listened for the wind. Before, in the daytime, passengers tore down the SRV flag, then tore it up—threw it in the ocean as they cheered. I told them wait a minute—save a piece so I can see which way wind comes. Now at night there was just this piece of red rag. Mechanic shined flashlight on it. I saw the wind blows from southwest. That's bad. That is the direction we want to go.

I used a ruler to measure distance on the map. I figured we were away from Cape Camau at least 500 kilometers. I was worried that strong wind might blow us back to Vietnam water.

Then came a terrible storm like the last time I was at sea. Sky and ocean were all black. When high waves came, sometimes water foam glowed like marks on the compass. The wild wind was like the whistle when a jet fighter takes off. This thirty-three foot boat went up and down like a little Ping-Pong ball.

But I heard nobody yelling for help or crying like in the other storm. I am sure everybody prayed at this time for the strong storm to leave us. Old memory came back of that storm in 1981. It was like it is happening again, the way some waves hit like sledgehammer, and bow is pushed into the sea.

I looked at my watch. Almost three hours we had been in this storm. I don't think we went forward much. This is not good for our fuel supply.

In the night the wind changed the way it blows. It slowed down and then back up again. I thought that means we had the worst part of it. We failed our schedule, but we can keep going if the boat stays tough. First thing when there is a break in the storm, I sent the mechanic out to look around. Wood was slippery from water, and he did not check the sides very good, but he came back and said everything is okay. When I told him about the 1981 storm, how a wave cracked the deck, he said he will go out and look again when the sun rises.

When light came, the wind was still strong but not as bad as at night. Passengers came up to throw over vomit. When they saw how big the waves are, they looked scared and go back down again quick! I was the only one who ate anything. I was not much hungry but need strength. I asked Dat for tea leaves— just mixed it with cold water and drank.

Morning passed but we did not see the sun much. I was sleeping off and on with my shoulder on the cabin wall. I told Dat to watch me. Sometime when I woke up I thought another day is past but it was only minutes.

I kept the boat right into the wind. We did not make progress but I didn't think we can blow back to Vietnam. This was not the course I planned but much safer than if waves hit us sideways.

In those long hours I did a weird thing. I think I was too tired. I had the idea that everybody must take off their rubber sandals. I told mechanic to fill a bucket with diesel. We will burn the sandals with black smoke. Then a rescue boat will see it and help us get to Malaysia.

Mechanic looked at me funny but he did it. Sandals were thrown up from below. Dat collected them on deck. Mechanic had a hard time lighting the flame. It didn't burn too good but there is smoke. Wind took it right away like nothing.

Then I had a big laugh and cannot stop. Mechanic laughed too, then Dat. They said passengers rely on me, and have good confidence so they did anything I say. I just kept laughing, on and off like the wind was doing. Craziest thing I ever did, this burning, but I think it made me wide awake again.

Pretty soon a father asked to speak with me. I said, sure, come on up. He was very respectful. He asked, where is rescue boat we make smoke for? I had to tell him I just imagined it.

I cannot believe how slow the time passes. About ten hours into the day, I can see a little bit of sky. Then maybe 10 percent was clear. I sent Dat to tell the passengers so they do not worry too much. I also told them we are maybe one third to Malaysia—the storm stopped our schedule for a while.

When the storm blew hardest my mind did not remember my loss of Lena. When wind became weak, these thoughts were back with me. I must try to think that I am very lucky among Vietnamese. My parents gave me money for eighteen escapes. Now I have good boat, good engine, and the storm is passing. I must be grateful for this, and that Dat is beside me.

Last wind left us. I thought how it will reach Vietnam, blow clouds over the delta in a few hours. It seemed to me now that clouds over the delta look like these at sea. Both places are flat. Already I was homesick for Vietnam. I remembered it like it had no communists.

The sea got calm before night. Clouds moved by the moon, and now the boat traveled like on a river. I put the ruler on the map and measured distances. With flat sea, we can get on schedule. That night I must curl up in a corner of the cabin. I made the mechanic and Dat sleep before that so they can watch the compass in the dark. That is hard to do very long. It sort of puts you to sleep, so I told them to watch together.

I told them to wake me after two hours. Nobody had a watch so they must guess. When they got me up, I was still very tired. The third night was the longest in my life. No storm to keep me awake, and my sadness made me want to sleep and sleep.

I don't remember anything about the fourth day. For twelve hours I kept on 210 degrees, then back to 180 degrees. I marked that on my map, so I must have done it. I changed course, I think, because it was better to land way down Malaysia and stay away from southern part of Thailand. I had heard they have pirates in the sea close to Thailand.

Fifth day I thought we could be close. There was fuel for rest of the day and one more night. The organizer was so cheap he did not put on more fuel, even for his father. I must decide what to do when night comes. Maybe not any lights on the coast of Malaysia. Dangerous to keep going at night and run into land. Map showed islands too if we are close to Thailand.

Dat cried out. I thought maybe pirate. I look very hard where he pointed. Something flat on horizon, too low for ship. Maybe submarine is so close to water. It disappeared. I steered away from where it was.

Pretty soon something else like it. Now I thought submarine had come up again. This was crazy but tired people think like that. I didn't want to say anything to make worry, but I asked mechanic if SRV had any submarines. He told me I should rest.

Then there were two things floating. I decided to keep on course. We were between them, but pretty far away. Dat shouted. It was a pretty big log. Other thing looked like stuff that floats out from land. Now I thought we may make it today.

But then there was only more sea.

We kept looking ahead, no place else. Sea made gentle waves at us but at one place, at edge of horizon, it did not move. I thought this little dark strip may be land. I steered right for it.

Pretty soon a bird came to look at us. It was a sea bird, but it must live by land.

We were watching that dark strip all the time. It got light at its bottom. That was a beach for sure! We shook hands and called for the fathers. Other passengers came out too and made offerings to Buddha. Some god had watched us for four and a half days. I said a prayer to that god, and hoped new luck will be with me. But how I wished Lena was beside me when I saw this bit of land. I wondered what she was doing during this minute and prayed we can see things together again.

I stayed away from this point of land and turned left to go parallel with shore. Four passengers kept watch that we don't run into something under the water.

Landshore went at about 120 degrees. It was jungle. I guessed we are between Patani in Thailand and Trengganu in Malaysia. For an hour I headed toward Trengganu. Then there was something on sea horizon. We looked awhile and saw it is a boat.

I was a little bit scared like a tired person is. This boat might be pirate. He turns when he saw us, and came in our direction. I decided to go by him next to shore. If he is a pirate, I can run my boat on the beach so we have a chance to get away.

I was not going fast so we can save fuel. Now when he came closer from southeast, I pushed the throttle to full speed.

He turned closer. I saw a foreign flag on his back. I didn't think he is a pirate anymore but want no risk, so I ran ahead of him down the coast. I tried to get to Trengganu, so if he is a pirate he will not go into harbor with me. He had a cannon in front. He blinked his light but my boat was too fast and he had to chase me.

Turns out he is Malaysian coast guard. He radioed to headquarters, and there were two more boats to meet me. I did good navigation because right ahead is Trengganu. All passengers came on deck. They thanked me when they saw a harbor ahead—even the organizer's father said thanks.

Now I followed orders from coast guard boats. They pointed to a long pier where they want me to land. I didn't know how to do that and bumped the pier pretty hard, made it shake. I thought, I do not make very good meeting with the Malaysian authorities. But this is a beautiful day with nice sun and cool breeze, a day to start happiness.

Chapter
Twenty-five

Cai pulled into Trengganu on July 16, 1984, completing the double escape he had envisioned when he nearly died from heat stroke in the Bien Hoa camp.

When I saw the dock where I am to land, I thought about the last days of April 1975, when my brothers said get out on a U.S. chopper. Five years I paid for my mistake in re-education. Four more as outlaw. For a while I thought that was all worth what I suffer because I met Lena and had her with me for escape, but that does not happen at the end. It was very hard to think how much I pay for my mistake, but I must remember that my life is not over, that in America I can work to get Lena out too. Then my mistake will not mean so much, and something much better can begin. Could be in the end this is best because my family and I will know how great freedom is because we saw when freedom died in Vietnam.

Trengganu was a refugee collection point, with a representative from the United Nations High Commission for Refugees (UNHCR). Like Thailand, to the north, and Singapore and Indonesia to the south, Malaysia was a reluctant haven for the boat people that had gushed out of Vietnam in the late seventies and still crossed the seas in a constant stream. In the previous six months, over 7000 had been processed, and most still languished near Trengganu.

When the first refugee jumped to the dock, he was knocked down by the police. The cop pulled out a .38 revolver and requested everyone come off the boat real slow.

The inhospitality of the SRV's neighbors was understandable. As observed by Nguyen Van Canh, "The massive refugee exodus (some 300,000 by the time Cai became one of them) is not a result merely of the harsh life in the SRV but is part of their diplomatic strategy in Southeast Asia. The refugees impose military, social, and economic strains on the countries that receive them."

Consequently, the beginning of happiness did not start on the day Cai's boat reached freedom.

Malaysian marines came with us when we go down the dock. One said follow guards into this camp on the shore. All around it is barbed wire like at Catum. I said to the mechanic, "What the hell is this? Are we free?"

When we are in the camp, an official asked in loud voice: "Anybody speak English?" One passenger stood up but he cannot understand the Malaysian. What he said was "I want list of all your names." I stood up and answer "Okay." Then he said, "Next to each name write the country where you want to go." I smiled all around when I translate that. I thought then we are safe— safe from being returned to SRV.

Armed guards observed the refugees' activities within the barbed wire. They were searched for valuables as well as weapons. The boat was impounded despite protests by the organizer's father. Malaysia had been fighting a small communist insurgency for thirty years, yet they regarded these escapees from communism with hostile suspicion. This was largely due to the fact that Malaysia's equivalent of the Vietcong were ethnic Chinese, which, to Malaysian eyes, were little different from Vietnamese. Cai, an ethnic Chinese, was singled out for quick and intense interrogation.

They took me to a little schoolroom. Refugees from boats before went through here. A lot of them still outside in old part of camp. They don't look too happy. I saw some Vietnamese bossing around others like they are guards.

Authorities told me I am illegal immigrant. I said, sure, all people in my boat are like that. We don't want to stay in Malaysia, just have to stop here to get to other countries. Okay, they told me, we will turn you over to UN people; that takes some time, and while we are here we got to pay for food and clothes and everything. How much gold we got? To get food for my passengers, the Malaysians took the compass and tool box.

I ask, "We land in Malaysia or North Vietnam?"

I looked around and counted how many are guards. Already I'm thinking about another escape.

After a while a major arrived. He asked if we need anything. I said, respectful, how about some water? He is a good man and sent marines to get two five-gallon cans. Then he asked if we got questions. A woman passenger requested that we go back to boat and pick up belongings. When we went back on board, everything valuable was already taken.

About 6:00 p.m. a bus comes. It was from the Malaysian Red Crescent Society (MRCS). They are like the Red Cross but because most Malaysians are Muslim people they call Red Cross, the Red Crescent.

This bus is to take us to camp inland. We were glad to leave the marines. I got on and I met a Chinese lady of the MRCS. Her name is Teo Beng Eng. We can talk in English so she told me what is going on.

She said after we are processed and checked for diseases we must go out to refugee camp on Pulau Bidong island. That's what happen to us. We were put on a boat and taken where there are

6000 refugees. Many of them were there for five years already because no country accepts them. They sort of made this island their own country and it has a little government by refugees. One thing is a big surprise to me. All escape boats are sunk. Refugees could catch fish for themselves but this is not allowed. Even a good boat like ours was taken out in ocean and sunk. I asked about this and nobody really knew why that is done. Malaysians said it is UN policy. UN people said Malaysians do not want competition for fishing and are afraid refugees will not come back to island and go somewhere else in Malaysia. I asked if boat owners cannot sell them so they have money to go to third country but authorities shook their heads.

When I got checked for diseases, they took x-ray of my chest. I told them I have bullet from battle in there. They said, okay, when we find it you can go to doctor and he takes it out. I was very glad for chance to get rid of this communist bullet that is in me so long.

After about a month I asked, when will I have my operation? They said, oh yeah, that's right—we will check your x-ray. They came back and showed me picture of my chest. Nothing in there. I said, must be mistake and show my scar where bullet went in. Nurse told me she don't know what happen, but they cannot operate if there is no bullet on x-ray. I said please x-ray again, but she said, sorry, too many refugees and it's too expensive. I didn't find out what happen to the bullet till I get to Montana.

Refugees who must stay here so long are mostly those with no education. A lot were just fishermen who could get away in their own boats.

They made a mistake when they said this because UNHCR decided they are economic refugees. Most countries will not give asylum for them. More better if they are political refugees. One of the things authorities asked me to do is talk to the Vietnamese about this.

I got an interview and told authorities I was a military intelligence officer. That sounds to them like I was an investigator for SRV. I said, no, no, but they said that's all right—they know I am not communist, but they need chief investigator for crimes in the camp. That will be me.

To tell the truth, this was a very tough job. The easy part is real criminals that came with boat people. They steal and make threats to good refugees. I just get their names and turned them over to Malaysian cops, and they beat them up.

But some refugees steal because they need food. It is against the law for them to fish or climb trees to get coconuts. If cops catch them they get beat too. I did not report thieves like that. There must be enough food. Everybody will work for it but there was nothing to do on the island. Big problem is that not enough food comes from UN.

The reason for this is that food was stolen before it got to the island. I cannot do anything about that. When it gets here, refugees are manpower to move it from boat to warehouse. Men stole some of it for themselves, especially rice and canned food.

I asked the authorities if I can talk to people about it. They said, "Good luck—here is a loudspeaker." I only want to talk with heads of families, but I must make speech now to everyone.

What I said is that food comes from many countries donating. People all over the world have a lot of sympathy for us. How can we not have sympathy for each other?

If not, we are like crabs in a basket, always fighting each other. We left all the things and persons we love in Vietnam because SRV made everybody cheat and steal from each other. Do we want to do that for the rest of our lives? If we come for new life let us be honest with everybody.

After the speech many people came to me and say they agree. What should we do? I said we should not be informers like people are in SRV. Let's be different and just stop people when we see them steal food that should be for everybody.

After a while this works pretty good. Food is shared equal. When that happens we laugh a little bit because that is what communists said they would do in Vietnam.

But some guys did not want to cooperate. At night they swim to Malaysian fishing boats and helped them fish so they can sell some to refugees. They also paid off Malaysian cop for this business. Because some authorities are corrupt, there's not much I can do.

Most refugees brought with them a little gold. An old woman named Tai came to me crying. She said she lost her only two ounces but could not remember how it happen. It was in her pocket but now it is gone. Pocket had a hole in it.

I told her in 6000 poor people, not much chance to get gold back but I will try. I asked my assistants and they agree. One of them said he saw two young men having big argument like they each found the same thing. I called on loudspeaker for these two, Ngo and Tung, to report to me.

First they deny they found anything. They argued about island lottery, they said. I talked with them for hours. I said if they found something and cannot agree who found it, then neither one can have it. Better turn it over to me. Finally, they agreed. They gave Tai's gold to me.

This was like a miracle. Tai is the happiest woman in the world. I am happy too because Vietnamese can be honest. I got on loudspeaker and told the incident to the whole camp. We are not crabs in a basket anymore.

A lot of problems came from organizers who did not collect all the gold from their passengers and want it now. I told them, sorry about that: when people risked their lives for a new life, that is enough to cancel old debts. Besides, no one here must profit from debts that never happen if SRV was not so cruel.

Authorities thought there is better morale on the island because of more honesty. They said I helped this happen, and asked me to be camp leader. I did not want so much responsibility but I will get a little house for me and Dat, so I took the job. While I was leader, I looked for someone to sponsor me in the States. It took many months, but I finally got a letter.

Cai's problem was that he had no addresses. First, he wrote back to his parents that at last he had completed a successful escape. They answered with equally joyous news: so too had his sister Hoang. She and his daughter had been picked up by a Spanish freighter and had debarked in Taiwan from where, after grinding through several bureaucracies, they made it to California, where his brother was providing for them. However, that did not ensure sponsorship for Cai. The policy of the U.S. Immigration and Naturalization Service (INS) was that siblings could not sponsor each other. Neither could a minor child sponsor a parent, though a parent could sponsor a child. Spouses could sponsor one another, but apparently the INS felt that if brothers and sisters could sponsor each other, vast permutations of immigration would result.

That left Cai with only unrelated Americans to contact. All of them had been in the 101st. So he simply wrote to those whose names he remembered after nine years; wrote to them, "c/o Pentagon, USA." He wrote about a dozen such letters, most of them to former enlisted men or junior officers. If there is a Pentagon dead letter office, they are probably there. However, one name, Hank Emerson's, must have been recognized because he had become a lieutenant general. It was forwarded to the addresses where he had retired, first in North Carolina and then Helena, Montana.

Under the circumstances, Cai's letter was rather indirect: he did not request Emerson's sponsorship; he merely advised that he had escaped, was well, had no passport but hoped to come to the United States. Cai was accustomed to circumlocution—he hoped Emerson would understand his predicament but felt diffident about asking forthrightly for sponsorship.

Emerson understood but replied in the same vein as Cai had written, stating his hope that Cai's future would improve. Meanwhile, Emerson got busy learning the sponsorship procedures. He first contacted the Lutheran Church, who got him into a refugee placement program. Six months passed and Cai had moved to the Philippines before he knew that Emerson had a place and a job for him in snowy Montana.

In my first letter to my parents I asked for information about Lena and her daughters. If she was here in Pulau Bidong, it could be like honeymoon for us in my new little house.

Since 1975 45,000 boat people had gone through here. Only 6000 were still here because no country gives them asylum. I tried to see some every day to tell them what to say to the UN. They did not understand the difference between economic and political reasons for leaving SRV. It was hard for me too because it is political system that makes economy so bad.

Some are peasants. They told the UN they left because their children die for not enough to eat. That's true but not good to say. They must tell that they do not have enough rice because SRV makes them donate rice "to build socialism." Yes, that's the truth the peasants know for sure—that's why people starve in SRV. I said, just tell that to UN so they understand.

There are also people who flee from New Economic Zones. UN thought that is economic reason. I told people who come from there that they must tell how NEZ are just concentration camps with economic name. They got my idea and more can leave the island.

UN asked, "Could you vote?" People said, yes, but they don't tell UN that people in SRV must vote or lose ration cards. They must vote with cadre looking, and there is only one choice. After a while the UN got a better understanding of life in SRV. One official said, "Your whole country needs asylum," and he is right.

The worst incident happened while I was in charge when a Malaysian cop forced Cao Dai monk for sex. This monk is named Thanh. He was very ashamed and beg me for help. He was very afraid he must serve this cop again because they both may be on island for a long time.

The cop's name is Marue. I had very good relations with his boss, Major Lopez of the police department, but if I just tell him, he may not protect Thanh. Cops do not think rape like this is very big crime. So I went to the UN representative, Mr. Fong, and get the MRCS to back me up. Then the incident was reported directly to the Malaysian government. Major Lopez was so mad at me, but I told him I got to protect my people. He did not say anything, but took Marue off the island.

Because of this incident, I saw some officials of the Malaysian government. I asked them urgently, "Are any U.S. military personnel around?" They said no, why do I ask. I said I should report to them about resistance to communists in Vietnam. They said they will tell someone at U.S. attaché office.

Couple of days later a man who called himself Hai Bach came down to see me. That is not his real name. He was from Defense Intelligence Agency of U.S. He had a file on me already, all about my service with 101st, MI school, and Twenty-first Division. He knew very much about Vietnam, all locations, and officers. I think all that information got out before Saigon fell.

I had a long story to tell him about conditions in Vietnam. He heard it before, about the camps and starving and all the terrible things that go on. He was interested in just a few things. One of them is weapons caches for resistance. I only know about one. Before Twenty-first Division surrender, we buried about 200 weapons and ammo under a pagoda. Resistance people will know this pagoda because the body of a very brave ARVN general was buried there. He commit suicide when he heard that the country surrender. His parents came for his body, but the VC said they cannot have it because people might get together at the funeral and maybe talk about resistance.

I told Hai Bach about the seven mountains region and how the resistance wants air drops there. He asked me, how many men? I said, I don't know, maybe battalion. If he gave me parachute and radio, I will go in and report to him. He said he cannot authorize operations like that. I asked maybe I can do it for CIA. He didn't say much about that, but I should know Air America and most CIA agents went home. This was when I got first idea that Vietnam is not remembered much anymore. It's like it was a exciting movie, but now it's over and people went out and do other things.

The war is not over! When I said this, my hands are fists. The ARVN resistance still fights violently against the communists. I told him about the raid of Long Binh ammo dump in 1977. He said, yeah, they even have some air photos of that. I asked him if Americans thought that was counterrevolution, but he did not want to discuss this with me.

Mostly Hai Bach was interested in U.S. MIAs. Only thing I know is in Long Trang, 1975 or 1976, cadre said they keep some U.S. troops to trade for U.S. aid. They said this with other bullshit about how strong and important SRV is in the world. I don't know if this is true about MIAs—lot of people ask me. Everything cadre told us was lies. If they still have MIAs that would be the only true thing they ever say.

Nobody I ever met saw any Americans in Vietnam since 1975. If any still there, they are kept in the north. Personally, I don't *think there are any more POWs. Maybe some AWOL GIs married Vietnamese and accept life there, but I never heard about anyone like that either. A few French guys still hang around, but they have been in Vietnam all their lives.*

Hai Bach wanted to know everything like this: If there are Caucasians around, how do we know they are French? I didn't see any at all, but at Catum some old prisoners were in the French Army and got captured before. They said the Viet Minh kept some French officers. Americans must be much younger; that is how these old prisoners knew the Caucasians that people saw must be French.

Hai Bach said there are rumors that NVA keeps some POWs to do maintenance on modern American equipment. I don't know about that either. He asked if that makes sense to me. This is possible, but NVA have so much Russian stuff I don't think they need U.S. equipment. Maybe in the air force this happens. When I hid around the waterfront, I saw ships loading U.S. airplane parts. Workers told me it was going to Middle East somewhere. I think SRV wants to sell all U.S. equipment to get dollars, don't want to keep any themselves.

I tried to make a deal with Hai Bach. If he will support the resistance, I will tell them to look everywhere for MIAs. I told him about the ARVN raid at Catum. If there were Americans in that camp, those ARVN fighters could get them out easy because cadre had panic. He laugh and said he does not have any authority for action like that.

I want to tell best plan about MIAs. I heard about it at Oh-deuce reunion in 1988. This is called McDaniels plan. People who start this plan promise money for reward to anyone who gets a MIA out. Million dollars is to be the reward! Nobody have to pay out money, only promise to pay if MIA gets out. I promised $500.

If we get the word back to Vietnam, maybe on Voice of America, for sure organizers start looking for MIAs. Million dollars is so much money, SRV officials can be bribed for escape from camp like I was.

Boat is no problem either. For so much money an organizer can buy best ship in SRV navy! But better if resistance finds

MIA and brings him across Cambodia to Thailand. There they can use money to buy ammo and medicine.

Other big thing Hai Bach wanted to know is about communists who are refugees. There was one guy on my boat like that. When he got off he looked like a very heavy man but he is skinny too. Malaysian marines pat him down and found couple of pounds of gold around his waist. He carried K54 pistol too in case we meet pirates.

This guy can only go to Norway because they let in communists. On the island he was very quiet and other people didn't like him, but he told me his story because I had good relations with Malaysian cops, and he wants protection. He was like a district chief for the SRV. That was the reward for his terrorism as VC. But he did very bad job in his district—a lot of people starving and SRV tax collectors got their heads chopped off sometimes. People are very pissed off and his commissar got that idea. So he told this district chief that the people will not elect him again. Election is just big show—the commissar select, not people elect—but this chief must take all blame instead of SRV who made the policy that is so bad for the country. So before the election, commissar told him, we let you get away, give you plenty of gold and make sure Norway takes you if you escape. You got to find your own organizer, and if you get caught, that's too bad for you—you will be executed after your confession that you tried to sabotage good SRV programs.

He thought that was a pretty good deal and escaped with me. Back in his district, commissar say, "See, he escaped. That means he was U.S. agent and that is why everything goes wrong here."

The first form Cai filled out, the one indicating the country he preferred for immigration, wound its way through the UN bureaucracy into diplomatic channels with thousands of others. When finally interviewed by a representative of the INS, he still had not heard from Emerson, so there was no fast track for him into the U.S.A.

His service with the 101st qualified him for Priority II immigration status. He could move up in priority by providing assistance to the refugee organizations as he had to the island. The UN recruited him for their central refugee processing center in the Philippines. In February 1985, Cai and Dat were flown to Manila.

After many months MRCS told me I will leave the island. To the people still here I said this is the gate of freedom. They should try to improve their education and understanding of the world so they can progress to another country. Then I went to the island cemetery for those who died here. I felt very sorry for them but was glad that at least they were more free than in life. One of the last things I tried to do is ask if their bones can be returned to Vietnam if families will receive them. Forever I remember the cemetery at Pulau Bidong.

The airplane was wonderful for me and Dat, like great luxury that I must remember. Air hostesses brought a meal like a restaurant.

In Manila there was a bus for us. It took us around a bay big as Cam Ranh to a peninsula called Bataan. Famous World War II battle was here. The camp is for refugees who someday may get to America. There were 10,000 from Laos and Cambodia and Vietnam. Camp is well run by UN.

UN said I will be a teacher here. Camp is for adjustment from terrible times of refugees so they can settle in life of America. Authorities told me I will teach basic English, but before I start that there is more need for case worker in Community Mental Health Services office. I thought this might be a good job, but I must take fifteen weeks of training.

These are very lucky refugees because after a while they can go to the States. But most were here a long time and there are many problems.

Nobody has much skill that they can use in the States. People with skill already gone. Like a mechanic, he can go, but cannot bring wife and kids till he is making a living in the States. That leaves many single mothers in camp. Some of them meet other guys and want to stay with them. Very hard to get a divorce if husband is in the States and the woman stay in Philippines. I got to try and and solve problems like that.

Other big problem is birthrate. Very much leisure time in this camp. Women get pregnant all the time. Some have a baby every year. Some men accuse that their wife sleeps around— will not take responsibility for baby that comes. All these babies screw up the paperwork for the families. Couple applies for immigration with one child. Before application is processed, maybe two more kids, then new applications must go in. I told families like that, "Look, if you want to get to the States fast, don't have any more kids here." One of the biggest classes was for birth control, but it didn't help much.

Most problems came from refugees who were a long time in the Philippines. They got accepted by the U.S. but first must pass English test and culture orientation. This is real hard for ARVN enlisted men who cannot even read Vietnamese language. I helped them as much as I can, but about only thing they can do is try to memorize English test. There are two or three of these tests; no one knew which one he will get. After the test, people write down questions they remember. If a person is lucky, he will get questions he memorized. People take tests over and over for years. I think they will have a lot of trouble in U.S. unless family takes care of them. They asked, who will take bribe so I can go over? I said, keep your money—no good for you in the U.S. if you cannot deal with life there.

On the day I leave Bataan, many people came to bus station. I looked at their wet eyes and can just say good luck, please remember you are luckiest people to escape and be accepted in the U.S.

One old woman knew she can never learn enough English. This will be her last home. She said, "Now you leave, who will speak for us?"

I do not know the answer. I think it will be merit for me to work for boat people all my life. Maybe I will do that after I see some things. I am a Southeast Asian. These are my people. Many things about them I don't like and make me mad, but I want to serve them, make them feel that way about other refugees, not just family. But I must get Lena and our children to America. Then maybe I will come back. I cannot forget how bad has been their life, and what they must do together. They are better than corruption. They can see that with help and example. But now I have years for new life in America. Many tests for me and I must do them right or I cannot help anyone.

They were still waving, as long as I can see them. I had to take a deep breath for holding tears.

Chapter
Twenty-six

In Cai's pocket were tickets Emerson had sent him—Northwest Airlines from Manila to Seattle via Seoul. He was amazed at how easily he entered the United States, the destination of dreams for millions of refugees. With a single-sheet form from the INS, he and Dat were examined for only a moment by immigration.

He looked at the sheet, stamp it, and say "Welcome to America."
Just like that—no big deal, but still I have to cry.

We went to another part of airport to catch a plane to Montana. This airport is called Sea-Tack, biggest one I ever saw. I never heard much about Seattle before but I think it must be the greatest city in the U.S. if it's got an airport like this. But nobody's around. Dat and I can lie down while we wait. If this place was in Vietnam, a thousand people will live in here all the time.

Next plane was to Helena, Montana, where General Emerson lives. I hope he will know what I look like because it has been eighteen years since we saw each other. In a letter he told me I may not be able to live in so much cold, but this is July [1984], and everything looked green and pretty down here.

Hank Emerson had been retired for several years. Since Cai had seen him as a lieutenant colonel, he had blazed through a colorful career. After leaving the Oh-deuce, he served a year in the Pentagon in the Individual Training Directorate, the army's program for preparing recruits for combat. Shortly after Tet 68, he commanded a brigade with the U.S. Ninth Infantry Division, the "riverines" who scoured the delta in boats as well as choppers and afoot. While watching his troops encircle a VC battalion, his chopper was shot down and he was badly burned.

For five months he was hospitalized, then commanded a brigade of logistical troops at Fort Bragg, North Carolina. This was an infamous unit filled with antiwar protestors. Emerson turned the brigade around largely through a program of competitive athletics and giving Saturday mornings off if work quotas and quality were satisfied during the week. The five-day week was unknown elsewhere in the army except for special forces.

Emerson brought in Vietnam amputees to command companies where the war protestors were strongest. The character and example of the amputees—doing chin-ups with one arm, running two miles with one leg—put to shame the pretensions of the antiwar GIs, who faded from the scene. His success in raising morale and performance earned him his first star and assignment as assistant commander of the Eighty-second Airborne Division. He was in this job when Cai wrote him his appeal in 1971 to attend OCS at Fort Benning.

Emerson stayed at Fort Bragg to command the Special Warfare Center, then was promoted again, commanding general of the 2d Infantry Division in Korea. His two-year tenure there was described in a long *Newsweek* article, "Peacetime Gunfighter," a tribute to his success in taming racial rage when it was at its height in the post-Vietnam army.

Awarded a third star, he came back to Fort Bragg to command the Eighteenth Airborne Corps, the most potent and fastest reacting force in the army. Emerson saw their most likely AO to be the Middle East, an environment for which the army at that time had little concern. The Commander of Training & Doctrine Command, General Depuy, was focused on Europe, where the Bradley Fighting Vehicle was to be the new Rolls Royce of mechanized warfare. Emerson could get little R&D money to develop reverse osmosis machinery to ensure water for his troops in Middle Eastern deserts—all the funds were going into enormous cost overruns for the overrated Bradley. At a generals' conference, Depuy publicly rebuked Emerson for his opposition, a humiliation that warned the other generals not to knock the Bradley. At cross purposes with the Pentagon, Emerson retired voluntarily in 1977.

Fifty-one years old, he went into business with a caterer to the overseas camps of construction firms. After two years, his partner died and Emerson retired again, this time to hunt and fish in the Rockies.

General Emerson looked just like before but with white hair. He hugged me and Dat, then took us to his home, called "Fade Away" from old army song, "Old Soldiers Never Die, They Just Fade Away." We talked till midnight even though I had no sleep for twenty-four hours. I told him there are resistance people who still fight communists in Vietnam, and I must try to help them because they expect to hear from me. I am willing to go back to help them because they fight in despair.

General Emerson said he did not have influence in the army anymore. What I do must be my decision. He gave me a thousand dollars for things I will need. After three days shopping in Helena, he took us to Dillon, Montana. He worked through his friend General Womack so I can stay temporary in his son's house, and got me a job till I start school at Western Montana College.

Maj. Gen. James Womack, the Adjutant General of the Montana National Guard, was one of Cai's principal benefactors. A close friend of Emerson's, he and the Lutheran bishop of North Dakota had untied considerable red tape to bring Cai into a state where sponsorship of Southeast Asians was a rarity.

My daughter Van was staying with my brother in California, and soon she came up to live with me and Dat. We are the only Vietnamese for hundreds of miles. Montana people never saw

Vietnamese before. Usually they think we are Indians from the reservation.

But everyone is very friendly and good to us. Local newspapers wrote things that I told them about the war, re-education camps, and communism. I learned about the 101st Airborne Division Association from General Emerson, and so I got a lot of phone numbers of old friends.

It was in this way that Cai made contact with me. But he was no longer Cai when he did.

Cai was the Vietnamese name my parents gave me when President Diem say in 1954 that all business must be owned by Vietnamese citizens. So I dropped the middle name I had at birth and put Cai in front. But Ben was my first name. It became my middle name while I was in Vietnam. I decided to make it first again. I went to a Montana court and asked them to say I will be Ben Cai Lam, so that is my name now.

College is very hard for me because my English is not so good as native people. Dat's is not so good either, but he does all right in high school. Van's English is perfect because she is so young.

I talked to my brothers in Louisiana and California on the telephone. They live in Vietnamese communities. Most people there took off before the communists won. They brought lots of gold, diamonds, and green dollars so they made success in America. It seems they want to forget what happened and just be in new life here. My brothers and sister and I work to get my parents out. I must also make money to repay my family for all the gold spent in my eighteen escape attempts, but most of all I need money for getting Lena and our daughters out. I hope my story helps do that.

Lena became a visceral cause for me as well. Getting her out without benefiting her captors would be a parting shot, a final flip of the finger to the SRV, the NVA, and all their habits. We called

Lena's rescue "the extraction," a term for removing people from a hot LZ. We had to succeed because the Oh-deuce never fails.

There was a conventional, relatively safe, but costly way to ransom them. Like most Saigonese, Lena could receive mail, usually within three months from posting in the U.S. Under American law, up to $200 per letter could be sent into the SRV. Since the communists set the cost of freedom at about $2000, by dribbling the money in legally it would take over three years before she accumulated enough.

The buildup of funds is even slower because the SRV takes a 50 percent cut of incoming monies—that's before local bribery. Normal procedure is for the addressee to receive notice from the post office that they are holding overseas mail for her. She reports, the letter is opened in her presence, and if it contains money she is given the equivalent in SRV currency at the official rate—after she "donates" half the amount to "help build socialism."

Opening the mail in her presence is of course a charade. Contents are examined meticulously when the letter or package first arrives in Vietnam. It was the nature of the examination that absorbed our interest, for we had rejected piecemealing the money to her as required by U.S. law, and in acquiescence to communist venality.

So we decided to transfer the ransom from a third country. Optimally, we would get Lena the entire amount in gold, saving it from diminution by currency conversion. We hesitated before the all-or-nothing choice because gold, if found, would be confiscated entirely.

How then to transfer gold without detection? I had some acquaintance with a governmental agency with expertise in such matters. They were not encouraging. They advised that the SRV must be aware of every smuggling method, for they had sifted through tens of thousands of letters and packages, alert for contraband, especially gold. They could tell us no success stories.

I decided our best chance was to integrate auric granules into another substance intrinsically worthless. That substance was the first consideration; how to impregnate it undetectably with gold was the second. The two problems were equally knotty.

What could we send in that might not be confiscated, or at least minutely examined? From the experience of earlier refugees, Ben learned that between half and a third of everything in a package was pilfered or required as a bribe by the post office in order for the addressee to get the remainder. Thus, anything mailed had about a one in four chance of being received: half went as a "donation" to the SRV, a quarter more to pilferage or the local postmaster.

What we needed was something of no intrinsic value that would not arouse suspicion for that very reason. For example, it would be transparently obvious that if we mailed a bottle of fish sauce there must be something else in it because fish sauce was available in Vietnam.

Books were automatically confiscated: there were no legal publications except those of the SRV. Exotic food would probably be taken out of curiosity. Even more vulnerable was an alcoholic beverage. Nonalcoholic beverages raised the question of why the sender would waste the weight and space, both restricted by the SRV postal authorities. Western shoes and clothing were almost as valuable as gold.

It was while considering a lamination of gold attached to a wine label that I thought of photographs. Here was something of no commercial but great sentimental value—not something the communists wanted but could understand being mailed from overseas. Ben checked with his brothers. They had indeed sent photographs to Saigon and all, as best their parents could recall, had arrived.

Even if photos got through, could they carry gold in worthwhile quantity? I enquired among some platers and learned there was a process called "electroleafing." About twenty "enriched" three-by-five photos might be worth $500. But to separate the gold from their backing required a chemical reversing process too sophisticated for Lena's resources. I was back to the drawing board.

While I looked for the technology, we tried a dummy run of photos. We sent Lena fifty. Each had a heavy cardboard backing, unusual for western photography but Ben felt the communists were too primitive to realize that. We wanted to see if heavy pictures aroused suspicion. For further assurance of receipt, Ben wrote sentimental messages across the cardboard, expressing nostalgia for lovely Vietnam, things like, "This is a picture of a Rocky Mountain. It is nice but cannot compare with the beauty of Moui Ba Dinh," "This is an elk. It is good to eat, but how we miss the wonderful shrimp of the fatherland," i.e., inscriptions that appealed to a communist's patriotism, or was kind to the image the SRV had of itself. This took immense imagination but Ben wrote something appropriate in Vietnamese on the back of each photo.

By a separate letter written in opaque Chinese, Ben told his parents to inform Lena to strip all photos for gold, and the code to be used for acknowledging receipt of the trial mailing of fifty photos. They got through, all of them. The postmaster even remarked to her how lonely it must be for Vietnamese in America. Now all that remained was my search for a reversible gilding process.

Meanwhile Ben struggled with the bounty and frustrations of America.

Student health insurance paid for a successful search for the elusive machine gun bullet that had knocked him out of the war. Indeed, it was not until the slug was surgically extracted that Ben determined the caliber and thereby identified its East German origin. Somehow the slug had traveled from where it had entered his chest, through his shoulder, and into his bicep. This explained its absence from the chest x-ray in Pulau Bidong.

M ontana doctor was very good. He had experience with bullet wounds from hunting accidents. He made joke and said, "Ten years for bullet to get into your arm—just wait ten more and it come out your finger!" I said please take it out, I don't want to carry piece of communism around with me anymore.

Eligible for several governmental loans, Ben went on a rampage of consumption, buying three vehicles, three TV sets, two computers, and a VCR. His opinion of *Platoon* was that he could understand why the SRV was so eagerly showing it. He thought the movie to be better propaganda for them than *55 Days*, the communist depiction of their 1975 conquest of South Vietnam, a film all prisoners in re-education camps were required to watch repeatedly.

With the first money he earned, Ben rented an apartment, then a house. A hundred miles away in Helena, Emerson watched his acculturation warily:

"He's got a lot of airborne drive," Ben's benefactor noted. "He makes friends easily, and he's adjusted well in Dillon. From what I know about the Vietnamese community in California, they help the transition of new arrivals into American society—explain things, show them the ropes. Ben didn't have that assistance here. He's independent, which is good, but he sort of landed on Mars and needed to find out for himself what's really going on. To put it another way, he's had to jump start his new life. Or you could say he's got a lot of balls in the air, and I don't know if he'll catch them all."

The first ball he dropped was in college. It was not the reading intensive courses that he bobbled but math and particularly statistics, requisites for an associate degree in business administration.

My English not so good that I understand statistics problems. First time I got "D." Now I take it again.

Everyone wants to help me, so I think I can make it through. Then I'm not sure what I do. Montana very good place for my family to grow up. Food and house is not expensive. During hunting season I see deer beside road, and just get out of car and shoot one. That's legal. People carry more weapons here than in war.

But pretty soon I will be a citizen. Next year Lena maybe will be here. In May, I must graduate. Then I must decide for sure what to do. Guys from reunion said, "Come to Wisconsin," "Great opportunity in D.C.," "Good jobs in Phoenix." I have big family pretty soon and must make the right decision.

"Reunion" was the dedication of a memorial to the dead of the Oh-deuce at Fort Campbell, Kentucky, in June of 1988. Giving speeches were Ben, myself, and John Del Vecchio, who wrote this about "the oldest eagle":

If a man can be simultaneously driven and serene, such a man is Ben Cai Lam. You can see the intensity in his eyes, hear it when he speaks, yet be caught by his easy smile, and feel no tension. These facets flash from deep and mixed experience. Perhaps a man is forced to learn a kind of control that a re-education camp unintentionally teaches. Perhaps so many years of soldiering adds something unique. Whatever the source, today, when he describes the flavor of elk jerky, or death of prisoners in a minefield, or the exasperation of calculus, Ben fairly bursts with a mixed love and apprehension of life.

In the nine months I've worked on this story, I've seen the love overtake the apprehension. The rain was pouring outside the Oakland airport. I awaited his flight at the baggage carousel. The crowd thinned, but still I did not recognize anyone resembling the twenty-year-old whom I vaguely remembered. Finally there was only one man, incomprehensibly older, wearing a loud yellow jacket. His carriage showed the pain, his clothes the optimism.

Jumbled feelings and experience spurted out as we drove home. We had spoken on the phone after Emerson had advised me that "Ben has a hell of a story." The story, whatever it was, would be an unwelcome interruption of a novel I was working on, but if Ben was willing to spend his meager earnings on airfare, I'd spend the time to appraise his story.

As it came out in fits and starts, I wondered how I could tell him that he had wasted his money. It took him three days to sketch the essentials. Dates, names, locations were scattered and incomplete. We tried taping but the flow was incoherent. I advised him to organize the major periods on paper, then we could talk through them, filling in, surfacing secondary recollections.

For three days he was our house guest, but he barely ate at all and could not sleep as memories dislodged. His written text was like a military after-action report: a lot of dry detail about disposition of units, names of commanders, tons of supplies and so on.

I told him the American public would not be interested in such stuff. How did he feel, how had he felt? That was the only way other people could share his experience. When he left, we were both discouraged. I told him I could not approach a publisher with what we had so far.

As soon as Ben got back to Montana, he sent me a short essay he had written for freshman English. It described his parents' house as he remembered it from his childhood. That unblocked something. From there he could reexperience as well as recall.

Every week or so, as his college studies permitted, Ben mailed

me an installment of his history, handwritten until he checked out
a personal computer after six months. I'd call him and we would
talk about the installment, my questions sometimes reviving complementary incidents. We live about 700 miles apart; consequently,
we had only three face-to-face sessions, the first in California, the
second in Kentucky at the reunion, and the last at Great Falls,
Montana. Perhaps there should have been more, for they seemed
to prime the pump of his memory, producing vignettes like those
of Thieu's bodyguards and the "Christmas Carol rebellion" in the
re-education camp.

"Where are we going to cut the book off?" I asked.

We were among dilapidated headstones in a frontier cemetery,
a grove of tall trees conspicuous on the sand-colored, low rolling
hills of the upper Missouri River. Ben had swept his hand proudly
around the vast vistas and distances of his adopted home state. True
to its advertisements, Montana is "big sky country," broader horizon
to horizon than the curve of the planet, and higher too, from puffy
clouds like ambling sheep, to feathery cirrus at ethereal heights.

"Up that mountain range is Missoula." He gestured north. "Vang
Pao lives there since he escaped from Laos."

"Know much about that war?"

"Not much. He has a helicopter and CIA bodyguards."

"Think he's going back?" Ben shrugged. "How about you? Is the
war over yet?"

"I like to go back, maybe to Thailand. Maybe I can help refugees
and resistance from there."

"The CIA wasn't interested in you."

"They say I must have college degree."

"Well, you're going to get one."

"I think war is pretty over for CIA. What do you think about
what Russell said at reunion?"

Retired sergeant Jim Russell had said that if the old Oh-deuce
got together again, he'd go back with them to Vietnam. I told Ben
I was sure Russell felt that way but he did not mean it literally.

"I got to do something. Up here there is no news. Sometimes I
get Vietnamese newspaper from California. It says some guys went
back. Communists say they killed some. People give money for
resistance but I think maybe there is corruption again."

"Same old story."

"This story can have new chapters."

"Will it ever be over?"

"Chinh said no. He said resistance now is like VC in 1960. Nobody thought they had much chance to win. Maybe resistance is like that. For sure it takes more generations before we win."

"The resistance doesn't have a Ho Chi Minh."

"He might be there. He might be in Thailand. Ho worked for many years. Very old before his army is powerful. He died before it win."

"Think your Ho Chi Minh might be in the U.S.?"

"Possible." Ben sounded like he meant barely possible.

"How about you? You got some pretty raggedy ass ARVN to follow you."

"Oh no!" Ben's laugh was short and loud as if a switch had turned on then off. "I fight for ten years. Don't have enough courage left!"

"How about Dat?"

"Too young. Don't remember enough."

"What would he have to remember?"

"Re-education camp. He didn't have that."

"He'd have to give up a lot too."

"That's right. That's why I don't think resistance leader will come from U.S."

"Getting cold?"

Wind had come up with late afternoon, and the air was dry enough to make my nostrils itch. The previous day, when I flew in, raging forest fires from Yellowstone Park had draped a giant plume of haze across four states. Now the wind had shifted, and the sky was a moving mural of a thousand widely spaced clouds. Flames and burning once again seemed far away.

Ben felt the evening chill and suggested a walk through the military section of the cemetery. It was circular, centered around a nineteenth-century cannon. Rounded white tablets, just like those at Arlington, were laid out in perfect arches, in final formation as if on stationary parade. We became intent on finding the headstone of someone who had died in Vietnam.

Most of the names were Scandinavian, or other north European, with a scattering of Italians. Small gray markers, flush to the ground and faintly etched, identified a few veterans of the Indian wars.

Many other veterans had died in 1918, perhaps, it occurred to me, from the apocalyptic flu epidemic, for they had not been awarded the Purple Heart. The last date for others was 1943, 1944, or 1945. They had been brought home from both theaters. No one in Great Falls, it appeared, had been lost in Korea or Vietnam, though they could be buried in the Catholic cemetery on another hill.

"Fifty-eight thousand names on the wall in Washington," I observed, perplexed that none were here.

"America very big. Vietnam War not so big."

"It sure was back then. Biggest event for the country in the second half of this century."

"Still not so big, Tom. Many big events in America. In Montana I watch them on TV. Change, change all the time. Everything starts in the U.S. Everything going on here. Everything moves on."

Including the extraction. About the time this book was being edited, Lena received a second sheaf of photos. She acknowledged that "Your pictures are a treasure for me." She's coming out with her daughters. Ben's parents arrived, then returned to their island birthplace in Hainan, China, to pay respects for the last time at the graves of their ancestors.

The cemetery reminded Ben that his parents would be visiting earlier generations. That was something he could never do, and an unmendable link had been broken. In his own life he had been uprooted twice and flung on foreign shores. Something remained behind each time, something that could never be recouped or reconnected as his parents would do in Hainan.

In place of roots, Ben has memories. The most bitter are consequences of his faith in America's commitment to Vietnam. But he understands that now; he understands that the GVN abused the commitment and prevented it from reaching the South Vietnamese people. That is now history, and the macrocosm of Ben's experience. Yet he was not mastered by events, and could always find the necessary opportunity.

"Sometimes when guys died in prison camp, I thought they were lucky. They were, but not as lucky as I am."

POSTSCRIPT

It was not my purpose in writing Ben's story to explain why the communists won their war, but inferentially that has emerged, so in this postscript I will make my opinions explicit.

The foremost and overriding reason that South Vietnam does not exist today is that it never existed as a nation except on paper. As a nation, South Vietnam was not even the sum of its parts.

There may have been too many parts: ethnic, religious, cultural and class-based segments of a society that had never historically cohered. There was no locus for nationalism except the Vietcong; no tradition of noblesse oblige; no sense of social conscience or civic responsibility. No enduring allegiances except familial.

After all allowances are made, after every extenuating and mitigating circumstance is considered, a country—any country—is responsible for and is reflected in its leadership. In that leadership there must be something more than venality before a country becomes a nation.

In that crucial characteristic, the GVN never became the government of a nation. The GVN was never of the people, much less for the people or by the people. This failure has been expressed in the aphorism that democracy cannot be exported. It can be nurtured from abroad but, essentially, democracy must be homegrown or it is quickly choked in tentacles branching from dictatorial philosophies of government.

In the sixties, the truth was not self-evident. Supporters of American intervention cited South Korea as precedent: an Asiatic, artificially divided land, autocratically ruled (i.e., Rhee-Diem) with no system or tradition of democratic values. Unquestionably, American armed intervention in South Korea permitted it to survive, and some thirty-eight years later it is growing into a genuine democracy. The difference in outcome is the difference in duration. If we had remained in South Vietnam as long as we have in South Korea, there might be a transformed GVN, as a new generation of local leaders grew militantly democratic, as in Korea.

Not that we should have remained in the partnership we ill-advisedly created in Vietnam—not that there should still be a GVN like the one we defended at such heartbreaking and bankrupting cost. The GVN, as we accepted it, had no redeeming features except that it was our baby. Like fathers, four U.S. presidents seemed blind to its fatal faults, never imposing (even privately) the discipline of an ultimatum: "shape up or we ship out." When we shipped out, it was without any indication from GVN that they would shape up. Like Ben, they always believed we would return to the rescue if clearly necessary.

The GVN was insupportable. That was the foremost and overriding reason why the communists were able to exterminate it. Yet, for better or for worse, the U.S. military could have prevented that outcome if our strategic sense had matched our armed might.

Not later than 1967, but probably before, it was evident that the VC insurgency would fail without increasing support from the NVA. It took no Clausewitz to perceive that to win the military war we had to block the NVA from entering the south. Along the South Vietnamese coast we did so, as the U.S. Navy effectively interdicted communist infiltration by sea. If we had extended this interdiction to the Cambodian coast, quarantining it as we did the Cuban coast in the 1962 missile crisis, the Ho Chi Minh Trail would have been the only remaining umbilical cord between the VC and NVA. Lon Nol's 1970 coup in Cambodia proved that.

But permanently cutting the trail was never attempted, though the means to do so were on hand as early as 1967. In 1968, the trail was particularly vulnerable as the communists reeled away from their disastrous Tet offensive. Four U.S. divisions (maybe three would have been enough) inserted on Route 9 would have caused the NVA to dash itself to pieces against our annihilating fire power. In a year or so, our superb engineering capabilities could have fortified Route 9 into a Siegfried Line, its flanks secure on the DMZ defenses (never ruptured while U.S. forces were there) and the Mekong, a river as formidable and impassable as the Mississippi. Behind such fortifications, our four divisions could be replaced by average ARVN troops. We could have gone home when we did in 1971, but with South Vietnam well defended all around from the primary enemy, North Vietnam.

That would have left ARVN matched against an unsupplied VC. In that circumstance, historical precedent much favored ARVN: Since the end of World War II, no insurgency has failed that had convenient access to external support, and no insurgency has succeeded that did not have such access.

Both propositions in this iron law of guerrilla warfare were validated in postwar Greece. While supplies and support flowed freely to the Greek communists, their insurgency flourished; but when Tito shut the open border, the Greek insurgency withered and died. Most recently, an open border (Pakistan's) proved essential for the success of the Afghan guerrillas. With Cambodia interdicted as it was, with the Ho Chi Minh Trail closed as it could have been, there would have been no open border for the Vietcong and they, as well as the Khmer Rouge, would have either expired or compromised.

At the time when cutting the trail was relatively so easy, General Westmoreland was prevented from doing so by President Johnson's policy against "broadening the war." Johnson's underlying reason seems to have been fear of Chinese intervention, as happened in Korea. It was an unwarranted fear.

In Korea, MacArthur advanced right up to the Chinese frontier. In Laos, an allied force on the trail was 400 miles from China. Today in Korea, China tolerates a strong American army 200 miles from its border.

Moreover, China and Vietnam have been warring neighbors for a thousand years. Over the centuries, China has "defended" Vietnam the way Germany has defended Poland. Moreover, in the late sixties China was convulsed by its cultural revolution, its armed forces focused on internal turmoil and a flaring frontier feud with Russia.

China was unfitted and indisposed toward retaliatory ventures as demonstrated by their shrug when Nixon finally mined and bombed the North Vietnamese port of Haiphong, which directly endangered Chinese shipping.

Seeing clearly that cutting the trail was the only way—and a feasible way—to defeat the communists, Westmoreland should have resigned when Johnson vetoed a war-ending drive across the Laotian panhandle. In turn, General Abrams should have resigned, bringing the strategic debate to a head. So too should the legion of generals who in retrospect grumble about how the army was not allowed to win the war. But not a single general was sufficiently committed to victory. The highest-ranking officer to resign in protest against the no-win strategy was a solitary colonel, Dave Hackworth.

American public opinion was anxious for such a decisive move. Even after the surprise of Tet 68, the polls showed a shift to a more, rather than a less, hawkish strategy. The people had the wisdom but our leaders lacked the will.

All the while, American fighting men gave their all, trusting in the professional dedication of their generals. The troops did not get all they deserved in return—the ultimate professional sacrifice— resignation in protest to a strategy that foreclosed victory. *Not one general was willing to put his career on the line the way he told his troops to put their lives on the line.*

This chilling hypocrisy reflects corporate rather than soldierly values. Generals have become managers of personnel more than leaders of men. Apparently, casualties take second place to careers. Evidently, a clause has been appended to MacArthur's ringing dictum: "There is no substitute for victory"—except a promotion.

Small wonder there has been no official history written of the Vietnam war, no in-house critique of its strategy, not even thirty-four years after our ground forces came ashore; whereas, the official U.S. Army history of World War II was completed six years after its conclusion. Generals hasten to publish the plans they accomplished, not the reasons why they should have resigned.

PENTIMENTO

Old paint on canvas, as it ages, sometimes becomes transparent. When that happens it is possible, in some pictures, to see the original lines: a tree will show through a woman's dress, a child makes way for a dog, a large boat is no longer on an open sea. That is called pentimento, because the painter "repented," changed his mind. Perhaps it would be as well to say that the old conception, replaced by a later choice, is a way of seeing and then seeing again.

That is all I mean about people in this book. The paint has aged now and I wanted to see what was there for me once, what is there for me now.

—Lillian Hellman

Ben's story continues to be filled with drama—as if he hadn't already participated in enough drama to last a lifetime.

In late 1988, upon reading this book in manuscript, Hank Emerson became apoplectic over the fact that I had included the "hachet incident" (p. 76). He begged and badgered me to omit it, but mostly he leaned on Ben, calling him often and at length, openly accusing him of ingratitude. Ben, in turn, urged me to take out the incident, not because he felt it was inappropriate in the story, but solely for Emerson's sake.

By agreement, Ben and I are splitting all proceeds from the book fifty-fifty. Emerson offered to replace Ben's share if he would withdraw from our agreement. But Ben did not, and I have not excised the incident. Though grateful to Emerson for his wartime leadership and support, I felt the incident should remain in the book for three reasons:

First, when juxtaposed with a typical communist pogrom, the hatchet incident illustrates how the two are not equivalent. Even what happened at My Lai—atrocious deeds by any standard—

amounted to routine practices in the communists' campaigns of terror both during and after the war. To my knowledge, this vital difference in *intent* (to say nothing of magnitude) between what we did and what they did has yet to be acknowledged by commentators. The hatchet incident provides an opportunity to contemplate the way in which atrocities are considered *violations* of U.S. policy while, conversely, they are viewed merely as a *means* to implement communist policy.

Second, as a narrator admitting to the facts of the incident, I am testifying that the rest of the book deserves to be taken seriously. In telling a true story, I am obliged to relate the facts impartially. Where I and others were wrong, I say so, not only for the satisfactions of confession, but for reinforcement of what was right—the two together demonstrating a desire for historial accuracy. Indeed, what are the historical facts that bothered him? I see none. Emerson, of course, did not order or encourage decapitation. He offered a reward, a bounty, for the first "kill" with a hatchet. He regrets that his offer was misinterpreted. That's war; that's history, no less than the other actual events related in the book. If the incident was cause for embarrassment, it would be mine perhaps more than his because the "hatchet man" was a member of my company as much as he was a member of Emerson's battalion. I should have foreseen the possibility of the bounty being misunderstood and reviewed its intent with my men in B Company.

Third, the hatchet incident has been related twice before: the first time by Malcolm Browne; the second, by Oh-deuce veteran Michael Clodfelter in his book, *Mad Minutes and Vietna Months.* Clodfelter was in another unit, absent on leave at the time of the incident, and, through hearsay, erroneously described it this way:

> The only "highlight" of the operation was the deployment of Hatchet patrols by the 2/502nd's CO, Lt. Col. Henry "Gunfighter" Emerson. Inspired by the mutilation of a fallen Five O'Deuce trooper by insurgent soldiers, Emerson equipped each patrol member with a hatchet and offered the incentive of a case of beer and a three-day pass to Saigon to any man who would bring back from the hunt a trophy of a Charlie's head. Pickings were sparse, however, but finally Emerson's reward was

earned by a young trooper who happened to stumble over a dead enemy soldier.

Clodfelter's perversion of the incident appeared as I was writing *Where the Orange Blooms.* I felt that the reputation of the Oh-deuce should be defended. Emerson's comment upon reading Clodfelter's account was, "Who's going to remember what some PFC said about it?" Emerson could have saved himself much grief by recognizing that his comment would be just as true as when applied to this book—the twice-told tale was incidental, not likely to be long remembered.

My manuscript was completed by the spring of 1989, when David Hackworth came to town on a promotional tour for *About Face,* his co-authored autobiography. He came to my house and we took up the matter of Emerson's reaction to my inclusion of the incident. As a "friend," Hack urged me to remove it to spare Emerson anxiety.

Hack then went on to say that he had saved some reputations of officers we both knew by omitting their transgressions or by using pseudonyms. I was revolted by one of his excisions: an incident in which a colonel who, when one of his units faced annihilation, exclaimed to Hackworth, "What will this do to my career?" Though I had not read *About Face* at this time, its reputation for hard-hitting, tell-it-like-it-was forthrightness was being hailed by virtually every influential reviewer. Now, having read *About Face,* I join in raising banners and ringing bells for nearly every one of his conclusions. I would vote for any presidential candidate who would name David Hackworth Secretary of the Army. I mean that sincerely, in spite of everything I say in the following account.

We have been colleagues both in war and in print. He wrote a blurb (as did Emerson) for my novel *Born of War:*

> A stimulating, suspenseful, and compelling tale. Taylor, a former Green Beret, has masterfully produced a provocative work that captures Gen. Orde Wingate, Britain's maverick warrior, in all his brilliance and madness.

During the previous four years, while Hack was working on his book in Austalia, we had exchanged more than nine lengthy letters in which I responded to his questions about my views and our mutual experiences. He thanked me for my "accurate recap" of the intelligence that led to Operation Gilbraltar: "God, it's good to get confirmation on so many foggy details," and added, "please, dear Tommy, shoot me down in flames if I'm wrong."

That's what I tried to do during our companionable afternoon in the spring of 1989. Emerson was wrong, I told him, in trying to remove the incident from history. There had been too much cover-up in the war already—it seemed to me that Vietnam was where the term originated. That wasn't the point, said Hack. Emerson was one of the really good guys (I quite agreed), and to diminish him would be to let down the small—the very small—brotherhood of good guys like us who fought the war as it should have been fought. In three of his letters, Hack had urged me to write Emerson's biography; now, in Hackworth's opinion, I was about to savage Emerson instead. Back off, he counseled; then added that he knew the top reviewers who could really give my book a boost.

It was clear that though Hack appeared fond of me, he was more fond of Emerson. There was nothing in that for me to resent. Instead, I was proud to be included in the brotherhood. But though judged to have paid the price of admission, I began to perceive that the cost of remaining in the brotherhood was astonishingly high. For there was the redoubtable David H. Hackworth—the clear-eyed iconoclast, so celebrated for rattling the army's mendacious mandarins, for sounding off with the truth loud and clear—speaking softly about keeping faith among the brotherhood.

It was clear from his comments that for a member to stay in good standing among the brotherhood, he must respond obediently to its catechism. And the first rule of that catechism is: do not offend an elder brother, no matter how well-intended the perceived offense might be. Though I didn't know it, I was off the reservation already. Hack had described me to Emerson as "a hack writer on an ego trip who is a fast-buck artist."

"Just bury the hatchet," Hack said upon leaving, and in a couple of weeks I began to suspect what the consequences would be if I didn't. For in the middle of April, he wrote me to say how pleased he was that I had taken his advice because, "there were guys getting ready to attack you with some pretty dirty garbage that could hurt the Taylor name, even if untrue—smears I know about!"

I called Hack in Los Angeles to ask him two things: why did he think I was removing the hatchet incident, and what "dirty garbage" was he talking about? Well, he said, he was sure none of it was true, but someone had said that I had hidden in an APC during the firefight and had run away from another. Also, people might interpret my sleeping in a tree as cowardice. Remember that night at Dong Ba Thien?

I did, and Hack, in an early draft, had put it in his book (then titled *Line of Departure*). Dong Ba Thien was a Special Forces camp near Cam Ranh where the brigade TOC stayed during the arrival of the troops in July 1965. The camp had a mini-zoo, featuring a tower-cage housing a boa constrictor and a giant sloth. Being slothful myself, I slung my hammock high up in the space between them in order to have the benefit of the sea breeze. I slept there every night, including one during which jumpy sentries opened fire on the innocent jungle and everyone in the brigade began blazing away as if we were about to be overrun by night-stalking VC. Only there were no VC, only shadows.

When a head count for "casualties" was taken, there were none, but no one knew where I was. Having been woken by the fire, I determined the safest place to be was where I was—between the snake and the sloth—and returned to sleep. Anyway, I was found among the treetops, and it was there that Hack remembered me.

As for hiding in an APC, I was never inside one in Vietnam, and would be more than curious to know where this incident was supposed to have taken place. I have a Silver Star, two Bronze Stars, and a Purple Heart (Ollie North's decorations) to memorialize my cowardice. "Hack," I told him, "I hope these guys speak up, because I don't have the publicity for my book that you do."

I assumed that Emerson was behind Hackworth's psychological maneuvers, so I called Emerson, telling him that this carrot/stick strategy wasn't working on me. He said he had nothing to do with it; that Hackworth had his tactics in peace just as he had had them in war, and that he, Emerson, did not know what Hack was up to.

That may be true. I hope it is. No one—least of all Ben and I —wanted Emerson to self-destruct. I would sacrifice anything but my integrity to see him spared. Since retiring to Montana, he has sought only his well-deserved privacy, now about to be stripped from him in a crushingly ironic way: the man he saved (by bringing him to this country) has collaborated with me, a comrade in arms, to revive the most mortifying event of Emerson's career. To cap his anguish, Emerson can remember that it was he who urged me to write Ben's story.

But the wound is self-inflicted. The reader can verify from his own reaction what a minor event the hatchet incident was among the cavalcade of hideous practices described in this book. It was Emerson himself who made the hatchet a cynosure.

He was betrayed, not by Ben or me, but by Hackworth who, if he were Emerson's real friend, should have told him, "Hank, the hatchet is no big deal. The story's been told twice and no one even noticed. People who read it again are going to forget it again. There's too much more that's far more important."

Instead, Hack forgot to listen to his own clarion call in *About Face*: "To tell all was a choice I made: I did not believe I had a right to discuss what happened to my Army if I did not honestly discuss what happened to me as well." The hatchet incident happened to me, twice.

Like the war in which we five Screaming Eagles fought, we are all embarrassed by the upshot of the hatchet incident. For Clodfelter, it is an example of how soldiers were *Pawns of Dishonor*, the original title of his book. For Hackworth, it was another opportunity to win by whatever means, none of which worked. For Emerson, it is a seeming betrayal by two of his own. For Ben, it created a dilemma, skewering him between two men who had befriended him. The dilemma remains a big, big part of his life today. For me, it is the source of uneasy reflection on how men, in spite of their union through searing experience, are really not philosophically united at all.

As we all used to say in Vietnam, "There it is."

GLOSSARY

ammo: ammunition.

AK/AK-47: the standard communist carbine; also known as a "Kalishnikov."

AO: area of operations.

APC: armored personnel carrier.

ARVN ("arvin"): Army of Vietnam (South Vietnam); also a soldier thereof.

AWOL: absent without leave.

BOQ: bachelor officers' quarters.

C&C: command and control.

CG: commanding general.

Charley: the Vietcong or North Vietnamese Army.

cherry: someone new to the war.

Chieu Hoi: literally "open arms," the name of the program to encourage defection by communist troops and sympathizers; someone who so defects.

Chinook: the largest cargo helicopter.

chopper: helicopter.

CIDG: Civilian Irregular Defense Groups, mountain militia.

CI: counterintelligence.

CO: commanding officer.

Cobra: an attack helicopter, heavily armed; also known as a "gunship."

COMUS MACV: Commander, U.S. Military Assistance Command, Vietnam; i.e., the commander of all American forces in Vietnam.

COSVN: Central Office for South Vietnam; the communist field headquarters.

CP: command post.

DAO: Defense Attaché Office (U.S.).

district: the South Vietnamese equivalent of a county.

DMZ: demilitarized zone.

DRV: "Democratic" Republic of Vietnam, i.e., the Hanoi regime.

DSC: Distinguished Service Cross; the second highest U.S. medal.

E&E: escape and evasion.

FAA: Federal Aviation Administration (U.S.).

FO: forward observer for artillery or mortars.

G (general's) staff: five sections—G1 (personnel), G2 (intelligence), G3 (operations and training), G4 (logistics), G5 (civil affairs).

grease gun: .45 caliber submachine gun.

GVN: Government of South Vietnam.

hooch: a native hut usually made of thatch.

Huey: the troop-carrying assault helicopter.

KIA: killed in action.

KCS: Kit Carson Scouts; communist defectors, usually NVA, working in the field with U.S. combat forces.

LZ: landing zone for helicopters.

M14: the standard U.S. infantry rifle prior to the introduction of the M16.

M16: the standard U.S. infantry rifle used in Vietnam.

M48: the U.S. tank used in Vietnam.

M60: the portable machine gun used by U.S. infantry.

M79: the U.S. grenade launcher, also called a "thumper."

MACV: see COMUS MACV.

MI: Military Intelligence.

MIA: missing in action.

MRCS: Malaysian Red Crescent Society (the equivalent of the Red Cross).

NEZ: New Economic Zones, i.e., communist penal colonies within Vietnam.

NVA: North Vietnamese Army or a member of it.

OCS: Officer Candidate School.

OPCON: operational control.

PFC: private first class, a U.S. enlisted rank.

point: the first element in a patrol or advance.

point man: 1. the leading soldier of the point, 2. an informer in re-education camps.

POW: prisoner of war.

prep: preliminary bombardment.

PRG: Provisional Revolutionary Government.

province: the South Vietnamese equivalent of a U.S. state.

PRV: Provisional Republic of Vietnam; communist South Vietnam before it was annexed by the DRV to become the SRV.

PSP: pierced steel planking. Strips of metal with large perforations designed to make runways for the air force but often stolen by the army to make tent floors.

PSYOP: Psychological Operations.

PX: post exchange, a U.S. military department store.

rally/rallier: a communist defector; the term used before, and sometimes carried over into the Chieu Hoi program.

R and R: rest and recreation; the biannual leave for servicemen in Vietnam.

ranger role: a technique of rolling clothes to secure them for crossing water, usually by swimming.

RF: Regional Forces; i.e., provincial militia.

ROK ("rock"): Republic of Korea or a member of its armed forces.

RPG: rocket propelled grenade (communist).

RTO: radio telephone operator.

RVN: Republic of Vietnam, i.e., the Saigon regime.

S staff: staff sections at battalion or brigade level corresponding to the G staff; i.e., S1, S2, S3, S4, S5.

Skyraider: A-IE U.S. Air Force single propeller, close support bomber.

SRV: Socialist Republic of Vietnam, the current name of the Hanoi regime.

Stratofortress: B52 bomber.

tri-border: the wilderness region where South Vietnam, Cambodia, and Laos converge.

VC: Vietcong; literally "Vietnamese communists," but applied only to the guerrillas fighting in South Vietnam.

VNAF: South Vietnamese Air Force.

XO: executive officer.

ABOUT THE AUTHOR

Thomas H. Taylor is a graduate of St. Albans School and West Point. His most recent book, *Born of War*, is a "docudrama" about the activities of the bizarre British general, Orde Wingate, during World War II. Taylor's previous novels are *A-18* and *A Piece of This Country*, both about Vietnam, where the author won seven decorations, including the Silver Star, two Bronze Stars for valor, and the Purple Heart. *Where the Orange Blooms* is his first work of nonfiction.

After leaving the army in 1968, Taylor received a master's degree in sociology and a juris doctor from the University of California. He practiced law in California and Saudi Arabia, but now writes full time. Taylor is a colonel in the United States Army Reserves, and was twice a national long-distance triathlon champion. He lives in Berkeley, California.